John Maynard's original and provocative study looks at sexuality and religion as alike creations of language, regularly connected in discourses that give them a single origin and mingled significance. In the elaborate and varied systems of sexual–religious interrelation in the Western Jewish/Christian tradition, Victorian writers found a central vocabulary for debate over sexual issues and for their individual refocussing of sexuality and religion.

After a wide-ranging introduction (drawing on myth, anthropology, comparative religion, and the history of sexuality), Maynard goes on to articulate and interpret the strikingly complex and varied ways in which the earnest skeptic, Arthur Hugh Clough, the Protestant clergyman, Charles Kingsley, and the Catholic convert, Coventry Patmore, placed the relation of sexuality and religion at the center of their work. In Clough, where inherited sexual and religious truths were tested and often burlesqued or overwritten by his skeptical intelligence, Maynard finds a foil to the simplicities of his age – and of our century's attempts to reduce Victorian sexual thinking to one thing, whether medical myth or a leaden prudishness. Kingsley by contrast attempts to unify and construct one new view, a variation on Christian marriage that places very unascetic spousal embraces at the center of the universe. Patmore, unknown in his experimental early poems and almost as ignored in his great odes, moves from Kingsleyan celebration of married love to a profound exploration of desire's failure and the creative absence that replaces it with human sexual relation to God.

A final chapter on Thomas Hardy's *Jude the Obscure* returns to the universal questions of the Introduction by showing one Victorian literally disintegrating into (body) parts the constructive visions of his predecessors. This implosion of language and meaning illuminates – as fiction, myth, mere human discourse – the tradition it destroys: capable of being thus deconstructed but, in Hardy's successors in the modern age, also subject to renewal.

VICTORIAN DISCOURSES ON
SEXUALITY AND RELIGION

VICTORIAN DISCOURSES ON SEXUALITY AND RELIGION

JOHN MAYNARD

CAMBRIDGE
UNIVERSITY PRESS

Published by the Press Syndicate of the University of Cambridge
The Pitt Building, Trumpington Street, Cambridge CB2 1RP.
40 West 20th Street, New York, NY 10011-4211, USA
10 Stamford Road, Oakleigh, Melbourne 3166. Australia

First published 1993

Publication of this book has been aided by a grant from the Abraham and Rebecca Stein
Fund of New York University, Department of English

Printed in Great Britain at the University Press, Cambridge

A catalogue record for this book is available from the British Library

Library of Congress cataloguing in publication data
Maynard, John. 1941–
Victorian Discourses on Sexuality and Religion/John Maynard.
p.   cm.
Includes index.
ISBN 0 521 33254 0
1. English literature – 19th century – History and criticism.
2. Religion in literature. 3. Sex – Religious aspects. 4. Sex in literature. 1 Title.
PR468.R44M39 1992
820.9'382'09034 – dc20   92-12820   CIP

ISBN 0 521 33254 0 hardback

UP

For Alex and for Ursula

Contents

Acknowledgments

It is a pleasure to offer thanks to the many friends and colleagues who have offered support, intellectual and often practical as well, to this project over a number of years: Richard D. Altick, Abigail Bloom, Jerome H. Buckley, Tom Collins, Nina daVinci-Nichols, Lloyd Davis, Heather Dubrow, Melissa C. Flannery, Linda K. Hughes, Ruth Johnston, Judith Kennedy, Nikki Lee Manos, Robert Martin, Renée Overholser, Beth Povinelli, Charles Ross, Mark Rudman, Warwick Slinn, Jeffrey Spear, Catherine Stevenson, Enid Stubin, George Thompson, Michael Timko, and Aileen Ward. In sadness I also record my debt of gratitude to three splendid scholars, thinkers, and friends who have passed away in the last few years, John Clive, Gordon Ray, and Geoffrey Summerfield.

Andrew Brown, Angela M. K. and L. W. R. Covey-Crump, and Joan and John Holloway were most hospitable during a research visit. The officials of the British Library Manuscript Room, of Balliol College Library, of the New York Public Library, and of the Princeton and Yale University Libraries have been extremely helpful.

I am very thankful to the John Simon Guggenheim Foundation for support in the earlier stages of this work, to the New York University Research Challenge Fund for later aid, as well as to Duncan Rice, Dean, and the late Robert Korchak, Budget Director, of Arts and Science, New York University. Professors Sergio Perosa and Rosella Zorzi most kindly offered civilized leisure from faculty business during a term at the University of Venice to allow final revisions. Mary-Beth Horn was a patient and most effective word-processor.

PERMISSIONS

Permission to reproduce drawings and to quote from unpublished letters by Charles and Fanny Kingsley was generously given by

Angela M. K. Covey-Crump. Drawings from "Elizabeth of Hungary" are also reproduced by permission of the British Library. Portions of this book, in somewhat different form, appeared in *Annals of Scholarship* (1990), *University of Hartford Studies in Literature* (1986), and *Pequod* (1987); and a section will appear in a book forthcoming with the SUNY Press, edited by Lloyd Davis. The publishers have kindly granted permission for partial reproductions here.

CHAPTER I

Introduction: *The Subject Somewhat Broadly Conceived*

This book looks at the rather substantial discourses on the relations of sexuality and religion in a number of Victorian writers. They were in the first instance chosen for the degree to which they placed this conjoint subject at the center of their thinking and writing. The names of three of them, Clough, Kingsley, and Patmore, well enough known to the Victorianist, will perhaps be only vaguely recognized, or even virgin territory, to that blessedly not extinct species, the curious general reader. Hardy, the subject of my conclusion, is of course a world-read modern writer as well as an eminent Victorian and I use him precisely to open the subject out from the Victorian English cases I primarily consider. But my other choices have their own importance quite apart from their usefulness to this topic.

Arthur Hugh Clough, always cast in a secondary role to Matthew Arnold as the Thyrsis of his elegy, is also always being rediscovered as the other Victorian poet of genius, whether as an anticipator of modernism when that meant T. S. Eliot's work or as, in a recent book, an intellectually more interesting Victorian writer on religion than the modernist's favorite, Hopkins.[1] Whatever the play in his reputation, he is a permanently exciting, unchangingly readable English poet. Charles Kingsley is something less, though also something more. An eminent Victorian rather than a truly major creative talent, he was also a person of intellectual importance of his day, a major force as muscular Christian and very popular novelist and sage in the creation of at least one segment of the Victorian and indeed – as a long-read child and adolescent's author – also twentieth-century mind. His representativeness and wide influence give his copious works an importance beyond the talent they display, which is nonetheless not inconsiderable, titanic in energy and output if not Olympian in control and formal artistry. Coventry Patmore will be least known, and then perhaps only because of a half-life granted him at the moment in the reflected light of some feminists' burning anger or glowing disdain. Not so much his work as the title of one of his poems – the once-famous *The Angel in the House* – survives as a household word for what he in fact never advocated, the limitation of woman to a domestic pedestal. That poem, so popular in its day, strikes me in any case as a very false direction of Patmore's poetic inspiration. But I do argue for the lasting value of his statements on loss and desire in his unknown experimental early poems and especially in his sometimes great – and barely known – odes in the late series, written after his conversion to Catholicism, *The Unknown Eros*.

These three offer a convenient display of Victorian religious centers: honest doubter, Anglican churchman, Catholic convert. But what has brought me in this book to these writers is primarily their passionate interest in those mega-issues of humanity that I wanted to try to look at. They have a double advantage in this effort. Unlike so many writers who can hardly not be involved here and there with the mystery of sex, religion, and their relation, but who often do not draw out their thinking to clarity, these Victorians make this combined subject the central focus of their works. Their fascination with the issue is abiding and even verging on the obsessive – as if they were all caught in the seductive gaze, or by the even more enticing language, of that serpent creature who has been the central symbol in Western culture for the unresolvable nexus of our sexual and religious perplexities. In their fascination these writers have also created quite full, unusually articulate discussions of these great topics, especially discussions about their perennial and not easily fathomable relation. In exploring the complicated work of three fine minds who had special talents for finding word for what is hard to speak, I have thought I might at least have the opportunity to probe the mystery of this subject.

Before turning to their works, it seems to me useful to look in this introduction briefly at the broader issue that underlies this inquiry, the general relation of sexuality and religion. The temptation would be to see these Victorians as merely sports from an age of strange growths, new eminent specimens to place in a Stracheyan gallery of God-mad or sex-mad, or perhaps God-and-sex-mad Victorian eccentrics. I can hardly deny the interesting eccentricity of some of their work. Their writings may offend traditional religious conformists who have an instinctive distaste for mixtures of the profane with the sacred. More likely, some of their thinking will offend modern readers by forcing them to consider the degree to which sexual discourse is still anything but free from religious issues and traces. It may well be that the only scandal that remains in the postmodern world is that of religious seriousness. And these writers were often very serious about seeking a religious basis for their thinking on sex – though sometimes, as with Clough and Hardy, deliciously irreverent as well.

Whether serious or joking, these writers saw in the relations of sexuality and religion not an eccentric but a central subject. And when we look into it, we find that they are right: this certainly has been a central issue in human thinking in all cultures and all ages. It is rather we who are eccentric, even from our own Western traditions, in looking to separate sexual discussions as secular phenomena from their usual religious affiliations. This introduction is my necessarily brief and sketchy essay to recollect that larger human discourse in its broadest form; I then outline briefly the more specific history of the Western discourse on sexuality and religion that was, as my individual discussions will show, very clearly before my Victorian examples as a history of controversy to which they reacted and in which they participated. For some readers this summary may only remind them of what they know already. But it seems to me especially necessary as a preliminary because there has been not only an inclination in the literature on Victorians to marginalize, or even totally overlook, such thinking on religion and sexuality; there has even been a wholesale tendency to place secular discourses on sexuality at the center of Victorian thinking.

As I show at the end of this chapter, the result has been a strange kind of mis-focus, in which all commentators admit that religion has been central, of course, to sexual thinking throughout the ages and into the Victorian period, but yet almost all then give undue prominence to the strange and highly fictional discourses of medical scientists – all the time admitting that the wild theories and gross prejudices of these primitive scientific mavins seem merely secular versions of various religious positions. The continuing importance of the religious discourse, from which all others still spring by agreement or difference throughout most of the century, will be clear in this account of Victorian thinkers who are much more centrally located, and more influential, than the pompous or fanciful men of science who occasionally left the horror and confusions of their hospitals or laboratories to pontificate on issues of sex, morality, and belief. As significant is the way in which even new ideas on sexuality seem necessarily to continue to articulate the universal discourses that bring together religion and sexuality – those two great and highly artificial arenas of language in which humankind creates meaning for itself. Hardy, who, as I show in the final chapter, never doubts that the two have been created and have flourished together, usefully focusses this age-old discussion by asking whether, and at what costs, they could both be dispensed with.

One brief word, before beginning, on my words: in *my* discourse I have followed our time-spirit and used the now popular term "discourse," especially because it has been a useful way to speak of how a creative vision can embody more fully than mere logical argument or essay an entire way of thinking about a subject. By using all the power of words at their disposal as creative writers – poetry, fiction, essay, or often a mixture of the three – my subjects have been able to articulate more of the mystery they insist on approaching than the mere writer of ideas might: not because of some magic in the aesthetic object (though there *is* magic we should not try to deny in the greatest art) but because they have a full toolshop of language with which to fabricate their different verbal creations. The term "discourse," which I sometimes alternate with the more everyday "discussion," also has its value in calling attention to the created, world-of-language, quality of both religious and sexual ideas. I also use the term, often in the plural, with the reservation that the modern mind is a more cosmopolitan thing than even a great historian of ideas such as Michel Foucault might wish to assume (because cosmopolitanism is necessarily untidy and resistant to systematic explanation).[2] Better begin by presuming only to explore the variety of different discourses put together by individuals, in reaction to earlier thinkers and to each other, and try only much later to define some unifying tendencies creating connections between the discourses of an age – and thus in the massive sum constituting *the* discourse. Otherwise we may find that in the quest for the hidden key to all discourses we have only a catalog of the obvious points that writers share and have missed the play of argument, point of view, texture, and difference that keep the debate of modern minds going unceasingly in a system of thought that contains – not necessarily blends – in its different moments all other earlier systems.

What is the fascination exerted by that old serpent that these writers, like so many others, should keep coming back, as this book does, to the issue of sex and religion? We hardly need an explanation for the interest of sex – with its obvious appeal to our senses awakened even by the word – or indeed for religion, which is after all the quieter place where we all agree certain mysteries lie and should, now or some day, be looked into by us. But what of their linkage? Why that garden story, which won't leave us, still joining nakedness, love, temptation, and our mortal and immortal destinies – despite all efforts of theologians to separate the sin from the sex? To the extent that we still look, as these Victorian writers did, through the special lenses of a Judeo-Christian Western heritage, we may begin with a sense that the issue is taboo, a dirty subject put against the clean holy of holies. Strong forces are still at work to insist that they be kept apart; Hardy's *Jude the Obscure*, the focus of the concluding chapter, actually had the honor of being burned by a bishop – because, as Hardy remarked, he couldn't find a way to do the traditional honors to the author himself. Martin Scorsese's interesting film interpretation of Jesus, *The Last Temptation of Christ,* could still inspire rage, anathema, and picket lines for bringing sex into the life of Christ. *E pur si muove.* The Magdalene has always had a central place and fascination in the Jesus tale. Sex – as the obsessive temptation of the hermit or the worrying preoccupation of the proscribing godly – and sexual desire – as the energizing force of fervid religious aspirations – have rarely been absent from Western religion. Especially after Augustine, discussions of man's fallen state have been hopelessly entwined with those of concupiscence or carnal desire. Our central arguments over avoiding sex – the eventual imposition of celibacy on the clergy in the Middle Ages and its rescission in the Protestant Reformation, the monastic and other ascetic movements, focus on the immaculate conception of Christ and Mary or on the perpetual virginity of the Virgin (how many siblings *did* Jesus have?) – all only underline the unavoidable inter-involvement of our culture's thinking on religion and sex. The very language of Western religious tradition testifies to this mingled discourse. The Old Testament affirms a God who himself affirms marital fruitfulness as a central religious duty and who increasingly brings into religious articulation the culture's practices of marriage and sex, from rules against sex during menstruation to the central introductory ritual of circumcision. In the passionate and lyrical love songs included in the received text of the Old Testament – the Song of Solomon (of Songs;

or Canticles) Christians, like some Jewish commentators, have found a language for the religious community's relation to God, or even that of the individual. The New Testament itself fervidly dreams of the union of Church and man to the Creator as a marriage – the great marriage of the Lamb in Revelation.

Although both Judaism and Christianity were created in difference from the polytheism of the pagan religions around them, they are not greatly distinct, in their insistence on connecting religion and sexuality, from the worship of those strange gods after which their devotees – in the sexual language regularly used – were so often given to whoring. It is indeed one convention of our century that the traditional distinction between pagan sexuality and Judeo-Christian purity should be overwritten and stress now placed on similarities between the Western tradition and religions that are more obviously positive toward sexual expression and more direct in combining sexual and religious symbols. This is certainly our heritage from James Frazer's *The Golden Bough*, with its even too-universalistic demonstrations of prominent similarities between, say, the Christian myth of death and resurrection and fertility myths in polytheistic cultures. And the stress on sexuality as a unifying motif across religions is one we inherit generally from the emphases of the Cambridge School at the beginning of the twentieth century in exposing the sexual nature of much classical ritual. Similarly, we read in widely popular anthropologists like Bronislaw Malinowski or Margaret Mead about the far more open sexual elements in religious ritual in certain cultures, though we may not have noticed sufficiently that Trobrianders followed especially controlling and prescriptive rules on sex. What we did hear, especially from Mead's Arcadian descriptions, chimed with a predisposition to liberate ourselves from earlier codes of reticence and decorum.

If one strategy of our century has been to try to uncover a universal religion beneath the surface of Judaism and Christianity, another, opposite one, has been to stigmatize Western religion as uniquely opposed to sexuality. A recent general critic can still rather naively (if rather eloquently) oppose sexual nature (the way of other cultures and traditions) to a Western religion set against nature (a Judeo-Christian religion trying to suppress sex but succeeding only in repressing temporarily a pagan culture of nature that now reasserts itself in force in our day).[3] This view, so common in our pro-sex, religion-wary century, overlooks the many ways in which Judaism and Christianity have always celebrated marriage and sex, if also, like most religions, tried to regulate them. And it ignores the many ways in which Christianity has built religion upon sexual language and experience: in the varied sexual discourses of the early Church, in Catholic mystic writers, or in nineteenth- and twentieth-century sexually liberal beliefs. And, as I shall stress below, it overlooks the essentially sexual orientation of the ascetic or controlling and regulating impulses themselves.

The more important critique of this kind of thinking, however, is that it valorizes nature, in which sex is regularly included, as a reality beyond discourse. In this it too willfully jumps over the prime hurdle to all investigation of the history of ideas on sex and religion: that *both* are manufactured discourses, mysteriously generated in humans' need to make some sense, or get some use, or both, out of their strongest experiences. They are perhaps the greatest products of humans' astounding ability to create a cultural world of ideas and symbols in the void of our meaningless physical existence on this planet. When we use the term religion, we are generally clear, whether we are conscious of it or not, that we are talking about a construction about god or gods, not a hierophantic or mystic experience itself; similarly we should be aware that sexuality is itself a discourse, quite separate from the facts of sex itself, which of course can only enter discourse as already language about sex, not sex acts.[4] Created out of humans' and societies' need to make some sense out of their greatest experiences, both discourses, of religion and sex, tend to parallel each other in articulating larger structures of meaning or organization around simple cores of ritual and symbol; and each regularly draws on the structure, detail, or accumulating power of the other to promote its discourse.

All societies, as far as our histories of religion or our anthropological studies of other cultures have been able to determine, build up cultural systems that articulate relations of religion and sex. And in this our Western traditions are unique only as all traditions are, in offering a highly individual intermingling and resolution of the two discourses. Depending on how one approaches this fact, either religion or sex may seem to be the by-product of the other. Religious comparativists may simply assume that it is of the nature of religion to become an imperial discourse to which nothing human is alien: "religion takes all the world as its province and turns its eyes upon the slightest manifestations of sex, as the history of the great world religions demonstrates."[5] Or we can focus on the myth-producing power of sexual energies and fantasies, which are thus seen in some sense as a major motivation or guiding force in man's need to create religion; sex then offers some major drive for the human need of religion and provides a good deal of religion's symbolism. As Balliol's celebrated Master, classicist Benjamin Jowett put it, "It has been imagined by Skeptics that all the more intense forms of religion are really bastard or illegitimate results of the relations of the sexes."[6] This process of course can take complicated and often obscure forms: notably in Freud's unclear ideas of religion as displaced or necessarily redirected sexual energies (sublimation),[7] or in Jung and his disciples' complicated compromise system, in which religious and sexual symbols are seen as arising from the same psychic centers and developing hand in hand.[8] One may hazard the guess that even the persistence of Jungian thinking, despite its central irrationalism – innate psychic symbols, or acquired psychic forms inherited by mankind in an almost Lamarckian process – is perhaps explained by its ability so well to read a plot for the development of religion and sex in the obviously sexual imagery of religion. Whereas Jungians find a way of connecting the two in their theories of genesis, other writers on the subject are apt to muddle into an or/and way of considering the primacy of religion or sex: is the chicken the system of belief and ritual spawned by man's thinking about eggs and their fertilization? Or is the world system the great egg of eternity that opens to reveal all other phenomena, including the birds and bees? One twentieth-century writer, creating a history of phallicism based strongly on R. Payne Knight's speculations back in the eighteenth century, opts, contrary to Knight, for the world egg – "It is not strange, then, that the successive physical acts that eventuate in birth, together with the parts of the human body that enact this greatest of dramas, should have served humankind at all known times and places as a basis for religious observance" – only to blunder later in his treatise into the opposite position: "Most religion, and all expression of spiritual idealism, as it relates to society, primarily got its start from the sexual embrace. Without sexuality the world would have been cold and passionless and men would have felt no need for the exaltation of religion."[9] Before such general confusion in matters hardly open to research, it is perhaps best to conclude that both discourses, on sex and religion, have tended to grow together and twine together. As Jung himself noted in his practice, sexual questions invariably turn out to be religious ones and religious questions always turn out to be sexual.[10]

The relation of sex and religion in the world's religions, including those of the West, takes a variety of forms; what doesn't vary is the fact that the two are significantly and importantly related. There is room here only to suggest the prototypical forms: first, there are religions that openly and directly celebrate the relation between the divine and the human as a sexual one; or they present it by a symbolism so strongly sexual that it virtually amounts to the same thing. This may be a direct myth of an intercourse. A good example of this is the Hindu myth of god of love Krishna and the cowgirl Radha, his chosen paramour who left her husband to join the god and with him explore and enjoy the archetypal positions of approved lovemaking. The idea of sex with God is still perhaps a shocking notion in the West, where so many less attractive ideas have ceased to shock, though Harold Bloom has reminded us that in its most powerful versions of him the Bible offers not a philosophical idea of God but a creature like ourselves, who began his relation with us by a form of intimate suscitation.[11] The idea of some kind of sexual liaison with God was in any case not unknown to Christian mysticism. An example would be those much-debated Canticles, when they are read not as the love poems of Solomon but, from within their position in a sacred text, as a way of speaking of the passionate relation of God and the soul. The general issue was indeed a central preoccupation of the subject of my fourth chapter, Patmore.

Or a sexual union between human and deity may be implied in ritual activity of a sexual sort. And such ritual is a central function in many religions. For instance, there is the frequent custom, in pagan religions of antiquity, in traditional Hinduism, or in contemporary cultures studied by anthropologists, of an initiation by ritual defloration, whether by a person representing a god or by a stone or wooden phallus. The ritual itself may vary from actual sexual act to open or even disguised symbolic representation, as for instance in the confirmation ceremony in some Christian churches, where the maiden is dressed in white and sponsored by a male friend of the family. Such a ceremony may serve a jointly symbolic purpose in extending meaning to human puberty: providing an introduction to both adult religious and sexual life. Another ritual, that of sacred prostitution, offers similarly a token of divine intercourse: the spirit of the gods flows through the prostitute, herself often believed married to a god, into the devotee/customer. In the process the more worldly desires of both customer and religion could also be served. Though the British in India were unable, or unwilling, to eliminate commercial prostitution, they saw such a religion as a fundamental, perhaps because too competitive, threat and extirpated the hetairai-like *deva-dasis* from traditional Hinduism rather thoroughly. Stories of the gender reversal of this practice, sex with a priest who conveyed the force of the god, seem to suggest it was less effective, except in the limited case of initial defloration, possibly because it was too easily abused by a charlatan priest.[12] Throwing maidens before minotaurs or young men before dragons can be understood as extremes of sexual initiation. Georges Bataille's suggestive speculations on all kinds of ritual sacrifice, so prevalent in most religions and yet limited to symbolic or outlaw expression in the West since the triumph of Christianity, call attention to a connection between sexual experience, the limits of human culture and control, and the experiences of blood and death in sacrifice.[13]

Finally and most obviously, there is the great unkept secret of phallic worship, whether in Hindu stories of lingam and yoni, or in those Etruscan tomb appointments D. H. Lawrence found so interesting, or in the numerous relics of phallic ritual in Japan, or in the wayside shrines of West Africa.[14] Nineteenth-century students of mythology and religion as different as Grote and Frazer assumed or argued a progressive and universal evolution in religion away from phallic cults, making these in effect special versions of an anthropomorphic and polytheistic religion of nature from which more civilized cultures were supposed to turn in order to submit to an abstract deity.[15] That histories of phallic worship cannot forbear to remind us – as Robert Browning did so interestingly in his *Fifine at the Fair*, where an old Druid phallic stone is explicitly compared to the modern gothic steeple which has only succeeded in reifying it in attempting to supplant it – of the hidden examples of phallic religion everywhere around us, only suggests how illusory this faith in upward progress has been.[16] Needless to say, another admirer of R. Payne Knight, Sigmund Freud, has broadly succeeded in once again releasing the forms of male sexuality into our landscape, though he did not adequately release the companion form that would have restored the female polarity to our vision. Though it is probably foolish to seek for one determining meaning of such an over-determined object as a phallus (or, as twentieth-century anthropologists have cautioned, for one universal historical pattern for the rise and fall of any worship), the almost universal inclusion of such direct sexual symbols in religions, whether overtly or covertly, certainly suggests some common function in humans' discourses on sex and religion. Here the god almost is the sex, the sex the god.

A second large group of religions tends to separate the world of deity from that of human life, but allows that world to mimic human sexual concerns. Such polytheistic religions imagine gods very much involved in their own sexual affairs, thus offering a kind of display of human sexual issues and energies in a larger tableau. The inference can be drawn that sex is a central source of motivation for the universe and, often, as in myths of origin, of creating force; or, conversely, that these religions insist on commenting on this subject as on all major human interests. The divine beings may be rather close to phallic symbols themselves, with great earth mothers representing the powers of fertility paralleled by phallic powers of heaven, earth by sun, or clouds by rain, or the general sexual principles of Chinese Yin and Yang; indeed, the Hindu fertility god Shiva and his lover Parvati appear both as beings and as their sexual parts, especially that lingam of Shiva that caused such trouble through the world when men dared to curse it. Or the world of divinity may be theatrical and quite human, as in the fully elaborated loves of Zeus or the Shinto procreative adventures of the generating god and goddess Izanagi and Izanami; or something in between, as in the varied names, bodies, and functions of Venus. Usually some sexual relations with humans are brought into these stories so that there is a somewhat suppressed version of the kind of religion directly focussed on divine–human intercourse.

Just as these pantheons maintain parodic or direct contact with human sexuality, the apparently unworldly or anti-worldly religions that style themselves as the end of a purifying evolution out of nature are very much created in special relation to the merely natural or carnal world they may seem to ignore or spurn. In dualistic systems in which sex as part of the human, earthly world is opposed to a spiritual, supernal world, sex is not a neutral term, not merely one aspect of the worldly things left behind. Rather it is normally made a central term in the antinomy: the main thing one is not to do in ascetic systems, for instance in monastic and conventual social structures as widely different in origin as Buddhism and Christianity. The negative term is stressed by its necessary absence to the creation and perpetuation of the ascetic system. As Foucault has so elegantly shown in his thinking about the development of a discourse of sexuality in the nineteenth century and earlier, the elaboration of religious negations of sexuality breeds an equal elaboration of sexual discourse. Conversely, and somewhat more generally, it is an obvious truth rather obscured to our view by its very evidentness, that anti-worldly religions are elaborated as antitheses of discourses of sexuality and in some sense only exist as discourses in this opposition.[17] Moses leaves his wife and goes up on the mountain, never to enjoy her again; Buddha resigns a married life and founds a monastic one centrally committed to shunning the kind of sexual life he has abandoned; Augustine cashiers the faithful mistress who ministered to the sexual demands of his body; takes on another; considers respectable Roman marriage, but abandons the project; finally, leaves all women (except mother) for the life of the West's greatest promoter of religion as the antagonist to sexual burning.

Sexuality may be configured in unworldly or fully ascetic systems in a number of forms. First, there is the familiar idea of a purely anti-sexual asceticism; and the focus is on what can be made of the denial; there is likely to be a stress on resisting the temptation of sexuality as the negative spiritual exercise that leads one to the positive spiritual plane – for instance, in the ascetic development of Christianity, St. Anthony in the Egyptian deep desert finding and then resisting the enduring sexual thought-flow at the very core of his nature; or Hindu hermits being tempted by actual women in the ascetic development of Hinduism. I use the second, less familiar example beside the well-known Christian one for a reason. That even Hinduism, often cited as the most worldly and sexual of major religions, can so easily develop an ascetic tradition based on rejection of sexuality much like the Christian one should suggest that we are dealing not with fundamentally different kinds of religion but with alternative states of a similar thing in non-ascetic and ascetic developments of a religion.[18]

This relation is more obvious in developments within an other-worldly or ascetic religious tradition which begin to allow the return of repressed sexual powers in controlled, usually symbolic ways. In these cases sexuality is not only the defining other discourse that enables the ascetic one; it also in effect leaks the excluded and thus amplified sexual concerns back into its system. Sexual concepts, or, in Freudian terms, sexual energies are consciously or semi-consciously redirected toward a spiritual world: in the medieval Catholic tradition of St. Bernard of Clairvaux, for instance, whose sermons on the Song of Solomon celebrated the union of God and man in sensual, sexual terms; or in the well-known raptures of St. Teresa of Avila, whose visions of angelic visitation, piercing her heart with a golden spear, were probably correctly made conscious by Bernini's statue as sexual in kind; or in the sensuous, rocking rhythm of the student studying the Torah in the Hasidic tradition, sometimes even spoken of as a kind of spiritual copulation. "There is no point at all in blinking the fact," one historian of mysticism has concluded, "that the raptures of the theistic mystic are closely akin to the transports of sexual union, the soul playing the part of the female and God appearing as the male. The close parallel between the sexual act and the mystical union with God may seem blasphemous today. Yet the blasphemy is not in the comparison, but in the degrading of the one act of which man is capable that makes him like God both in the intensity of his union with his partner and in the fact that by this union he is co-creator with God."[19]

Such a statement itself trails with it, of course, a certain cloudy but still perhaps attractive after-glory of modern Christian idealistic and liberal sexual–religious attitudes, as well as less durable male assumptions about the primacy of paternity in the human as in the cosmic sphere. But the underlying dependence of other-worldly formulations on intertwined ideologies and attitudes toward religion and sexuality is especially apparent in activity far less easy to accommodate to such idealistic modern sexual values. This is the tendency toward a full reversal of asceticism by apparently deliberate violation of its codes, and indeed of many codes present in non-ascetic systems. In those provocative studies of sexuality and ritual sacrifice, Bataille indeed suggested that sexual activity generally was conse-crated to religious uses because of its violation of normal boundaries and controls: a quality of all sex experience that he found to be especially evoked in religious ritual.[20] We could look at the persistent allegations of sodomy, written even into the six-letter words of our language, in the heresies of the Middle Ages; or at the enthusiastic and sexually aberrant groups, those so-called Ranters, who surfaced in the confused period after the English Civil War; or even at the various, weird sexual–religious sects that emerged in the United States and keep emerging to this day – though now they appear more often on television than in black masses or mass heresy trials.[21]

The best example is perhaps the complicated development within a number of major religions known as Tantrism. Within the openly sexual practices of Hindu religion Tantrism developed as an extreme of mingled sexual–religious practices, including special focus on the sexual nature of cosmic powers, a quest for sexual ecstasy as a religious goal, and the sacralization of actual sexual intercourse. Even in a Hindu context there was a tendency to explicit violation of taboos, for instance of restrictions on sex during menstruation; or there was a willingness to engage in actions normally considered excessive, such as orgies or partner swapping. As the ideas and practices of the cults spread into the Buddhist world, and eventually as far as Japan, they offered an essentially antithetical expression of the original inspiration for Buddhist asceticism. Tantric Buddhists sought to become Buddha by worshipping the ascetic leader imaged in a perpetual yoni. In place of ascetic rites there were demonic sexual initiations based on deliberate reversal of the religion's original asceticism.[22] In such religious groups and rituals we can actually see the completion of the process everywhere at work in asceticism: first, the development of a new sphere of other-worldly or spiritual life created precisely out of the repression of the sexual discourse present in worldly religions; then a second level diversion of energies and language to the fashioning of a spiritual world; and finally the achievement of a new kind of religious experience, perhaps often closest to ecstasy, by deliberate reoccupation of the shunned sexual territories for a specifically religious aim. And this, of course, draws upon all the special force, discursive and emotional, that comes from knowingly – even against great inner resistance – violating normal taboos in the service of religion. The Tantric cults suggest why the concept of sublimation is in fact so difficult to pin down; on the one hand, their special stress on retention of semen as a way to promote and preserve spiritual ecstasy seems to follow almost precisely the classic idea of a deliberate channeling of sexual energies for spiritual aims. Yet the important use of taboo-breaking activity of an emphatically sexual nature seems to reverse the entire concept until one can ask, with those who will seek to stop such behaviour, whether the religion isn't being sublimated into sex. In fact, the entire system of asceticism, taken to this extent, reveals its nature as a complicated version of other religions that directly join sexual and religious celebration. Both types use sexual symbolism, ideology, and ritual to celebrate divinity; the difference is perhaps mainly a matter of immanence versus dualism. One situates itself within the apparent or experiential universe and makes of this a sexual celebration; the other uses sexual discourses to celebrate a removed divine world, even to bring it within reach for a time.

Such intimate and complex intermeldings of religious and sexual rites and myths exhibit sufficiently clearly their habitual connection. It is worth noting as well how closely the two are linked even when no complicated symbolic practices or mythologies bring them together in a unified discourse. For instance, in ethical religious systems that place stress primarily on a "way" of living or conduct of life, sexual activity is nonetheless a central object of regulation. And in the process there is really a subtle shaping of a discourse of sexual meanings, even as this is maintained at the level of daily practice rather than extraordinary myths of origins or ultimate destinies. Sex generally rears its attractive head, along with those somber facts of life, of death and burial, as what most needs organization and control, and through control, definition. As a symbolism of the cosmos, Confuscianism could tolerate the traditional Chinese sexual system of Yin and Yang. Yet as a philosophy of life concerned mainly with organization of daily living it insisted on prescribing its own rules for rather sedate and controlled sexual practice. The potential threat of female sexuality and power was literally boxed off in the home and bed-chamber, thus highlighting a view of sex as a force before which its rational and political way of living stood at risk. Or in classical Greek society, where the system of traditional myth, still formally honored, was becoming second in practical importance to various systems – Stoic, Epicurean, medical – for daily living, elaborate regulations and precautions structured the enjoyment of sexual pleasure: so that, as Michel Foucault has elegantly shown, Greek attention was not on the facts of a bisexual, pederastic-heterosexual system of sex that so strike and interest us but on the healthy and honorable manoeuvring of the individual within these givens.[23]

Such focus on regulation and definition of sex experience is equally obvious in religions where there may also be a prominent controlling mythic figure, especially in a monotheistic system such as ancient Judaism, where the patriarchal word in a written text has become the center of religious activity.[24] In the interpreters' idea of God there is little direct sexual content and indeed a great uncertainty about God's possession of a body. Often there is a fear of danger to us of seeing or naming it – even though we are made in his image. Potential mates in earlier or neighboring female earth deities have been driven away so that the definition of God as supreme patriarch often seems paradoxically to render him beyond gender or sex, a behemoth of power to Job or an almost science-fiction fantasy of wheels, wings, and fires to Ezekiel.[25] Yet we know a God by his works, and his show a tremendous interest – more of a Jewish matriarch than father – in every detail of his creations' sex lives, from rigid prohibition of sex during menstruation to rules against sodomy (but *not* through the eponymous tale of the manhandling of the angel-visitor, which was pruriently misinterpreted much later), to pro-hibitions against birth control and in favor of family service to a diseased brother's wife – both conveniently summarized by the story of Onan and Tamar. One reads, indeed, an ordering system generally focussed, in both its prohibitions and injunctions, on maximizing procreative sex; and one reads through such a system a narrowly patriarchal but positive celebration of life on earth.

Of course even in elaborately ritualistic and mythic religions there is usually a series of practical regulations, very often including ritual contamination during menstruation or after childbirth or elaborate systems and handbooks of sexual positions or emission controls – as in Hindu or Taoist traditions. Even quotidian sex activities are instinctively felt by most cultures to belong in a realm shared with or supervised by religious powers and discourses. Sexual energies seem not only especially worthy of regulation but even serve as natural focal points for divine penetration into daily human life. As we study the vastly different sexual folkways and implicit attitudes to sex manifested in different cultures, we can be certain that these constitute a major axis of cultural and individual self-definition and self-production.

In face of so many, and many rather overt, relations between constructions of sexuality and of religion there is a natural temptation to go beyond the phenomena of their conjunction and to try to find some causal link between them. Students of literature, who are ourselves used to the ineradicable excess of interpretive possibilities stimulated by a given text, are prone to a strange reversion to positivism when dealing with phenomena from the worlds of religion and myth, perhaps because these "real-life" cultural activities are seen as lying somewhere outside of the magic circles of artistic hermeneutics. So we have been tempted, as we generally aren't in literary interpretation, to seek a single-minded causal explanation when we glanced over at those nearby sites of symbolism: anthropological fields, archaeological digs, or those massive anthologies by students of comparative religion or myth. In the process, we have uncritically treated the now antiquated work of James Frazer as both latest and true word in the history of myth; we have, some of us, singularly honored Freud and Jung when they have been largely ignored by anthropologists.[26] Of course we – as structuralists in those brief years when that seemed the only game in town – were delighted to jump on the Lévi-Strauss bandwagon, even if it meant clearing the myth board of all the usual kinds of meaning we generally work in. And as a radical corrective we were delighted with the work of Clifford Geertz because it treated social, cultural phenomena so much like works of art.

Social scientists tell us that they are generally used to working with a surplus of explanatory systems or causes, a situation that we shouldn't find so different from our usual over-filled basket of interpretation: they can explain cultural and social phenomena very adequately by one system . . . or, as adequately (at least in the opinion of other researchers), by another. If we pursue the theoretical context of a subject such as the present one seriously enough to find out what anthropology says of the conjoint appearance of religious and sexual discourses and rites, we are likely to learn mainly to be skeptical of universal explanations and the attractively simple stories that we like to tell when out of our own discipline.[27] Our once darling Frazer, out of date in his anthropological thinking even at the time of his massive and influential (and, yes, fascinating) compilations, offered Westerners an only too attractive form of evolutionism, in which all societies, past or present, were on one track of religious development leading ultimately to the wasteland of his own positivist thinking, a view we now need to historicize as much as the linguistic-racial "solar" theories of the influential German-English Victorian Max Müller. Against Frazer we need to note that religion in fact hasn't died out; and many of us now admit that so-called primitive societies may be as close to religious truth as our own eccentric monotheistic traditions. Nor does Frazer take much interest in the large area of social uses of ritual. Mircea Eliade, that other darling of ours of some years back, appears even more grossly evolutionist, with his constant efforts to find in other cultures the filaments of spiritual yearning that will lead to modern Christianity. His project indeed seems almost a perverse attempt to prove Christianity by re-interpreting all other religions as arrows pointing in his direction.[28]

Or our current enthusiasm (by revival), Joseph Campbell – like Frazer and Eliade most impressive in his omnivorous, giant ambition to ingest and then write a history of all mythologies – persistently argues a historical line of diffusionism (a few cultural inventions spread like wildfire across the globe) as a way of avoiding problems of interpretation and explanation in particular cultures (what anthropologists generally *do*); his is, incidentally, another kind of evolutionism that fossilizes primitive societies as mere provincial holdovers from earlier stages of development.[29]

Such simplifications are what we should expect from those who seek, alone in the library, to draw the big picture in fields where they have limited expertise. Their collections remain in themselves interesting depositories. But no more than those other armchair students of all cultures, Freud and Jung, do they offer usable explanations for the phenomena of religion and sexuality they all so frequently observe. To take one great example for all, I am afraid we need to retire that theory of a thousand faces (and more than nine lives) presently so attractive to some feminist thinkers: of an evolutionary religious development (or regression) from earth-mother matriarchal religions to sky-father patriarchal ones. Such developments there have been in particular cultures, or in reverse direction. But we can't hook our personal preferences in culture to some great law of necessary evolutionary development or some new myth of a fall in the pathway of universal cultural development. If it is clear how richly intertwined religion and sexuality have been in the long histories of so many, many human cultures and how universal a need, of individuals, societies, or both, their union seems to fulfill, it is not apparent that this phenomenon is susceptible of easy explanation by one or another reductionistic system.

What one can be clear about is just how fundamental the process of symbol and meaning-making is to the creation by humans of their selves and societies. To think for a moment, as Foucault has usefully asked us to do in his *Introduction* to his (alas never to be completed) *History of Sexuality*, of sex without the human discourse – the sexuality of some particular culture or way of defining human sex – is to realize how alien such thinking generally is. Foucault reminds us, brilliantly and shockingly, of the obvious fact of sex: it is not discourse but some literally unspeakable play of "bodies and pleasures."[30] If Masters and Johnson have shown us in detail that the body play is not without a certain complicated articulation of the body itself – levels of excitement, blood pressure, and the rest – it is still true that the physical facts don't leave much except such additional physical facts to talk about. There was the same sense of shock, of essential scandal, in Kinsey's earlier attempt at a clarifying sociological discussion of sex. To obtain the raw data of sex experience he was obliged to ride over distinctions of tremendous cultural meaning. Very different "sex acts," masturbation, homosexual intercourse, heterosexual intercourse, orgies, became only so many statistics, susceptible of percentage compilation. As with Foucault's philosophical clarity, or Masters and Johnson's physical explicitness, such statistical clarity gives us truths that seem harsh, unnatural.

Brute facts? Not necessarily brute or anything else; mere facts, without the meaning and ritual with which we are used to express them. The feeling of scandal that surrounded Kinsey or Masters and Johnson, that generally attaches to this way of thinking, comes not from anything prurient in the writers but from the fact that we normally don't think this way. We want to talk about our human sex in other ways than this bare bones record of sexual acts. And this is really Foucault's point: that most of what we intend when we talk about sex is just that: talk about sex, not sex: a discourse of sexuality. The brutes – animal creatures around us – are a case in point. Notice how our discourse changes radically when we discuss their sex (even to say their sexuality is too much). With them, it is indeed simply bodies and pleasures, a play of the parts; we are not bothered when we find all meaning, except the benefit or inconvenience of the results of animal mating to us, emptied from the sex discussion. Incest, that central human warning-marker around certain kinds of sex, is not even in question, unless it be the mere danger to the physical stock of too much "inbreeding" – a convenient word that never seems to strike us as a euphemism for incest.[31] Once a regular dog-walker, I can testify that I have had entirely friendly, superficial conversations while my dog and my neighbor's dog were engaging in play of the parts whose implications would have been tremendous if our children rather than dogs were at issue. Or look at the equally revealing, because so obviously crossed and confused, language where humans attempt to use animals to symbolize their own sexuality, as in totem thinking, or in the comic discourse of polite animal breeding.[32] If dogs really could talk what they might say about *our* sex practices would be more interesting. While we simply respond to a bodily signal and make puppies, they would say, you humans must make an enormous business of sex: complicated ceremonies, dances, songs, social structures; above all, you talk, talk, talk about it: stories, myths, jokes, psychoanalysis, church confession, earnest discussions that you foster on the birds and the bees, endless talk – and endless books, too!

A dog's-eye view of religion would only repeat such a radical critique: we come into the dog world willy-nilly, we run in the sun, we mate, we die: what need for your temples, churches, processions, ceremonies, rituals, myths, far less your animal or human sacrifices, self-denials (catch a dog turning from what pleasure he can find!), and your holy wars. The final chapter, on Hardy's *Jude the Obscure*, will suggest that such a dogged process of unconstruction, radically alienating us from the constructs of discourse we make on the sites of sex, death, and mystery, is always possible, that the fabric is always having to be respun, always liable to rents and runs and total unravelings. On the site of our absence, perhaps, our sense of the meaninglessness of central events in our lives – birth, coming of age, joining the ways and beliefs of our society, mating and procreation, aging and death – humans tell stories or make social events of order or meaning. Desire, momentarily stilled in sex, finds its object as often in fabrication of gods or sexual ritual, even systems of deferred or denied desire itself.[33]

After my limiting remarks on Frazer and company I will not now turn and try to provide a theoretically better history of humans' creations of sexuality and religion. But two examples from rather good and also rather open-minded and theoretically eclectic contemporary anthropologists may serve to suggest the richness of discourse in rite and myth and the extent of possible interweaving of religious and sexual discussions. Looking at the common (though not universal) ritual of initiation at puberty, which she broadly terms maturity rituals, British social anthropologist Jean La Fontaine reviews the various explanations and interpretations offered by different commentators: some see the often very lengthy, complex, certainly central, and sometimes quite painful procedures of various cultures primarily from the point of view of the individual: a rite of passage into adult life, the necessary separation of the boy from mother and integration into male society, or the more complicated admission of the girl into a new role in woman's society; at a psychological level, for boys a fending off by ordeal or sexual mutilation of anxiety over incest wishes for the mother or, in

Bettelheim's revisionist Freudian reading, a blood-letting that allows boys to assume some of the female's reproductive power. As a social event, the forms and stories of the ritual have been seen as asserting the power structures and values of the community: the wayward strength of adolescent growth is structured into the hierarchies of adult leadership; class may be defined; the community is brought together in a public assertion of shared values. Feminist analysts have seen in some rituals (most obviously in the terrible practice in some cultures of clitoridectomy) an exceptional subordination of girls as they become women in a process which in any event manifestly and massively creates gender differences.

Analysts of meaning in the rituals and stories themselves have found assertions of fertility (Frazer and company), the assimilation of the power of nature into the human community, a meaning in the structures of language and ritual themselves apart from conscious content (Lévi-Strauss and his followers), or even a variety of meanings to different participants and observers (Audrey Richards: a kind of anthropologists' reader-response interpretation). La Fontaine can comfortably buy into most of these, with the important caveat that some work better for some societies, others for others. When she attempts to say what can be said in general, she comes back to the rather obvious but rather important central occasion, which is the coming into adult sexual life of the adolescent: "The overt concern of many initiation rituals marking adult states is adult sexuality, and the rituals imply the particular ideas about human reproduction held by the people who perform them."[34] Sex education *per se* may or may not be part of the ritual but the process generally defines sexuality for the culture as it enables and celebrates its emergence in the individual. In that sense, adult human nature is being created by a complicated set of acts and language that reach out into other areas of meaning or cultural production, social roles, gender roles, unifying cultural tales. Sex or rebirth often appears in the rituals; and La Fontaine notes that almost all interpreters share a "common element": a concern with sexual symbolism and generation.[35] Finally, she remarks the religious element commonly present, whether as a sense of "mystical power" seen in male potency and presented as analogous to powers of gods and mysterious forces or as a parallel sense of female mystery in "hidden powers of generation. Sexual intercourse, in creating new life, mobilizes mystical power."[36] As an interpreter particularly committed to finding the social mobilization of such structures, La Fontaine stresses how they are used to enable the society to cohere and function. One could as well stress how they create religion in its most basic form; or, from another point of view, note how social and religious structure have come together to define and produce a certain kind of sexuality as discourse and a particular kind of adult human nature. We come again, appropriately enough, to the religio-sexual symbol of the great chicken and egg. What is important for our purposes is the centrality at such a moment of adult-making of the linking of religious and sexual rituals and meanings. That the kinds of unions, the predominance of religious mystery, sex education, or social function will vary from society to society seems a necessary, and to my thinking not unattractive, limit to any abstract theoretical definitions of their connection.

In another recent study, M. E. Combs-Schilling offers an equally broad and eclectic theoretical view but then focusses on a single cultural case, especially interesting because it is in a large, complicated, and relatively Western society, the North African kingdom of Morocco. He finds a particular configuration of Islamic religion and monarchic power coming together in a few central rituals that both create and deploy a particular kind of sexuality.

As in many religions, especially biblical Judaism, from which it borrows heavily, Morocco's version of Islamic ritual centers on a sacrifice (indeed the willingness of Abraham to sacrifice Isaac and the substitution, permitted by God, of a ram). The king sacrifices publicly each year on Prophet Muhammad's birthday, dressed in a glowing white robe, as a symbol of the patriarchal submission to the will of Allah in each household in the land. Such admission to one (male) God in the name of one (male) prophet brings power, authority, structure, cohesion to the society and to the small family societies of which it is made. The patriarchal system, which clearly subordinates women to men, both creates and is empowered by a parallel sexual system which is made equally central to ritual and belief. Each male who arrives at the second initiation rite of a society, in this society the central one, of marriage, is permitted to play king for a day, indeed is empowered by society and its leader to become a patriarchal ruler as he takes on the mature role of head of household. He is symbolically treated by family, friends, elders of the community as in the place of the king for his wedding day. The wedding night ritual is then a parallel sacrifice (recalling Bataille's general equation between animal sacrifice and sex) of the virgin bride, with a parallel and central public exhibition of the ritual letting of blood (in defloration or, in a liberal milieu, if this has already occurred, by sacrifice of an animal or an elaborate ruse that allows the bride to lose a second time what, we say, no one can lose more than once). Such a clear marriage ritual of male authority then has obvious cognates with the larger, heavily structured and rather firmly fixed sexual ideology of the Muslim religion. Men are to control and limit (presumably errant and dangerous) female sex-force here on earth. In return for thus putting Allah first in this as in all things they will be rewarded in heaven by that rather arrant case of (partial) asceticism (fully) rewarded: sex with those crystalline virgin houris, with whom the faithful male will find none of the worries and troubles he has had with real females below. Indeed, they are happy to join happy males for orgasms of up to twenty-four years!

As in La Fontaine's analysis, Combs-Schilling's stress is not on locating a single perspective from which to view this amalgam of ritual and myth but on the extremely full and complicated way in which sexual event and discourse are structured into social order and ideology, production of adult individuals and family groups, creation or ratification of religious vision. Combs-Schilling rightly points out to his Western audience not only the staying power and effectiveness of this structure (Morocco held the line against both Christian and modern Western intrusions and appropriation) but also the particular price paid in gender differentiation. Below, obviously, and in heaven by inference (since their men will have abandoned them for uncomplicated gratification with those pellucid houris and they are given no apparent place there) women have become an instrument to male authority and power. In some sense the religion has appropriated the mystery of female sexual power for a male end. The female's power in nature is ignored or slighted and attention is redirected to a male power above, as if to make males the central creative force in the universe. Combs-Schilling concludes with an interesting parallel between the three monotheisms of the West, Judaism, Christianity, and Islam. All three have used central moments of male sacrifice (Rosh Hashanah, Christ's crucifixion, Abraham's sacrifice) to leverage systems in which a lone male God is out of the natural universe, away from female power; and where ultimate fulfillment is in heaven, also out of nature.[37] Having fairly stressed the dignity, drama, and effectiveness of this Islam culture, he also notes the way in which order has been achieved by the postponement of sexuality out of life, with the result that neither male nor female looks for much personal fulfillment in human sexual life in this world. The young are not much in each others' arms, except for ritual blood-letting. A system that focusses on sexuality out of the natural universe has organized and harnessed sexual forces for its grandiose but rather abstract ends.

It is not difficult to credit such coherently presented generalizations about a large and complex historical culture that most of us know virtually nothing about. The parallels to Western Jewish/Christian traditions are doubtless more surprising and for most of us run up against a firmer sense of our own diversity and complexity, exhibited across so many varieties of belief and so many centuries. But if we are likely to say *some*, and some very major, Christian traditions have indeed worked in a similar patriarchal manner and then insist on the diversity, we should also hardly deny the larger parallel: that Western Christian beliefs and rituals have been very much involved in a continuous, if finally very diverse and complex, discourse on sexuality. Recent general studies have taken us back to the very fructuous and creative moments of Christianity's beginnings in the first four or five hundred years following the presumed preaching of Jesus and the proclamation of Christ. Historians Peter Brown[38] and Elaine Pagels[39] especially have broadly illuminated for us different ends of this world.

Pagels has emphasized a mainstream before Augustine that stressed, in sexual as in other matters, the freedom of Christians to follow conscience and reason against both the secular power of established pagan religion and the inner force of temptation. In this earlier mainstream, Christianity largely followed the traditions of self-control of many pagan sexual discussions and joined to this a traditional Jewish concern with limiting sexual activity to a fairly constricted, but fairly positive, expression of humans' God-commanded destiny to be fruitful and multiply. But a second, originally even fringe set of attitudes developed beside these views. And these, in many ways predictive of the strongest forces of the future Church, insisted in diverse ways on creating a new vision of human sexuality as an outlook central to the emerging world religion. Martyrs, holy hermits, monks, ordinary Christians who renounced family or sexual relations with their spouses began to see in sexual absence a great new source of religious presence. For some, like St. Paul, continence was merely a better alternative to the complication of marriage – necessary nonetheless for most people – in a time when the kingdom of God was anxiously expected. To others it was an especially important way in which the baptized Christian's control over temptation could be exhibited. To some it signified a level of commitment to the new religion, a continuation in some ways of the practice in the late Jewish world of a few holy persons – the Essenes, for instance – who manifested their devotion to religion by breaking away from all usual connections to a mere normal life of this world. They could become, as they were sometimes termed, athletes of the strenuous religious life.

For some others, however, as Brown so vividly recreates this world, ascesis came to take on a full meaning of a location in absence of a hope for fulfillment elsewhere. Denying the body's demands here could be the best way to ensure the true joy of a risen angelic body in another world. If there were no houris waiting there, they would in any case hardly be necessary. The risen body could experience the greater sexuality of moral weightlessness, trouble-free possession of the entire self: a dream of a fulfilled body beyond all mere genital gratification. The context was being set for the major fabricator of Christianity before the Reformation, the Augustine who turned from the confusion and anxiety of his own sexual experience to a career as the supreme formulator of sexual discourse in Christianity. As Pagels has so well suggested, Augustine inherited a Church no longer growing in martyrdom and opposition but possessing supremely the powers both of spiritual authority and of secular subsidy and support. Christianity was ready for a religion of obedience and its failures rather than of freedom and its successes. The sexual traditions that led to Augustine encouraged his full and further development of an ideology of sexuality as a site of a fallen will, a will in man that turns again and again against the aims of his religion and his higher self. The old sexually charged myth of the Fall, of course, provided the place for this central turn of Christianity. Sex did not constitute the Fall, as the persistent vulgar myth and occasional serious belief might suggest;[40] but man's present sexual nature was a result of the Fall. And Augustinian Christianity defined the lust of sex, its indiscriminate and uncontrolled drive for pleasure and fulfillment, as precisely its fallen quality. In paradise procreation would have been a rational, if not necessarily pleasureless act. Here below, man was condemned to burn, as Augustine had burned, as precisely his sexual parts and desires represented his self-opposed fallen nature and alienation from God. When he possesses God, the Word as Flesh, there will be no place for sexuality itself, the distressing production of desire by words that runs on and on in its alienation from the true aim of all man's desire.[41]

With such an ideology of sex as a central constituting tenet of the Church, Western Christianity began a long process of interaction with the sexual mores of the societies it inhabited, which were obviously at some level responsive to its message but, at another, equally obviously resistant. It was only a confirmation of its overall outlook that this now major tradition, emphatically anti-sexual in its central self-definition, should find itself in a long conflict with a diverse, greatly fallen world in land after land in which it worked. Fornication, the adverse term given to all sex other than marital sex undertaken for procreation, was everywhere only too evident, whether by folk custom before marriage, in adultery, or prostitution. Married couples were only too prone to positions or frequencies of sex that showed the modest aims of necessary procreation were hardly foremost in their minds. The clergy themselves (one of the Catholic Church's best-kept open secrets) were often strongly resistant to the new view that they should all become ascetics and provide leadership in totally controlling sex. The campaign to enforce virginity universally on the regular clergy, as opposed to monastic celibates, didn't really begin in earnest until the twelfth century and it faced massive opposition for more than two hundred years, particularly intense in some areas, from a priestly class very much used to its wives or concubines and to the passing on of priestly power within the family.[42]

As in its canon law and written discourse Christianity developed into a particularly controlling religion in sexual ideology, an extreme regulating force that intended to settle and organize every sexual issue by its master discourse of lust, it also revealed itself as especially preoccupied with sexuality. This fact is, of course, one that tends to hide behind the aggressively negative view of sex that often even leads to a prudish covering over of its own discourse. Foucault's general *Introduction* to a history of Western sexuality has been enormously helpful in unmasking this obvious preoccupation. If we have been denied his full analysis and explication of the medieval sexual discussion,[43] we have been fortunate in other broad studies of Christian sexual thought. We have not only histories by Pagels and

Brown for the earlier period (and of course a great deal of more specialized work on which their summaries draw), but also a number of works on the Middle Ages, from Le Roy Ladurie's classic if somewhat inaccurate study of priestly sex records in Montaillou[44] to John T. Noonan's study of the Church's attitudes to contraception to John Boswell's still controversial look at attitudes toward homosexuality[45] to the broad survey of marriage and sexuality by Eric Fuchs to the massive and useful studies of the development of penitentials and the canon law on sexuality and marriage by Jean-Louis Flandrin and James A. Brundage.[46] Most obviously, what we are finding is that the whole, really rather varied discussion in many lands in the entire period from early Christian times to the high Middle Ages positively reeks of sex. We have again a great chicken-and-egg issue that probably can't ever be resolved: is the Christian focus on controlling and stigmatizing sex a result of a broader tightening of sexual morals, a European *Zeitgeist* in which the Church participates and which it serves primarily to articulate? Or is the sexual issue a crux of Christian thinking and self-definition that then shapes the world it tries to guide and affect?[47] Certainly there is a diverse world of sexual opinion that includes a continuous disagreement between Church and sectors of the population in different lands, so that where the Church is effective one could conclude that it was because it was in tune with the times. On the other hand, once begun, the Church's tendency to define itself by its increasingly more ramified, often tortured reflections on all aspects of sexuality certainly created one of the fullest integrated religious–sexual discourses that the world has ever seen.

Note first that there is some reason to believe that a focus on sex, rather than specifically on driving out or controlling sex, was the first Christian inspiration. The overall direction of Christianity was of course away from the regulatory text of Judaism and toward a bodily presence in Christ the Word become flesh, or Christ of the Mass.[48] In the Word become Flesh there is necessarily a potential entry of the fleshly. At least persistent rumours of a left-wing movement toward free love communities among the early Christians, balancing the ultimately prevailing ascetic ones, as well as the generally experimental attitudes among the Gnostics (though often, in fact, very anti-corporeal) may suggest that the general direction of sexual interest was once in question.[49]

Second, even where we find a position fairly well settled within the medieval Church in an apparently strict, anti-sexual form, we find it has in fact complicating facets which lead to a vibrant rather than frozen discussion. Married sex, for instance, was determined by virtually all parties to be permissible, as we all know, for procreation only, and individuals were forbidden all practices – diverse positions, oral manipulation, anal sex – that might arise from a quest for marital pleasure. At the same time, the second cardinal rule almost set itself in dynamic opposition to the first. Because marital sex was bad, but not nearly so bad as adultery, the Church insisted strenuously on the concept of the marital debt: from Paul's own words in his famous First Epistle to the Corinthians on the sharing of bodies in marriage, married individuals were strictly told that they *must* grant sex rights to each other on demand.[50] The effect was to create within a generally negative attitude to sex a view of marriage that made the central issue the right to sex; more importantly, it built a system that presented sex as a most dangerous force that must, at all costs, be appeased. The underlying structure of thinking is one that empowers and celebrates sex even as it seems to deny it: a kind of steam pressure system with marital sex the control valve that alone can prevent moral catastrophe. And of course the ascetic similarly empowers sex when he or she creates an entire world and language in the tremendous life-long effort to control and finally vacate this power not oneself from within oneself: it is, in effect, the strongest thing in the world (and therefore) worth conquering for God. Prohibitions on intercourse for married couples, never on Sunday, never during Lent, but also not before other major celebrations of the Church year (sometimes up to nearly half the days in the year), suggest not only a ritual banning of defilement but even an attempt to bring all Christians into at least a part-time ascetic role. The substitutions, for married couples or ascetics, *either* sex or religion, would have made the connection between the two extremely clear to all members of the society.

Whatever the realities behind those rumors of liberal sexual practices in some areas of early Christianity, it was inevitable that a system which so empowered and developed sexuality as a force would eventually take some turns toward more directly harnessing those energies in a positive direction. The newer religion of Islam perhaps followed the logic more directly and easily: houris in heaven for those who kept sex from getting out of control on earth. But in its own way Christianity either followed such a movement more subtly[51] or enabled a secular version of the redirection of sexual pressure upward. The latter is perhaps one of the complicated factors in the genesis of that perplexing and much debated phenomenon of the Middle Ages, courtly love, a divisive force from the twelfth century forwards which, its classic historian Denis de Rougemont tells us, is still present in Western love whenever it takes either of its two great archetypal turns, toward the death-love of Tristan or the compulsive degradation of Don Juan.[52] Maybe. Whatever its origins and ultimate impact, about which specialists will keep quarreling,[53] as a phenomenon it certainly displays a division one might predict in a tradition where sex is seen as the most compelling and most dangerous game in town. That is, sex is made problematic, perhaps, perhaps not, the ultimate goal of love; but its force is in any case celebrated: perhaps a purely spiritual kind of love parodying religious forms and language in its classic mode of desire held at a ritual distance: the fascinating cat with its claws pulled out; perhaps a prelude to a more continuous denouement/defilement to come: the suspension that leads to death (Tristan)/the transgressive embrace of Venus that threatens damnation (Tannhäuser). *Or* the path to heaven itself: Beatrice and Laura both lead their lovers through the mixed experience of earthly spiritual love and on to contemplation of heaven.

The earthly spiritual realm of love in courtly love is perhaps best seen not as the single root of all Western confusions about sex and love but as one of many versions of the production of a realm of romance in our culture, with various weightings of anti-corporeal idealization and reversionary guilty, though often accentuated, gratification. Similarly, developments of a sexualized realm of religious fulfillment in the Middle Ages prelude other similar moves, in diverse places, sects, and times, in the long history of Christianity since. Perhaps only the very bad odor in which sex on earth was held kept Christianity earlier from more broadly and fully developing the typical formation of deferred fulfillment. Early Christians more often developed that half-way house: the body, without specific mention of sex, risen perfect in heaven: weightless, sinless, pain-free.[54] In the Middle Ages the sexualization of a relation to God took more indirect routes, in a context of increasing humanization of God through focus on both Christ and Mary as intercessors. Then a thinker of the twelfth century such as Bernard of Clairvaux could come back to the sensual biblical text, the Song of Solomon, and find in it a full vision of man's relation to God as that of lover. As in the parallel tradition of love set free from sex, the relation to God could similarly be written suggestively somewhere between soul and body. Their uncertain definition of love allowed some writers in the courtly tradition to extend their ambivalent lovemaking to heaven. Similarly, mystics after Bernard could express their longings for God in a language filled with a sensual rhetoric of earth. In the thirteenth century Mechthild of Magdeburg and Gertrude of Helfta wrote down their dreams and visions of a union with Christ that was much like that of lovers.[55] Hadn't even ordinary married couples been encouraged to think of religion as a place for an alternative use of sexual energies in the Church's complicated systems regulating intercourse against religious observances? Hadn't marriage itself been made a sacrament, contrary to earlier practice, on the view that Christ had used it as a way of speaking of his relation to the Church?

Such openings of alternative, more positive, connections between sexuality and Christian sensibility could hardly predict the wholesale recasting of the issue at the time of the Reformation, when a matter such as celibacy of the clergy, only fairly recently settled in the Catholic Church, was returned to a crucial spot in the intellectual and political battles of Christianity. And, of course, the validity of the entire great tradition of asceticism was equally put in question. The distance between the early Christian world, in which enthusiasm for denial of the body even led some ascetics to effect cohabitational "spiritual marriages" of Christian fellowship in renunciation, and the Protestant world, in which such practices would be anathema of anathemas, is a great one. Not that the initial direction was toward a more positive idea of sex in marriage itself: Luther, and to some extent Calvin, took only an even more skeptical view than the medieval Church of humans' ability to live without the remedy for lust of the marital debt – hence the abolition of all systems of celibate vows as vows that would inevitably be forsworn and hence the more permissive views on divorce and remarriage. And, of course, in a limitedly reformed church such as the Church of England much of the older system of canon law remained long intact.

The first 1,500 years of Christianity contain far more diversity in attitudes to sex than are usually ascribed to them, and within its normal parameters, far more interplay and conflict than is usually thought; and the initial revolution of the Reformation left much unchanged. Still, it opened the possibility for debate and change that has never closed since. In a longer time-frame, the period since the

Reformation has been one of far more experimental thinking in Christian attitudes toward sex, which has as often moved as radically in other directions as the Church initially did toward asceticism and formally anti-sexual positions. This is a fact often covered up for us by the simultaneous, strong continuation of those earlier traditions within and without the Catholic Church and, perhaps even more, by the emergence of secular discussions of sexual issues that tended to assume anti-religious positions or to provoke hostility from religious institutions. The antipathy between sex-positive attitudes and traditional religious views, which continued from the appearance of small groups of seventeenth- and eighteenth-century libertines to the masses of liberated thinkers of the twentieth century, has tended to mask the extent of disagreement among Christian thinkers themselves as well as the interinvolvement of secular and religious thinking.[56] Indeed, the writers discussed in this book may still surprise some readers for their scandalous sexual attitudes – the scandal being not their rather modestly expressed language and opinions but the fact that they are often connected to sincere and devout expressions of belief.

Inasmuch as this book will thus explore in some detail a few particular examples of diversity in a major period since the Renaissance, I will not try here to present a summary history of that diversity. Perhaps two examples, offering a brief reminder of the range of positions present on any major subject, will suggest the degree of open-mindedness that is required when we approach the broader discourse of religion and sex in our time. Take the issue of attitudes to marriage. We know how much controversy there has been within even the Catholic Church on the issue of contraception, with the official position still enforcing concepts of the proper nature of married sex as an instrument of procreation. This hides, however, profound movements toward a far more positive view of marital sex, beginning as a concern with the marital relation itself as opposed to the mere prophylaxis against adultery in the old concept of the marital debt, and developing especially in the liberal instructions for parochial counsel of St. Alphonsus Liguori, which were widely adopted in the early nineteenth century.[57] With Foucault, we can note more especially how the Church in the nineteenth century intensified its already enormous involvement in scrutinizing, regulating, and articulating its members' sexual experience.

Outside of the Catholic Church, even before the general celebration of the joy of sex in marriage by most Protestant sects in the twentieth century, the diversity is enormous. While the Anglican Church incorporated some of the traditional language against "carnal lusts and appetites" in marriage in the Book of Common Prayer, there seems to have been at least a major tendency among some thinkers to exalt, if not exactly sex in marriage, then an aura of love and desire. English love has been defined as a new unification of spiritual love and sexual desire within marriage. Within this broad, if nebulous tradition, Puritanism itself has been, controversially, offered as a contributing force, a reading of the record that historian-author Charles Kingsley, a strong advocate of loving, sexual marriage himself, helped to found – as we shall see. If the dating for the emergence of a modern marital system based on affection and sexual bonding remains a matter of argument,[58] what is also clear is that serious views of marriage as a site of sexual love, rather than of controlled lust and procreation, were available among Protestant believers for centuries. In the sexual radical Milton, advocate of rational divorce centuries before the traditional legislation against divorce would be finally abandoned,[59] there is also a very positive reading, against Augustine's, of the central myth of sex in paradise. Adam and Eve enjoy in their bower loving and pleasurable sex that the narrator celebrates as a model of "wedded Love": "the Rites / Mysterious of connubial Love." More significantly, such very positive married love still exists as an ideal for a Christian marriage – "Perpetual Fountain of Domestic sweets" – that the narrator contrasts to the misuse of sex in unmarried, unloving, and lustful situations.[60] For generations of English and American readers, Milton's rereading of the founding myth of sex and the Fall would become the best-known one, a major alternative to Augustine's and in many ways a clarification and replacement of Genesis.[61]

A parallel field of expanding and diversifying sexual ideology, which again I can only point to here, is that of the conceptualization of an afterlife. If some early Christians thought of heaven as a place of happy, if not especially sexualized bodies and some medieval mystics could imagine union with Christ as a sexualized ecstasy, the usual notion was Aquinas' rather static one of the full person's contemplation of God. But as McDannell and Lang have shown in their pleasant history of heaven, beginning with the Renaissance it was possible to imagine heaven as a more sociable location, even as a place of warm greetings and, in pictorial representations by Italians such as Giovanni di Paolo or Signorelli or Dutch Jean Bellegambe, as a kind of garden of bodily delights adjoined to a center of divine contemplation.[62] The Reformation, as well as the Counter-Reformation, initially brought a return to stricter, more God-centered visions of heaven. As Joseph Hall succinctly put it, "here [in heaven] is no respect of blood; none of marriage: this grosser acquaintance and pleasure is for the paradise of Turks, not the heaven of Christians."[63] Yet the issue remained in play in the ever widening, more diverse discussion of sexual subjects in the emerging modern but still Christian world. Some Protestants continued to stress the materiality of heaven.[64] Perhaps the most memorable image is again Milton's, of the blushing angel Raphael – "Celestial rosie red, Love's proper hue" – and his description of love in heaven, not quite sex as we know it but a blending of total angelic body into body: "Whatever pure thou in the body enjoy'st / . . . we enjoy / In eminence, and obstacle find none / Of membrane, joynt, or limb, exclusive barrs: / Easier than Air with Air, if Spirits embrace, / Total they mix, Union of Pure with Pure / Desiring." Or in Catholic tradition there is the increasing prominence of the Virgin in the cosmology of the heavenly family, a centered, but far more humanly centered, object of eternal contemplation. And of course with Swedenborg and Blake in the late eighteenth century there is a radical reopening of the question of a heaven that very much elevates and celebrates earthly sex. Human aspirations and relations were continued into Swedenborg's ever evolving heaven; in Blake, last judgment was a place of very warm bodily reunion of lovers.

Such large traditional issues of sexuality and Christianity – the definition of marriage or the question of sex in the great beyond – were, typically, passed into the nineteenth century as sites of disagreement and passionate diversity. Ascetic beliefs or attitudes, stemming ultimately from Augustine's time, highly suspicious of sex, still hung heavily over Victorian discussion as a conservative orthodoxy; yet quite opposing points of view could exist side by side, whether in arguments between controversial opponents or, as we will see in Clough, in the more agonized dispute within an individual's own divided mind, which thus became a microcosm (as indeed Augustine's was for his time) of the society's general division. In Kingsley we see a much more decided *parti pris*, married Christian sex set in a controversial relation to the alternative ascetic positions – which had nonetheless once asserted a considerable psychic attraction. Or in the more experimental and experiential Patmore we will find a restless movement through a variety of positions, including something like Kingsley's Protestant glorification of sex in marriage, to ultimate recovery of a Catholic mystical vision of sexual energies turned from the creature to God himself.

In the discussion of sexuality and religion, as in most areas of nineteenth-century thought, we can thus speak of a discourse only in a very special way. All cultures display a diverse set of positions among which individuals and groups in society can choose particular configurations for particular occasions. As I have been suggesting, the Christian discourse on sex was characterized in its origin and development by both diversity and an inherent inner dynamic, or even instability. By the time of the English nineteenth century, where there is such a rich mixture of diverse Christian sects and traditions with newer discussion claiming a non-religious secular identity (though often merely restating earlier positions in disguised form), the inherent diversity in the discourse demands some new, specific recognition. We are dealing with a distinctly cosmopolitan discourse in the sense I have already suggested as appropriate generally for studies of modern thought, one which is made out of a great diversity of contemporary positions – a discourse composed of varied dis- courses – and which, at the same time, is distinctly in possession of its own history. It is a discourse that doesn't, as in earlier times, merely embody the current orthodoxies and certain modifications currently being proposed but broods and builds upon its awareness of the many alternatives built into its long and complex history – here close to two thousand years of Christian thinking about, and controversy over, sexuality.[65]

It is a prime intention of this study to break beyond our own century's limiting conception of the discourse of the nineteenth century – that original location of our own cosmopolitan thinking – so that we can see the complexity and multiplicity of the age's discussions. In this, like a number of other writers on issues of nineteenth-century sexuality, most notably Peter Gay and Foucault himself, I have had to think through the stereotypes of Victorian thinking that we have inherited from the Modernist children of the Victorians. In "modernizing" their own discourse on sexuality, writers of the early twentieth century initially created a myth of Victorians' prudery and anti-sexuality that located their discourse somewhere very close to Augustine's – not without evidence, because those positions were very much available in some areas of nineteenth-century discussion and still occupied some strongholds of orthodoxy; indeed, in the late 1830s and 1840s the traditional positions seemed to many observers to be making a comeback in the return of Church tradition in both the Oxford Movement (and its accompanying restoration of nunneries among Protestants!) and new interest in conversion to Catholicism. And not without reason, because a new secular discourse, inspired by a quest for social and sexual respectability and promoted even by some medical thinkers, mimicked much of the traditional conservative Christian involvement in scrutinizing and regulating all areas of sex experience. Not only was sex seen in this discourse as a necessary evil, and varieties of sexual expression, including masturbation or birth control, as an interference with the proper aim of sex in procreation – as in the conservative Christian tradition – but there was even a relatively new stress on women as capable of sexlessness (but also as incapable of passionate sex without corruption), probably in a complex way a secularization (and gender assignment) of the Church's traditional celebration of celibacy in both men and women.

Gay in much detail and Foucault in a brilliant overview have summarized much of the specific research that has been showing this conservative discourse for what it was: one among a great diversity of Victorian positions all set in controversial relation – and itself taking a variety of forms.[66] In the time of Steven Marcus's groundbreaking *The Other Victorians* (1966), we could still conceptualize the period as an orthodox Victorianism of prudery and control – one remembers those Victorian diagrams of mechanical contraptions for controlling nocturnal emissions, themselves a scientism of an age-old concern of monastic writers, who considered triumph over involuntary ejaculation, far more than mere avoidance of masturbation, a great victory for total chastity of mind – set beside a subversive underworld of other Victorians' license and pornography – itself a shadow of the medieval reality of authorized prostitution, tolerated gang rapes, and the unholy pursuit of pleasure.[67] Marcus's contribution – an important one – was to call attention to the latter, the large Victorian underworld of sex, especially as seen through the clear lenses of that magnificent diarist and pornographer, the voracious Walter of *My Secret Life*. But he set this against a conventional modernist view of a normally prudish Victorian world, which he exemplified in the works of a Dr. William Acton. Acton's views on female disinterest in sex (for

Acton part of a complicated argument in favor of tolerating and regulating prostitution as a necessary outlet for male sexual drives) were in fact only a variant of the larger conservative discourse of the age – a discourse to which Peter Cominos has usefully given the umbrella term of sexual "respectability." But this tradition in which Acton, though with special qualities of his own, broadly fits is in no sense *the* Victorian view, as Marcus implied, but is merely that familiar conservative outlook that modernists had labeled Victorian from among many competing (and often far from fully coherent) Victorian perspectives.[68]

Marcus's use of Acton had an unfortunate additional effect of placing an obscure medical writer at the center of further discussions of Victorian attitudes to sexuality and of thus seeming to separate off a new secular discussion from the broader religious approaches of the time. Since Marcus's study, there has even been a tendency for historians to lose the firm sense of the connections of sexual ideas to religious ideas that exist even in apparently secular discussions such as Acton's and that were still so obvious to the rebellious modern children of the Victorians. Indeed, as this study will show for these central writers, most of the various Victorian discourses developed on sexuality – not only the conservative, but also liberal, innovative, or original discussions – were generated against the backdrop of the varieties of religious discussions inherited from the past.[69] The odd thing is that we knew this already before the focus on the man of science, Acton, obscured the obvious. Even in the too-simple earlier view of Victorian sexuality, it was assumed that Victorian pre-occupation with religion would orient thinking on sex. Since Marcus we have been in the uncomfortable position of somehow at the same time of course knowing this and yet not knowing it.

Readers who still assume that there is a monolithic Victorian attitude on sex will find in the first study, of Clough, a display of a vigorous dialectic between the simplicities of the conservative "respectable" position and alternative points of view. Clough is proficient, as many twentieth-century writers are not, in the roots of this discussion in earlier religious positions so that, as I argue, his own experience, beginning in reaction to the revival of patristic tradition in Tractarian Oxford, is cast as a revisit to the archetype: Augustine's sexual burning itself. The succeeding chapters, on Kingsley and Patmore, should continue this opening into the diversity of Victorian positions by exploring the large and complicated discussions of sexuality developed not by a Victorian skeptic like Clough but by two committed Christian thinkers, who end in very different positions, Kingsley as the sex-affirming Church of England opponent of ascetic Tractarian Oxford and Catholicism alike, Patmore as the extender of medieval Catholic mystic visions of sexuality turned from earth to God. My hope is that this approach, whether for those new to this Victorian discourse or for students of the diversity of the period, will bring the concerns of these writers seriously before us. It would be easy to dwell far more briefly on a greater variety of individuals and in the process to create summary discussions that might seem to offer only another panopticon of Victorian absurdity. I trust that this very brief survey of the larger subject has suggested that these interests of my subjects are hardly absurd; rather they are individual versions of universal and ubiquitous concerns of humans and their cultures. Shall we dismiss as absurd Kingsley's intense hopes for a love life that extends into the next world, when so many religions offer a land of sexual heart's desire beyond this? Shall we merely find scandal in Patmore's hope for sexual relation with Deity Himself, when such a conception is so prevalent in so many religions and when it has such a rich history in his own, Catholic, tradition?

It will also be easy to take such discussions apart, and indeed I have ended with a nineteenth-century writer who, always sadly, sometimes furiously, insists on exposing the merely constructed, Rube Goldberg, quality of religious–sexual discourses, both the traditional Christian ones of Jude's beloved Tractarian Christminster and the seemingly opposing neo-pagan ones of his also beloved Sue. Hardy's view of large cultural traditions laid out and deconstructed literally into their sexual parts, an early version of the mere play of bodies and pleasures of a Foucauldian, radical view of the bases of all sexual discussion, is in any case an unavoidable perspective for us.[70] Yet it must also be set against the inevitable human need, so clear in the religious cultures of the world generally, as in the Jewish and Christian Western traditions, to make once again some whole of individual and social meaning that is greater than the mere sum of the parts. As a science of sex has finally succeeded in this century in actually being scientific by showing us the mere mechanisms of body parts and their functions, or the mere varieties of sexual activities in our society or in cultures everywhere, it may be apparent that most of what humans wish to hear about sex, whether said by doctor or psychologist, priest or writer, falls not into science but into the area of verbal activity where myths and necessary fictions provide some coherence and allow some belief. And that rather returns the discussion, albeit somewhat more self-consciously, to the mythic or religious bases in which it has usually been found in human history.

An approach to sexual discussion through the liaisons between religion and sexuality seems to me a somewhat new subject in nineteenth-century literary history.[71] I hope the reader will find it a useful optical instrument to help him or her see more clearly the complicated and often conflicted discourse that we find. By the same token, I am aware of the danger of all gadgets in literary history. They may encourage us to rig up reducing and overly simplifying explanations of what are necessarily multi-faceted and very complex phenomena. The decision to articulate and interrogate the major discussions of a relatively few individuals has allowed me room to place them fully in the broader intellectual history. To keep my sometimes dazzling double subject in clear focus I have also been particular about locating individual writers' thinking within their biographies and in the context of their entire literary careers.

CHAPTER 2

From Cloister to "Great Sinful Streets": Arthur Hugh Clough and the Victorian "Question of Sex"

I begin with Arthur Hugh Clough because his poems stage and enact our own efforts, as we try to understand Victorian sexual and religious discussions, to realize the varieties of attitudes and opinions available in the age. Clough's skeptical, probing mind insists on exposing limits and weaknesses in any would-be orthodoxy it considers; his restless craving for successive antithetical views of any phenomenon makes his work a virtual anatomy of the differing positions of an age in fact far more unsettled on sexual and religious issues than we have wished to think. Clough offers the clarity of debate, satire, contrast; he is also intensely akin to the majority of writers on sexuality in his age, certainly to the subjects of successive chapters, Charles Kingsley and Coventry Patmore, in displaying a very deep commitment to the interconnection of sexual and religious experience, even as he works at a problematics of both. His work allows us to appreciate the profound interdependence in most Victorian thinking of sexual and religious issues while providing a cool diagram of the possible positions that other writers often occupy with single-minded and obscuring fervor. Briefly, he shows us the logical alternatives that are easily overlooked in such a passionate combination of subjects: sexuality and religion can both be affirmed together as a mutually supporting system of thought and belief; either can be asserted in exclusion of the other (and Clough's way of thinking follows that of most in his age in seeing this then as a relation in which one must deny the other rather than simply exist as a separate entity); and of course both sexuality and religion can be in some sense denied, rejected as not representing any values either for the individual's life or as general ways of organizing experience. As we shall see, such a simple, systematic formulation hardly exhausts Clough's ingenuity as a dialectical thinker. Just because he thinks of the two discourses as essentially connected, he can see how their relations can take the form of appropriation of one by the other, sexual energies redirected into religion, religion used as a medium for sexual mythology – as we shall see massively in the later Patmore – either sexuality or religion injecting the other with enthusiasm or discouragement. His own position is consistently tinged by a distancing skepticism, a habit of mind that looks always for alternatives or dissonances. But it is not generally despairing: the possibility of sexual or religious assertion always exists beside his sense of the likelihood of falsity – he would say factitiousness – in the system of values we spin in these areas of desire seeking fulfillment.

Since Walter Houghton's important revaluation of Clough back in 1963,[1] critical attention has focussed on defining the nature of Clough's achievement rather than deploring what had seemed to his contemporaries and his early critics to be a failure of great promise. His merits as a satirist have been amply recognized; the degree of positive assertion in his poems and prose has been stressed against the old view of Clough as a self-paralyzed doubter.[2] More recently, the quality of his doubt itself has been explored and celebrated in critical studies that see Clough's affinity to the problems of making any statements at all that have been so fully raised in the contemporary revival of skepticism in post-structuralist criticism.[3]

I need not argue Clough's importance as a Victorian commentator on central issues of faith and doubt. He has, of course, been enshrined as the very good poet of Victorian doubt and religious perplexity. At the same time there has been recognition, but oddly embarrassed and uncomprehensive recognition of Clough's equal concern with issues of love and marriage.[4] Here there is still some need to be more emphatic against our age's continuing reluctance to recognize sexual issues when we find them, not in the pornoepic *Secret Life* of an underworld Walter, but in a serious and earnest Victorian poet. Without seeking to deny the other qualities that have been far more fully recognized in Clough's writing, I suggest that we should carefully observe a preoccupation with problems of sexual values and sexual adjustment that speaks clearly in his personal life and runs centrally through most of his work, from *The Bothie of Tober-Na-Vuolich* to the late second poetic life in the *Mari Magno* tales. It is not too much to say that Clough was as concerned with the problems of sexuality in the context of his time as a D. H. Lawrence or Ford Madox Ford in the twentieth century. Put in broadest terms, the issue Clough found in his life and kept wrestling with in his poems is

just what we might expect an earnest but sane Victorian to be facing
privately: how to reconcile his sexual needs with the various
restrictions and religious and moral ideals of his society. More than a
Walter, he is sensitive to both his society's repressions and ideals.
More than the young Ruskin, he is aware of his sexual feelings and
the possible modes, respectable and underworld, of obtaining their
gratification. Clough seems in this exploration, as he does generally
in his self-debate over earnest morality and worldly pleasure, to take
on, in our hindsight, a representative quality. His struggle to find his
own stance on sexual issues seems especially familiar to us – far more
than Kingsley's remarkably earnest liberal one or Patmore's surprisingly experiential one will – because it begins in an attempt to
negotiate the gap between two areas of experience we have tended to
stress in our view of Victorian sex lives: a religious and social world
that seems to offer little room for sexual pleasure, in Clough's case the
proper world of morally earnest Arnoldian Rugby and the celibate
world of Oxford tutors and dons, and a beckoning other world of
forbidden but in fact very accessible gratification. He thus necessarily
begins by attempting, not always happily, but, as ever in his works,
very candidly, to bring into dialogue Victorian extremes: some of
the acknowledged worlds of Victorian religious idealism and control
and some of the known but unacknowledged underworlds of
sexuality.[5]

If Clough's work ultimately provides a broad display of the various
combinations of religious and sexual thinking at work in the Victorian
world, his life first follows a somewhat simpler and more familiar
story of sexual exploration. In this he initially needed to find his way
from his inherited religious system, which seemed to exclude sexual
expression, to a clear recognition of the claims of sexuality. And this
is a manifest theme he writes into his work. We know the pattern
well from works at the turn of the century and beyond – *The Way of
All Flesh, A Portrait of the Artist, Sons and Lovers* – that chronicle an
individual's subversive struggle for sexual realization against inner
and outer religious and social restraints. Clough is both a much
earlier voice and one that is finally less comfortable with the solution
of a new secular sexual morality than the twentieth century generally
has been (and both Joyce, at an emotional level, and Lawrence in a
more explicit way could be said to join him in this). From his personal
exploration Clough moves not to one new and simplifying assertion
but to an ever-broader view of the different possibilities for sexual

and religious discussion and to a fuller understanding of the nature of that discussion.

Certainly in both life and works Clough's first move is a rather decisive recentering of the discussion away from one in which religion leaves little place for sex or explicit discourse on sexuality. The reticence of Clough and his widow editor-biographer, Blanche Smith Clough, prevent us from knowing more than a brief and perhaps incomplete outline of his actual sexual experience. But his biographers let us at least see broadly some of the situations that lie behind the more dialectical and psychological explorations of his poems. Whereas Clough's critics have been surprisingly indifferent to the large amount of sexual content in his work, his important biographers, Chorley and Biswas, following the Stracheyan and Freudian traditions of Victorian biography, have hardly ignored his sex life.[6] Chorley's attempt, in Edmund Wilson's manner, to establish a childhood wound that explains the "failure" of Clough's life at least leads her to look for passages of sexual revelation.[7] It also tends to explain away Clough and to lead her to ignore the degree to which Clough undertakes a deliberate and self-aware discussion of sexual issues. Biswas's fuller and critically more sophisticated study follows Chorley in a preoccupation with interpreting a passage of sexual discussion as a psychological crux of castration or of excremental vision rather than as literature. He provides, however, a balanced assessment of Clough's sexual growth and, alone in full discussions of Clough's writings, he gives sufficient emphasis to Clough's preoccupation with sexual issues.[8] From the biographers' accounts we can at least see that Clough, the son of the respectable, withdrawn merchant class, the very good student of Dr. Arnold, the outstanding scholar at Balliol College, Oxford, the serious fellow and tutor of Oriel College, unsure whether to take orders and become a don for life or to pursue a high-minded profession in the world, was a person obviously susceptible to the new religiously dominated sexual morality by which some Victorians were attempting to distinguish themselves from the looser days of the Romantics and Regency. The good Rugby boy, the serious student and college tutor existed in a milieu in which he would tend to equate sexual abstinence with religious purity.[9] In this ethos, the world of Walter, of prostitutes and assignation houses, was definitely out of bounds, much as its temptations might intrude rather often in the form of sexually exploitable or exploiting servants or soliciting prostitutes. In this world the exceptionally approved sexual expression was, of course, wedded love, though among respectable, moral Victorians of his class there was frequently question, as there had been in Catholic tradition since before Augustine, as to whether even such love should have much of a sexual side.[10] But as he seemed to be moving toward the career as don for which his academic talents certainly qualified him, Clough was also moving toward an almost celibate role in still unreformed Oxford. We need only think of the life of the fellows as we find it in the *Apologia* of Clough's senior at Oriel, John Henry Newman, a religious leader to whose aura of self-denial and personal holiness Clough was profoundly attracted – despite his strong allegiance to Newman's major opponent in the heated controversy over Newman and Pusey's Oxford Movement, Dr. Arnold – to realize how close the social life was to that of a priestly society of gentlemanly celibates. In the same way, Clough's tutor Adam in *The Bothie* functions almost as a Catholic priest might. He blushes as a maiden at his students' discussion of possible affairs, reproves loose talk, but provides sensible, fatherly guidance when a student resolves to marry.

Unlike Adam and unlike his admired Newman, who braved Charles Kingsley's further displeasure by admitting that he had always personally found it good to abide as he was, celibate, Clough was troubled in this milieu both by sexual curiosity and emotions. In a letter to his sister he acknowledged that he could be at times quiet as a Puseyite, yet, "I could be provoked to send out a flood of lava boiling-hot amidst their flowery ecclesiastical fields and parterres. Very likely living in this state of suppressed volcanic action makes one more exasperated than one should be when any sort of crater presents itself."[11] However Clough's symbols here are read, they certainly suggest more than an intellectual discomfort with the Puseyite role of submission and celibacy. His curiosity beyond those ecclesiastical fields is revealed in his friendship with the more worldly Thomas Burbidge, with whom he corresponded over experiments in "eroticophilosophica." After they published their poems together in *Ambarvalia* Clough defended Burbidge's blunt speech against the criticisms of his "prude" friends.[12] He read George Sand; he became acquainted with more worldly men such as Monckton Milnes, statesman, connoisseur, collector of pornography, with whom he breakfasted in Paris; and in Rome he became a friend of Margaret Fuller, who had abandoned American properties for a passionate and secret marriage with the young Count Ossoli.[13] With Emerson himself, with whom he became friends, he noted in 1848 in his diaries: "[de sexualibus]" – evidently a discussion of the question of sex, about which Clough would write a few months later.[14] More furtively, Clough's own emotions found some outlet. To his wife he would confess some kind of sexual experience beginning at age twenty. Whether this was only a matter of the masturbation which he compulsively confessed to his private diaries and noted with large stars, or some experience with a local girl or prostitute isn't clear.[15] Certainly the battle against "that wretched habit," which had begun a good deal earlier than age twenty, played a major part in his early, rather Augustinian sense of forces within working by their nature against his religious desires, his general "exceeding wickedness and abuse of God's grace from my very childhood."[16] It certainly contributed to his profound and early sense of conflict between the values of his milieu and his sexual drives and a persistent feeling, which would perhaps be the hardest cultural legacy for him to master intellectually, that his conscious and sexual selves followed rather different values and laws.

The diaries keep coming back to that key word in Clough, dipsychus (here usually in Greek, δίψυχος), his sense of a psyche divided against itself; in one instance this is explicitly connected to his going "full length" so that we can see the sexual base of self-division in the great poem of his maturity already established in his early conflicts over gratification and religious inhibition.[17] Clough's awareness of women certainly penetrated his cloistered Oxford life, a life that was in fact under constant siege by Oxford's numerous town prostitutes, over whom the university exercised paternalistic police authority.[18] A poem, "Natura Naturans" in *Ambarvalia* makes a great deal of the feeling generated by an hour's ride next to an unknown girl in a railway car.[19] Whether based on a real incident or not, it shows Clough attuned to the ordinary arousal of such raptures. Certainly, as Chorley showed, Clough had some crossed love relation in 1846 with a girl he hoped to marry.[20] It isn't clear that she was a Highland girl. But the persistent interest in Highland lasses in his poems suggests that he may, unlike the sage Adam in *The Bothie*, have become himself involved romantically during one of the summer vacation parties he led to the Highlands in 1846 and 1847. Certainly the *Ambarvalia* poem "ὁ θεὸς μετὰ σοῦ" (Γοδ βε ωιτη θου, π. 38) taking chaste leave of an attractive girl, with its extensively reworked manuscripts, suggests reflection over either a real attraction to/affair with "my Highland lassie" or a very vivid imagination of the possibility.[21] If Clough avoided yielding to whatever temptations he felt for a "life in some black bothie spent" with a "cheery" Highland girl, he was not so easily rid of the sexual needs which perhaps surfaced most strongly whenever he left religious Oxford, first in the Scotland summer holidays, then after he threw himself into the world by resigning his college fellowship.[22]

Clough saw the world, as so many Victorians did, especially in Italy. He was in Italy in spring–summer, 1849, in Rome and Naples; he went to Venice the autumn of the next year. There are further biographers' rumors of some kind of emotional crisis in Italy, but again no substantial information.[23] There is no question, however, that what was on Clough's mind and imagination in Italy was rather different from the preoccupations of Newman three years before as a Catholic convert preparing for the priesthood. Not a Catholic himself, of course, but certainly aware of Rome's symbolic resonance as the seat of Catholic Christianity, Clough deliberately used his pilgrimage to embrace Rome's most worldly side as a decisive step away from the English religious center of Oxford that he was abandoning for good.[24] Whatever his personal experiences at Rome may have been, he wrote a fine poem, *Amours de Voyage*, about a young Englishman in Rome, interested, maybe, in a young English-woman he meets there. Naples he used as a setting for a major poem, "Easter Day. Naples, 1849." The specific occasion is a discussion with a pimp about the local wares offered to tourists. Whether Clough ever actually listened to a pimp's solicitations, or responded, we don't know. But the same subject has a central place in the poem he wrote the next year at Venice, though the cicerone offering the local female attractions is now elevated to Mephistopheles himself.

Having considered the world of other Victorians in Rome, Naples, and Venice, a world that was certainly available to him in London's tens of thousands of prostitutes as it had been in the town–gown prostitutes of Oxford,[25] Clough opted, instead, for the longest journey. He met the respectable Miss Blanche Smith, a cousin of Florence Nightingale, about 1850 and settled his sexual life in the official manner with love, marriage, and children in 1854. Or did he? *Amours de Voyage* states, with Clough's characteristic honesty and second thoughts on second thoughts, the arguments against committing oneself to the tenure of a Victorian marriage with any particular individual one happens to meet. And Clough's letters to his future wife reiterate many of the scruples of his milktoast hero in *Amours*.[26] Clough's marriage was apparently happy, though his wife's prudish reaction to *Dipsychus* may leave us suspecting that this marriage may have been forced by her more into the conservative mold of respectability and religious sexual repression than allowed to develop into the liberal vision of married lovers that Clough often imagined and Kingsley would champion all his life.[27] His marriage certainly was coincident with his unhappy virtual abandonment of poetry. Curiously, his return to poetry in the Chaucerian framed tales of *Mari Magno*, written just before his tragically early death, is equally coincident with the first prolonged breakup of his marital relation: his final voyage in quest of better health. The subject is marriage; the tone is approving according to Victorian ideals; the most interesting stories, however, are about marriages between strangers and the guilt of an unfaithful husband traveling to regain his health. Did the dying Clough commit adultery? Probably not. Did he think about the problem? Certainly; openness to different possibilities, alternative positions on seemingly settled issues were the strongest points of his mind and imagination, after as before 1854.

With the exception of *Mari Magno*, which goes back to old questions of marriage and opens some new ones, Clough's poetry about love and sexuality is written, as indeed his very extensive output of poetry not related to these issues is, out of the rather brief period, roughly seven years from 1847 to 1854, of sexual and religious indecision that preceded his marriage. From the biographer's point of view we could say that Clough uses his poetry to debate different possibilities in his personal life with particular focus on the inter-twined issues of sexual expression and religious values and belief. What we find in his poetry, however, is not a journalistic record of his experience, whatever that was, but something close to an analytical display of sexual opinions and attitudes of his day, each looked at with individual perspective and critical intelligence. Each proposes some large aspect of Victorian sexuality, usually in relation to religious thinking and ideals, and explores its strengths and weak-nesses, the latter often by a precise satirical incision or persistent intellectual curiosity over incongruities. The group of poems is finally valuable not for the resolution Clough moves toward but for his subtle understanding of the subject before him, human nature in two of its most complex aspects. Clough argued in a review of Matthew

Arnold and Alexander Smith that modern poetry should follow the novel in its fruitful descent into ordinary realities of "everyday life": "general wants, ordinary feelings, the obvious rather than the rare facts of human nature." Poetry, he asserted, should "divinely condescend to all infirmities; be in all points tempted as we are; exclude nothing, least of all guilt and distress."[28] At the meeting-place of ordinary sexual need as he experienced it and the system of beliefs and values which most often seemed to him to constrain that need Clough found the core of his subject. He does not always write about the intersection of sexuality and a controlling religion as a generator of guilt, though rather often this *is* his special turf; his work almost always insists on the wants and facts of human nature.

Though most of the poems in the *Ambarvalia* volume predate *The Bothie of Tober-Na-Vuolich*, *The Bothie* was published first. It was relatively popular in its day but sometimes has been criticized in our century, especially by contrast to Clough's later work, as simplistically romantic. As a case study of Victorian mating it is, however, not so much simplistic as radical, an attempt to look at Victorian sexual issues from a new perspective. This central concern, which has often been overlooked by Clough's commentators, is clearly written into the text, as we will see. Ironically, it was also written into Clough's original Scots title for the first (1848) edition, which Clough saw as a very embarrassing accident. But, as a kind of symbolic Freudian slip of the collective unconscious of his age, in some ways it *is* most appropriate to his subject. Misunderstanding a boatman as explaining the Scots name of an old hut as the cottage at the bairds' well when in fact he probably said the beard's well, Clough titled his poem *The Bothie of Tober-na-Fuosich*: that is, the cottage at the bearded well, or cunt.[29] Appropriate: because the poem is about a return to basics in social life emblemed in the simple cottage, a communal living-place for laborers, and also about a return to realities in sexual matters – which the guffawing and embarrassment over the title shows as badly needed.

The initial inspiration for the poem came from Clough's own vacation study tours in Scotland. These were for Clough a chance to get out of Oxford and out of the quasi-priestly role he was forced to assume there. Whether in fact, or only by the illusion of the tourist's special freedom, probably by a combination of the two, Scotland must have seemed also a release from some of the proprieties of English sexual mores.[30] In the poem as in Clough's other poems with

Scottish settings, lassies seem far more ready than English maidens to be kissed and kiss back. They seem more ready to accept love, associated with marriage or not, as a good in itself; and they seem less preoccupied with fears that the girl who gives herself too trustingly to her lover will fall into prostitution. These fears are, as we shall see, present, but they are the fears primarily of the English students and their tutor as they are the fears of the English speaker of Clough's Highland lassie poem ("ὁ θεὸς μετὰ σοῦ"). The situation is slightly analogous to that of the high-minded Englishman trying to preserve his fine sense of honor among Tahitian natives. Indeed, perhaps by an association set up by Clough's admiration for Tom Arnold, Matthew's brother, off to a new life in New Zealand, the world of Scotland seems naturally to Clough to open to the even less formal world of faraway New Zealand and Australia (Southern California perhaps became the twentieth-century equivalent for the British intellectual pushing outside the manners of his society). In the *Mari Magno* "The Lawyer's Second Tale," the seduced girl, unintentionally abandoned pregnant by her conscientious lover, finds not prostitution but respectable prosperity, suitors, a husband, and a large family in Australia. In the story of *The Bothie* the hero Philip, poet, Oxonian, gentleman, radical idealist young talker ("The Chartist, the poet, the eloquent speaker"), consummates his talk of a new and better society by committing himself to his marriage and setting out with his bride to New Zealand.

The poem thus tries to look at sexual relations from the perspective of a different society and an open future for the principal characters. Other societies with other standards were always a standing threat to the solidification of the more conservative Victorian sexual attitude and the restlessly intellectual Clough was not likely to miss the challenge of other cultural structures or of a new culture being formed in the antipodes. His success in presenting these issues in *The Bothie* is more surprising. The poem is quite well organized, especially for a first long work. More than any other work by Clough, it creates a full group of individualized character-speakers, the lively, urbane, young Oxford students and their sage tutor, with a nice sense of the social ambience. Clough gives moral authority to Adam the tutor; but his imagination would seem to be on the side of the pleasures of being a young gentleman with the world open before him. Indeed Adam is virtually a portrait of a road for Clough about not to be taken: the "grave man" who would not leave Oxford and who becomes a picture of talent and feeling locked into a controlling celibate mold: "white-tied, clerical, silent, with antique square-cut waistcoat / Formal, unchanged, of black cloth, but with sense and feeling beneath it" (1.20–22).[31]

What is best is the way in which the social and sexual issues that Clough raises are integrated into the story. As in the intellectual problem drama of Bernard Shaw and his contemporaries, the issues are dramatically underlined at the opening and then made the explicit subject of a discussion scene. At the opening banquet given to the English student visitors by their Scots hosts, Philip's non-conformity to his society's values is set out dramatically and it finds an answering ring in at least one Scotsman who invites him to stop at his bothie if he should ever come his way. Philip's generally independent cast of mind as something of a democrat and something of a disciple of Carlyle on the value of work (as indeed Clough was, at times, too) is then focussed in the succeeding discussion on a sexual issue. There is in fact an important shift from what seems to be a political problem poem of its turbulent time to a poem about sexual attitudes and adjustments.[32] In the discussion, Philip displays his radicalism by announcing that his amorous instincts follow his democratic social opinions: he prefers girls whom he sees doing ordinary work to the artificial finery of conventional girls of his class. From the way Clough handles it, we can see that such discussion of sexual preference came close to passing the borders of Victorian propriety. The tutor is embarrassed; Clough himself, whose revisions from manuscript of the 1848 edition to the 1862 edition show him, as often in his poetry, progressively pruning back his more explicit statements,[33] seems to suggest that he, too, felt some embarrassment over the candor of his discussion. To us, it is clearly not comparable to Molly's night thoughts in *Ulysses*. But in Clough's milieu the candor is unusual. Philip explains his position by providing a brief account of his sexual growth. He saw an ordinary capless maiden "Bending with three-pronged fork in a garden uprooting potatoes" (II.44). Suffice it to observe, without speculation on what sadistic, masochistic, or other impulse may have been aroused at the sight, and with no Freudian comment on that three-pronged stimulation of potatoes, that for Philip's level of awareness the experience was sexually electrifying. He discovered something about himself: "a new thing was in me" (II.46). In Clough's revised edition this is explained as "the feelings between men and women" (II.39). The manuscript version was more explicit: "Never, believe me, revealed itself for me the sexual glory" (p. 598).[34] In the 1848 edition there was, as well, a surprisingly explicit reference to the prior confusions of adolescent sexuality (the "celled-up dishonour" can hardly be anything but that Victorian unmentionable masturbation that had so badly troubled Clough himself):

> a new thing was in me, though vernal emotion, the secret,
> Yes, amid prurient talk, the unimparted mysterious secret
> Long, the growing distress, and celled-up dishonour of boyhood,
> Recognized now took its place, a relation, oh bliss! unto others.
>
> (p. 598)

To know Philip's direct attraction to the girl we have to go back even further, into the manuscript early draft of the first three books where "Longing to take her and lift her, and put her away from her slaving" (II.47) is:

> I longed to raise her,
> Circling the soft yielding waist to uplift her, away from her . . .
> Circling the delicate waist look up in her eyes, and, it might be,
> Might be, perchance, peradventure enfold her and not be resisted.
>
> (p. 598)

The essential issue raised in the discussion may be put as simply as, may a young man who knows what he wants go out and find it? In the upshot, Philip sets out, along with a touring party of the students, to do just that. At the end of the discussion the wit Hobbes suggests that Philip soon may, "smit by the charm of a lovely potato-uprooter, / Study the question of sex in the Bothie of *What-did-he-call-it*" (II.270–71). And he is reported in Book III, "Studying the question of sex, though not at What-did-he-call it" (p. 605, III.103, 1848 edition only).[35]

Complications, however, are introduced into the discussion and subsequently in the plot (explaining why Philip does not study the question of sex at the bothie immediately). These are of less general interest and perhaps help account for the failure of the poem to find many twentieth-century readers. They are the areas where Clough's imagination of a freely expanding sexual development runs up against conservative scruples. Such scruples take the form both of prohibitions and inhibiting idealisms. In Clough's structure they are so many obstructions through which the path of Philip's true self-realization through relation to another must run. One prohibition is the one obvious to Philip's friends and tutor, against marrying below his own class. Adam is not adamant on the issue but on the whole counsels that Philip do his duty in his station. Although Philip wavers in the tour of available women that follows the discussion, even at one time coming back to momentary belief in the superiority of elegant society women, his initial repulsion from the, to him and us, Victorian nonsense of "Boudoir, toilette, carriage, drawing-room, and ball-room" (II.89) – which he sees as the places of women's alienation from both nature and their sexual selves – proves strong enough to maintain his initial quest.

Seeking love in a cottage runs up against a still-deeper prohibition than the social one. This is the decent young man's fear of being that worst of attractive Victorian gentlemen, the seducer of innocent maidens. Scotland proves to Clough's hero, as it possibly did to Clough himself, a dangerous place just because the maidens and their guardians seem not only innocent, but also somewhat indifferent to the whole issue. Philip's first Scottish lass, a girl named Katie he meets at a farm, fills his need for a girl of the earth and she seems only too ready to complete his education. Walter would persevere, but Clough portrays Philip barely rescued from a moral trap. If he makes love to her but decides she is not a "help meet" for life, what will happen? The conventional conservative answer is obvious and Philip sees it visually in a dream:

> dressy girls slithering-by upon pavements give sign for accosting,
> Paint on their beautiless cheeks, and hunger and shame in their
> bosoms,
> Hunger by drink, and by that which they shudder yet burn for,
> appeasing,–
> Hiding their shame – ah God! – in the glare of the public
> gas-lights. (IV.134–37)

The picture is, almost literally, a Victorian stereotype, the fallen woman as the fruit of sin, and Philip rehearses the conventional moral that needs rehearsing because it carries the nexus of conservative confusions over female sexuality:

> Maiden reserve torn from off it, grows never again to reclothe it,
> Modesty broken-through once to immodesty flies for protection.
> Oh, who saws through the trunk, though he leaves the tree up in
> the forest,
> When the next wind casts it down – is *his* not the hand that
> smote it? (IV.148–51)

Women, in the conservative, "respectable" litany, are hardly sexual.[36] They are "passive," as Adam replies, but once deflowered in their passivity they change into passionate devils. (The odd image of a *tree* cut down seems to tell us inadvertently the problem with this: he who denies a woman's genitals shouldn't be surprised to find her preferring scandal to gentility.)

The reader may well ask why shouldn't every Jack in Philip's egalitarian world, who takes sufficient liking to his Jill to bother to seduce her, also marry her. Here the problem comes out as an idealism in Philip and, apparently, his author that represents the difficulties inherent in the more liberal Victorian sexual position that was the main alternative to the conservative "respectable" one. This is that of idealized married sexual love, a position popularly represented by the two writers examined in succeeding chapters, Kingsley and the Patmore of *The Angel in the House*, as well as, in less explicit form, by more mainstream writers such as the Brownings.[37] It offered the obvious advantage of reversing religious scruples about sexuality generally by identifying a special sphere in which religion, now liberal on sex in this one aspect, could authorize sexual gratification. But one problem in this way of rendering sex acceptable by the sacrament of marriage to one's true love is that it put its adherents under the burden of finding an angel and true love as the legitimization of sexual release. Philip's bluntness about his sexual drive was perhaps rendered tolerable to his Victorian readers by his reliance upon the language of sexual idealism. In the discussion he insists that, while intending to marry a healthy woman who will labor with him in life, he also intends to put her on a pedestal: "Grand on her pedestal rise as urn-bearing statue of Hellas" (II.81). This aspiration, the only scandal in the poem to modern ears, leads Philip's friends to laugh at him as a Pugin of woman, trying to idealize a "gothic," primitive kind of woman for modern consumption. The criticism is acute and shows how well even in this poem Clough can acknowledge alternative perspectives on the idealizing position. Yet the poem, as much an idyll in plot as it is realistic drama in dialogue, is committed to celebrating the idealist position. Philip believes there is *one* Jill for him, not a selection of many. When he becomes involved with the wrong one, Katie, he is miraculously rescued by one glance from a keen-sighted attractive stranger. Philip sees the hazard of his flirtation with Katie, flees her, finds his way accidentally to the bothie to which he had been invited in the first scene and meets, of course, his true Jill, the stranger he had seen, Elspie, his one and destined love. The romance world of the poem suspends our disbelief and provides at least a temporary solution to the conjoint problems of prohibitions and idealism that Clough would keep coming back to in his succeeding poems on sexual adjustment.

It is worth noting, in contrast to the relative simplicity of the story, how seriously Clough continues his exploration of sexual psychology in his presentation of the courtship of Elspie and Philip. Their conjunction may be a fortuitous one constructed by a busy plot; their mating itself is in quite another fictional world. As in that other psychologically perceptive romance, *Jane Eyre*, their mating is presented as a series of attractions and repulsions, or repressions, leading finally to successful union. Love-making is really initiated by the lassie, who communicates her own sexual aspirations in an innocent revelation of her dreams. It is a loaded shot at Philip's imagination and heart and a loaded gun to the post-Freudian reader.[38] However, her dream image, that of a bridge, functions so clearly as a metaphor for sexual union that it can hardly have been innocent to Clough or his readers. It is, rather, one way of getting around Victorian conventions against explicit sexual descriptions. Elspie says she feels at times like a bridge support raising herself on one side of a river to the height of a larger support on the other:

Sometimes I find myself dreaming at nights about arches and bridges, –
Sometimes I dream of a great invisible hand coming down, and
Dropping the great key-stone in the middle: there in my dreaming,
There I feel the great key-stone coming in, and through it
Feel the other part – all the other stones of the archway,
Joined into mine with a strange happy sense of completeness.

(vii.67–72)

The "sweet idea and image" serves to bring them together and the evening ends in an embrace.

The next day Elspie feels a strong maidenly reaction from the opening of the previous night: "I am shocked and terrified at it. / Yes, it is dreadful to me" (vii.117–18). Again with intuitive justness and innocent consciousness, she finds from another dream a simile to express her fear. It is again a simile into which Clough and the reader, and even Philip, can easily read a more explicit meaning. Philip seems like a sea pushing up into an inland stream (burn):

> You are too strong, you see, Mr. Philip! just like the sea there,
> Which *will* come, through the straits and all between the
>   mountains,
> Forcing its great strong tide into every nook and inlet,
> Getting far in, up the quiet stream of sweet inland water,
> Sucking it up, and stopping it, turning, it, driving it backward,
> Quite preventing its own quiet running: and then, soon after,
> Back it goes off, leaving weeds on the shore, and wrack and
>   uncleanness:
> And the poor burn in the glen tries again its peaceful running,
> But it is brackish and tainted, and all its bank in disorder.
>
> (VII.120–28)

There is just a hint too much of the earlier fears of irremediable pollution of maidens. But on the whole the description effectively takes us into Elspie's natural fears of the male force she has released in Philip. The sexual parallels in the imagery are obvious and, in terms of the age, very frank.[39] The inversion of the usual equivalence between sea and women should not lead us to glib theories of a parallel inversion in Philip or his author; the metaphor is appropriately applied from the fast-running tide in Scotland.

Philip doesn't force Elspie's feeling and soon an equally natural release of repression takes place, "a revulsion passed through the brain and bosom of Elspie" (VII.144). The narrator continues Elspie's simile to describe her awakening sexual feeling:

> the passion she just had compared to the vehement ocean,
> Urging in high spring-tide its masterful way through the mountains,
> Forcing and flooding the silvery stream, as it runs from the inland;
> That great power withdrawn, receding here and passive,
> Felt she in myriad springs, her sources, far in the mountains,
> Stirring, collecting, rising, upheaving, forth-outflowing,
> Taking and joining, right welcome, that delicate rill in the valley,
> Filling it, making it strong, and still descending, seeking,
> With a blind forefeeling descending ever, and seeking,
> With a delicious forefeeling, the great still sea before it;
> There deep into it, far, to carry, and lose in its bosom,
> Waters that still from their sources exhaustless are fain to be added.
>
> (VII.154–65)

Clough's intuitions in psychology, expressed here in something like the pulsing, repeating language of passion Lawrence defended in his Foreword to *Women in Love*, offer something close to a solution to the formal Victorian anxieties of plot and discussion. In both the similes of bridge and burn, the female element, far from being Victorianized and passive, is equal and strong. Philip may have thought he was seeking an angel to put on a pedestal. His honest following of feeling led him instead to a woman with as complex sexual responses as his own. Their story ends with an embrace of mutual passion – "Stooping, knowing not what, put her lips to the hair on his forehead : / And Philip, raising himself, gently, for the first time, round her / Passing his arms, close, close, enfolded her, close to his bosom" (VII.169–71) – followed by emigration to the shared life of toil in New Zealand. Concerns of social status yield easily, at last, to fulfilled passion. The last word is given to the wit Hobbes. His comic epithalamium, a fable from the story of Jacob's two wives, again offers a metaphorical insight into the relations of the sexes that is not available in the conscious reasoning of the students and, one suspects, the author. Philip has sought an ideal, a Rachel, but Hobbes warns him that real life brings more often a Leah, sexual, as she is in Clough's own "Jacob's Wives," but not his intellectual ideal, no angel for the pedestal. Hobbes's advice is to keep on working : by accepting the Leah in his wife and in marriage he may yet realize his ideal. The poem "Jacob's Wives" (pp. 211–14) similarly suggests the possibility of a final, if uneasy, harmony of romantic and sexual aspirations, as Jacob sits in his tent doorway under his palm tree and beside his spring after hearing out the claims on him of both his wives. It is a truism that conservative Victorian sexuality tends to project its division into romantic ideal and passionate reality through female alternatives, blonde angel or dark-haired fallen woman. In his exploration of one person's exit from Victorian society and con- servative standards by following his natural sexual growth, Clough seems as naturally to reach out to images of balance and the harmonizing of alternatives.

The concluding homily, based on the favorite Victorian device of a typology of personal life from the Bible, reminds us of a context of reference, even in this comic form, that conflicts throughout with the movement of the poem away from religious constraints on sexuality and indeed away from England entirely. For the moment of the poem there is a kind of magic which cancels the inherent conflict. Along with the type from the life of Jacob[40] there seems to be imported a kind of providence working in Philip's life that brings together his moral, even religious seriousness with sexual fulfillment. In the romance of the plot, where the author can stand in for providence, there is at least an imitation of a new covenant in which God helps those who help themselves to the sexual goods of this earth. The final book has many references to a kind of providence, with Philip doubting Adam's assurance, yet then finding his own good destiny in his mating. The poem even ends with an allusion to Origen as the fountainhead of such allegories as Hobbes reads over Philip and Elspie's espousals.

Origen, fervid advocate of religious continence, probably self-castrated, is, however, not so easily reconciled with the celebration of marriage in this world; and, on the other side, as the very names Hobbes necessarily suggests, the accommodation of secular thinking to traditional religious conservativism is no easy one. The poem keeps reminding us of limits to its apparent easy solution, limits that will be a central focus in Clough's work outside the magic circle of this genial and seemingly realistic romance. The counterpoising weight in the poem is located especially in the indulgent but nonetheless properly serious and moral tutor, Adam. His name may suggest the promise of a new man that Philip in fact seems to be on the way to fulfilling by the end; Adam himself presumably returns whence he came to the life of gown and cloistered colleges, a life still not so far from that of Origen's priestly class. Clough is obviously drawn between the two male figures, officially an Adam poet but subversively on the side of Philip, in many ways where Adam's sympathies, like his name, also lie. Subsequent poems find Clough moving the center of narrative consciousness progressively away from a donnish or clerical role, following and working out his own changing position about the quasi-religious role in which he had begun as well as about his sexual life.

Clough did not follow his friend Tom Arnold to the antipodes. Nor was he able to wish away, or dissolve in poetic myth-making, the sexual scruples and ideals he inherited from his society, which, ironically enough, he was quickly returned to by the embarrassment of the inadvertently obscene title. After fussing for many years over a choice of new title, Clough bothered to change to the meaningless but unscandalous "Vuolich" in the new edition he planned. He was very capable of such embarrassment over sex; but also his nature was such that he was not able to drop the whole troubling business of sex that the accidental title in fact so well signified.

Clough's next publication, the *Ambarvalia*, offering the poems of himself and his friend Burbidge, consists of shorter poems written mostly before *The Bothie*. The good number of poems on issues of love repeat the problems that conjointly stand in the way of Philip's development in *The Bothie*, the fear of degrading a woman by involvement and the unreal quest for an angelic mate. Though the poems look like love poems, they are really poems about the difficulty of becoming involved with anyone, just as they stand beside religious poems that are really about the difficulties of finding any adequate belief, even a belief in not believing. The Highland lassie poem ("ὁ θεὸς μετὰ σοῦ"), whatever its biographical content, contrasts to *The Bothie* in that scruples prevail over aroused feeling. The speaker is tempted by a new life of the soil in Scotland with a happy lass but fears he may merely be rationalizing a seduction. He resolves to repress his inclinations, as the more explicit manuscript variants make clear: "Sweet would seem the vivid dream of oblivious hasty love: / But I look into thine eyes – oh their bidding, 'tis obeyed, / Eager passion cowers rebuked and the rising gale is laid" (p. 588). To borrow the spirit of Clough's own Mephistopheles, we might set Clough's essentially religious scruples here over a maiden's chastity against Walter's annoyance that, in his experience, there were no innocent working-class maidens to be seduced because working-class boys had their maidenheads before the professional seducers were on the scene. Certainly the poem's formulation of female sexual life, like that of the conservative "respectable" position of his society, seeks not to acknowledge any reciprocity in sexual desire.

Another poem, "ἐπὶ Λάτμῳ" (on Latmos), puts this conflict on a more abstract level. The speaker prefers the unreal ideal love of the Endymion legend, mortal projecting his feelings to the moon, to what he has found of earthly love. The problem with earthly love, he admits, is not earthly maidens who were "fair to look on" and kind, but his relation to them: "But the life, the life to me / 'Twas the death, the death to them" (p. 39). With this approach to it, he finds this a "curious cruel world" that turns flowers "unto foulness, / And the odour unto stench." That the flower-pollution issue is the usual one of deflowering is clear from the manuscript lines, "the bliss to sorrow turns / And the joy to shame and grief" under the impact of others, "spying, prating prying" (p. 591).

The stench may seem to be primarily in the nose of the smeller; the speakers of other poems, who look not quite for the moon but for the perfect love, seem to exist in such a rarified atmosphere that fears of bad smells may well yield to fears of asphyxiation. "When panting sighs the bosom fill" is a poem of reflection and moralizing over the title situation. He considers the tolerant, if materialist, position that sexual feeling is as natural in humans as in beasts, though raised by sympathy to a "passion prized for Reason's sake" (p. 6). Yet the prudent operation of reason seems to put a practical block in the whole proceeding: the speaker fears he may commit himself now and find "Too late, the veritable thing." Though it takes the form of a lesson to the self, the poem really develops to the point where it poses a problem, the conflict between romantic ideals, expressed as usual in religious images, and realistic gratification: "the things are good: / Bread is it, if not angels' food; / But Love? Alas! I cannot say" (pp. 7–8). Another poem, "Thought may well be ever ranging," warns against involvement that comes from "caprices of a day" (p. 26) or from a misplaced sense of duty. The advice is good in itself, yet the insistence that hearts "Must or once for all be given / Or must not at all be given" in "life-long bliss" seems to create another impossible duty, of perfect life-long love.

What is especially interesting in these poems, and in Clough's work generally, is not only that he feels these idealizing constraints and scruples but also that he keeps hearing and admitting so clearly desire's cry for food (bread rather than angel cake). In "Natura Naturans," the interesting fantasy on a girl in a train, the anonymous hour's release of feeling apart from ordinary restraints opens up an almost dithyrambic strain of sexual celebration. The sexuality of the entire universe flows for the moment through them:

> In Libyan dell the light gazelle,
> The leopard lithe in Indian glade,
> And dolphin brightening tropic seas,
> In us were living, leapt and played. (p. 37)

As with a greater poet under sexual restraints, Eden, here the Eden reached through innocent imagined relation, opens an outlet for erotic celebration. For Clough the myth even allows a momentary passionate assurance that cancels all conflict between religion and sexuality. The terrain of Jewish and Christian origins becomes the locus for overriding usual social constraints. The contiguous passengers' innocent glow was like that

> in Eden's sinless place
> The hour when bodies human first
> Combined the primal prime embrace,

> Such genial heat the blissful seat
> In man and woman owned unblamed,
> When, naked both, its garden paths
> They walked unconscious, unashamed. (p. 37)

The poem may make us wonder whether there wasn't buried in Clough a fine erotic poet unable to find an opening for singing of primal matters. In this poem Clough writes over the biblical text, as he will do again and again in his poems, most notably, as we shall see, in "Easter Day"; but the writing is still within the normal bounds of interpretation, rather than cancellation. Paradise is presented, in language reminiscent of Milton, in the anti-Augustinian tradition of *Paradise Lost*. Sex was passionate, a heat as the speaker finds it still; but this genial desire was in no way sinful in itself (as Augustine would also agree, though denying the passion of the Edenic experience of sex) and it can be restored, at least in the speaker's imagination, even today, a recreation of that unashamed "primal prime embrace" (as Augustine would in no wise agree, though Milton would).[41]

A curious Latin work, an "Addenda to the Apocalypse" never published by Clough and left only in a manuscript now in the Bodleian, shows similar radical thoughts of sexual renovation, here more boldly adding his own words as the final word in the Bible rather than rewriting. The Spirit now offers to the speaker of Revelation not the New Jerusalem of heaven but the opportunity to lie with "body and flesh" in the form of Pandemia, an emanation of the bodily rather than spiritual world.[42] Yet she is validated as a fellow–servant of God, a purveyor of one of the great mysteries: "And there stood before my face a woman slender and tall, of about thirty years of age. And she said unto me / I am Pandemia whom thou seekest. / Lo, I am not spirit, I have body and flesh and limbs and substance. Blessed are those that lie with me." At least in hidden myth-making, Clough could dream directly of an easy reconciliation of self/spirit and world, of sex and religion.

His later poems, however, especially the major *Amours de Voyage* and *Dipsychus* show Clough laboring, in an evidently fallen, not Edenic world, under an increased burden of conflict and self-division that takes him far from a lyrical mode. Clough's well-known tone of self-division in these long poems of his poetic maturity builds especially on his increasingly conscious working at a set of interrelated perplexities, especially those of religious belief and religious values (what beliefs if one *can* believe) and sexual values (what kind of gratification, if gratification *can* be pursued). The problem in both of these related areas of thought involves that of choosing one belief from many; and this becomes increasingly connected in Clough's imagination, especially as he looks at the alternative of religiously sanctioned marriage, with a similar difficulty in attaining satisfaction because of personal difficulties in making any kind of commitment to one person. As with the young T. S. Eliot, to whom Clough has frequently been compared, as also with the young Augustine who stands behind both as a cultural achetype of sexual-marital-religious irresolution, sexual uncertainty is part of a general breakdown of personal and metaphysical security and a stimulus to a style of introspection, self-division, and agonized self-consciousness.

The sexual issue is clear enough in the title and the mottoes to *Amours de Voyage*. One of the mottoes is, in fact, "Il doutait de tout, même de l'amour" and if the poem, as most commentators have agreed, is like "Prufrock" or *The Wasteland* in presenting a consciousness divided to the point of paralysis, it stresses, like those poems, or like Augustine's *Confessions*, a central paralysis from perplexities in love and sexuality. Underlying and parallel to this crisis, there is then a more general paralysis of value in religious uncertainty. As in *The Bothie*, Clough looks at the world through the consciousness of an intellectual Victorian from his own sophisticated university milieu. This time, however, his subject lacks all revolutionary fervor and all Carlylean will to work. He is a certain gentleman with the effete name of Claude who is making the grand tour with a yawn and has settled in Rome to study, without any apparent enthusiasm, sculpture. That Claude can study the great tradition of the naked, natural, and Greek (even with figleaves at the Vatican) without enthusiasm is indicative of the world he lives in, or rather creates in his apprehension of reality. Like that of the nineteenth-century idea of Hamlet, like that of Prufrock or Pound's Mauberley, it is a world in which possibilities of commitment or action seem all outside the self, incapable of activation. Claude moves through a museum world littered with the fragments of great actions. His mind works by ironic, self-mockingly heroic allusions to the past: "I have made the step, have quitted the ship of Ulysses; / Quitted the sea and the shore, passed into the magical island" (1.234–35). Parallel to this mock-epic reference to great secular action there is a muted but significant rewriting of religious literature of pilgrimage, a broader version of Claude's, and his author's, habitual overwriting of biblical texts. For Protestants the Catholic grand tour culminating in the eternal holy city always had its mock side; one went, as Browning portrays himself in his *Christmas-Eve and Easter-Day*, as much to criticize as marvel. Yet no degree of Christian schism could entirely efface the essential pilgrimage; and the studious, really unworldly Claude, still trailing clouds of quasi-clerical dust from Clough's own recent role as tutor and the portrait of the equally quiet Adam in *The Bothie*, seems more naturally to inhabit the role of a Newman-like religious scholar in Rome than that of a Byron in Greece. Rome's own contemporary throes, a very real conflict between contesting forces of secular modernism and medieval religious power, fit Claude's personal conflict quite precisely and suggest the broader tension between religious and secular roles that underlies and conditions his uncertainties as a lover.

He tells his experiences to us through letters in Clough's colloquial but intellectually loaded and syntactically complicated hexameters, a further development of the deliberately unregular meter he had opposed to Longfellow's regularity in *The Bothie*. He writes to a close male friend in England, Eustace. It has often been remarked that the tradition is that of Richardson; but Claude's relation to the tradition, as to other traditions, is one of distance and contrast. He is a burlesque Lovelace, writing of his passional lacunae, of his willful inactions and his barely willed actions. He plots, but is no plotting villain, except in his schemes against his own heart. Claude exists in a social milieu fallen from action; he meets a part-gentry, part-middle-class English family through a university friend who courts one of the daughters; he finds nothing to inspire a sense of decisive commitment in his friend's drift into conventional marriage; when we read the letters of his friend's fiancée we can't help agreeing. Yet there are Fortinbrases astir in his time as in past times. As Claude lives his little concerns through the heroic months of the siege of Mazzini's Roman Republic, he finds it all absurd. He is never sure whether he could even play his little part as a tourist defending his friends from soldiers' rape: "Am I prepared to lay down my life for the British female?" (ii.66).

Without underlining it by bringing on stage a Mazzini for comparison, Clough thus contrasts Claude's life to that of heroic action.[43] Philip took action in love, if not in battle. Claude's battlefield is similarly that of love; but his campaign fails entirely. He becomes interested in the sister, Mary, of his friend's fiancée, courts her, if this is even the right term, in a most lukewarm, indecisive way, hesitates to act when she moves on to Florence, finally decides to pursue her only to find, in a hasty chase north, that he is unable to trace her. He gives up. The campaign might really be said to be another siege, a burlesque of the historical siege, in which Claude successfully defends his citadel of bachelorhood by a series of aggressive feints.

Claude acts foolishly; he lacks backbone and ordinary virility; but he is not simply a self-ignorant fool in the manner, say, of Emily Brontë's Lockwood. Others see him in a far better light than he presents himself in, as "*most* useful and kind" (ii.227) during the Roman crisis, as withdrawn and intellectually cold but not silly. His thinking, too, is not silly. It serves as a vehicle for Clough's serious examination of many of the issues he had already raised in his earlier poetry. And he is, like Clough himself, like Prufrock too, distinguished by the honesty of his positions and the candor of his self-evaluation. Clough's portrait of him is good evidence that Clough could see, like his friend Matthew Arnold, the larger destructive consequences of restless striving for intellectual answers to the knotty problems of his time.

It is not, however, that Claude must find solutions. It is that he waits only too honestly for the spark from heaven, the *coup de foudre* that will guarantee his commitment as a lover against the "factitious" involvement. Factitious indeed is his favorite word, used to stigmatize self-deceit arising from convenience, momentary enthusiasm, or a sense of duty. This is, of course, the concern with finding "the veritable thing" in love that we have already seen in *The Bothie* and the *Ambarvalia* poems. Its primacy reminds us again of a barely submerged religious identity in this lover. He is a lover like a Protestant of fine conscience who looks for the true faith among a welter of offering tenets that promise indeed spiritual gratification, as various choices of women offer sexual, but only at the expense of abandoning the narrow path of the true way. Energies from a religious tradition that admired the glories of Roman Christianity but found them finally false – preferring "Christian," Gothic architecture, as Pugin would, to the glories of Renaissance and baroque Rome – seem to invade an apparently secular, sexual choice.

Here, in a world where the romance assurances by plot of *The Bothie* or *Jane Eyre* are not to be expected, the problem of correct choice occupies center-stage. With logic that could wreck any marriage, Claude repeatedly asks how any Mary we happen to meet on the way in life can be the veritable thing – a version of Clough's simple but perturbing religious question, how the religion we are born into happens to be the right one. His scruples against love arising from mere "juxtaposition" (III.107) leads him to break the normal process of emotional involvement: "I am in love, you say; I do not think so exactly" (II.263). "I do not like being moved," he writes, "for the will is excited; and action / Is a most dangerous thing; I tremble for something factitious, / Some malpractice of heart and illegitimate process" (II.270–72). Instead he waits, an Adam waiting for his Eve in the "Eden" of his passivity, for God to provide the perfect mate: "Let love be its own inspiration: / Shall not a voice, if a voice there must be, from the airs that environ, / Yea, from the conscious heavens, without our knowledge or effort, / Break into audible words? and love be its own inspiration?" (II.278–81). The wholesale transposition of language and images from the realm of religious conversion – "not my will but Thine, oh Lord" – again suggests the general crisis of faith that manifests itself as a problem of sexual choice. Claude keeps finding his hopes for love's fulfillment in passages from the Bible, which, like his author, he keeps overwriting. But without the romance plot provided for Philip in *The Bothie*, the allegories of religion for the private life don't seem to work for him and his world: "But for Adam, – alas, poor critical coxcomb Adam! / But for Adam there is not found an help-meet for him" (I.150–52).[44] The chain of logic in his position is hard to break unless one strikes at the fundamental assumption that equates choice of mate with an act of spiritual election. But waiting for God to help him to help himself to a wife of course leaves our hero at the end a self-admitted coward in "the perilous field in / Whose wild struggle of forces the prizes of life are contested" (v.82–83).

There is perhaps no better way to call in question a form of idealism than to take it completely seriously. Clough lets Claude be a martyr to the idea of seeking the perfect angel mate, the liberal sexual view that paid for its positive version of sex with the religious idealization of the coupling of man and woman in marriage. He follows it truthfully and suffers the consequence: absurdity. He is also used to raise a number of correlate issues. Such is his fear of miscommitting his heart that he takes a negative position on the frequent Victorian idea, as we see it in Charles Kingsley, or in the

Brownings, of continued soul-mating after death. He believes no bridegroom could sanely go through with it if he didn't see the "funeral train" in the distance that will give him "that final discharge" (III.117, 119). The fantastical absurd perspective not only calls in question "Talk of eternal ties and marriages made in heaven" (III.112) but the whole idea of life-long commitment to "perfect" relations under which Clough and his hero labor. Claude sometimes sees that the entire strain in his culture of idealizing and intellectualizing sexuality, of which he is the finest flower, puts man out of relation to his nature, almost as much as the alternative conservative repression of sexuality it opposes. Could the grain sprout, he asks in a couplet that anticipates not only "Do I dare to eat a peach" but also some of Hardy's grim reflections about sexuality and advanced consciousness, "would it endure to accomplish the round of its natural functions, / Were it endowed with a sense of the general scheme of existence?" (III.45–46).

At the crisis of his story, when he hesitates and loses Mary as she goes on to Florence, Claude is even driven for a moment to a more realistic assessment of his position. That is, he admits he has a desire for Mary or someone that is more fundamental than the apparatus of love, special election, and marriage raised upon it: "could we eliminate only / This vile hungering impulse, this demon within us of craving, / Life were beatitude, living a perfect divine satisfaction" (III.179–81). He may even be attracted by the idea of "*Mild monastic faces in quiet collegiate cloisters*" (III.189).[45] The phrase reminds us how close Claude has been all along to the only somewhat more worldly version of monasticism in England's collegiate world, the place from which his author began writing. To recognize for a moment a simple force of craving, separate from religious and social channeling, is also to remember the reverse alternative of sexless devotion to religion. Claude's brilliant, if heavy and rather clerical-seeming analysis of the problems of meaning and willing, continue to attract us by their play with the meaning of meaning and their intellectual humility.[46] They also let us know that something can begin to go wrong, as Clough sees it, when we try to build too-elaborate systems of discourse on the basis of simpler drives and alternatives: here sexual gratification or denial. Clough's sympathetic but ultimately highly destructive enactment of an idealist sexual view brings him even to the borders of the far more profound sense of overripeness and failure of systems of language that we will find in Thomas Hardy's *Jude the Obscure*. To some extent Clough finally evades the issues he has raised by, at long last, letting Claude put his long-delayed novelistic plot in motion. He eschews the impulse to monastic misogyny, which soon gives way to a triumph of nature as Claude begins his ridiculous, failing pursuit of the fleeing but willing female. Despite the loss of repose, Claude ends his correspondence still insisting that there may have been something factitious in the failed affair. But the reader is left with the firmer intuition that Clough has shown us something more factitious in the system-building that sexual and religious thinking have performed on the old site of the marriage game.

Though often known only by a few of the Spirit's irreverent songs or by its reputation as an early response to the Higher Criticism, *Dipsychus* has been deservedly considered Clough's most important work. Despite relatively greater recent critical attention to the interesting perplexities of the *Amours*, *Dipsychus* deserves that position in Clough's canon and, as a major poem in a great European tradition, has a right to substantially more attention from readers of English poetry. Drawing upon the example of Goethe's *Faust* (Dipsychus originally had the name Faustulus in Clough's drafts) and probably on other works of irony or self-division such as Byron's *Don Juan*, Tennyson's "The Two Voices," or even parts of *Sartor Resartus*, Clough finds a less overloaded, more pithy and lively way to express his complex ideas than that of allowing the intellectual, self-perplexed sensibility of Claude to expatiate directly. T. S. Eliot obtains point and economy by moving the monologue inside the mind and using it as a vehicle for symbol and private myth. Clough objectifies confusion and self-division into dramatic dialogue. The perplexity is clarified into an open-ended argument in which one character, Dipsychus, attempts to set out and maintain beliefs and the other, the Spirit, later called Mephistopheles, undercuts, ridicules, and laughs away those beliefs. The process works as a dialectic, forcing Dipsychus to adjusted positions. It also effectively allows for expression of a wide range of positions, including extremes, thus providing an ideal medium for Clough's restless openness to the strong points in different ideas as well as his rather merciless exposure of weak ones. Less original a thinker than Goethe, he is especially good as a refractor and critic of the varied and often confused ideas of his time: a splendid mediator and interrogator of his age's mind rather than another voice proclaiming a single truth. The approach to truth through dialectic and critique, disturbing as it was to

Clough's contemporaries, now gives an especially attractive and durable, even contemporary quality to his work.

At the same time, Clough prevents the poem from becoming merely a discussion by two persons by leaving unclear the relation of Dipsychus to the Spirit. This troubling focus on the relation of ideas to the subject considering them is thus always foregrounded – yet another way in which Clough's work seems more familiar in our age than it was in his: truth is found in the conflict of ideas in the world of the subject but exists only as rejected or welcomed by the subject's personal anxieties or desires. The Spirit is in a sense a kind of inner voice with special access to what is troubling Dipsychus. In this sense, if Dipsychus (an Englished version by Clough of the New Testament term he applied so often to himself in his diaries) is, by name and attitude, a person divided by his uncertainties,[47] the Spirit speaks for one side of his psyche and merely objectifies an inner conflict. Dipsychus raises but leaves unanswered this question of the Spirit's function: is what he hears "My own bad thoughts, / Or some external agency at work"? (II.19–20). As the reader watches Dipsychus understand his own attraction to the Spirit's positions and, with the Spirit's help, define those positions objectively, the reader senses a process of externalization of the Spirit into a more conventional tempter, a process signalized by the adoption of the name Mephistopheles and the epithet of Cosmocrator or The Power of this World. Yet even this increasing definition of the Spirit is finally undercut by Clough's "Epilogue" where he playfully suggests that "perhaps he wasn't a devil after all." If Dipsychus represents the "tender conscience," as the "Epilogue" suggests, it may naturally, as it sees the world's position, "exaggerate the wickedness of the world" (p. 292). Clough's own Latin "Addenda to the Apocalypse" had indeed suggested that wedding with the world – which is what the Spirit is selling – is the one thing needful, as it had been for the happy bridegroom Philip in *The Bothie*.

Finally, Clough finds in *Dipsychus* another kind of formal freedom: he brings his poem simultaneously near to both personal confession and objective drama. Both Dipsychus and the Spirit are explicitly related to the author of their dialogue, the former by his assertion that he is the author of Clough's own poem "Easter Day," the latter by the personal notation to the Spirit's famous song on the pleasure of money: "(Written in Venice, but for all parts true, / 'Twas not a crust I gave him, but a sou)" (v.196–97). Such points confirm our general sense, from Clough's life and other work, that he is struggling with problems important to him personally, yet the dramatic form gives him the freedom to try out different positions through Dipsychus or the Spirit without the embarrassment of giving them personal endorsement. Clough's surprising powers of dialogue and dramatic interplay, first shown in *The Bothie*, come into force again in *Dipsychus*, here as sprightly drama of ideas with sudden contradictions and antitheses such as we have become more used to in abstract modern drama.

The ideas so dramatically presented in the poem range over philosophy, views of society, and the individual. They center, however, in Dipsychus' unresolved sexual dilemma, which provides the situation for much of the dialogue (looking over Venetian women) and the motivation for bringing in related issues. The sexual crisis is now so severe that it brings into open discussion the conjoined religious upheaval. Religion had been present in the earlier works mainly implicitly, in the quasi-clerical role of Clough's central characters or in the repressions or ideals attached to different sexual attitudes. Sexual difficulties, problems of marital choice, seemed to point to less clearly stated religious problems. The relation between sexual and religious crisis is now directly faced at the same time that the Clough figure in the poem finally takes a clear step toward a more secular role. For the first time we also have a direct statement of the personal crisis as a variant of a problem in the relation of sexuality and religion that has accompanied Christianity since its early history.

The work opens with Dipsychus alluding to a poem "Easter Day" which we read, along with "Easter Day II" as the separate work of Clough's, "Easter Day. Naples, 1849" (neither the "Easter Day" poems nor *Dipsychus* was published in Clough's lifetime).[48] Both "Easter Day. Naples, 1849" and *Dipsychus* share an uncertainty about received religion – "Christ is not risen." But the allusion from *Dipsychus* to "Easter Day" stems more immediately from an identity in the speakers' situations and directly links the seemingly commonplace statement of Victorian crisis of faith to bluntly sexual issues. Both speakers (or the speaker of both poems, to follow *Dipsychus*) observe the unredeemed world directly in the "great sinful streets" and street-walkers of worldly Italian cities: "At Naples then, / At Venice now. Ah! and I think at Venice / Christ is not risen either" (1.31–33). Both speakers also, in their own ambivalent responses to the immediate sexual release offered by the sinful streets, find Christ not surely risen in their own hearts either.[49] The speaker in "Easter Day" presents himself in a state analogous to that of the city: "Through the great sinful streets of Naples as I past, / With fiercer heat than flamed above my head / My heart was hot within me" (1–3). When we find from "Easter Day II" that he was actually in the company of a "blear-eyed pimp" offering his seedy wares (a "beautiful danseuse," a lady "in the green silk there," or the commodity so highly valued by Walter of *My Secret Life*, a "little thing not quite fifteen"), it is hard not to interpret the flaming heat in an Augustinian sense. The speaker in *Dipsychus* is rapidly forced by the Spirit, who torments him with self-knowledge, to admit his attraction to Venetian women and girls.

Dipsychus properly picks up from this similar situation because "Easter Day," while an excellent poem and one of Clough's most blunt statements of religious skepticism, still shockingly blunt, in fact, leaves the full implications of the speaker's involvement in the scene somewhat vague. He finds some relief in proclaiming his skeptical message but in some sense he does not get quite to the heart of what troubles him so in those sinful streets. The parallel with St. Augustine is a helpful one and probably was, explicitly or intuitively, in Clough's mind as he wrote both poems. In his own battles with the seemingly independent and uncontrollable power of sex within him as he had experienced it ever since boyhood guilt over masturbation, Clough had approached an Augustinian experience of division through sexual temptation, an experience closely tied to his early preoccupation with the term "dipsychus" as a way of describing his own psychic state. Certainly the poem creates and then contrasts a Christian reading of sex to the alternative in a world of religious uncertainty. The young Augustine found himself burning with sexual passion in a great southern city and learned the necessity of striving to subdue and redirect the passion into a passionate religion. The skeptical Cloughian speaker, troubled by reading in Strauss, is also troubled by the flames of passion, seemingly not under his control, that tormented his great predecessor. The date of the title even gives us a clue to the personal poignancy of the poem and its subject. Actually written in August, the poem was deliberately retitled from the earlier manuscript "August 1849" to "Easter Day. Naples, 1849." Clough had noted that his fellowship, which he had given up earlier, was actually due to expire at Easter 1849 in any case.[50] The day thus probably stood in his mind as the final day of spiritual reckoning. Had he chosen religious retreat from the world, as Augustine did, Easter 1849 would have found him in holy orders rather than exposed to the world.

His poem, however, is less personal than the *Confessions*. Out of his skepticism and his experience of sin without and within, he nonetheless attempts to write a kind of updated litany. This he does now by fully overwriting the biblical texts in this his most decisive biblical revision, one that exceeds interpretation and essentially substitutes a deconstructive, and then competitive, opposite reading of the texts it writes over.[51] His new text bears the message that the Christian myth is cancelled; more, it insists that we must now abandon the Augustinian solution of turning from sexual energies to religious devotions, and even suggests that these forces may have been identical. Whereas the fishermen of Galilee are told to go back to catching fish, not men, the "Daughters of Jerusalem" are ordered more explicitly to return their emotions from Christ to ordinary sexual feelings: "Go to your homes, your living children tend, / Your earthly spouses love; / Set your affections *not* on things above" (104–6). Good believers generally are warned not to turn "pleading eyes, / And sobs of strong desire, / Unto the empty vacant void" (129–31). As so often, this message is made most clearly in a rejected variant, here an addition after line 85 in an early draft, which speaks explicitly to the general process by which early Christians turned away from sexual pleasure in the hopes of the full bliss of the risen and happy self.[52] Christians' early certitude made the plucking out of the fire easy. Now the fire seems inevitable.

> Well might it be before
> When we had hope those after joys to win
> To talk as then we talked of crucifying sin!
> With the new birth
> And life to come and bliss unspeakable in store
> Twas little for a day so quickly to be o'er
> To mortify our members here on earth.
> But now, upheld no more
> There is nought for us but to sink sink in
> Down down into the sea without a shore
> Sea without shore or bark
> One flood without one ark!
> For the whole world, and there is none but this,
> The whole world lies in wickedness
>   Christis is not risen.   (pp. 674–75)

Ironically, this of course leaves him rather precisely where Augustine was in his continuing and intense sense of sexual desire as a sin. Only he now lacks Augustine's faith to help control his Augustinian sense of the power of lust. Save for the obvious inference that he is clearly not going out of his way, in his present company, to mortify his flesh anymore, the speaker does not explore his position too clearly, so that Clough leaves it to us to see the quandary in which the freethinking rewriting of the ascetic tradition of Christianity has left his protagonist: namely with Augustinian fears of the power of lust but without an Augustinian remedy. The speaker then further confuses all by the reversal in "Easter Day II," where the former poem is ascribed to "one that somewhat overwildly sung" (14), as if he hoped to cancel his cancellation and retrieve a degree of traditional Christian control. It is fair to observe of the speaker, as Mephistopheles might have had he been present, the following: first, that his religious faith seems to fall or rise with the propinquity or distance of sexual temptation: the more he feels the world unredeemed, the more he believes it in fact is; the statement that "Christ is not risen" threatens to turn into Christ is not risen for me because of my sin, thus shifting his axis of sensibility from freethinking to morbid religious despair. Second, the speaker, when he counsels abandonment of religious exaltation and acceptance of ordinary sexuality, seems still of two minds: either this is still sinful and bad, making the whole world wickedness, or it is the best we have, though meager in the face of mortal suffering: "Eat, drink, and play, and think that this is bliss!" (77). Wherever we say the speaker stands on the issue of faith, whether with the strong voice of doubt of the first poem or with the less persuasive, if "graver word," of the second, we can say he remains confused and upset precisely because he finds crucial issues of faith so intimately tied to excruciating problems of sexual gratification. Thinking to rewrite totally the conservative Christian tradition on sex most fully (and in quite extreme form) articulated by Augustine, he ends up very much in the experimental position Augustine was in before his conversion – finding that his own lust seems a central problem needing solution.

I don't think that *Dipsychus* solves these sexual or religious problems. But with the issues finally directly stated in the Easter Day poems, Clough's insistently prying and questioning dialectic now works strongly to clarify and, if possible, move to some resolution of all that still seemed hidden in "Easter Day." With the pimp, rendered as the suavely worldly Spirit, brought right into the poem, Dipsychus can't avoid going to one heart of the matter: that he experiences a difficulty in his unfulfilled sexual nature that does not seem to go away. It is with him in Venice as in Naples, then as now. In the discussion that ensues in *Dipsychus*, with the Spirit an excuse for continually baring issues normally not discussed in Victorian literature, Clough gives us his fullest anatomy of the sexual issues and perplexities of his time.[53]

That a nice Rugby boy like Clough should look fully at the issues of sexuality only in a poem where the celibate speaker finds himself unable to resist the attractions of prostitutes is itself a full comment on the confusions in sexual ideologies he has been trying to sort out. In other poems we have seen Clough or one of his personae resist the temptation of seducing respectable young ladies or more available Scots lasses. Having done so, he follows a certain kind of clear logic in offering the ultimate temptation as what remains available: girls who solicit (or procurers who solicit for them) the nice young man's long-restrained release. The situation that Clough dramatizes – his speaker driven from the reserved moral position of tutor Adam, through the agonized inactions of gentleman-traveler Claude, finally to seek satisfaction of his needs in the *cloaca maxima* of the nineteenth-century prostitute system – plays out the illogic of the various and confused sexual attitudes he found in his age and mimicked in his work. Eventually the absurd strategy of encouraging a growing class of prostitutes (often literally girls themselves) in order to keep other British maidens undefiled would erupt in the public battles over medical regulation of prostitutes, in which reformers under Josephine Butler attacked the morality and logic of building Victorian houses as a way of preserving Victorian homes.[54] Clough attacks the same system subversively, by showing that the self-feeding dichotomies of purity and degradation on which it is built are mainly empty rhetoric.

The pleasure of reading *Dipsychus* is especially in experiencing the continuous play of one kind of language against another. Dipsychus' slightly unsure assertions of the received moral view of things are set against the Spirit's restatements in worldly but common-sense terms as he strives incessantly to break down Dipsychus' restraining ideals and bed him with the world. It would take as long as the poem itself to follow all the nuances of argument in the long discussion, from the opening to the end of scene three, around the attractions to/

repulsions from going off to have sex with one of the inviting dark-
eyed Venetian women. The general logic of their discussion is
apparent enough, however. Whether at the Piazza San Marco, or at
the public garden, or at the quays, the Spirit keeps turning the
subject to the young women, with a clear sense that they are very
much present already on the unacknowledged periphery of Dipsychus' mind: "There was a glance, I saw you spy it" (II.66).
Dipsychus' initial reaction is to try to fend off recognition of his
feelings. His prayer against his own lewd feelings implicitly calls
attention to the ridiculous overstatement in the angelic ideals that
Clough's earlier works sometimes criticized but still struggled under.
It builds up hysterically a catalog of domestic purities like a bulwark
of defense against fornication:

> O moon and stars forgive! And thou, clear heaven,
> Look pureness back into me. O great God,
> Why, why in wisdom and in grace's name,
> And in the name of saints and saintly thoughts,
> Of mothers, and of sisters, and chaste wives,
> And angel woman-faces we have seen,
> And angel woman-spirits we have guessed,
> And innocent sweet children, and pure love,
> Why did I ever one brief moment's space
> To this insidious lewdness lend chaste ears.   (III.14–23)

The over-defensive stance only gives the Spirit an opening for
presenting a different view of prostitution by allowing him to occupy
the vacant place of ordinary common sense. He rightly sees
Dipsychus' fear of lewdness and invocation of angels as a romanticism
based on unreal, black-and-white alternatives that survive from a
version of the religion he thought he had cancelled. He answers
Dipsychus: "O yes, you dream of sin and shame – / Trust me, it
leaves one much the same" (III.29–30). If Dipsychus, like Augustine,
and like the conservative position of Clough's age, overstates the
dread force of fornication, he also over-idealizes the idea of love itself:
"You think I'm anxious to allure you – / My object is much more to
cure you. / With the high amatory-poetic / My temper's no way
sympathetic" (III.35–38). Dipsychus' fears of sexual contact derive
from his hidden romantic over-estimation, a kind of prudery layered
upon Byronism's melodramatic association of love and death: the
unspoken "thing" growing in significance precisely as it no longer
dares speak its direct signifier.

> I know it's mainly your temptation
> To think the thing a revelation,
> A mystic mouthful that will give
> Knowledge and death – none know and live!
> I tell you plainly that it brings
> Some ease.   (III.41–46)

The Spirit then turns his persuasive powers to the purpose of offering Dipsychus some ease in the nearest way. But here Dipsychus is not so easily driven into silent submission. He has strong views on the subject of woman's sexuality, views that he, like Philip in *The Bothie*, doubtless received from the sexual discussions of his time rather than arrived at himself and which reflect all their confusions over sexuality. His position seems almost a deliberate parody of dubious theories of sexual respectability propounded by some Victorian sexual conservatives.[55] The litany, seeking its assurance, as usual, in a version of the central sexual myth of paradise, begins with the assertion that women are different: "I know; / Not as the male is, is the female, Eve / Was moulded not as Adam" (III.74–77). "Stuff!" the Spirit answers, "The women like it; that's enough" (III.77–78). But the problem, as in Philip's thinking and the confused thinking of sexual conservatives generally, seems to be that those chaste angels come to like it too much. He is very tempted by the idea that women, as he will admit men can, could simply enjoy sex as recreation:

> Could I believe, as of a man I might,
> So a good girl from weary workday hours
> And from the long monotony of toil
> Might safely purchase these wild intervals,
> And from that banquet rise refreshed, and wake
> And shake her locks and as before go forth
> Invigorated, unvitiate to the task –   (III.79–85)

"But no," he concludes, "it is not so" (III.86). The woman who tries sex becomes an addict; once down, she descends ever lower:

> The swallowed dram entails the drunkard's curse
> Of burnings ever new; and the coy girl
> Turns to the flagrant woman of the street,
> Ogling for hirers, horrible to see.   (III.92–95)

The Spirit correctly evaluates this as a standard rhetorical mode, answering more a need of the speaker than a reality: "That is the

high moral way of talking; / I'm well aware about street-walking"
(III.96–97). Dipsychus is undaunted and proceeds with a full dress
rehearsal of the Victorian whore's progress (III.98–113). This speech,
like his appeal to angel powers of purity, tends to show up its own
fatuity ("the frolick pulses stilled, / The quick eye dead, the once fair
flushing cheek / Flaccid under its paint," etc.). The Spirit's answer
is, first, to laugh at the unreal language: "Fiddle di diddle, fal lal lal!
/ By candlelight they are *pas mal*" (III.114–15), then to point out that
prostitutes are neither dark angels nor animals but people:

> Well; people talk – their sentimentality.
> Meantime, as by some sad fatality
> Mortality is still mortality;
>
>   . . .
>
> As women are and the world goes
> They're not so badly off – who knows?
> They die, as we do in the end;
> They marry; or they – *superintend*.   (III.162–71)[56]

With the deflation of the stock Victorian myth of prostitution,
Dipsychus is driven to manufacture a welter of arguments to fend off
temptation. Could he believe any daughter of Eve with "cherry lips
and chubby cheeks / That seem to exist express for such fond play"
(III.122–23) were not further degraded . . . could he believe that
the male as stronger person didn't have the responsibility to refuse
her . . . could he believe that any woman was beyond redemption
or that he didn't make it harder for her by having sex with her . . .
then, the implication clearly is, he would. And, with this admission,
the Spirit has him, as he really has had him from the opening. He may
not get over the conservative arguments about women's sexuality
and prostitution; he may lose these small skirmishes but he has the
main point, which is to push Dipsychus into admitting that, unlike
the shy Claude, he most certainly wishes some kind of sexual
existence. Dipsychus' last resort is to ascribe his chastity, so far, to
heavenly miracle; but the Spirit deflates this angelic intervention:
"Cry mercy of his heavenly highness – / I took him for that cunning
shyness" (III.192–93). He then caps the discussion by pointing out
directly the extreme susceptibility we have already seen in the idealist
celibate: "Ho, Virtue quotha! trust who knows; / There's not a girl
that by us goes / But mightn't have you if she chose" (III.197–99).
    Such an undeniable truth about Dipsychus really closes the
discussion, even if Clough has only disturbed, rather than totally

reformulated, "respectable," conservative ideas of female sexuality and prostitution. Dipsychus has lost the main argument to self-knowledge and finds himself forced to retreat to a new position: finding prostitution still unpalatable, he will try his society's alternative:

> welcome then, the sweet domestic bonds,
> The matrimonial sanctities; the hopes
> And cares of wedded life; parental thoughts,
> The prattle of young children, the good word
> Of fellow men, the sanction of the law,
> And permanence and habit, that transmute
> Grossness itself to crystal.   (III.204–10)

The Spirit's answer is succinct: "Go home and marry – and be d—d" (III.218). He is happy to preside over either form of damnation. The problem, of course, is that Clough can hardly present social marriage Victorian style as anything but damnation or legal prostitution.[57] Having rejected prostitution, declared other forms of sex impossible, and admitted his hero's need for sex, he has him back in Claude's position with deeper vengeance. Like Claude, he resents the hypocritical social roles which, the Spirit assures him, he will be forced to play in the mating game. Like Claude, he finds his very ideals betray him when he faces them honestly: how can he commit himself for a lifetime through the marriage market when the ideal angel love is just possibly (not likely) around the corner:

> love, the large repose
> Restorative, not to mere outside needs
> Skin-deep, but thoroughly to the total man,
> Exists, I will believe, but so, so rare,
> So doubtful, so exceptional, hard to guess;
> When guessed, so often counterfeit; in brief,
> A thing not possibly to be conceived
> An item in the reckonings of the wise.   (X.30–37)

The only way out still seems to be born sexless: a full retreat to the monastic ideal from which Clough has been finding his way in his series of poems. Dipsychus' language is a very close echo of Claude's on the demon of craving: "could we eliminate only / This interfering, enslaving, o'ermastering demon of craving" (v.66–67).[58] But short of self-mutilation *à la* Origen, which in all Clough's exacerbations in *Dipsychus* over sex he doesn't really suggest to his hero, eliminating the need has been shown to be emphatically impossible. So, after much splendid poetry laughing at the way of the world but even more at those who think they can avoid it, *Dipsychus* comes around on this central issue to its beginning. Sure of his need, unclear about both prostitution and marriage, Dipsychus yields only to the need to do something. The devil takes care of the rest and they depart for San Marco after dark. For a moment the restraints of repression and idealism are themselves held back; in the same lifted mood Clough gives the Spirit some of his lightest-hearted statements of skepticism over religious belief and simple worldly pleasure.

In *Dipsychus Continued* we find that Dipsychus has twice yielded his innocence to worldly streets and gratification, presumably to a prostitute in San Marco the evening of the final dialogue and later to marriage and Victorian success. The brief, unfinished, and indecisive continuation adds little more to the story.[59] There is no picture of happy marriage; his pre-marital affair, though it apparently started his career going, comes back to him thirty years later only as guilt, so that the poems end with repressive religious feeling – clearly not banished, merely laying low for a while – having its say again, though it is clear that the woman took his innocence, not he hers (II.17). The continuation suggests what *Dipsychus* itself shows, that Clough vigorously and courageously exposed and clarified the complicated and intertwined sexual and religious issues of his day without finding any easy solution to the problems he stated. Despite Clough's often joyful, sometimes even riotous demolition of the Augustinian tradition, it seems finally to make its full claims on the flesh of his hero and perhaps on Clough himself, who did marry and does seem to have been damned (or at least dammed up) as a poet until close to his early death. Nothing that is said in the poem about honestly facing sexual desires and the logic of their satisfaction seems to attack the deeper feeling, which Dipsychus seems indeed to share with Augustine, that desire itself is something shameful, a "vile" craving, something "gross." More, even if the skeptic looks for accommodation with, rather than eventual mastery of this demon, he shares Augustine's sense that this is a force alien to the subject self, a "demon" within, a separate law of the members which must be recognized but is not easily accepted. Such a central Western tradition of thinking on sex, which had been so powerfully inscribed in Clough's own early experience by the conflict he had experienced between his earnest aspirations to moral Christian behavior, even at times to a kind of Tractarian sanctity, and his inability to control even his habit of masturbation, is too powerful for even Clough's sprightly efforts at self-liberation.[60]

With *Dipsychus*, Clough's brief career as an important poet really closes and along with it Clough's major contribution to his age's writing on the confused subject of sexuality and its relation to the equally confused subject of religion – perplexities at the heart of so many of the age's major cultural and social preoccupations. Clough is certainly far from a revolutionary, even in the terms of his age. He had no part in distributing birth control information in the street or writing tracts for free love. But the weight of his thinking clearly comes down on the side of exposing simplicities in his culture's confused strains of thought and on opening up a freer and a better-articulated discussion. If he does not write his three major poems in a directly confessional mode, it is still clear enough that he works in his poetry toward a standard of basing sexual and religious discussion upon honesty to one's own self-understanding. To keep on writing in his age about the problems of the young celibate was in itself an act of courage in exploring his own perception of experience as against the various received views of the time. Unsure what to say about sexuality, he still says that the subject cannot be merely swept under the rug of public reticence and he is not afraid to reach back and interrogate central myths of Western culture in his search for better understanding. "Ignorance," as he remarks in a letter of 1850 reflecting on his personal voyage away from the security and protection of a don's life, "is a poor kind of innocence."[61] His position in "Adam and Eve," a dialogue sequence that, unusually for Clough, does not focus directly on the apple as sexuality, is perhaps indicative of the general direction of his thinking. Adam feels, in contrast to Eve's hysteria over guilt, that man may suffer a sense of impurity in his quest for knowledge. But the alternative, of hiding from experience, is far worse: "That which we were, we could no more remain / Than in the moist provocative vernal mould / A seed its suckers close, and rest a seed. / We were to grow" (1.13–16).

Clough himself grew, for all his Claude-like scruples, to the sexual and other than sexual involvement of marriage. He left some sincere, even passionate but not very good poems to his future wife.[62] Perhaps, as his biographers have argued, the growth to married sexual intimacy repressed as much as it released the restless energies that we feel in his major poems before marriage. It seems to have

forced upon him, or he let it force upon him, the public codes of
reticence in sexual issues against which his poetry works so persistently. We have a long period of silence after his marriage. The
silence is ostensibly that of the Carlylean worker in harness doing that
which lies nearest to hand in supporting wife, family, and society. But
the work Clough was born to do is thereby put off, and it is further
delayed by all that important service to Strachey's abomination, the
saintly "Flo" Nightingale.

Eventually, before Clough's death, there is a partial return from
Victorian marriage, family-making, career, and charitable works, to
poetry. He allows *Amours de Voyage* to be published at last in the
Atlantic Monthly in 1858. He works with Norton on plans, unfulfilled
at his death, for a collected edition of his poetry. We naturally think
of his poems as statements of the time of writing. But to begin to move
toward publication of the works that had not appeared in the
published *Bothie* or *Ambarvalia* is itself another major step in Clough's
poetic career. The stress should be not on his hesitancy but on the
renewed courage of a married Victorian in even these tentatives
toward putting all his views before the public. We need only think of
the ordeals of Hardy, Joyce, or Lawrence as they tried to publish
their candid observations on sexuality or religion in a far more
divided and generally less reticent age to realize fairly Clough's
situation. Thackeray, in the well-known Preface to *Pendennis*, had
even despaired of ever being able to publish his candid observations
of sexual "temptation": "Since the author of *Tom Jones* was buried,
no writer of fiction among us has been permitted to depict to his
utmost power a man. We must drape him and give him a certain
conventional simper. Society," he concluded, "will not tolerate the
Natural in our Art."

Thackeray perhaps implies that more could be done in the less
popular form of poetry than in fiction. But the difference was only
relative to the more limited readership for poetry. Publication in the
Atlantic Monthly was coming into the more public area in which moral
censorship prevailed. Significantly, in his final act as a poet, the
unfinished series of *Mari Magno* tales written before his death, Clough
adopts a more popular, more novelistic style than in his earlier work.
This series has been written off as a tribute to a happy marriage and
acceptance of Victorian mores. Stylistically, it has been looked at as
a concession to the taste of the day for the domestic, familiar kind of
poetry that we will meet in Patmore's *Angel in the House*. The popular

manner of the poem certainly has dated more than the intellectual, metaphysical and allusive, styles of *Amours* or *Dipsychus*. Clough's intention is, however, not to yield his independent thinking to the age but to place it more obviously before the age. He signals his intentions in his form, a series of frame tales of voyagers on a transatlantic passage that obviously alludes to the more open, more worldly discourse of another age in the *Canterbury Tales*. The general subject he gives his Victorian pilgrims to discuss is his own old one, sexuality, with the usual cross-connections to religious values. If his speakers are closer to a public Victorian language than Philip, Claude, or Dipsychus, they are nonetheless used by their author to ask probing, disturbing questions about orthodox positions.

Even this familiar device of employing different narrators suggests Clough's aim of providing varied perspectives on issues of marriage. Certainly the tone of any one tale, as in reading Browning's dramatic monologues, should be ascribed in the first instance not to Clough but to the character of his chosen narrator. Closest to Victorian orthodoxy is the English clergyman, who tells two long tales. He is described as a sober and serious man of fifty, grave but with a wide knowledge of the world. He is not the mature Clough but the figure he might have been had not *his* religious thinking taken him far closer to the ordinary world. We see his outlook in his deep-mouthed Tennysonian interjection to "The Lawyer's Second Tale": "if the women don't sustain / The moral standard, all we do is vain" (243–44). His own tales are far from conventional in subject, but are rather conventional in point of view. The first looks at a hesitant Claude-like lover, and raises most of the uncertainties about recognizing real love that for so long so bothered Clough. However, the real problems thus raised are then washed away by a romance tale: the hesitant lover's family becomes bankrupt, he voids his engagement from honor, and forgets his problems of determining true love in hard work. Finally he meets his old lover by accident and they are happily united without further worry over scruples. The effect is to raise disturbing questions even though an answer is given to them. This effect is much stronger in "The Clergyman's Second Tale," where he is a moral vehicle for his author's disturbed story about a man, like himself, traveling for health. The issue raised is adultery; the married man, Edward, is preyed upon, to follow the Clergyman's way of telling it, by a *femme fatale*, one of those "Beings who seem for this alone to live, / Temptation to another soul to give. / A beauteous woman at the table d'hôte" (80–82). The Clergyman is as clear about her attractions as her badness and rather deconstructs his own moral position in his descriptive rapture: "Her throat and neck Junonian in their grace; / The blood just mantled in her southern face: / Dark hair, dark eyes; and all the arts she had / With which some dreadful power adorns the bad" (96–99).

Their adulterous affair is as clearly presented as a strong sexual release as it is characterized as a moral fall: "There [at her hotel room door], with the exultation of a boy, / Read in her liquid eyes the passion of her joy; / And went in with her at the fatal door / Whence he reissued innocent no more" (132–35). True to Dipsychus' ideas of women's sexuality, this pretty bad penny turns up later in London degraded by her passion into a prostitute. Edward, after excessive self-punishment for following his passion, is welcomed back to his loving, forgiving family. The perspective is very conventional, far from that of a Ford Madox Ford tale of passion. But Clough raises in a new form for him – that of adultery – the problem intrinsic to the conservative approach to sexuality he had so long been interrogating: the disjunction between passion and goodness. The Clergyman poses no solution to the problem of the "bad" woman's very real sexual attractions. But he does allow Clough to raise what still seems to him a dilemma.

Even a Clergyman in these tales is allowed to undercut his moral saws by recognition of passion and its complications. But the usual point of view is very clearly not that with which Clough began as a poet, of tutor and religious leader, but of various secular voices that surround the Clergyman. Clough contrasts the grave approach to marriage problems of the Clergyman to those of these other speakers. Two more ready men, an American with "racy tales of Yankeeland" and a Seaman, the Mate, tell tales closer to fabliau realism. A girl gets into bed with an unknown young man in the wrong room in an American hotel and, with this unusual but chaste introduction, their relation blooms to happy marriage. In the Mate's story a French girl, left stranded in Liverpool, accepts marriage at first sight from a gallant captain who befriends her. Both marriages, which put practical relation before considerations of ideal love, suggest an easier, less agonized functional view of marriage that implicitly undercuts the moral structure Claude or Dipsychus had confronted. The Mate's story ends with a worldly joke by a listening Artillery Captain about how sailors' wives accommodate to a husband with wives in every port: "Of course the women would at times suspect, / But felt their reputations were not wrecked" (72–73).

"My Tale" tells merely of a pretty girl seen and admired briefly in the Pyrenees years ago. It suggests generally that erotic feeling knows no ordinary social bounds. The theme is taken up more vigorously in the two tales of the Lawyer, especially the second. Of all the individualized speakers, he seems closest to Clough's usual undoctrinaire perspective; he is also close in his subjects to two of Clough's personal preoccupations. His first tale, a story of an intellectual young man who finds too late that he loves his cousin Emilia, takes a position that Clough's period of thrashing out sexual issues had at least brought him to decisively: that the young hero should not choose the college fellow's life of religious-like celibacy and withdrawal from emotions. The second, more interesting tale goes back to that, for Clough, erotically charged area, the Highlands and their lasses. Interestingly it is now the college fellow, rather than his students, who is made the center of amorous interest. His students away on a trip, he falls in love with a young woman, tries moral forbearance, but yields to her nightly visitations to his room. Without moral coloring, the Lawyer continues this tale of premarital involvement. He goes home with her to her uncle and, in effect, lives with her unmarried (the uncle is a practical man). Alas, a misunderstanding leads to disaster: she, pregnant by him, emigrates to Australia and he is unable to locate her despite his good intentions. Eventually both marry others and have large prosperous families, only to meet again by chance in middle age. On top of its merely factual, amoral presentation of the details of this love story, over the Clergyman's objections, the poem is morally probing in its treatment of the familiar romance theme of the end. Though the action follows a reverse pattern from that of Hardy in *Jude the Obscure*, where a bad marriage precedes (and indeed also follows) the discovery of genuine love. Clough's perspective certainly anticipates Hardy's interrogation of the idea of marriage as a binding contract. The lass writes to her first accepted lover, indicating that he is still first in her heart. His response suggests that same is true for him: "O love, love, love, too late! the tears fell down. / He dried them up – and slowly walked to town" (510–11).

On that sad, thoughtful note, accepting the fact of emotional infidelity as the Clergyman's "Second Tale" accepted that of sexual infidelity, Clough's last poem ends. Clough's work ends where writers such as Hardy, Ford Madox Ford, Lawrence, or even the Joyce of "The Dead" and Molly Bloom begin, on the complications of physical and imaginative sexual feeling within marriage. (Or one thinks more recently of Updike's tales for grown-ups of grown-up relations.) In this last try at poetry before his death, Clough does not fully explore this large subject, as he does rather fully explore the problem of the unmarried Victorian male. But, fairly considered in Clough's context, *Mari Magno* is yet another indication of his finely probing temperament and his restless undermining of orthodox simplicities about human sexual nature.

Fertility in finding more, and more complicated, issues for sexual discussion, boldness and honesty in pursuing their implications even when they bring him into very controversial territory, unwillingness merely to wish away moral and religious difficulties, these qualities of Clough's last poems are also those that characterize his work as a whole. As even this rather curtailed survey shows, he left an impressively full record of his inquiry into sexual issues. Even more impressive is the range of issues, especially the varied relations of religious and sexual thinking, that he puts forward for Victorian discussion. He offers not so much a coherent system for sexual thinking – this we will find in the other two writers on which this study focusses – as a highly articulate dissection of the varieties of sexual issues, in each case brightly illuminated by his curiosity and by his skepticism of received dogmas. Merely to summarize the questions he raises is to display a catalog of issues that could serve individually as central subjects in others' works. Each indeed really represents an entire way of defining sexuality, so that we have in Clough a kind of wonderful bazaar of competing, often irreconcilable sexual ideologies forced to submit to the democracy of their association and comparison. A vision of happy natural sexuality, as offered in "Natura Naturans" and in the descriptive scenes of *The Bothie*, exists beside a different image of the untroubled, non-sexual life as its own paradise, whether of happy fellows at Oxford or of those "mild monastic faces" at Rome. Stereotyped Victorian ideas of falling and fallen women are first presented seriously, then held up to comic scrutiny. Romantic ideas of sex as a mystic moment of love and death are balanced by Mephistopheles' concept of "some relief" to male frenzy and the Seaman's and Mate's notions of practical, realistic marriages. He casts an especially interested and skeptical eye on one Victorian solution to the age's increased fascination with sex and its sometimes increased prudery, the happy marriage to the angel wife, an ideal we will find hugely elaborated in Kingsley. As *Amours* itself so thoroughly shows, marriages that must be made in heaven seem not to function very well on earth; looked at from Mephistopheles' triumphant dialectic, what are they but an idealized version of prostitution? Even adultery, of body and of emotions, comes in for Clough's scrutiny, with the usual display of problematics rather than dogmatics.

Perhaps most striking is the way in which Clough recenters religious perspectives around sexual alternatives. As in the poems of T. S. Eliot, we have throughout Clough's work a sense that we follow the psychic figure of the author, even as his various objective characters serve to distance his specific experience. The major poems seem to offer the inner history of the crucial period in Clough's life when he moved from celibate don, occupying almost a priestly traditional role, to the awakening to an opposing, seemingly natural sexual life of "Natura Naturans" and *The Bothie* – a poem where the don seems half participant, half enthusiastic voyeur. Confrontation with the world and with his own sexual desires is then in far more earnest the subject of *Amours de Voyage*, the two "Easter Day" poems and *Dipsychus*. Clearly he chooses the world, indeed decides Christ is not risen as he decides to rise to the bait of pimp or Mephistopheles in Naples or Venice and to the further solution of conventional marriage. But the action doesn't so much secularize his point of view as it gives a broader, worldly cast to his continuing focus on relations between religion and sexuality. He must be, in effect, a new priest of a world in which sexuality looms larger than religion and must come first. Fishermen are to catch fish first, the women of Jerusalem to return to their husbands. Even in *Amours*, a poem set *in Rome* that deflects issues of conversion from traditional religious concerns to marital and sexual ones, Clough's speaker is the pilgrim of fine conscience, driven by an ultra-Protestant concern not to yield to the "factitious" in this holy city of another Christian creed.

In *Dipsychus* Clough attains his classic status as the Victorian wit and skeptic of religion only as the fruit of his growth to sophistication in sexual issues. As much the sensible, seductive Mephistopheles as the nice sexual scrupler Dipsychus, Clough creates a world in which religious and sexual desires are alike problematized. Traditional visions of guilt and defloration may be correct, or prostitution, or if you prefer, marriage, may be the necessary and realistic way of the world. Certainly, he is still recognizably in his tradition's most fundamental mode of conceptualizing sex in seeing it exactly as a craving demon that must be treated as a problem to be solved. Clough ceases to uphold his society's varied connections between religious systems and sexuality, whether the translation of sexual energies to religion of the early Christians, the repressive version of Christianity's Augustinian tradition, the angel-love idealization of the perfect, but perfectly unlikely, Christian marriage, or the revisionary myth-making of a new Eden of nature; they are all possible, all rather absurd. But he also refuses to drop the issue. He finds sexuality, in its various ideologies, often linked to religious views. He can't accept any one system but he can't merely ignore ways of thinking that he finds prevalent and interesting. In his final poem the mere Clergyman has only one, and a conservative, lesser part in the contemporary discussion that Clough stages on sexuality. Yet this is not because the issues are not connected to religion; they continue to be very much questions that span sexual and religious values. But they are too important therefore to be left only to the official religious representative. Questioning of all religious and sexual dogmas, Clough also is especially conscious of the ways in which they have been combined or associated. And because he seems to have experienced them personally as systems that stood or fell together, he tends to accept their mutual implication even when he is most skeptical of the systematized forms of both. Clough's works thus initiate this study of some Victorian elaborations of sexual–religious discussions with a broad display of varieties of such Victorian thought, all presented with strong sympathy for the human desire that they seek to channel to fuller or lesser fulfillment and with a most engaging skepticism about their credibility.

CHAPTER 3

Sexual Christianity: Charles Kingsley's
Via Media

Clough tests and questions his culture's sexual and related religious attitudes by raising them, in the frictional process of his ceaseless dialectic, to explicit formulation. His limitations in this respect are those that so irritated D. H. Lawrence in those two dialectical temperaments who preceded him in discussing sexual and meta-physical issues in the twentieth century, Shaw and Wells. Like Shaw's similar de-sentimentalization of prostitution in *Mrs. Warren's Pro-fession*, like Wells's skepticism of conventional maidenly sexual roles in *Ann Veronica*, not unlike even Strachey's way of offering up sex as *another* subject for Bloomsbury conversation by pointing accusingly to a spot on Venessa Bell's white dress and pronouncing "Semen?" Clough explores sexual and religious issues by a process of ideas, a process even of naming what many in his culture would forbid from such open-ended discussion. Like them, like even Lawrence himself in his campaign to restore our oldest words to literary use in *Lady Chatterley*, Clough seems more often to have his sex in the head as language than in the blood as direct experience. The work is centrally a play of ideas; desire, temptation, damnation, real as they doubtless were in Clough's agonized personal vacillations, are more often conceptualized than fully realized. Clarity, if only about his own and his culture's confusions, is attained by working up to an intellectual perspective on the emotions and sensations discussed. Current sexual beliefs are questioned and analyzed; certainly there is the pressure of the poet's need to find a way to live with sexual desire and a concomitant wish for a lasting solution; but in fact no new center of conviction is created, whether about sex, religion, or their relation. Clough's unsettled state remains his glory and defines his limits.

This was not the approach of another Victorian writer who placed sex in as central a place in his thinking and artistic vision as Clough did, and indeed as twentieth-century writers such as D. H. Lawrence or Henry Miller have: Charles Kingsley. Like traditional writers on Christianity and sexuality, Kingsley was a thinker not content to rest uneasy in perplexities but sought his own definitive formulation. But like a Lawrence or Miller, he also insisted on expounding a philosophy or religious point of view that arose out of, and justified, his personal experience. In Clough, personal experience merely helps to disintegrate the settled views of the past or the confused thinking of his age. In Kingsley it is the new ground on which to found a new revelation, albeit one that he worked hard to locate in, and justify by, religious texts and tradition. His work is less flexible, less open-ended, less provocative than Clough's; by the same token it presents a more consistent, much more fully articulated and deeply held position. In him, sex has become – first in his personal experience, then in his beliefs – the center of a new vision of life, an emotionally charged conviction, about which religion, as well as morality and social issues, must be reoriented.

Charles Kingsley, the muscular Christian and author of a variety of nearly major works from the socially aware *Alton Locke* to the long-popular *The Water-Babies*, was perhaps best known in his day for the three historical novels, *Hypatia*, *Westward Ho!*, and *Hereward the Wake*. He was an eminent Victorian rather than a completely major Victorian, though he was an eminent Victorian of great talent, perhaps even bordering on the lower levels of genius. A man of importance in his day, Kingsley was perhaps betrayed out of the fullest realization of his abilities by their very multiplicity. He was a decent artist, an impressive and moving preacher (despite a bad stutter in private conversation), a good poet, an enthusiastic if none-too-professional instructor and professor, a moralist, an amateur scientist, a great writer of descriptions and a good architect of fast-moving adventure plots, a committed if none-too-radical social reformer, a leader of movements and generator of public opinion, a tireless crusader for sanitary improvements. Such abundant talents and breadth of interests earned quick recognition in his day. He was given ecclesiastical preferment – to Dean of Westminster Abbey – academic recognition – by appointment to the Regius Professorship of history at Cambridge (a position for which he was barely qualified, or not at all, as a writer of historical novels and enthusiastic amateur) – and social recognition, first as a royal chaplain, then as tutor and even friend to the Prince of Wales. And there was intellectual recognition, as he was elevated from a public nuisance as a clerical fellow-traveler of the Chartists to a public man as an author, moralist, preacher, even sage: the important if somewhat diminished heir to the roles of his idols, Carlyle, Maurice, and perhaps even Dr. Arnold.

What remains of all this is that to us Kingsley is still a novelist of importance to be looked at, with Bulwer-Lytton or Disraeli or Reade, after the absolutely major writers of the age, and to bring into special studies of the Victorian novel of politics, of religious assent, or the physician in literature.[1] But his continuing significance must surely be even more as a representative literary man, one who works interestingly and seriously – at the frontiers of understanding or knowledge to which his age had led him – at issues as various as faith, science, socialism, history, or health. Perhaps most interestingly, he grappled mightily, if not always charmingly, with what used to be considered the Victorian untouchable, sexuality. His reactions, his observations, his tentative theories, as in the other areas of his thinking and imaginative writing, do not generally lift him beyond the frontiers and out of his age. Broadly speaking, his commitment was clearly enough to the liberal but idealizing strain of his age's thinking that Clough captured so well and criticized so cogently. Yet his thinking is unusually broad, suggesting the ramification of his sexual vision in most areas of life and, most emphatically in this clergyman and influential religious popularist, in his formal religious beliefs. It is also relatively consistent and clearly articulated.

A full scrutiny of Kingsley's discourse is especially useful in helping us to avoid simplistic or reductive thinking about Victorians' sexual attitudes.[2] Here is an eminent Victorian, a representative religious voice of the period, who clearly insisted upon finding his own way in his sexual opinions and who as clearly insisted upon making his views apparent to his age. As in his other thought, he is liberal, an accommodator of conflicting positions. To us he is thus doubly interesting as an example, even a case, of how an intelligent Victorian found ways of reconciling sexual needs with the peculiarly strong idealisms, restraints, and pruderies of his age. Whether comfortable with the discovery or not, we can also find displayed in Kingsley, sometimes perhaps a bit too clearly, a full elaboration of what doubtless continues – especially in its glorification and defense of lifelong, monogamous marital relation as the center of value – as the most common idealistic sexual position within and without formal religion today.

Kingsley is today best known for none of this. He exists rather, as an early reviewer anticipated he would, as the too-bold, too-busy Protestant parsonical fly gone down to history embedded in the clear amber of Newman's *Apologia*. For of course Kingsley did rush in and he did even dare to tread on an angel: to call John Henry Newman's personal integrity into question as he asserted the age-old Protestant prejudices about papist lies and Jesuitical dissimulations. The deed, performed unthinkingly and offhandedly in a review of Froude's history, was at least twice foolish, obviously in tackling a mind and personality far more subtle and formidable than his own, less obviously but perhaps more importantly for attacking a Catholic churchman who was anything but a Bishop Blougram and indeed far from being even an unpolitical Jesuit or ordinary priest, who had in fact gone to extraordinary lengths to preserve his intellectual freedom within the complex administrative machinery and politics of the Church.[3]

What brought this distinguished writer, thinker, and public man to such a gross error with regard to a man whom he himself confessed had had the power of mind and personality to exert a major influence on him? The answer seems to have been not merely the common blindness of one sect with regard to the virtues of another, especially the virtues of a renegade. As Dwight Culler has suggested, the issue between these two distinguished Christians, one a celibate Catholic priest, the other a respectable Anglican clergyman and devoted family man, seems to have been broadly that of sex.[4] Or at least that was the area where Kingsley was betrayed by strong emotions and prior commitments into a decidedly damaging controversy. Newman himself perceptively and not unfairly accused Kingsley of "nothing worse" than being "furiously carried away by his feelings."[5] Without going into the details of the controversy and its various letters and pamphlets that ended definitively with the *Apologia*, we can at least see clearly that Kingsley's feelings went back to a time when Newman's tracts, written by the then eminent Anglican theologian, had strongly attracted Kingsley, as Newman and the Oriel College world once had Clough, toward a different view of his calling as a clergyman from that which he eventually took up. He even admitted privately that his "own heart . . . strangely yearned towards" the Oxford Tracts "from the first."[6] But in Kingsley's reflection, theirs was a view that would have separated the worlds of sexuality and religion that he devoted his mature life to joining.

Asked by Newman to justify his charge that Newman did not consider truth for its own sake a virtue, Kingsley recalled a sermon, when he himself was only a beginning clergyman, which allowed him to shake off "the strong influence which your writings exerted on me."[7] Forced to be more specific, he cited a variety of sermons from that time in which Newman presumed that "Celibacy of the clergy" has a note of the true church, nay worse, that "the humble monk, and the holy nun," those other neuter religious persons, are "Christians after the very pattern given us in Scripture."[8] "Monks and nuns the only perfect Christians," the mature Kingsley scorns; and that scorn was present in his initial accusation that Newman believed in cunning: "the weapon which Heaven has given to the saints wherewith to withstand the brute male force of the wicked world which marries and is given in marriage."[9] Later Kingsley would moralize, as a Freudian psychologist might, over the sexual hysteria of a poor Carmelite sister Newman mentioned, who had given herself the stigmata, and he would accuse Newman of spreading "misery and shame into many an English home," as if he were as determined a destroyer of the family as any handsome horsebreaker from Hyde Park (or is the implied comparison to that other Victorian destroyer of happy family life, the hidden vice, masturbation?). Against accusations of such devious, sexually driven dealings, Newman had only quietly to protest his general integrity from the open record of his life and as quietly answer the specific charges by noting that he had merely, when a Protestant, chosen to follow St. Paul's assurance that it is "good to abide even as is," that is in celibacy.[10] Newman of course – as was glaringly before the Protestant churchman Kingsley – went on after his conversion to Catholicism to bind himself by traditional vows of celibacy. But perhaps the greater threat had been the presence in the Church of England of a most talented and articulate group of thinkers who could assert the conservative tradition, never repudiated by the Thirty-nine Articles, of respect for chastity and celibacy that was very much a part of the tradition of Church Fathers whom they studied as models of piety and sagacity.

The strength of Kingsley's reaction, in 1864, to sermons that Newman wrote twenty or more years before can be understood best from his biography, where the rejection of asceticism, as biographers have shown, was tied up closely to the major emotional resolutions of his life.[11] An intense, somewhat indrawn boy from an upper-class but unaffluent clergyman family, the young Kingsley vented his feelings in a bad stutter and in the better outlets of horseriding, rowing, fishing, or just rambling. At Magdalene College, Cambridge, in 1838, almost as much as Clough at Newman's Oxford, Kingsley, the future clergyman, couldn't fail to be drawn into the atmosphere of contest between the newly forceful conservative visions of religion and Church history of Newman and Pusey's Tractarian group and the renewed Protestantism attacking back. But Kingsley also devoted himself to the man's world of sport and he made a close friendship with a Charles Mansfield, so close that one biographer has detected homoerotic attraction.[12] Close male–male attachments in un-coeducational Cambridge or Oxford were hardly unusual and usually similarly unclear.[13] Kingsley in any case had felt the attraction of heterosexual intimacy even before going up to Cambridge. A prose fable called "Psyche" has a maiden observing two fond lovers' naked limbs "writhed round each other, and their lips mingled in sleep, while their white breasts heaved together in mutual throbs."[14] The expression may be romantically derivative, but the warmth of attraction to such sexualized sleep seems real enough. And so is the fear, which the fable goes on to express, that such bliss may not last forever. The very attractiveness of this vision seems to leave him vulnerable to the idea of attaining such bliss only to lose it. The intense desire for a kind of sexual paradise, and the concomitant fear of its loss, are thenceforward central to Kingsley's sexual experience, with his stress increasingly on finding a way to banish the loss forever and dwell continuously in a world of sexual presence. The young Clough also dreamed and wrote of a sexual paradise regained, doubtless expressing what was on the minds of a majority of young men then and now. But Kingsley differs in desperately seeking a way to make his dream a permanent reality.

As already noted in regard to Clough at Oxford, sexual paradise of a very brief and post-lapsarian sort was available to university students, despite elaborate regulation by the university, from street-walkers in town and at regular brothels in nearby villages beyond the university's control.[15] Kingsley apparently tried it once, as he later confessed to his bride, and decidedly didn't like it. Or, if he did like it, his intensely guilty reaction didn't allow him to acknowledge it nor, presumably, repeat it. As he spoke of it to her, it was a matter of being spotted, of having sinned and fallen.[16]

It is possible that it was the guilty reaction from first sex that led Kingsley's thinking a distance down the cloister path of celibate

Tractarianism. Meeting during a summer vacation with a Fanny Grenfell quickly put him on the more ordinary track of love and sexual interest that would emphatically bring heterosexual sexuality back into his religious thinking. Perhaps it was about this time that he drafted a detailed account, now lost or destroyed, of why celibacy was impossible for him.[17] They fell immediately and passionately in love. Even with the rigorous limits on intimacy of his day, he found it practically impossible not to seek a physical side to his relation with Fanny. They found some way at least to kiss passionately. Fanny wrote enthusiastically of "strong arms" that "bound me, while my willing limbs were entangled with yours, + my lips clinging to yours, + the warm life flowing into my very soul." During the four years before they married they devised complicated rituals of sleeping together by imagination as they lay in their distant beds – "feast" or "festival" times with what Fanny called "delicious nightery" of "strange feelings." "Never control any desire of pleasure because I am not there to share it with you!" Charles instructed, "I am there, if *you* are there!"[18] When, after much painful forced separation, they were finally permitted by her family to plan the wedding, they spent a day in the country in which the Victorian equivalent of what in the United States used to be called heavy petting took place rather spontaneously: he writes to celebrate one occasion: "my hands are all perfumed with her delicious limbs, + I cannot wash off the scent – It has made itself what it should be, a part of myself! And every moment the thought comes across me, of those mysterious recesses of beauty, where my hands have been wandering."[19] Their imagination was filled with plans for their first meeting in bed after marriage; Charles imagined that he would "undress you with my own hands, from head to foot, + cover you all over with burning kisses til you were tired of blushing + struggling, if you *did* struggle, wh I pray you would not."[20] Fanny was troubled by "spasms" for which the pre-Freudian doctor wisely recommended speedy marriage, strongly seconded by her future husband.

A less modern quirk appears as Charles decides to put off full consummation until a month after the wedding – to prove he is capable of "self-denial," but perhaps also out of anxiety.[21] But this was to be no Ruskinian marriage – indeed Kingsley professed contempt for Ruskin on just this point: contempt perhaps especially because he had overcome a similar temptation to evasion.[22] The delay was in any case even what the sex therapist might have ordered for such an inexperienced couple: a month in bed naked warming to each other before full intercourse. We also may wonder if this planned delay actually took place; Fanny's own letter anticipating marriage shows little bridal hesitation: "we will kiss + love very much . . . you will take me in your arms, will you not? And lay me down in bed + then you will extinguish our light + *come to me*! How I will open my arms to you, + then sink into yours! + you will kiss me + clasp me + lay blessed [*sic*] body to me." Man proposes; woman disposes. Later Charles would dream of reenacting "our marriage night."[23] In any event, sooner or later, the result seems to have been a decided success. A child was conceived; as for Kingsley, he found the begetting "the most delicious moment of my life – *up to that time* – Since then what greater bliss."[24] It is a pleasure, as it is in reading the Mosher report, to hear such an authentic voice of Victorian sexual gratification to set against the modernist stereotypes of universal sexual blocking and repression in the period – even when we hear it in Kingsley's rather treacly language.[25] Here, certainly, is a Victorian who enjoyed sexual intimacy – and did so with enthusiasm. At moments in their letters he even attains an eloquence that we can hear and admire over the passage of time, as in this profession written even after many years of marriage:

I do love you utterly – your image haunts me day + night, just as it used before we married + the thought of that delicious hidden sanctuary of marriage, when we shall clasp + be clasped in blessedness, please God, on Monday night, gives me a proud + yet humbling thrill every time it flashes across me. I cannot believe my own happiness + honour . . . that *you* you, pure + passionate at once, beautiful + wise in my eyes + in the eyes of all who see you, should love *me*! give yourself up to *me*, body + soul! have given me two such children of your own beloved delicious body! – I feel that one gift so great a debt to God.[26]

What is even more interesting is the complicated ways that Kingsley found to justify and rationalize this joyful sex experience against the restraints and conservative ideology – especially religious ideology – that were as much a part of his milieu as they were of Clough's. There were, of course, the ordinary middle-class and upper-class standards for courting that forced Charles and Fanny to think of full sexual experience only in marriage (though Charles reminds Fanny in a letter before marriage of how much can be achieved in an unchaperoned instant).[27] More interestingly, in Fanny's family, a family composed of older sisters, Charles found a

I. DRAWINGS BY CHARLES KINGSLEY PASTED OR INSERTED LOOSE INTO THE NICE DIARY KEPT BY FANNY GRENFELL KINGSLEY DURING HER ENFORCED ABSENCE FROM CHARLES KINGSLEY, 1842–43

Reproduced by courtesy of Mrs. Angela M. K. Covey-Crump

1. Drawing of Charles and Fanny tied up and making love on a cross bound over waves to heaven

2. Drawing of Charles and Fanny embracing naked, probably as Eros and Psyche, rising to heaven. "She is not dead but sleepeth." (Luke viii.52)

3. Drawing of Charles extracting a thorn from Fanny's foot. "'The Thorn!'
C K July 28/43!"

4. Drawing of couple, with infant, harvesting naked. "C K Oct. 31/43." Inscription on back: "The Harvest truly is plenteous, but the Labourers are few! Pray ye therefore the Lord of the Harvest, that He would send in Labourers *into His* Harvest!" (Matthew ix.37–38: which reads "will send forth labourers")

5. Drawing of Charles prostrate and mostly naked on floor by Bible and bed. "CK Friday! *10 o'clock.*" Inscription on back: "Charle's [*sic*] Fest! [*sic*; probably for Fast] Every Friday. Eversley Cross – 1842–3."

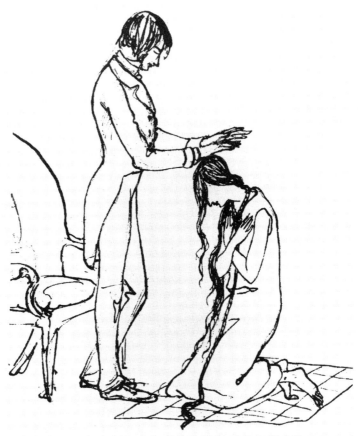

"I absolve thee" from all thy Sin
In the name of the Father, the
Son & the Holy Ghost!"
Amen!

6. Drawing of Charles, elegantly dressed, absolving Fanny, appearing before him barefoot, loose-haired, ill-clad, with a rope for scourging around her neck. "'I absolve thee from all thy Sin In the name of the Father, the Son & the Holy Ghost!' Amen!''

7. Frontispiece drawing: Elizabeth on a cross with grotesques.
Inscription: "Elizabeth of Hungary"

Fanny! my beloved, my ___, my sister, my wife! Why do I ___ ___: not only to delight your eyes and ears in happier days: if it ___ not touch it: I have been too long idle: I must look. — You do ___, my garden shut up, my fountain sealed, there. I must be ___ — happy toil! Therefore I write; for you, even then ___

8. Introduction, with Fanny as illuminated F as on a cross, wearing a halo

9. Drawing of naked boy and girl kissing on a pillow-cloud. Inscription: "OF SUCH IS THE KINGDOM OF HEAVEN!"

10. Drawing of grotesque men killing Elizabeth's mother, the queen; a child (Elizabeth) observing (corner left)

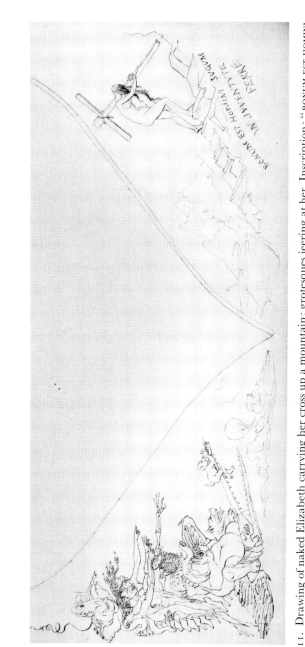

11. Drawing of naked Elizabeth carrying her cross up a mountain; grotesques jeering at her. Inscription: "BONUM EST HOMINI JVGVM IN JVVENTVTE FERRE" (it is good for a man to carry a yoke [submit to a cross of sin] in youth)

12. Illuminated letter: married Elizabeth as half-naked woman harvesting. Tools for work above

13. Drawing of female stigmata (rape position) on a page of text

14. Drawing of female bodies being raised to heaven. Suffering humans below

15. Drawing of naked female on cross. "Darling!" written over her body

16. Drawing of Elizabeth being whipped naked by a woman with a raised whip. Inscription:
"RIPE UNDER MY BODYE AND BRYNGE YITE UNTOE SUBIECYON."

17. Drawing of Elizabeth sleeping alone while her husband looks on. A dragon
being slain in the back (probably suggests his sexual desire put aside for love of the
ascetic Elizabeth)

more actively anti-sexual attitude at work that nurtured religious feeling to the total exclusion of overt sexuality. Without going so far as actually to join an order, the sisters had been attracted by the idea of a Protestant nunnery or beguinage that had been one outgrowth of the Tractarian movement. Fanny and her sisters had made a kind of half-commitment to join the community at Park Place, Regent's Park, inspired by Edward Pusey, Newman's co-leader in the Tractarian movement who remained within the Church of England. When Charles and Fanny fell in love, this idea of a life of voluntary virginity came to be a major obstacle, symbol of the sisters' emotional opposition to sex and marriage as well as their practical opposition to Charles as a relatively poor young man without great prospects. For about a year, Fanny was even sent away to the Continent and the two forbidden to communicate – except in their pre-arranged festival night intimacy by imagination.

It seems clear that the pressure of a passionate sexual desire working against a quite discouraging social context – one of the most conservative sexual milieux of the Victorian period and one that specifically defined itself in relation to the ascetic Christian tradition – drove the young Kingsley to an extraordinary awareness of sexual issues. Ultimately it drove him to develop a rather specific set of positions somewhat precariously situated between an ascetic Christian viewpoint and a naturalistic sexual permissiveness. In the process Newman and his sermons inevitably became associated with an entire set of opinions that he not only opposed intellectually but resented personally as the cause of his immediate sexual frustrations. And this was only aggravated by the appeal that Newman and his work held for Kingsley as for so many of his generation. Whereas Clough moved almost regretfully, step by step, away from a celibate religious role with some nostalgia for the "mild monastic faces" that Claude finds in Rome, Kingsley felt a direct and immediate threat in ascetic religion and in some sense used his relation with Fanny and her family to make a full break with the ascetic Christian tradition which had at first attracted him. After admitting his yearning for the Oxford Tracts he goes on to explain to Fanny that, had he not felt "a secret warning" that "they struck at the root of our wedded bliss, I too had been ensnared! Love saved me!"[28] In this process, inner temptation becomes objectified as external threat. In his analysis, he quickly identifies the resisting force in Fanny's world with the Christian ideas embodied in the celibate orders. He tells her that her case is a "peculiar" one, of a woman "brought up from child-hood in a *nunnery* [my italics], living, not as women should, in the hope of marriage but in the present enjoyment of *sisterhood* [his italics]."[29]

Against this idea of celibate Christianity he forges not an anti-Christian naturalism but a pro-sexual Christianity. The enemy is now placed historically and as an ideology: "the old ascetics," "Mani-chean Popish fancies," as well as the more recent versions in "Popery and Puseyism"; Fanny is warned to avoid the later tradition of Church Fathers where Catholic attitudes to sex had taken firm form in favor of celibacy, with marriage seen mainly as a cure for fornication: "a few self-conceited fools shut themselves up in a state of unnatural celibacy + morbid excitement, in order to *avoid* their duty, instead of *doing* it . . . Avoid the *fathers after Origen*, (including Him)."[30] Against the tendency of ascetic religion to separate body from soul, he boldly asserts to Fanny the holiness of matter, "God's holy matter awful glorious matter." "Let us never," he proclaims with a boldness equal to a twentieth-century celebrator of the animal in human nature, such as D. H. Lawrence, "use . . . those words animal, and brutal in a degrading sense." Unlike Lawrence, Kingsley does not merely transfer religious values to an animal realm, in effect moving away from Western dualism and toward religions that celebrate sex in this world. He attempts to construct a sexual continuum in which there is no essential difference between physical sexuality in this world and spiritual communion in the next. Heaven will be a place of "resurrection of the flesh, wh is the great promise of Eternity – no miserable fancies about . . . souls escaped from matter, like poor Henry More – but bodies! *our* bodies, beloved, beautiful bodies, ministers to us in all our joys."[31] Sex becomes a spiritual rite now and gives us a foretaste of the pleasures of interpersonal communication in the hereafter. "Our toying becomes holy, our 'animal' enjoyments religious ceremonies."[32] Guilt is staved off; sexual needs are rationalized as religious acts; and, because sex is authorized by the highest religious and ethical values, there is no question, as there was in conservative Victorian thinking on sex, that it is a joy in which women indulge as fully and happily as men. Fanny should go to bed, pretend to be naked, open her lips to imagine his kisses, and "spread out every limb, that I may lie between your breasts all night!" Such a fulfillment, one that few in the twentieth century would say is not devoutly to be desired, is here actually justified devoutly by a parsonical reference: " (Canticles I, 13)."[33] In addition he recommends that she say the Te Deum aloud.

The unfinished manuscript of a prose life of "Elizabeth of Hungary," prepared for Fanny as a wedding present, stated his case to her for wedded bliss over celibacy in a more formal lesson, complete with vivid illustrations of St. Elizabeth's self-torturing preference for ascetic rites over happy marriage to her husband. Beginning with his dedicatory letter admitting his own temptation to the Oxford Tracts, Kingsley casts the issue as an ultimate choice of religious systems based on the status of love and sex: "Is human love unholy – inconsistent with the perfect worship of the Creator? Is marriage less honourable that virginity?" Really raising once again fundamental concepts debated by Pelagius' defender Julian against Augustine at a crucial point in the development of Christian attitudes to sex, he sees this as an issue of the status of nature: "Is nature a holy type, or a foul prison, to our spirits?" The contemporary version of the debate is between Protestantism and marriage on the one hand and "Romanism, *and* a nunnery" (quoting Fanny herself) on the other. Doctrine thus determines life style: "No woman worthy of my Love, could marry, holding Popish or Tractarian doctrines, without degradation, and a wounded conscience!"[34]

Fanny evidently found Charles persuasive as parson as well as lover (or perhaps as parson because as lover); in her Diary before marriage the former near-nun now looks on Catholic priests in Nice with horror: "It is an unnatural state . . . These thoughts have brought me to see the horrors of that system which makes Celibacy a *Law*, more broadly [?] than I cd. have conceived possible a few years ago. And my love too, has taught! Oh! no one shd talk of Celibacy, + its blessings, til they have loved! To think of giving up all this – the heaven implanted instinct! . . . To quench the bright flame wh. must consume *body soul* spirit or light us on to Heaven + God! Poor wretched Priests! To be shut out from love!"[35] On the wedding night Fanny plans not only undressing and kissing but reading from the Psalms and prayer in nightdresses; after the naked laying of his body on hers they will "both praise God, alone in the dark night, with His eye shining down on us." The promiscuous mixture of foreplay and piety bears extraordinary witness to the forces of id and superego that are ultimately reconciled in the Kingsley's marriage: "Oh! What solemn bliss! How hallowing!"[36] For Charles even the marriage-bed itself is an "altar" in the "bliss of full communion" in sex.[37]

Communion indeed is the word he and Fanny use regularly for sex, as well as "sacrament" or "religious ceremony." In return for allowing *such* communion, the superego is given not only the guarantee that marriage will legitimize the ceremony but even assurances that it will be a marriage perpetual and eternal.

Charles confesses that he can't imagine "communion with you" as a "mere temporary self-indulgence."[38] Indeed the thought is so horrid that he could hardly dare to touch her body if it were not to be forever. The direction here is oddly both restrictive – sex only in marriage forever to one person – and expansive – bliss shall be now and eternal, a "heaven on earth" as Kingsley calls their bedroom.[39] And the thought of more and more satisfying sexual bliss to come can even augment the erotic force of the present. Away from his wife, he dreams of loving her soon on earth and forever in heaven: "remember, what a happiness it is to have a body at all – how lonely, cold, barren it would be to be a disembodied Spirit. Not that we desire to be unclothed but to be clothed upon – To have a spiritual deathless griefless life instilled into that darling body, wh. is my garden shut up, my fountain sealed, and soon to be opened to my embrace!"[40] As putting off consummation for a month raises the pleasure by anticipation, so the "thrilling writhings" of earthly delight shall be "dim shadows of a union wh shall be perfect."[41] A strongly sensuous drawing (Illustration 1, following page 100) shows two lovers, recognizably Kingsley and his Rubenesque bride, entwined in a close copulatory embrace, floating on a large Christian cross to which they are bound by ropes, billowed up on waves whose whipped-cream airiness suggests an easy passage to eternal bliss. Another (Illustration 2) has Charles with wings of Eros closely embracing naked Fanny as they rise up over the sun toward the higher heavens. What more pleasant transportation can one imagine to the Last Judgment?

There are problems in this resolution of Kingsley's sex life, problems, as we shall see, that emerge in more objective ways in his writings. One is that the erotic energies channeled into the respectability of marriage do not accord that well with the realities of a Victorian clergyman's family life. Fanny became an exemplary helpmate, laborious to order repairs on the old rectory at Eversley, assiduous with problems of her children, intrepid and enduring as amanuensis for her literary spouse. But the sexual heaven seems sometimes to threaten to trail away its glory. Within five years

Charles is chiding her, when away on a trip, that he longs to be back in her arms "while all you long for, you cruel cold darling beauty, is I find, to sleep by my side." This is relaxed and we can be fairly sure that the warm bride did not turn a cold wife; other letters speak of "wallowing" naked in a "very narrow bed" together.[42] But in some way Kingsley sensed and feared the erosion of his high valorization of sexual love by ordinary experience. As a kind of defense, he often stayed away on extended travels or took up residence elsewhere. His very sincere letters, expressing his longing for Fanny but nonetheless indicating that he will stay away longer, seem driven by an unacknowledged need to renew their early experience of desire in absence when their relation was forbidden. In one letter Charles even turns on himself for an instant and admits he must seem a "humbug," writing of his longing but staying away.[43] He suffered from periodic breakdowns, apparently mild depressions. She became increasingly wedded to the rectory and her life there. A final entry to the passionate diary she had kept during their pre-marital separation shows passion commuted into a much quieter feeling: "I am a wife + a Mother! + oh! so happy – in such a sweet peaceful home"; her husband is writing his sermon nearby and there is a child in the garden; "the whole place is getting gradually into order."[44] So happy there that she refused even to join Charles at Cambridge during his time as Regius Professor.

Even if the information were available, it would take too long to try to chart out the complexities of a long marriage. One can only note that such high hopes place great demands on the reality of Victorian domesticity and perhaps open the way to much psychic conflict and sexual frustration. Again without really understanding what he is doing, Charles seems to have focussed more and more on a heaven of sexual joys as a way of compensating himself for whatever limits or failures he found in his little paradise at Eversley. Letters to Fanny, now a wife of many years, begin to sound like compulsive repetitions of the pattern of courtship, longing for the good days of union and full sexual presence to come: only these are now beyond marriage in a new marriage in heaven: "What would life be without you? What is it with you – but a brief pain to make us long for Everlasting bliss. *There* we shall be in each others arms forever – without a sigh or a Cross – but how long first! How long." Earlier, before marriage, Charles used almost a contemporary language of presence and absence: when they are married he hopes they will not be "*startled* by

the *presence* of enjoyment because we never feel the void of its *absence*";
in any event, "in Heaven, our Love will be without oscillation, ever
at the same glorious full-tide of delight!"[45]

At least such faith in the eternality of love – by which Kingsley
could banish thoughts of absence or limits to love – seems to have
endured to the gates of eternity, as the sad comedy of his death
suggests. Fanny had seemed to be on her deathbed, leaving Charles
so careless of his own health that he was soon actually on his. Charles
joined her sickroom from his own for one final kiss, then returned to
die in the assurance that they would float away to paradise together.
He apparently never knew that Fanny recovered and lived long –
years enough to edit his letters and record their plans for a tombstone:
a circle representing eternity, enclosing a spray of flowers, representing their love, with a Latin inscription proclaiming their love,
past, present, and future. To Fanny went the sad work of living with
love's loss in the fact of mortality; her husband seems to have
generally persuaded himself that he could enjoy a little paradise of
sexual love, in a continuum that stretched from earthly marriage to
its replica in heaven – with a minimal awareness of the cleavage that
normally must be spanned in the movement from this world to next
in such thinking.

Second, Kingsley seems to have been subject to a minor pathology,
not a full-blown perversion but what, for want of a better term, must
be called a kink, one that we shouldn't blow out of proportion but one
that we also can't ignore. His attraction to asceticism then repulsion
from it in the context of his close association between religion and
sexuality seem to have opened a way for an element of sadomasochistic fascination with flagellation. Rather than accept the
possibility of pain and absence as an aspect of love and sexual
relation, an awareness that is often cultivated in the ascetic's
postponement of desire to a higher sphere, Kingsley seems to have
preferred to banish asceticism formally, then allow much of its
apparatus of conscious pain subversively back into his paradise as
unrecognized sadism. Kingsley's mild version of the English vice, a
vice that did have strong roots in the English school system of
birching,[46] thus comes out as a kind of positive parody of the anti-
sexual traditions of asceticism. This seems to have been primarily a
product of the clearly difficult period of sexual excitement without
release when he loved Fanny with no hope that their love would find
consummation; yet Fanny herself, that attractive almost-nun in an

almost-nunnery, doubtless attracted the young Kingsley, already interested in the renewed idealization of celibacy in the Oxford Movement, for reasons he didn't fully understand. He found some outlet for the frustrations of unfulfilled sexual desire in mild self-scourging, in occasional nights out on naked thorns. These nights, called by the lovers "fasts," are clearly masochistic parallels to the feast or festival nights of mutual imagined sexual bliss. After the most severe Charles reported, "when I came home my body was torn from head to foot – I never suffered so much as that night. It was like St. Bernard in the thorns but with very different feelings! . . . I then began to understand Papist…visions, and their connection with self-torture." The association with the Catholic system that he consciously so strongly opposed is also striking in a half-plan, half-daydream he related to Fanny of going to a monastery in France in disguise – "barefoot + in sackcloth" and there confessing all his life's sins. At the end of the plan he stood "before all the monks, + offered my naked body to be scourged by them!"[47] While striving to turn Fanny away from her family culture of celibacy, Charles contra-dictorily encouraged her to join in his ascetic paraphernalia and involved her in light sadistic fantasies, essentially of Fanny coming to him as a barefoot penitent to place herself in his clerical power (see Illustration 6) or of her putting on hair shirts and scourging herself in her turn.[48] Oddly, he seems to have found his way to such traditions through her background – she admitted that "'Crucifying the flesh,' – 'Mortifying the body' – 'Dying daily' – +c" had a "mysterious charm, an inexpressible beauty to me for years" – then found her, persuaded by his arguments, worried about *his* ascetic excesses.[49]

Except for one reference to a sexual communion more pagan than Christian with himself as priest and she as victim, this element seems to fade gradually from his life after marriage.[50] Yet it had already found a track in his imagination, in those rather good grotesque and sadistic drawings that he did to accompany that wedding present for Fanny (which she planned to read on their wedding night), the unfinished prose life of "Elizabeth of Hungary," where the critique of asceticism also allowed him to indulge sadistic material of the saint's life.[51] The drawings (Illustrations 7–17) seem continuous with those personal ones, of Fanny and himself combining love with crosses or casting Fanny as a barefoot penitent or as a naked worker in the fields of life, that Charles gave to Fanny for her Diary (Illustrations 1–6). Indeed Fanny is specifically asked to see Elizabeth as a stand-in for herself, were she to choose the other road, of asceticism. An illuminated letter F puts Fanny on a cross (Illustration 8); in another, Charles wrote "Darling" over a naked Elizabeth on a cross (Illustration 15). Charles himself is a stand-in for Elizabeth's concerned husband, who watches her scourging and agonies with sympathy, but who thus also has a voyeuristic relation to them (Illustration 17). The author-illustrator was rather clearly, and literally, of the devils' party as he shows grotesque figures killing Elizabeth's mother by plunging a dagger in her stomach (Illustration 10), jeering at Elizabeth herself on, or carrying, her cross (Illustrations 7 and 11), or as he himself places her stigmata on the page in a rape position (Illustration 13). Whereas the moral of the story itself – that Elizabeth should have been content to have "her cravings for celibacy" overruled in the "tumultuous tide-wave of her bliss" in marriage – is rather preachy, even patronizing, the description of the facts and "penitential tortures" she chooses *after* such marriage become almost as vivid as the illustrations: "And she knelt down before them, + bared all her budding loveliness" to be beaten with a rod (also in Illustration 16).[52] Elizabeth's life would also be the subject of his longest published poem, where his wife and mother and father persuaded him to cut some of the "coarser passages."[53] As we will see, the interest in torture and violence would find its way elsewhere, even more subversively, into his writing even as it disappeared from his conventional married life.

The presence of such problems and difficult areas shouldn't obscure the main point, however: that the same feelings which would lead Kingsley to overreact so unfortunately in response to Newman were really central to his life and conception of himself. Unlike in the modernist view of Victorianism – which in any case ignores the entire history of Christianity's relation to sexuality in one form or another – as repressive religion in conflict with sexuality, Christianity and sex had become for him very much cooperating agents, not competing powers. Religion was made to affirm sex in at least one special form; sexual fulfillment in turn provided the optimism and energy for a muscular clerical life. In fact his doubts had disappeared through his loving talks with Fanny; he had left her warm lips with the assurance in his faith to go speak to a bishop about taking holy orders.[54] In his case the central conversion of his life, the moment of eternal yea/saying, was one of joint religious and sexual persuasion. Clough, who had rejected the special holy orders of a celibate don, apparently never seriously considered the orders that lead to the traditional wedded life of the Anglican clergyman: sexual and religious perplexities led only out into the great world of more temptation and more perplexity. For Kingsley, the union of sexual and clerical commitment that Protestantism allowed became the cornerstone of his existence and his site point as a writer.

Although Kingsley found many other issues to write about in his poems, sermons, speeches, and novels – especially social issues of labor and justice, sanitation, science, history, man's need for religion, war and national glory – the sexual issues and resolutions that were essential to his personal life are writ large in his work. Like other Victorian writers who found sex at the center of their experience of life and insisted upon talking about it in their work – for instance Charlotte Brontë, George Meredith, Hardy, or Clough himself – Kingsley had to confront the difficulties of maintaining an open sexual discussion in face of his age's fairly strict standards of decorum for published material. In his letters, even those published by his wife (much more those still in manuscript at the British Library), he could be fairly explicit about his beliefs; poems also, as writing normally aimed at an educated few, were granted a traditional license of erotic imagery and sensuous feeling. Sermons and lectures could talk about an issue only in broad terms. Novels, especially, as written for a mass public, were expected to have love interests, but were also expected to avoid a too-serious confrontation of sexual issues. (Before we sneer too easily at Victorianism here we should consider that the novel was as much in the Victorian public realm as television has been in the last half of the twentieth century and probably subject to about the same degree of control of expression in sexual matters, at least during hours when children watch – also the controlling audience imagined by censors of novels.)

Although we find almost nothing in Kingsley's public writings that approaches the direct and frankly erotic comments on his relation to Fanny in his letters and private drawings, I think we can also say that Kingsley probably managed to communicate the gist of his sexual vision to his age. Only the succeeding age was blind to it because of its presuppositions concerning the ubiquity of sexual repression among eminent Victorians. Kingsley was a very popular, successful writer, whose liberal sexual attitudes, like his liberal social ones, struck a major chord in some parts of his society, especially when presented with his nationalistic, somewhat insular good tidings for

England and its unique traditions. Indeed we must presume his version of sexual liberalism gave no offense even in the very highest circles, from whom he obtained preferment, even that position as history tutor to the future king. If its suitability for children was the ultimate test of the respectability of a Victorian discourse, his had the nation's top seal of domestic approval.

Still, Kingsley was aware of fighting a battle with forces in his society that would have wished to silence him on sexual issues. He warns readers of *Hypatia* in his Preface that, unlike the usual novel written to avoid raising a blush on the maiden's cheek, this one is best kept away from the young and innocent. In return, the outspokenness of the book was cited by the Puseyite party as a reason for denying Kingsley the D.C.L. at Oxford. As clearly, Kingsley lined up with the bolder respectable writers of his day who dared the censoring voices of conservative reviewers: with Clough himself, whose least questioning, most affirmative sexual statement, *The Bothie*, he greeted with a very positive review; with Mrs. Gaskell, whose presentation of prostitution in *Ruth* (bold in its day though somewhat sentimental to us, as it was to Clough) he praised; and with Charlotte Brontë, whose masterful openness on sexual issues he first criticized, then came to identify with as he read Gaskell's life. Using the general imagery of Brontë's own preface to *Jane Eyre*, he declared that her life and work should shame the prudery of our "not overly cleanly, though carefully whitewashed" age.[55] All of which is not to say that he wanted to open the floodgates of sexual candor in fiction fifty years before the waters rose. Kingsley looks for a liberal receptivity to ideas he considers central to the religion and morality of his day, not for radical license in sexual discussion. Eventually he himself would write an essay justifying Puritan opposition to the license of what he calls the adulterous theater of the seventeenth century.[56] And he is there content with the, to us, ridiculous anomaly of being unable and unwilling to cite in print for his age the printed offenses of the earlier age, so he can only point to unnamed enormities and assure his unscandalized audience that they would be as scandalized as the Puritans were if they took the trouble that the Puritans did to find out what the Cavaliers were saying on-stage. Yet he is careful to show that he (like, in his view, his Puritan subjects) is no prude in his sexual morality, by ending his essay with a picture of demure but clearly sexual love between a Puritan couple of the time, Zeal-for-Truth and his cousin and virgin bride-to-be.

Kingsley is able to present his sexual opinions rather clearly in much of his work, despite his society's limits on published expression and his own scruples, because he is by and large content with presenting a sexual program rather than a fully imagined vision of sexual psychology or sexual experience. For the same reason we can look at that program schematically, across many works, without feeling that tremendously important insights into the art of specific works are thereby lost, as they would be in the novels of a more subtle artist of sexual issues such as Charlotte Brontë. Although I enjoy reading Kingsley's works and recommend the novels as interesting reading (some to grown-ups, others especially to adolescents with an historical imagination), I am content to make the case that Kingsley is an important Victorian man of letters who offers an interesting, and quite coherent, set of sexual–religious attitudes. They represent a very significant other "other" Victorian position – a rather central one – that challenges our received notions of respectable Victorian sexuality and provides one genealogy for a considerable section of even contemporary thinking on issues of sexuality and religion.[57] If emphasis on this side of his work serves to make his writings more accessible as works of creative imagination, that is, of course, as it should be: acknowledging his major interest in sexual issues allows us to see Kingsley more nearly as he really was and helps remove him from the realm of mere boys' (and adventure-loving girls') author. But in identifying Kingsley as a writer very occupied with sexual issues, I would not wish to mislead those on the prowl for Victorian softcore work into thinking that the thousands of pages of Kingsley's works will prove happy hunting-grounds. Like the American man who wrote Hardy to complain that he had been persuaded by the notoriety of *Jude the Obscure* to spend a dollar on a damned ethical tract, they would find that Kingsley offers ideas about the thing – interesting ideas for those who like them – and strong emotions about it, but not usually the thing itself.

Central to the discussion of sexual issues in his work, as it was in his life experience, is the opposition of marital sexuality to celibacy. This theme is repeated again and again in letters, poems, novels, and essays, years before it surfaces in the debate with Newman. In fairly public letters, a number thought fit for print in his day by his memorialist wife, Kingsley spells out his theories quite explicitly. He pronounces that the question of celibacy versus marriage is indeed the central one in the religious life, just as the Malthusian doctrine is in economics (which perhaps is less a logical comparison than a demonstration that Kingsley finds his way right to a sexual core in any discipline, from theology to economics).[58] The issue is central because it really defines man's nature and his place in the material and spiritual universes. He takes his stand, in a resonant term, on the "divineness of the whole manhood" – that is, on the worth in the eye of God of both man's physical and spiritual natures, of both this universe and whatever life is to come.[59] He sees God's work in man's physical nature just as he can find it even in the natural facts of the physical universe. His belief in the sacramental quality of the physical world is especially clear in his ability, as amateur scientist clergyman, to accept the very unpalatable details of evolution in Darwin, whose work he welcomed.

By contrast, he sees the ascetic theology that he tends to identify with Roman Catholicism as rooted in the belief that man is essentially a spiritual creature only alienated for a time in a body; man is destined in heaven for a different life that turns its back on all earthly relations for a single relation of soul to God.[60] He opposes this view, which he sees as a foreign substance in the ointment of Christianity, by appealing back to the Old Testament; like early Christian critics of the development of asceticism in Christianity, he sees the injunctions of the Jewish tradition on proper use of the body and the normal duty of marriage and reproduction nowhere canceled in the New Testament.[61] God approves the good of this life, sends man forth to multiply, to act in his image as husband, father, or son.[62] He rationalizes Matthew xxii.24–30, that there will be no marrying nor giving in marriage in the resurrection by, essentially, arguing that marriage is given here but continued hereafter[63] – though the point of the question Jesus was answering, about a multiple widow's multiple husbands in heaven, would continue to bother him. He sometimes hesitates to say simply that we shall rise in the body, join the sheep, and copulate in heaven as the goats do here. But fleshly love is at the very least a great foretaste and symbolic shadowing forth of the greater intercourse, the "still more intimate union" in the world beyond, whatever form that shall take. On the whole Milton, whose sexual ideas in *Paradise Lost* provided a dignified and respectable rationale for a positive idea of sexuality throughout the eighteenth and nineteenth centuries, seems very much present in Kingsley's thinking. To Fanny he had recommended him as the best answer to the ideal of denial and martyrdom: Milton, "the Healthy

Man, the Champion of the marriage bed of pure humanity in an Age of Popery + Puseyism + Comte Skepticism and licentiousness."[64] His speculation about sex life in the hereafter finds some support in interpreting that difficult (for him) passage in Matthew by the report in *Paradise Lost* that angels copulate by total mutual encroachment.[65] In Kingsley's reading, both Milton and the two last chapters of Revelation encourage us to go on dreaming of a sensual hereafter.

He follows Milton also in attacking the Augustinian tradition that sees sexual desire – "the law wh makes beings unite themselves, + crave to unite themselves" – as a result of the Fall. The law of sex is rather one of purity, which should "hold in the spiritual world, as well as the natural": a full reversal of Augustine's sense of craving, as Clough still uses the word, as a law of the members *against* God's law.[66] In this world, in any case, paradise lost is to be regained by the effort of loving, and man and wife may be happy even here, in the garden of their sexual love. The sexual animal man may give himself to love and gain admittance to the very garden of the Lord. Though Kingsley stresses, as Freud will, the need to combine love and work, his position is perhaps easier than Milton's view of the Fall, where wedded love is still a positive ideal realizable in the fallen world but also where Adam and Eve, as Douglas Bush remarks, seem more like Mr. and Mrs. Doe embroiled in domestic quarrels than partners working to recover paradise. For Kingsley the union of a loving couple may indeed become a type of their eternal union beyond. Finally, because of his belief in the continuity of unions here and here to come, Kingsley opposes all forms of polygamy, whether con-temporaneous or serial. The Bible shows a quick evolution from harems to monogamy; we must now learn to avoid these em-barrassing complications in heaven with which Jesus' interrogations in Matthew were concerned by not divorcing or even remarrying after a spouse's death.[67]

This fairly coherent, if not always entirely common-sensical, program in favor of sexual marriage and against celibacy is reflected in most of Kingsley's more formal published work. In his first novel, *Yeast: A Problem* (1848, in *Fraser's*), Kingsley brought some of the conflict of his personal life between sexual desire and ascetic Christianity into his story. The young hero Lancelot establishes an immediate bond ("eye wedlock") with the lovely and intellectual Argemone. Her maidenly hesitation in committing herself to Lance-lot is blamed on the workings of a villainous religion and a somewhat villainous, popishly inclined vicar. Ultimately she follows her heart and sexual feelings toward her lover and away from the almost gothic-novel threat of celibacy in the vicar's plans for a Protestant beguinage. "All that is prudish and artificial," Argemone comments, has fled before love; like Fanny she embraces her husband-to-be nightly in imagination.[68] With the second hero, the proto-Lawrentian gamekeeper-preacher Tregarva, who takes an equally proto-Lawrentian fancy to the upper-class sister of Argemone, the idea of marriage in heaven is similarly underlined. His beloved Honoraria dies, as indeed does Lancelot's Argemone. But the Epilogue assures us that such incomplete marriages on earth may be completed in heaven. For this world and the next the book champions what Kingsley calls, in a reference to "Mahomet's heaven," "honest thorough-going sexuality" (p. 137).[69] We should not be surprised at the model offered for Christian thinking; liberal, anti-ascetic Christian thinking on sexuality necessarily moved toward the more directly sexualized vision of the afterlife in Muslim monotheism.

Kingsley's best-known novel, *Alton Locke, Tailor and Poet: An Autobiography* (1850), is essentially a *Bildungsroman* focussed on social comment. It brings its tailor hero only to a Pisgah sight of wedded sexuality, as he learns before his death to love a woman his intellectual and spiritual equal, not the merely pretty lady he has pursued for so long. By the same token we are told incidentally that he eventually came to understand the power and modesty of the biblical ur-story of sexuality: "the man and his wife were both naked, and not ashamed."[70] In *Hypatia or New Foes with an Old Face* (1853) a turbulent, and often impressively vivid, historical novel of fifth-century Alexandria, Kingsley comes far closer to placing issues of sexuality and asceticism at the center of his novel. He has the correct instinct, both as historian and theologian, to return to this period in which the long ascetic development of Christianity was being confirmed in the crucible of public controversy and agitation. The broader issues at contest in the warring factions of Alexandria as Kingsley portrays it (and indeed in the actual history of the time) are essentially those philosophical or theological ones that Kingsley had linked to sexual issues.[71] Hypatia, the lovely female philosopher, is the last spokesperson of the Neoplatonic pagan tradition that contemned the flesh and ordinary uses of mortality for an ideal of non-worldly spirituality. Another character, Philammon, is a young monk who sets out to see the world after being awakened by inadvertently glimpsing paintings of beautiful women in an old temple. He emerges from the new Christian unworldliness, Christianity built on Neoplatonism rather than on the Old Testament celebration of ordinary living. The values he explores and the choices he makes, as well as those made by the second hero, the Jew Raphael Aben-Ezra, are as much, perhaps even more, choices among sexual attitudes than among religious ones. Indeed they often appear identical. A recital of the various and complicated points made about these sexual issues in the novel, with which it is saturated, would be long. In brief, not only is Hypatia killed (by a rabid Christian mob who in fact share her fanatic contempt for the world) but her philosophy is discredited. Christian asceticism is accepted as the historical new wave; but it is not allowed the last word as a value. Philammon is tempted by Hypatia's philosophy but eventually returns to his monastery; the author's final suggestion is that he may have a more worldly connection to Hypatia in the world to come.

A more positive center of value in the book emerges with Raphael's conversion from harem-owning, to asceticism *à la* Hypatia, to marriage (and incidental conversion to Christianity more along lines Kingsley can value). His mother, a somewhat incoherent witch and mother-earth figure, is given very strong lines asserting the Old Testament values (as Kingsley saw them) of the earthy fruit of the womb against celibacy: "You are all in the same lie, Christians and philosophers," she scolds, whereas the Old Testament men lived their lives: "they did what you are too dainty to do, and had their wives and their children, and thanked God for a beautiful woman, as Adam did before them . . . and believed that God had really made the world, and not the devil, and had given them the lordship over it." Kingsley uses her to answer the ascetic revival of his day that he had long identified with Newman. Marriage and human relation are a central part of the Christian religious way. Newman would disagree – and he did, in his *Callista* of two years later, also set back in time in North Africa but specifically excluding personal relation from the Christian search.[72]

Two Years Ago (1857) also asserts Kingsley's central points clearly. Tom Thurnall the adventurous doctor, one of Kingsley's best characters with his grown boy's toughness and cunning resourcefulness, eventually yields the armor of his personal indifference for a warm relation with the religious schoolteacher Grace, while she in turn abandons her preacher-like ascetic role for personal love. "You

and I never part more in this life, perhaps not in all lives to come,"
Tom declares at the end.[73] As to Kingsley before him, love brings to
Tom a new religious faith. And this in turn grows out of his
acceptance of his vulnerability to chance, death, and emotional loss.
Kingsley indeed comes close here to analyzing the function his
sexual–religious system plays in protecting him from fears of fate and
loss. Kingsley even sees in Tom's final position as a lover a kind of
normal neurotic weakness that creates the need for sexual fulfillment
as a reassurance. In the same novel we are shown the education of the
agreeable but removed clergyman Frank Headley to the value of
sexual as well as social commitment. His love for the aristocratic
Valentia leads him away – somewhat as his author had been – from
his Puseyite leanings toward celibacy of the clergy and puts him into
touch with his parish. In the process he discovers his own capacity for
true self-sacrifice in fighting typhoid fever.

Kingsley's last novel, *Hereward the Wake: "Last of the English"*
(1866), an historical novel of England at the time of the Norman
invasion, is not much, in terms of pages, about love and sex, rather
about battles and Hereward's old Viking valor; yet what there is is
central. Hereward's fortunes follow his happy choice of a wise and
noble wife; his downfall, as Kingsley arranges the historical record, is
directly related to his abandoning her for another woman. In the end
his hopes of heaven rest with his last-minute turn back to his first wife,
whose name he shouts at his death, who comes to claim his body
majestically – "leave the husband with his wife" – and who prays for
him daily, and who presumably will reestablish marital relations in
the Christian Valhalla above.[74]

The opposition of ascetic and sexual values receives one other
strong statement in Kingsley's work, in the verse drama *The Saint's
Tragedy* (1848), and it is also repeated in some of his other poems.
Although *The Saint's Tragedy* earned him some attention in its time,
mostly because of the anti-Tractarian position that it was, rightly,
presumed to take, Kingsley is not an important poet or poetic
dramatist. Yet these works, also, are interesting for the intensity of
Kingsley's commitment to sexual themes. *The Saint's Tragedy* grew
directly out of Kingsley's personal conflict over celibacy and sexual
marriage in his relation with Fanny. As we have seen, the formal
point of that earlier, uncompleted prose life of St. Elizabeth of
Hungary, with its grotesque, rather sadistic drawings, had been to
make a kind of anatomy of celibacy as a religious ideal in order to

open the way to recognition of the advantages of sex and marriage. In the earlier work the didactic aim seems in great conflict with the sadistic celebration of asceticism that seems to escape subversively from the author's pen, both in text and drawings. Kingsley's later, completed and published, verse drama has the strength of representing in a more open and explicit way the opposing positions of asceticism and marriage. Lewis loves Elizabeth, sees in her eyes a type of the heaven to which he aspires, but fears that wedlock may be a kind of treason to her purity. She does in fact love him and they marry. Perhaps Kingsley then draws on some of his – and Fanny's – own earlier experience of a conflict between religion and sexual fulfillment in portraying her uncertainties in taking up the bride's role wholeheartedly. She, as Kingsley planned himself, put off consummation, in her case, in words rather like those of Jane Eyre, to avoid losing sight of God in his creature. She is disturbed by the thought that she has two husbands, God and Lewis, and wonders if the earth and its bride-beds are made to tempt us from God. Yet for a while she and Lewis find a heaven on earth, a renovated Eden, in their fulfilled love: "The self-begetting wonder, daily fresh; / The Eden, where the spirit and the flesh / Are one again, and new-born souls walk free."[75]

Set against this acceptance of the earthly as a type rather than the antithesis of the divine is the ascetic world view of the Papal Commissioner for the Suppression of Heresy, Conrad. He is a strong and interesting character who makes a plausible case that Elizabeth should turn herself to the higher occupation of sainthood rather than that of wife or motherhood: "Wife? Saint by her face she should be" (p. 45). Under his influence, Lewis chooses a crusade, where he ingloriously dies. Elizabeth eventually abandons her children for the occupations of a saint. Conrad's view of "Passions unsanctified, and carnal leanings" (p. 83) is set in debate against the ideas of a practical worldly spokesman, the counselor Walter. He sees the idea of ascetic sainthood as itself a diversion of normal sexual energies, which must then cover its origins by abusing and denying them: "prurient longings [for] celestial love, while you blaspheme that very marriage from whose mysteries you borrow all your cant" (p. 132). Conrad's apparent triumph (Elizabeth dies to all appearances a saint) is belied by her deathbed thoughts of her husband, whom Conrad can't erase from her mind. Conrad himself is murdered by those his fanaticism has angered. Kingsley succeeds in this drama in at least making asceticism credible (without being carried away by its sadistic material); but the effect of his analysis is to define it as a distortion and misappropriation of energies that should by rights be directed into a heterosexual relation.

Another poetic work, a narrative dramatic monologue "Saint Maura" (1852), also shows Kingsley's instinct to revisit the complicated history of Christian sainthood and martyrdom and fight the glorification of asceticism at its historical root. It rather too explicitly makes the point that true sainthood is a religious not a celibate quality. A soon-to-be-sainted wife addresses her husband, from her cross across from his, renewing their love and religious faith at the extreme moment of earthly matrimony. Ahead waits "Another body! / – Oh, new limbs are ready, / Free, pure, instinct with soul through every nerve, / Kept for us in the treasuries of God" (p. 298). Other shorter poems celebrate the order of nature and sexual marriage, or they directly invoke images of established religious asceticism – usually nuns – to symbolize the failure of love.[76] Kingsley's explicit and quite constant critique of asceticism, so often based on a review of Christian history, in many ways is his central position as a Christian thinker. If he was only a casual scholar of Church history, he nonetheless knew enough to understand the very strong ascetic traditions that had grown side by side with Christianity from almost its beginning, and he places his own Protestantism squarely in a tradition of reaction from a religion that centers its unworldliness in a suppression of sexual energies or their redirection into religious sentiment. This is not merely an aspect of his muscular worldly version of Christianity, but its central defining position.

I have used the term "liberal" for Kingsley without intending any direct associations between sexual and political attitudes. But like a political liberalism, Kingsley's sexual position between Victorian conservatives and radicals did force him to defend his position from the left almost as much as from the right. In this, though his advice is not unlike Clough's – that fisherwomen should go back to their husbands – his instinct, unlike Clough's open, problem-accepting, and experiential approach, is to develop a full position, to create an ideology of his sexual beliefs. Kingsley offered his Christian sexuality as an alternative, socially respectable and justified by appeals to religious history and theology, to the notions of total or partial celibacy that were frequently present in his society, especially in the conservative "respectable" position.[77] After that initial experience with a prostitute, he seems not to have been much bothered by sexual complications in his personal life. If there was some Ellen Ternan somewhere in his life he either resisted the attraction successfully or hid it competently. His latest novel, *Hereward*, does deal with material of adultery and divorce but there is no reason to believe Kingsley himself ever strayed far from his chosen, Fanny. Whatever the ease of his sexual fidelity in practice, in theory and imagination he nonetheless waged a hero's warfare against indescriminate lust and promiscuity. The force of sexuality that he accepted, even magnified and idealized, in loving marriage seemed to him as potent for ill outside of this accepted area as it was for good within it. It is as if he had circumscribed an area of sexual experience and sanctified it by its connection with his religious system; anything outside that circle had no such aura and was condemned with much the same prudish feeling that more conservative writers of the age condemned all sexual experience. By a kind of liberal's instinct, Kingsley positioned himself in a self-chosen middle from which he could accuse both "extremes" with equal vehemence – one of celibacy and the other of sexual promiscuity.

Had there been a Victorian advocate of free love who had suffered from Kingsley's attack as Newman did, he (or she) might have been equally surprised to find how easily a sexual disagreement could become with him grounds for assassination of character. Certainly Kingsley, like the conservatives of his society, looks on forms of sexual experimentation – to use a term he would never choose – not as possible alternative choices for other people but as failures of character. As early as *Yeast*, non-marital sex comes pre-coded by the more conservative conventions of his day. Lancelot's early sex life before he met Argemone, presumably with prostitutes, is treated with the same contempt with which Kingsley treated his own early experiment at Cambridge. The narrator preaches directly to educators and guardians of young men not to let them go Lancelot's way (and, incidentally, doubtless the way of many educated young men of the day), the way of allowing reading in licentious Latin poets to take the place of all sexual education. For Lancelot, the consequence of this education is that he naturally falls into sex the easiest way: "What was to be expected? Just what happened – if women's beauty had nothing holy in it, why should his fondness for it? Just what happens every day – that he had to sow his wild oats for himself, and eat the fruit thereof, and the dirt thereof also" (p. 5). Later a suave, worldly Colonel Bracebridge warns him to avoid forming "*liaisons*, as the Jezebels call them, snares, and nets, and labyrinths of blind ditches, to keep you down through life, stumbling and grovelling, hating yourself and hating the chain to which you cling" (p. 23). In fact the Colonel is more than self-destructive in his sexual explorations. We see him finally as a stock villain, leaving a local girl whom he has seduced to bring their child forth in a brothel while he travels fashionably on the Continent. In a more than melodramatic, certainly unconvincing, touch, when he learns from her that the child has died, he makes an end in guilt-driven suicide. His bad history can then serve as a lesson to Lancelot, who reads and ponders his suicide note.

Alton Locke is less directly concerned with alternate forms of sexuality. Alton's interest in the wrong girl, the demure but seductive Lillian, leads him only to a political fall, as he betrays his class to associate with her. Eventually she marries Alton's philistine cousin, the parvenu George, who sees her in coldly predatory terms, which do not adumbrate sexual marriage in heaven: "'She's a duck and a darling,' said he, smacking his lips like an Ogre over his prey" (II, 114). When Alton discovers these two ducks swimming in each other's arms on a sofa, he (and the reader) finds nothing attractive (II, 270). Even couples heading, formally, for marriage seem debased into some merely animal lust in Kingsley's vision if the marriage is not one that has the emotional potential for being made again in heaven.

In *Yeast* the artist Claude Mellot, with rather clear endorsement of the author, remarks that "extremes meet, and prudish Manichaeism always ends in sheer indecency" (p. 57). Using his usual liberal strategy, Kingsley again positions himself at a reasonable center; motion from that center leads indifferently in either direction to essentially the same aberration. This perspective is repeated in *Hypatia*, where the mother-witch figure Miriam tells the ascetic Christians, "Ay, you may root out your own human natures if you will, and make yourselves devils in trying to become angels" (II, 294). The pattern is indeed built manifestly into the novel. The world of Alexandria is divided between Christian and pagan ascetics on the one hand and the traditional popular licentiousness on the other. A Christian "fair penitent" (I, 151) even brings them together by dressing herself up in religious symbols used lewdly. Philammon and his sister Pelagia more extensively illustrate the family connection of extremes as Kingsley formulates them in his novel's discourse. Two Greek orphans, they, like Greek civilization, have moved in opposite ways, he to the role of monk (and sometime student of the ascetic philosopher Hypatia), she to that of sexy dancer and courtesan. The profession of hetaira, or talented courtesan, was of course accepted in the ancient world but it is not acceptable to Kingsley who, as we shall see later, must re-render Pelagia as a Victorian prostitute before he can redeem her. The danger Kingsley sees in her role as a stimulant for sex without love is apparent in a major historical scene: the attempt of the pagan politician Orestes to reestablish the pagan religion at a great public show. Pelagia has been enlisted to appear as a Venus on the half shell (delivered by an elephant), visible symbol of the sensual excess of the pagan world. Her "mystic cestus," her "dripping perfume" (II, 153), the dance she performs of "delicate modulations" (II, 153) have the crowd aroused and worshipping at her feet. It is a fairly innocent version of the *tableaux vivants* that Kingsley might have seen in Paris had he chosen. But the novel caps the performance with a heady judgment. As we shall see in more detail, her brother, driven by intense shame, breaks in to rescue her from all that; she in turn changes from satisfied performer to a guilt-stricken sinner. For all Kingsley's attempts to recreate the pagan scene in its historical brilliance, he seems totally at odds with its spirit.

In *Westward Ho!* (1855), a novel most directly concerned with the adventure of Elizabethan nationalism, alternative sexual styles are ascribed to England's foreign foe, and specifically to the ascetic opposite, the Jesuits. They are blamed for teaching the villain of the piece, the licentious English convert to Catholicism, Eustace (obviously a fairly direct side-swipe at converts of Kingsley's own age), Continental ways of love as Kingsley defines them: "That all love was lust; that all women had their price; that profligacy, though an ecclesiastical sin, was so pardonable, if not necessary, as to be hardly a moral sin."[78] This Jesuit-sponsored licentiousness is pointedly contrasted to the happy English married love of the hero Sir Richard Grenvile, whose sexual rigor extends to avoiding the French and Italian habit of flirting, even very innocent flirting, with women. All should be reserved for the bride, who otherwise takes only the "very last leavings and *caput mortuum* of her bridegroom's heart" (I, 197). In the next instant we see that his thoughts, even as he speaks, are on his wife in the terrace below: she smiles and his stern face melts into a "very glory of spiritual sunshine." As in the essay on the Jacobean stage, Continental sexual mores are identified with adultery. We see a fine Spanish gentleman, Don Guzman, captured by the English and treated civilly as a prisoner in house arrest, casting about with a liquorish eye on faithful wife and virgin maid alike to see where he should make his advances. With Grenvile's wife, we are told, he wouldn't have gotten into the batter's box. On licentious womanhood Kingsley is even harder, here following the usual distinctions of the conservatives of his day. Mary Queen of Scots, a hard woman and Catholic who has used her sexuality to manipulate others, seems to be put to death more for this than for her political position – surely a misjudgment of Elizabeth's *Realpolitik*.

Another unreal scene, of attempted rape in *Two Years Ago*, in which a booby squire is interrupted by the hero doctor Tom as he is in hot pursuit of the saintly Grace across an open field, is used to point a heavy moral. No sooner does Tom rescue Grace than he lets his own instincts out of hand and steals a kiss. It is part of his background as an independent adventurer that he knows how to do this kind of thing. But he must learn a lesson of true love, indeed that his flirtatious behavior is on a moral level with that of the rapist himself. When he sees she loves him and realizes his own love for her, he repents mightily and resolves to shield her as much from himself as from the impassioned Squire Trebooze. Later the oddly modern money-loving doctor must resist the temptation to marry someone else for money, in Kingsley's eyes a self-rape as abominable as rape itself.

Kingsley gives seduction and adultery no quarter in the final novel, *Hereward the Wake*. As Hereward is drawn away from his helpmate by the superior physical attractions of the younger Alftruda, there is very little imaginative comprehension of the force of sexual passion. Hereward simply says flatly that no one who once enjoyed Alftruda could live without her. The narrator finds it sufficient merely to note the "storm of evil thoughts" (II, 98) that goes through him when she tempts him and to show the disastrous consequences of his fall: "He was besotted on Alftruda, and humbled himself accordingly" (II, 291).

Perhaps the central myth of Kingsley's imagination, interestingly enough that also of another sexual liberal of his age, Robert Browning (as it was of many other male writers, who could easily find in it a combined assurance of sexual potency and gender identity), was the story of Andromeda. He writes in a letter that he has done a whole series of drawings and finds the beauty of the old myth "un-fathomable."[79] His poem "Andromeda," an epyllion in the rich sensuous style of the English Ovidian tradition, is really a celebration of Kingsley's myth of marriage itself. Unlike Browning, who stresses the rescue of maiden from dragon, Kingsley focusses primarily on the immediate sexual issues in this unusual boy-meets-girl situation. Perseus is so taken by the lovely tresses and probably naked beauty of his rescuee that he begins to woo her even before he takes care of the dragon. However, his hasty kiss is followed by the saving assurance that "to chaste espousals / Only I woo thee" (p. 208). Although he goes on to slay an actual fire-breathing dragon, the more real dragon seems to be that of simple lust, itself raised by the poor bound maiden's complete accessibility to airborne Perseus. Fortunately their quickly developing mutual passion after the dragon's death is channeled by supernal interference. Aphrodite gives balm both to increase longings and to create chaste content in espousals. Athene joins wisdom to love under such marital organization, with an added warning of "woe upon woe when the people / Mingle in love at their will, like the brutes" (p. 216). The very sensual poem, like Kingsley's work in general, strongly endorses sexual feelings in marriage, but as strongly attempts to forbid all sexuality that doesn't lie within that god-blessed circle where a religious ritual, even when here a pagan one, has sanctified and clearly organized the sexual mingling. Because of his need to stave off the danger he sees in a purely secular, sensual world, Kingsley's overall aim must be to produce a new, settled, and complete discourse joining sexuality and religion to replace the one of asceticism that he rejects. Even in a pagan context he must imagine such as discourse; his world and the pagan are indeed not so far apart, inasmuch as both accept sexuality as an aspect of religious feeling. But probably far more than a pagan sensibility, he feels an aggravated need to control sexual freedom by religious prescription, ultimately creating a system of marriage for his imagined pagan world identical to his own.

Around this central vision of sexual fulfillment in marriage, chastity in all else, Kingsley created not only a Christian and classical myth but that equally strong nineteenth-century pattern, an historical myth. Kingsley was popularly accepted in his day as something of an historian even to the extent of being given that appointment as Regius Professor at Cambridge, though this was doubtless more a recognition of his religious than historical eminence.

He certainly read widely in the history of his day. In addition, as we have seen in his attempts to revive and revise the history of Christian attitudes toward sexuality, he had a talent for broad historical generalization, which didn't advance his reputation among professional historians but was an impressive tool for stamping large patterns into an historical novel or a set of undergraduate lectures later offered to the general public. When we look closely at this process of pattern-making, we also find that a great deal of it has a sexual basis. His reading of history is at once oddly modern in its stress on changes in social structures rather than political events and yet dated, almost racist, in its British chauvinism. The sexual morality and family structure of the societies he looks at are taken as keys to their essential qualities. The sociological premise is essentially the one we have already seen in Kingsley's patterns of sexual value. A healthy society will reflect the strong bonds of idealized marriage that Kingsley himself champions. Failing societies will present one or both sides of the coin of asceticism or licentiousness. The one, indeed, easily flips over into the other. A strong settled marriage, untroubled by flirtation and adultery, allows members of society to focus on their work and the raising of children, making the society itself strong against others devoted to debauchery or monastic discipline.

When applied to history, this sociology leads Kingsley to some odd redirections. The ordained historian is forced to see the time of Christ as, in some sense, not too important. Rationalizing St. Paul's lack of enthusiasm for marriage, he observes in a letter that that was a time when sexuality was essentially reduced to harlotry, at least at Corinth.[80] He can find better stuff in the older days of the Old Testament, as Miriam's strong words in *Hypatia* show. Old Testament people moved vigorously from early polygamy to a strong monogamous family structure, in Kingsley's view frankly sexual and otherwise uncomplicated. The major event in history, however, is not in the Bible at all but in the emergence of a new sexual morality among the barbarian peoples threatening Rome at the end of the Empire. They appear in *Hypatia* as a small band of Goths considering establishing their power in Alexandria. Southern luxury and the charms of Pelagia, who becomes mistress to their prince, have them temporarily off balance. But their native values are those of a strong marriage based on their conception of the woman as the Alruna-woman, the hero wife, wise in counsel beside the hero man.

The Goths never established an influence in Africa; and it is Kingsley's point that Africa went to the ascetic/licentious dogs mostly because no such new influence was exerted on the degenerating sexual life of the time. These Goths eventually murder a yard full of fanatic Christians and then go back home. In the published Cambridge lectures, *Roman and the Teuton*, Kingsley sees the decline of the Empire as the result of Gothic, Teuton, Lombard, and, of course, Saxon virility, based on their sexual mores and chivalric ideal. "National life is grounded on, is the development of, the life of the family"[81] and the Northern tribes honored the family by keeping their sex in the bounds of marriage. The Saxons may have been cruel, but they were "venerable for their chastity"; the Visigoths were loutish but "they were chaste, and therefore they conquered" (p. 43). By contrast, the Romans had been corrupted by the availability of their own slaves and their lax sexual morality into total slackness. The lesson is plain to read: "As in individuals so in nations, unbridled indulgence of the passions must produce, and does produce, frivolity, effeminacy, slavery to the appetite of the moment, a brutalized and reckless temper, before which, prudence, energy, national feeling, any and every feeling which is not centered in self, perishes utterly" (p. 38). This pagan license "flipflops," as Rome declines, to Christian "dignity of celibacy and the defilement of marriage," which Kingsley is bold to assert is one of the most "practically immoral" set of doctrines ever preached to man. The Roman priesthood, being essentially an export from old Rome to the Europe of the Middle Ages, really only passes on the ancient Roman immorality and contempt for women.

In this view of history, one should rather say sexual myth of history, the stage is obviously set for a further conflict between the Roman ways and the indigenous Northern ways. Hereward woos his first wife by the old laws of chivalry and she becomes a true Alruna-woman, strong in counsel and bold even in battle. Hereward's enemy is as much the Latin clergy, who come over with William, as the invasion itself, inasmuch as they threaten more permanent change of English life. In *The Saint's Tragedy* the conflict is explicitly between the new courtly ideal of love and the celibate ideals of sainthood sent up from Rome.[82]

When he comes to the Renaissance, Kingsley naturally rewrites the Protestant Reformation as a conflict of sexual positions, in this anticipating the grounds of major debate in later twentieth-century social history.[83] This is what we have already seen in *Westward Ho!* and the essay on "Plays and Puritans," where sexual license and adultery are associated with Catholicism and the Romance countries; a full-grown marital sexuality – married love – is the pride of the English, who seem, by a connection between the marital and martial not made clear, to be able to take on three or four times their number of Spaniards, whether soldiers or ships in the Armada. Fierce in battle with men, the English are still renowned – at least in Kingsley's account – for abstaining from rape when they conquer. Captain Amyas Leigh's fictional band of men in South America swears an oath against atrocities, just as in Guiana Kingsley found that "no woman was the worse for any man" of the crew of the real Sir Walter Raleigh.[84]

Kingsley's historical system naturally leads up to his ideals for present-day England. In fact, the whole has the Whiggish cast of the patriotic school of historians of his day. He looked back to find in history the origins of the present sexual system in which he saw the strength of England. In this perspective it is perhaps less surprising to find that the three novels about his contemporary England, all focussed on a current problem, dwell so fully on the issue of sex and marriage. To Kingsley the real problem is maintaining the proper domestic relations. England's happy and resolute people will then naturally take care of her problems and preserve her position in the world. *Yeast*, a novel focussed on what idealistic young leaders can do about the social problems of England, mostly fights off the dragons of celibacy in Tractarianism, another foreign influence that threatens to bring in the sexual aberrations of the Romance countries. With these problems solved, the hero Lancelot can be privileged to hear from an impressive stranger a prophecy of new learning in the East and future leadership. This is all very vague, as if providing leadership for his country were hardly a problem for a man who has found his orientation in love that lasts beyond death itself.

In *Two Years Ago*, the public problems are simpler ones, typhoid fever and the Crimean War. In this interestingly diffuse novel, the concern with the characters' sexual destinies is again not merely to provide love interest to bolster the political and social preaching. Frank Headly becomes effective in fighting the fever as he abandons his faith in un-English celibacy. His love for Valentia acts as a generating force that energizes his reform activity. By contrast, the self-indulgent poet Elsley Vavasour moves away from English patterns into Continental ones. He has changed his name from the simple English John Briggs to the suspiciously Continental one that he now hides under. Though married to a fine woman, he seems determined to suffer from a French marriage rather than enjoy an English one. He carries on a flirtation with her sister; then he becomes consumed with unwarranted jealousy over the honorable admiration an old major has for his wife's good qualities. He creates the Continental adulterous affair in his imagination even when it isn't there. Kingsley comments that traces of jealousy for a reasonable (English) husband are naturally and regularly washed away in "sacred caresses" of intimacy (II, 174). Elsley instead flees into a suicidal jealous rage that Kingsley interestingly locates in the Romantics' Snowden mountain region. He moves entirely out of the healthy structures of his society and ultimately to his death, a thoroughly useless person.

Doctor Tom Thurnall's case is more interesting. Although his sanitary work and his opening love for Grace go hand in hand, he is really not completely converted to Kingsley's system of love until the Crimean War lands him in prison and shakes his self-assurance. Here the external threat is offered as a kind of warning and goad: a wise man will learn from the realities of the world to arrange his sexual life fittingly. Kingsley makes the same point in a very stereotyped scene of prostitutes that Tom passes outside a theater in London – "Gay girls slithered past him" (II, 320). They are all struck into their better selves for a moment as the news of the English victory at Alma (September 1854) passes through the crowd: "sinful girls forgot their shame, and looked more beautiful than they had done for many a day, as, beneath the flaring gas-light, their faces glowed for a while with noble enthusiasm, and woman's sacred pity" (I, 320).

Only in *Alton Locke* do the social problems loom larger than the sexual issues. Alton's choice of the wrong woman, it is true, cripples his attempts to be an effective voice or leader of the working class, and the idea of the better woman Eleanor is some consolation to him in his early end. The ostensible moral is that such personal regeneration, not revolution, is the only sure way to social improvement. But here Kingsley is too good a reporter, too aware of the economic problems of the lower classes, to seem himself convinced that a new sexual orientation alone can really solve the massive problems symbolized by the plight of the sweated tailors. Perhaps just because it is not so successful in working its author's thesis, the novel survives better than other Kingsley works as an unusually vivid account of the social conditions of the time.

Kingsley's fairly coherent program of sexual–religious ideals and its elaboration as a system of history has, more generally, the problem of all theses in art. If it gives his vision consistency and clear point of view, it also tends to limit his sensitivity in certain areas of experience where he is, in effect, already committed to particular emphasis or approaches. Most people since the massive influence of Freud and Kinsey on our century's thinking about sex would begin with a critique of Kingsley's sexual position as too restrictive. The positive view of sex in marriage would in itself probably appear favorable; it is, after all, the bias of thinking even in sexologists like Masters and Johnson. But the chaining of all sexual expression and exper-imentation to marriage would seem decidedly reactionary. The liberal in sexual matters in his time would appear rather a conservative in ours. His ideology also conflicts with that of many persons in our time in the whole area of women's rights and women's roles. In this area of his thought it is of course easy to mistake his position – liberal for his time – for a reactionary one even in his age, especially if we cue our response off of our own age's feminist catchwords about women in the nineteenth century. Kingsley often speaks of woman as angels, whether in the house (or bedroom) or up in his oddly sexual heaven. But this does not make him quite the cad on women's issues that the angel in the house tag would seem to indicate. His letters to John Stuart Mill on the rights of women are quite directly in favor of expanded rights for women, if not yet fully for suffrage.[85] He was forward looking enough to propose medicine as an especially good area for women's careers.[86] Nonetheless, while supporting at least some practical steps for the equality of women, he continues to see them in a distinct category. And this is in turn probably very much determined by his conceptions of women's roles in his ideals of marriage. In one letter to Mill he goes on to express his preference for women who conceive of their freedom as an op-portunity for self-sacrificing altruistic endeavor, without any sense that such a role might conflict with the aims of winning careers and independence, and without any seeming awareness that if one sex gives a benefit altruistically the other may be receiving it selfishly. Although he is not against independent careers – and this is much for his day – his real ideal, as he makes clear in a quaintly titled lecture

"Woman's Work in a Country Parish,"[87] is the homewoman who devotes herself to the duties that lie nearest at hand.

Further, he sees a "primeval mission" for all women that is very much connected to his sexual–religious ideas. Women are, in effect, to use their sexual attraction to civilize and Christianize men, to bring out the chivalry at least latent in English culture.[88] Women can perform this function because, again, their natures are fundamentally different from men's. Like Tennyson in *The Princess*, Kingsley does not deny women's intellectual capacity. Yet he believes their special quality to be spiritual more than cerebral. Their responses are finer as their strength is weaker. Aspiring to intercourse with a woman, in both senses, a man is forced to develop his nobler capacities. Eleanor, who is a person of education and strong mind, is even more important as a spiritual guide to Alton Locke. In *Hypatia*, the Jew Raphael is converted from his pagan meanderings to Christianity and monogamy by a noble wife – a conversion that restores him, in Kingsley's view, to the best aspects of Old Testament good life. In his Alruna-woman Hereward has a guiding light, almost a personal religious leader. But the presentation of this idea is perhaps most interesting in the modern *Yeast*, just because it rather inadvertently reveals the essential situation in this assignment of roles. There we find young Lancelot earnestly persuading Argemone to play the role of civilizer that the author would presumably consider hers by nature. He fears all his dreams of "Alrunen and prophet-maidens" will find no home in a real modern maiden. "Has woman forgotten her mission?" (p. 65). Will she refuse to charm modern man into being better, as she "charmed our old fighting, hunting, forefathers into purity and sweet obedience among their Saxon forests?" Kingsley makes palpable in his dramatic presentation what he can't see in his own thought: that this is a matter of men pushing a role on women that they wish to play themselves but can't quite find the courage to take up without a special excuse.

Kingsley's chivalric idealization of women's role in fact threatens, as Clough sensed it might in his critique of idealized sexual relations, and as it does even more obviously in Ruskin's similar ideas, to submerge the original sexual impulse. In the more common Victorian middle-class "respectable" position, women's moral and emotional higher nature went hand in glove with diminished sexual interest. For Kingsley this further angelization of women is neither necessary nor desirable. Yet his emphasis on women's social role in a chivalric system does tend, in practice, to render his vision of women somewhat desexualized. Good women, good wives like Hereward's Torfrida, seem to lose their sexual attraction as they become finer Alruna wives; less dutiful women like Hereward's second wife Alftruda seem more seductive and attractive even as they fail to inspire their men with nobler passions than lust.

Kingsley's commitment to a particular sexual attitude, and his need to differentiate it from simpler forms of lust, also weakens his work more centrally, in its presentation of sexual experience itself. There would be, for any Victorian public writer, a problem of limiting descriptions of sexual experience to acceptable public standards of reticence. But compared to a fellow Victorian writer such as Charlotte Brontë, who shared his focus on sexuality, or even to a more schematic writer such as Clough, Kingsley is relatively unsuccessful in presenting any aspects of the central experience of sexual initiation or awakening. Brontë cannot provide sexual scenes such as we find every thirty or forty pages in our contemporary best-selling novel. But she makes a great art of her analyses of the psychology of sexual unfolding.[89] Kingsley constructs his stories so that they usually center, as Brontë's do, on the opening of a sexual relation, usually the first for both of his hitherto chaste lovers. But his didactic aims, including his care not to seem to write with bawdy or lustful interest, make him fail imaginatively just where he should signally succeed.

Kingsley's hesitancy in approaching this subject even seems writ large in the very plots of his first two novels. Both seem obviously structured upon the central coming together of male and female characters. Yet they in fact never quite get together. In any event, sexual union is postponed to a heavenly honeymoon. Alton, having loved the wrong woman, is frustrated a second time by the premature ejection from this world of both himself and the right woman. He must find what content he can with his "blessed angel" (II, 308) in her angel home. The lovers in *Yeast* are less ethereal, but the evasion of final union in this world is the same. Argemone dies before she and Lancelot can do more than plight their loves. We do see the process of their courtship, but here again Kingsley seems to shift his attention from their central attraction. Instead, he focusses on the didactic religious issue so important to him, discrediting nunneries and celibacy in favor of marriage. No sooner does an interesting scene commence, with Lancelot drawing a vow of love from Argemone and forcing her will somewhat with his masculine determination – the kind of thing that makes a good scene of psychological exploration – when the conversation shifts radically in tone to allow Lancelot to lecture against the manipulating Tractarian vicar who has been pulling her in the other direction: "So 'celibacy is the highest state!' And why? Because 'it is the safest and easiest road to heaven?' A pretty reason, vicar!" (p. 194). This is followed by the former agnostic's sudden testimony that their love was designed by providence and then by Argemone's total emotional surrender, presumably a tribute to Lancelot's masterful presentation of Kingsley's major doctrines on celibacy and sacramental sexual marriage. A pretty scene of love-making, rector! we may be tempted to rejoin as we finish the chapter.

It isn't clear whether Kingsley veers away from the scene of sexual introduction because he prefers to lecture on his favorite sexual–religious topics or because he finds it difficult to write about the psychology of intimate relations, or because he felt he should avoid a too explicit scene of passion. In practice, he certainly chooses the clear formulation of a religious doctrine on a sexual issue rather than the persuasive presentation of sexual experience. In *Hypatia* Kingsley wrote, by the public standards of his age, a more shocking book, one that cost him that honorary degree at Oxford by giving his enemies a handle against him. Yet even here there is an odd swerve away from the central scene of sexual initiation to which the novel seems obviously building. Philammon had left his monastery to explore the world, attracted by those drawings of women. The woman to whom he is then most attracted is the philosopher Hypatia. He goes to her lectures to assert Christianity against her; he stays as disciple and admirer; eventually he waits outside her window at night only to get a glimpse of her. Hypatia herself has scorned physical involvement, preferring the abstractions of the Neoplatonic tradition as Kingsley understands it. She has consented to marry Orestes, the Roman prefect, as part of a plot to restore the ancient pagan order, but she finds her personal involvement unpleasant. With Philammon she feels something, however: at first a Platonic liking of master for pupil (1. 298).

It is at this point that the spokesperson for physical love, Miriam, enters the relation. She has her own poor ulterior motive (to get a ring back from Hypatia that proves she is Raphael's real mother). But Kingsley allows her matchmaking between the monk and the philosopher to be justified by his own rhetoric of love. She tells Philammon he would have been making love to Hypatia months earlier if he were a true man of the old stock. With Hypatia, she plays a more interesting role, a kind of accessory to her awakening sexuality. We see Hypatia stricken in her faith in the old gods, existentially overwhelmed by a sense that all is only flux and change. When she tries to renew contact with the old gods she is visited instead by a face from within. To her surprise, the face is that of Pelagia, the sensual courtesan, a person whom she has treated with contempt in her preoccupation with cerebral and celestial matters. The repressed returns now as her own need for the other half of her nature, which Pelagia represents. This need is then played upon by Miriam, who answers her frantic prayers to Pallas Athene by giving her instead a love potion. Hypatia goes into a most unphilosophic trance, awakens with hair disheveled, and is offered by Miriam a chance to embrace Apollo himself.

All is now prepared for the matchmaker to bring these recalcitrant celibates into first physical relation. But at this point the author seems to lose his nerve or his enthusiasm for such a union. Philammon is prepared by Miriam's strong talk about the old biblical ways with woman for the tryst in which Hypatia will be brought to him. Though these general observations are not undercut, Kingsley allows Philammon, who has hitherto worshipped Hypatia for her fine qualities, to dismiss the coming business as mere poison of the *carpe diem* variety, a mere sweet indulgence. When Hypatia enters and clasps his feet, he enlightens her as to his status as a mere mortal instead of accepting her embrace. Both fall away from the rendezvous, demeaned in their own eyes, offered no further intimacy except the final assignation in heaven that the ending of the novel vaguely suggests. Characters and readers alike have been led on and teased. Instead of the sexual accommodation and growth that we are prepared to expect, Kingsley leaves his celibates as they were. Hypatia's initiation, as we shall see, is transferred from a directly sexual one to a scene of extreme violence and total violation. Kingsley seems more interested in showing the ill consequence of celibacy than in presenting sympathetically his own sexual ideals.

In *Westward Ho!* two women enter into marriage. But again Kingsley gives us little experience of the intimacy that was central to his own beliefs. Rose, the beauty of the West country, refuses all English beaux but succumbs to the Spanish Don Guzman. The marriage is presumably happy enough but it is seen entirely from the outside, as a scandalous elopement. The Amazon nature child Ayacanora falls in love with Amyas Leigh, the bold English captain, who yields to her love at the end of the novel. But Kingsley submerges the interesting theme of conflict over dominance between the free woman of the forest and the strong leader – the kind of subject Charlotte Brontë would have treated so intensively and so well – in a mere political issue: Amyas must get over his hostility to the Spanish blood in Ayacanora (she is actually no Indian but half-English, half-Spanish) before he can accept her love. Their final reconciliation is only hastily sketched in, with the exotic free woman now reduced to a proper English lady.

In *Two Years Ago* there are suggestions of greater psychological subtlety. Tom Thurnall's original pass at Grace, his self-control through love, and his final acceptance of love as an aspect of his new sense of vulnerability are interesting. Yet the conversion itself, which Brontë would have developed in intense dialogue between the characters, is merely relegated to offstage action in a Russian prison. Their warm mutual acceptance then comes as a sudden, brief, undeveloped climax of the work. That relation of Frank, the one-time celibate clergyman, and the well-to-do Valentia is put more fully before the reader. Valentia herself is a lively, rather successful female portrait in Kingsley's none-too-impressive gallery of female characters. Kingsley conveys well what he had experienced at first hand, the attraction and apparent hopelessness of the educated poor man aspiring above his station. It is a kind of reverse of the poor governess theme in Victorian fiction. Yet the interest, as it is occasionally in *Jane Eyre*, is too much on asserting equality in God's and man's eyes, too little on the growing relation between the two. When they confess love to each other, an awkward fifty pages of exciting narrative of the runaway jealous husband Elsley intrudes; their relation then proceeds not with "love-making" (II, 264) but with practical mutual support in an emergency. One passionate kiss and then they must be off to deal with the present crisis. Again, it is not that we should look for sexually intense scenes inappropriate to Kingsley's age and audience; what is missing is the psychological and dramatic presentation of lovers' intimacy.

This persistent deflection of interest from the apparent and rather natural center in intimate relations of lovers is continued in *Hereward the Wake*, even though this book deals most maturely of Kingsley's

novels with marriage and even with adultery and divorce. The initial
romance of Hereward with Torfrida is indeed handled with unusual
concentration and delicacy. We see how Torfrida, dreaming days
away in her house at St. Omer, begins to dream only of Hereward,
whose strong deeds have been reported to her. When he rides under
her window and sees her dark blue eyes and raven locks he too begins
to think only of her, not of sultans' daughters and princesses of
Constantinople. Their first embrace, as Torfrida gives Hereward her
favor to wear, is also nicely portrayed. Hereward mistakes her
meaning, then realizes he is favored; her hands tremble with passion
as she binds the favor on him; he exults in their love by a warlike cry
of triumph that forces her to quiet him lest he bring scandal on her.
Hereward pledges to love her and, perhaps more in line with the
author's theories than with the needs of the scene, also pledges to
respect her virginity until marriage. Torfrida then symbolically
enacts the contrary by opening to him her private treasure hoard.
Her nurse warns: "Too fast! Too fast! Trust lightly, and repent
heavily." She replies: "Trust at once, or trust never" (I, 219) and
opens the door to her stronghold. Her gift, a magic armor, nicely
symbolizes their sudden closeness.

There follows an equally acute account of the ego adjustments on
both sides as these two strong-minded people realize that neither will
simply serve the needs of the other, as each had rather expected.
Torfrida fears that the Viking Englishman is not civilized enough for
her dignity; eventually there is a quarrel; the magic armor is
returned; and before they can make up their differences, he has set
out for battle with no protection at all. Presumably both have been
tempered by their suffering when they are reconciled after the
campaign, she by guilt, he by sulking and fighting in a dirty robe that
he refused to change. All this is psychologically more insightful
writing than we normally find in Kingsley. But he then wrenches us
away from this material. A wedding announcement ends the lovers'
estrangement and we are asked to move along to the view of Torfrida
that we have thereafter, as a model helpmate and warrior's
companion. The center of their life, as we are to presume, in the close
relation worked out in marriage is virtually ignored.

When we come to Hereward's adultery with Alftruda and his
divorce from Torfrida, the weakness of realization is much more
apparent, quite in contrast with Clough's imaginative openness on
this subject in his *Mari Magno* poems. We see almost nothing of

Alftruda's attraction, which is ascribed mostly to superior looks and youth and these we do not experience along with Hereward. The failure of the ideal marriage with the Alruna-woman Torfrida is ascribed only to a general sense of the hardness of their life during Hereward's winter quarters as an outlaw in England. It is almost as if Kingsley can't acknowledge that there might be serious psychological or sexual problems in a married couple's intimate relation that could lead to estrangements. As we have seen, he wishes to assert that in the end Hereward really belongs to the former wife who claims the body. Alftruda is necessarily reduced to a mere physical temptation upon which he "besots" himself.

The same weakness is clear in the poems and need not be belabored. "Andromeda" becomes so preoccupied with expounding the author's faith in chaste nuptials that the early sensuous relation of the lovers is put on hold and never taken up again. In *The Saint's Tragedy*, the interesting initial study of two lovers each rating the other as too far above him or her is not further developed. The issues of ascetic sainthood versus love and duty to family quickly come to dominate the verse play. In all these rather various cases, Kingsley often seems to have some good reason to deflect our attention from the psychological and sexual awakening of the lovers to other scenes or concerns. Yet the total record suggests he really fails as an author to bring alive the central experience upon which his philosophical glorification of married sexuality depends. And this, rather than any unpopularity of his opinions, probably accounts for the relative lack of vitality his novels hold for us as imaginative visions of love and sexuality.

To most modern readers Kingsley's treatment of sexual subjects will also seem both too reticent and too prudish on a number of special issues. Here one can only say that his open-minded and interesting views on marital sexuality did not extend to a number of other matters that troubled the sexual conservatives of his age. On one issue, as we have already seen, that of remarriage, Kingsley is probably more rigorous than the precisians of his age. Divorce has no real place in his view, as the effective erasure of Hereward's divorce suggests. Remarriage even after the death of a spouse is barely permissible but not really acceptable because of the complications it introduces in the heavenly remarriage. More than this, Kingsley seems to see something impure even in loving more than one person fully in a lifetime. His ideas on sexual purity, beginning with his reaction against his own early experiment at Cambridge, are in no way liberal. Premarital sex finds no place in his world of marital sexuality. Whether in "Andromeda" or *Hereward*, good characters explicitly denounce it. In his letters he insists that a major quality of the ideal Englishwoman, along with the earnest religious life, is "virginal purity."[90] He does not pretend that a young man like Tom Thurnall had lived for years without sex – presumably mostly with prostitutes and courtesans. He can be quite realistic, as in *Alton Locke*, in showing how poverty leads to prostitution among poor girls. He even portrays sympathetically a girl driven to prostitution to help her sick friend (I, 278). Similarly, he is not shy about mentioning the resorts of prostitution, in London, around the theaters.[91] Yet there is no question that Kingsley does not conceive of prostitution, even as a conservative medical writer such as Dr. Acton did, as a necessary evil, the relief valve of male sexuality.[92] Because Kingsley, unlike Acton, does not see respectable women as essentially sexually unresponsive, he counsels young men to preserve their sexual purity for marriage. Keep clear of Venus, he tells the Cambridge under-graduates in the lectures on *The Roman and the Teuton*, and you shall have a strong healthy maturity like that of the Teutons themselves (p. 46). Extra-marital sexuality, with prostitutes or otherwise, is of course anathema, as his observations in "Plays and Puritans" on adultery on- and off-stage in the seventeenth century makes clear. These are all simply different versions of that old evil, fornication, something unconditionally to be avoided in Kingsley's system as it had been in so many hundreds of years of Catholic theology.

On other standard issues of Victorian sexuality Kingsley seems, as far as his reticence allows us to judge, also to be much with the conservatives. A possible allusion to the attempts being made to introduce birth control techniques to the working class is entirely negative. *Alton Locke* refers to certain advertisements in workmen's newspapers that "no modest woman should ever behold" (II, 33). About homosexuality, still conceived in his day mainly as certain acts rather than as the full identity for which the word "homosexual" would be created at the turn of the century, he is more explicit, though just as negative. Sodomy, which was still a crime punishable by death in his age (and within his lifetime actually punished by death), is apparently for him appropriately so punished – at least at the level of rhetorical castigation. In the undergraduate lectures there is an unmistakable reference to the wicked Roman sensual slave trade in beautiful boys and girls. He goes on to observe that the Teutons put to death perpetrators of the crime for which "like us" (p. 77) they had no name and similarly had to borrow one from Latin. By contrast, that love dared speak its name in any Roman city, indeed could be not only spoken but enacted with impunity.[93] As already noted, biographers have suggested that Kingsley may have feared a homosexual urge in himself, especially after his novelist brother became involved in a scandal that was possibly homosexual in nature.[94] Be this as it may – and repressed homosexual urges are the easiest things for a psychobiographer's imagination to detect and the hardest thing for him or her to establish to the satisfaction of the rest of us – Kingsley is not unusually harsh for his age in this language, only far from the liberalism of his own attitudes on marital sexuality.

Finally, there is the favorite nineteenth-century bugbear of masturbation. And here also Kingsley would seem to join with the more conservative, though not the hysterical, opinions of his age. His admonition to Cambridge undergraduates to steer clear of Venus in youth, as the Teutons did, and grow strong and healthy into adulthood certainly encompasses masturbation, the usual sexual debilitator, as well as prostitution. It has been argued, perhaps correctly, that the undesirability of masturbation is the moral of one rather especially odd section of Kingsley's classic fantasy for children, *The Water-Babies*.[95] Tom the chimney-sweep has become a water-baby and felt, in the loving cuddly Mrs. Doasyouwouldbedoneby, some of the human affection usually denied to him. He now goes after her lollipops on his own, taking them from her cupboard on the sly. Such a joystick, longer than it is wide, would suggest a sexual interpretation only to a confirmed Freudian image-abuser. But Tom's changed appearance must give all of us pause: he is "horny and prickly"; "all over pickles, just like a sea-egg."[96] Tom has attempted to hide his sin but, as so many adolescents have feared, the sin has shouted itself out in pimples. Kingsley's moral is blunt, that when Tom's soul grew "all prickly with naughty tempers, his body could not help growing prickly too" (p. 157). It is hard to imagine all this relates only to a stolen lollipop, though hard also to believe that Kingsley would have felt such indirect, coded discussion could have meant anything to his childhood, not teenage audience. He was perhaps writing more to the parents who read the work aloud to their children. His position, as we might expect, is a moderate negative one. Lollipops are bad because they misuse a good thing, the natural warmth of the mother-figure. Parents need not pursue the child's sin by inquisitional methods, because nature will show forth the abuse of nature. It is indeed nature's way of giving us a small burn on our fingers so we will keep them from the fire (presumably that of mature illicit sexuality). The theft separates Tom from normal loving relations and from the community of water-babies. When he confesses his fault, far from being punished he is redirected in nature's right way by being given a little girl to teach him his prayers. His spots fall off; when he grows up the little girl becomes his lady beloved.

Kingsley's position, if this is a correct reading of this little tale, is not that of the hysterical opponents of masturbation in the nineteenth century, who even devised those elaborate (and perhaps over-discussed) machines to sound an alarm at nocturnal erections.[97] He has more faith in nature and in the easy redirection of sexual energies onto his main path. Yet he is, as he says, "in serious, solemn earnest." Masturbation, like the other sexual outlets, to use Kinsey's inelegant way of speaking of the varieties of sexual experience, is to be totally closed up, leaving only the way of married sexuality.

The tensions inherent in Kingsley's position as he attempts to affirm a strong ideal of sexuality in one circumstance while denying virtually its every other manifestation, sometimes emerge in his work as peculiarly troubled or disturbed moments. Where he feels a particular pressure between the extremes he wishes to avoid he sometimes veers heavily off the narrow path he has laid out for himself. These places certainly mark some of the low points of Kingsley's art, where we feel he has not got his materials under control. They also suggest the perils inherent in his simultaneously intense and highly constrained position. Kingsley has his feelings highly involved in the sexual issues he raises. The effort sim-ultaneously to suppress sexual expressions of which he disapproves and to celebrate what he does approve exposes him to unruly moments in which either he presents sexual feelings in hidden, inappropriate forms or allows his fears of sexuality to lead him into rituals of excessive repression. The narrow path he has set for himself in sexual matters makes it hard for him not to stray to one side or the other. His inability, in the experiential situations posed by his fictions, *not* to stray suggests why it was so important for him normally to circumscribe sexual experience by a clear, fully formulated ideology, where his own theology and religious belief could offer firm, unambiguous support in controlling his feelings.

Of the first kind of straying, covert expression of uncontrolled sexual energies not officially allowed in his system, we could say that the large accumulations of violence and slaughter that first enliven, finally encumber, some of Kingsley's novels are generally examples. Especially in the historical novels, where (paradoxically) Kingsley's imagination can work freely, there is remarkable stress upon violent conflict and accumulating heaps of corpses that suggests that Kingsley himself was working with excess energies he didn't entirely understand and also tapping them in his readers (still very much there to be tapped if the Anglo-American world's huge capacity for fantasy violence – English television murders and American "action" films – in otherwise fairly chaste popular culture is any indication). This sense of a general turning from sexual control to physical violence, especially in works that usually have a central sexual issue that is left incompletely explored, is of course intrinsically vague, a feeling on the part of the reader that the author's energies are being deflected from sexual to violent themes. It is compounded by our sense of a certain minor pathology in Kingsley in his interest in flagellation before his marriage: some evidence that his feelings had already found a path from sex to violence. We can be more precise in certain places in Kingsley's work, beginning with those grotesque and violent drawings in the unpublished prose "Elizabeth of Hungary." Obviously he himself sees a connection, and explores it interestingly and coherently in the further and published look at Elizabeth's self-flagellation in *The Saint's Tragedy*. In other places the connection appears less self-conscious. When Pelagia is scheduled to appear as a nude Venus before the crowd in *Hypatia*, it is not clear that Kingsley would have known why he wrote a scene of remarkable, indeed peculiarly disgusting, violence. A group of fifty Libyan men, women, and children are slaughtered on-stage by gladiators, even down to a little boy and his dog. If someone had asked Kingsley why this scene is so closely juxtaposed to the erotic one that follows – including the detail of Pelagia staining her dancing foot in the blood of the young boy – he would probably have said something about the odd mixture of excesses in the pagan mentality. We can't help sensing, instead, a mutual stimulation of sexual and violent imaginations somewhat out of his conscious control.

The effect seems most noticeable in those cases where, as in

Kingsley's own recourse to flagellation, direct sexual expression seems abnormally blocked. Then the author provides violence as an alternative, and does so almost as a kind of punishment. The most prominent example is probably that of Hypatia herself. The failure of her sexual initiation leaves her back where her critical creator found her, a celibate who scorns the involvement of loving sexuality. For this ongoing sin against the ark of Kingsley's foundation she is given a terrible, almost ironically parallel initiation. The Christian mob, who identify her with the pagan revival they wish to destroy, catch her up, rush her into church, strip her and tear her to pieces, a kind of ultimate rape. Kingsley would obviously disown the apparent moral, put out or be shut up, and ascribe the sexual element in the lynching to the violence of the hypocrite Christians in what was, after all, actual history. Yet the point does seem to be there in the fiction's plot, a dire if somewhat disguised warning against women who spurn sex and take up the cause of celibacy.

A similar observation can hardly help being made about Kingsley's treatment of that belle of the West Country in *Westward Ho!*, Rose Salterne. Although she is a respectable young lady who simply rejects all the acceptable young heroes of English blood who throw themselves at her feet, Kingsley's opinion of her is clear enough in the "slattern" barely hid in her name. When she elopes with the Spanish nobleman Don Guzman, it is as if Kingsley can't forgive her the combined slight to national pride and to all those fine local boys she refused. He sends a quixotic party of former admirers after her. They profess the most honorable intentions but it is clear that they would have looked to the Spaniards like a gang of cutthroats and desperados. To Rose they are fatal busybodies, who succeed only in compromising her not-unhappy marriage. This in turn leads to her mutilation and death at the hands of the Inquisition. It is hard not to feel that at some level the text tells us that this is what Rose gets for having held back from so many reasonable English offers of Kingsleyan married sexual felicity. Kingsley seems unaware that his heroes' precise concern for Rose's honor has actually destroyed a very honorable relation – by Kingsley's own standards – between her and her husband. In the same novel it is hard not to see Captain Amyas's final accident and blinding, as he pursues his hate of Spaniards and ignores his future bride, as a punishment for coldness. Once he is blind, he warmly accepts Ayacanora.

The treatment of Ayacanora herself and of her jungle home

suggests rather the opposite effect. Kingsley imagines scenes of uncontrolled sexuality and then, in his own reaction against their attraction, suppresses liberty by violent actions. His fears of uncontrolled sexuality lead to violent rejection of his own licentious imaginations. In the case of Ayacanora the suppression takes the fairly simple form of depriving her of her freedom as she learns to accept the restrictive codes of her recovered English identity. The free bird of nature is gradually adjusted to a cage of English domesticity. An interesting scene back in the jungle is more explicit in the restraints Kingsley finds he must impose on the emergence of an uninhibited, apparently natural sexuality from his imagination. Amyas's men, like Tennyson's lotos-eaters, are tempted to roam no longer. They take up with native women and settle down to enjoy bliss in a jungle paradise. The idea is obviously as tempting to Kingsley as it is to his hero. A sexual paradise regained, as we have seen, is a central and recurrent idea in his thinking. This one is, however, illicit, and not just in the technical sense of its lacking parsonification. It is also illicit because it is an escape from ordinary social life rather than its center. Just as Amyas himself, drawn by Ayacanora's beauty, feels temptation besetting him like a "gaudy snake," gliding in and wreathing "its coils round all his heart and brain," he is rescued, quite savagely, by his author. A jaguar rushes in and kills one of nature's brides, awakening her English consort from his dreaming state to realize he has left his sword behind. The attack is clearly a judgment, as surely from the author as God of this universe (South American jaguar but British *ex machina*), against stepping over the lines of accepted sexual union. Just because these are hardly cities of the plain, Kingsley's violence, with its details of the poor little dead girl, seems excessive, the result of a threat to him that demands vigorous suppression.

It should not be surprising that Kingsley's least well-controlled sexual scenes should turn around a figure whom he identifies as a prostitute. This had been his one personal temptation and fall; and though he doesn't record his temptations in the way Clough does, there was doubtless some residual or continuous attraction toward this most available of Victorian temptations that he suppressed. His presentation in *Hypatia* of Philammon's sister Pelagia as a fallen woman and ultimately as a magdalene figure is remarkable in the first place because Pelagia isn't really a prostitute at all. She is what the Greeks called a hetaira, an artistic, intellectual courtesan, and what in Kingsley's time was called a horsebreaker (and sixty years later a home-wrecker), an extremely attractive woman who lives with a man in return for support at the level to which she wished to become accustomed. In her case her man is Amalric, the prince of the group of Goths who have come to Alexandria in the hope of making hay out of the current political unrest. From first appearance, when Philammon meets her lolling on a boat with her Goth friends, Kingsley presents her very much as a Victorian "stunner"; our first view of her is indeed of her virtually naked beauty; and she soon favors us with a song on the shortness of life and the pleasures of "Sleeping by me!" (I, 59). She is then regularly nude and Greek, as in her appearance as Venus Anadyomene. Like the ideal Greek hetaira, she is an accomplished dancer, pantomimist, wit, and musician. This doubtless attractive view of her is qualified by Kingsley's assertion that she lacks a sense of right or wrong, perhaps also suggested by the allusion to the heresy of denying original sin built into her name: Pelagianism. Yet part of him can portray the emergence of a deeper emotional self in her relation to the Amal, who has become the center of her world. One part of Kingsley could thus look on her as a case of education by a loving relation: the light, sexually immoral woman grows into lover and companion.

But this lenient approach, to which Kingsley somewhat inclines, is thwarted by his suppressive rigors against all irregular sexuality. The conflict in the author is acted out in the complicated and excessive reaction that Philammon has to Pelagia once he discovers that she is not just a courtesan but his own sister. This reaction could have been one of the most interesting things in Kingsley, a study, like Hardy's Angel Clare in *Tess of the d'Urbervilles*, in the harm of sexual puritanism. The problem is that Kingsley doesn't sufficiently separate himself and the overall vision of the novel from Philammon's suppressive vision. Even before Philammon begins to recognize in Pelagia his long-lost sister, the novel has begun to reevaluate her, in Victorian terms, as a prostitute rather than a woman of pleasure of the ancient (or modern) world. The monk Arsenius quietly tells her she must go someday to hell: "Have you forgotten what you are?" (I, 317). This is not entirely the author speaking, but it is a quiet, reasonable voice. What she is in this perspective is of course a settled and labeled commodity, a whore, and this is certainly her brother's point of view. Both cast over the pagan love relation a pall of censoriousness that redefines it as intense sin. Philammon finds her "most sinful" (II, 16); he begins to rant against sexual variety: "What's beauty without chastity? Beast! fool! wallowing in the mire which every hog has fouled!" (II, 26). He resolves to "rescue her from this infamy to purity and holiness" (II, 28).

Philammon is indeed driven by a frenzy of shame and brotherly horror to incredible exertions to redeem her. His mission becomes in fact that of the Victorian rescuing the magdelene. At the public ceremony in which she dances as Venus, he vaults over rows of the audience, leaps on the stage, and attempts to reclaim her by an appeal to their new found siblingship. We are to believe that this violent intrusion upon her professional exertions suddenly makes her soul come alive. The scene, quite incongruously, seems like a pre-Raphaelite painting of the awakening of conscience, as Pelagia is suddenly rapt by a vision of her long-departed childhood innocence back in Athens. Later brother confronts sister with the lesson taken from Christ and Mary Magdalene. There is forgiveness, but she must acknowledge her sin, and, like the Magdalene, consume the rest of her life fasting and praying in the desert (II, 187). Philammon resolves to get her to a nunnery; he fights with her Goth lover; the stronger Goth is killed when they both fall out of a building. He essentially has his way as Pelagia now takes up a life as penitent and hermit. He and his sister die together, in a chaste family kiss.

Kingsley is uneasy with this story that he has created of sin made conscious, brought to an end, and repented until death. He insists upon a sympathetic treatment of Pelagia, similar to a liberal Victorian vision of the prostitute fallen through youth and innocence. He has Philammon implicitly criticize Hypatia's scornful dismissal of her as merely a sensual, low, earth-bound type. Yet he cannot seem to see the way to accepting her trespass as less than a serious one demanding some kind of grave consequences. Her pathetic pleas that God doesn't punish the little birdies for doing what comes naturally (II, 282) will not entirely do. The natural alternative, that she should proceed from pre-marital cohabitation with her handsome Goth to mature commitment and marriage, is considered but not accepted. Despite the sense of sin and hellfire that Philammon raises in her, this is her desire, and it is a desire based on the kind of strong personal love and sexual union that Kingsley himself endorsed so firmly in marriage. Here he gives this more experimental version of his philosophy of strong union a voice, especially in the comments of the earthy old crone Miriam. She declares that it will be better for

Pelagia to make an honest man out of the Goth by marrying him than to be terrified by Philammon's images of punishment for sinners. Yet this doesn't happen and the author, though aware of the violence that Philammon's conscience does to Pelagia's love, ultimately endorses the book's vision of life-long penitence followed by the full rehabilitation of the magdalene at the moment of her death. Because Kingsley could take a fairly practical, reasonable look at the social causes of prostitution in *Alton Locke*, we may guess that he would have described his own position here as one of a more moderate rehabilitationist. Living in sin is wrong but need not be countered by such a sexually puritan vision as Philammon's. But the novel shows him unable to give imaginative form to this vision. Instead, the emotional pressures engendered by his conception, that of sexual relation set rather tantalizingly just outside the heavy borders that he put around his garden of marital sexual delights, seem to have overwhelmed his artistic control. The contradictions built into a liberal sexual world of marriage set within a restrictive, moralistic, closed universe of sexuality come here too close to the surface and threaten to destroy the entire construction upon which Kingsley so heavily depended. And the very threat of that destruction, really deconstruction, makes it the more necessary that he affirm, not explore openly, the religious ideology he created to structure his thinking and control his own instincts.

Such cases, as the opposite case with which we began, Kingsley's excessive reaction to the threat/attraction of religious celibacy in Newman, indicate the perils of Kingsley's entire sexual enterprise. Eighty years ago I think it would have been hard for a modern thinker, trying to free him- or herself from inherited ideas of sexuality, to look on Kingsley as anything but a peculiarly unpleasant kind of hypocrite: a person who supported and promulgated many of the restrictive or frankly prudish ideas that, in the modern myth of Victorianism, came to be considered typical of Kingsley's period while withholding a small area of needed sexual satisfaction for himself. Today I think I can offer his thinking and its imaginative embodiment in his work as a peculiarly interesting version of the complexity of Victorians' treatment of sexual issues – especially in his insistence on integrating sexual views with his larger, fundamentally religious vision of life until the two become virtually one system of belief. Kingsley stands before us as a person and a writer caught, like a kind of sexual Waverley, in an awkward but sincere position between large forces that he can't entirely understand. We can see in him the strange ways in which his culture asserted its respectability, its new sanitary vision of controlled reasonable human existence, by insisting on minute scruples over sexual issues. And we can see in him the opposite impulse, toward a free and frank acceptance of the good of sexual experience, indeed a displacement or restatement of traditional social or religious ideals by a new more conscious preoccupation with sexuality as a kind of center of life. In this he is in many ways a clear predecessor of an early modern like D. H. Lawrence – a writer who indeed shares with Kingsley both a unique emphasis on sexuality as a quasi-religious center of life and rather puritanical scruples about variant modes of sexual expression.

The comparison, however, immediately suggests what especially distinguishes Kingsley among liberal writers on sexuality: his insistence, unlike a writer such as Lawrence, who reaches outside of his culture for new religious ideas, on structuring his thinking within a recasting of traditional Christian discussion. Working with a general historical idea of the movement within early Christianity toward increasing asceticism and negative views of sex itself, Kingsley tries rather consistently to restore something close to the non-ascetic early traditions. These, which he rightly sees as close to the Jewish traditions in which Christianity was originally situated, combined positive attitudes toward marriage and procreation with rather close controls on other kinds of sexuality – though rarely perhaps as positive as those of Kingsley himself.[98] Like Milton's celebration of married love before him, his is not a foolish or, in itself, inconsistent revival and adaption of this tradition. He updates it by avoiding stress on biblical taboos no longer relevant to his culture while emphasizing, indeed underlining and celebrating, the central positive attitude toward marriage in God's injunction to fruitfulness. He works close to later Christian tradition in condemning every sort of fornication outside of marriage while insisting on cancelling the ascetic and Augustinian tradition of suspicion of sex within marriage. If Clough takes on the Augustinian tradition more directly, Kingsley seems more able to put it behind him emotionally and accept sexual gratification as a good. The assurance that he provides for those who walk within the narrow path of his system – that they are not in sin when they enjoy the delights of married sex – is at least effective in staving off the return of Christian conservative tradition, as we feel it in Clough, as non-specific guilt and anxiety in sexual matters. It was perhaps just because his system so well accommodated itself to traditional Christian thinking, displacing Augustinian suspicions of sexuality with a limited celebration of sex in marriage while maintaining a sense of prohibitions and control, that Kingsley's sexual middle way apparently appealed so broadly. If it may seem to us in many ways an odd confection of liberalness and restrictiveness, in its day it could stand for a major alternative position to the conservative "respectable" one. Kingsley's great popularity and wide social acceptance in his society suggest he effectively represented a broadly attractive alternative, one which we find also, though less clearly articulated, in many other writers of his time.

In a broad perspective, we may see Kingsley, in the development of his system and in his successes and failures in applying it to a view of life in his novels, trying to walk a narrow line between forces, within and without him, of sexual need and sexual restraint, libido and its suppression, personal discontents and the restraining structures of his particular civilization. From this perspective, his earnest attempts to give their due to both sexual need and sexual limits are a moving, if sometimes pathetic, sometimes ridiculous, version of human attempts to find a system of language about sexuality that will please the conflicting Peter and Paul (or Hyde and Jekyll) within. The difficulty of his balancing act is clear enough from the lapses or absurdities into which he occasionally falls. It even seems clear enough that the prognosis for such a blatantly antithetical system of sexual values, in which a very open, positive ideal of sex in one situation – given every kind of religious sanction – is combined with restrictions – also backed by the authority of religion – in all other areas, is not that good. Kingsley's manifest division on sexuality leads to moments of confusion in his art; generally it may contribute to the larger problems of his work, where we so often feel a failure to confront the interesting issues he raises: a diversion of energy and interest into catalogs of social abuses or sanitary violations in his contemporary stories or heapings up of adventure and gore in his historical works. Above all, the pressure to maintain his precarious system denies him the exploratory, iconoclastic play of mind on sexual subjects that we find in Clough. Clough can toy with his earnest subjects, sexual or religious, can seem increasingly more able to stand back from the conflicts of sexual need and sexual ideals that he finds within and place them in a clear broad context of understanding. Kingsley is too immediately involved in his sexual system and in the religious beliefs by which he affirms it and simultaneously controls himself for such freedom.

Yet when all this is said, the interesting figure that Kingsley represents, the liberal Victorian who insists on finding a place for sex in both his sexual and religious worlds even as he essentially lives within the limits of those worlds (as Clough refuses to), is also an impressive figure. He is sometimes confused on sexual subjects, sometimes, to twentieth-century tastes, more irritating than interesting; but he is never dull or blasé, any more than he is on the social causes that also strongly occupied him and led him often into similarly difficult liberal positions between extremes. Despite the static, holding-the-line nature of his sexual–religious beliefs, he is also capable of growth. *Two Years Ago* finds him beginning to explore problems of sexual jealousy interestingly in the study of the poet Elsley Vavasour. *Hereward the Wake*, like Clough's latest poems, shows the parson beginning to acknowledge the problems of marital infidelity and divorce, albeit not with Clough's fresh and open-minded attention.

Above all, Kingsley commands our respect as a serious writer, a clergyman and social sage, who refused to evade the problem of working out and expressing his opinions and vision of sexual experience, both in relation to his ideas of society and his religious beliefs. In this, like his less earnest, more playful contemporary Clough, he importantly shows us that Victorian sexuality was not the simple monolithic thing that modernism tended to take it for. He speaks to us on this issue, as other Victorians long have on others, as a complex human, someone faced with the universal problem of accommodating sexual needs to all other aspects of experience. For many readers his solutions may no longer appeal; we may decide that his liberalism has gone the way of most stopgaps between great and changing historical and psychological forces or that his religious vision, not absurd in relation to the universal history of relations between sexual and religious ideologies in human cultures, may nonetheless seem restrictively of his period, even quaint. Or his position may live strongly today for other readers, especially for many Christians, in continuations or reconstructions of a liberal sexual position within strong religious traditions: preserving marriage as a protected confine for approved sexual expression while controlling other forms of sexual liberation. If he is thus closer to some readers of our time, he speaks clearly to all of us not as a wooden figure carved out by the dogmas of his age but as a living intelligence and personality, striving, as perhaps all must, for difficult accommodations in complex situations.

CHAPTER 4

Known and Unknown Desire: Coventry Patmore's Search for Eros

The nineteenth-century British poet and essayist, Coventry Patmore, has been a somewhat enigmatic figure, scourged lately as the conformist Victorian creator of the poem called *The Angel in the House*, revered as the (convert) Catholic mystical poet of his maturity. His angel, as his specialized advocates keep telling us, is not, in fact, oppressed Victorian domestic woman but the love between Victorian man and wife. But, as we shall see, there are reasons for feminists and other readers to suspect that poem. His religious poetry offers good reasons for other suspicions on the part of the conventionally pious reader but also, as I will argue, generally unrecognized but great attractions for the lover of distinguished poetry.

His early work, which made something of a splash when the very young man published in the 1840s but which sank virtually without a trace as Patmore edited and censored it into oblivion, reveals an interesting, open, largely experimental approach to issues of sexuality. As much as Clough, but with more emotional involvement and generally without Clough's intellectual distance and control, he allows the confused and conflicting language of sexual discussion and representation of his age to flow through the early work. In this quite early preoccupation with sexual choices and sexual themes Patmore is like both Clough and Kingsley. Like them, he seems to dedicate himself above all to sorting out issues of sexuality as his major mode as a writer – so much so that he prematurely, and somewhat absurdly, tries to take on the role of English Petrarch in *The Angel in the House*.

In contrast to both Clough and Kingsley, the young Patmore is not too much concerned with religion in any direct way. He begins from a more secular tradition, following, if also disturbed by, his father, a man of letters and friend of Hazlitt. Again unlike with Clough and Kingsley, there is never a suggestion of a call to the priesthood. He was not at Oxford or Cambridge and did not feel as directly as they the conflicting forces of the Oxford Movement and the strong reaction to it; he, unlike them, would eventually convert, as the Oxford Movement's spiritual leader Newman had, to Catholicism; but though his poems express great admiration for Newman, he finds for himself a very different tradition of Catholicism that shows little direct adherence to positions dear to Newman and offers many views that Newman found, or would find, uncongenial. If anything, sexual issues take on religious meaning for Patmore not through the religious discourse, or debates, of his society but in an existential way, through the boy and man's own sense that there is some special significance in sexual experience that introduces humans to a supernal sphere. It is intuitive and personal and something to be progressively explored.

Whereas Kingsley goes through a very brief period, in his grown life, of experimentation, then settles down to his life's work of building, rationalizing, and defending his system of sexual–religious belief, Patmore is closer to Clough in developing his position in successive works. But even here Patmore works over a lifetime of progressive exploration; Clough's voyage is mainly in the few years of resolution in his life as he moves from possible permanent don or pastor, to worldly young gentleman, to married citizen. Clough also works constructively to balance and evaluate; he expands his own and our understanding as he develops his range of analysis. Patmore rather tends to work through positions: to state them as strongly and vividly as possible and then, when he finds their limits for him, to move on to a position he finds more adequate to command his commitment. There is a gain in scope, as in Clough, but the new vision doesn't open the mind to a variety of possibilities so much as attempt a grand synthesis. His exploration takes him initially from the uncommitted and probing poems of his earliest publications, where he seems almost to let the various languages of his time on sex play themselves out into contradiction or dilemma, to the premature commitment that the moralizing of *The Angel in the House* represents. In that too-popular poem he reduces his awareness of the complexities of sex and sexual statement to a superficial version of Kingsley's system of restrictive married sexuality. And, like Kingsley, he legitimates his ideology with the doctrine and authority of his Protestant religion. But Patmore's central interest continues to be in the experience of sexuality and its language; and both his new choice of subject in his writing – in exploring failed love after the idyll of *The*

Angel in the House – and his personal experience – especially the death of his wife – lead him back to concerns with sexual desire itself rather than with prescribing a system of norms.

The apparent, almost schizophrenic shift in style and statement in the great odes of the 1860s and 1870s indicates a logical if startling confrontation with earlier problematics. Death, now, locates the central issue of sexuality in absence. In intricate, often enigmatic and highly expressive, odes, ranging from intense stories of personal loss and fantasy to mythic constructions – Adam and Eve, Cupid and Psyche – he presents the situation of desire separated from its object. The focus is now on determining the nature of sexual desire itself as a central phenomenon of human nature. In many different versions, Patmore's conclusion is that sexual desire is both the source of man's humanity, the essence of human nature, and also the connection to the divine. Now, more than seeking religions sanction and sanctification for a strong experience of this world, Patmore looks to reconstitute a modern chain of being linking man to God – through sexuality.

In this process religion becomes an increasingly central means of organising and explaining the complexity of sexual experience that he approaches in a personal and very emotionally involved way. His work recapitulates Western versions, especially those in mystic traditions, of the movement from natural love to sacred; but as we shall see, his is a rather special as well as certainly a well-stated version. If his associations between sexuality and religion begin very close to Kingsley's position, he eventually arrives, in his splendid odes, in seas of emotional and religious depth that Kingsley wished never to plumb.

In Kingsley, desire's opposites, as we have seen, exercised potent but unwelcome attractions. Inspired by the purity of Newman's piety, Kingsley was bothered by the ideal of sexual purity itself, which he admitted that he had not maintained before marriage and wished to assure himself he could achieve in his sex-filled marriage by excluding all unmatrimonial desires. He found ascetic practices, the self-torturing fasts that corresponded to the feasts of his imaginary communions with Fanny, exciting – and painful. He pursued his attraction to/repulsion from ascetic practices in studies of Elizabeth of Hungary that demonstrate equal parts of condemnation and curiosity. The high point of his passionate love with Fanny Grenfell was in some sense their enforced year's absence before marriage.

Thereafter, fully persuaded that he was deeply satisfied with his marriage, Kingsley nonetheless became preoccupied with a higher love, that of Fanny and him in heaven, that he could not yet reach. On earth he even contrived to spend long periods away from her, writing her periodically of his passionate wish to come to her. His approach to this awareness of two facets to sexuality – broadly speaking sexual presence and its absence – is generally to solidify their opposition, claiming that he chooses only presence – including believing that earthly and heavenly love are somehow on one continuum already present to him – and denigrating all those who accept or dwell upon absence: who indeed become the various villains of his many pieces, from holy but celibate Newman to the most malevolent hypocrites and torturers of his fiction.

By full contrast, Patmore's instinct is from the first to accept the entire experience of sexuality, positive and negative, present or absent. And his works move from an experiential view of combined presence and absence in his early work through a Kingsleyan period where he briefly looks for simple, binary opposition, to the full articulation of their essential interrelation in his masterpiece, *The Unknown Eros*. Indeed he ends even celebrating virginity, not as the dead alternative to a rich sexual life that Kingsley took it for, or the mere release from the pressure of desire for which Clough sometimes craved, but as the highest expression of sexual feelings in a mature state of realization.

THE LIFE

In reading Patmore, as with Clough one is struck by the inescapable figuration of the author's life in his works. The early works are clearly about young men, like the author, confused, upset, excited by sexual tales. No one reads *The Angel* without finding in it some reflection, strong or dim, of Patmore's own celebrated "perfect" first marriage. Some of the odes, though very possibly pure fictions of a personal life, cry out to us their lading in the pain of adjustment to the death of his first wife and his remarriage. And, like John Singer Sargent's well-known visual rendition of the aged, aloof, and patriarchal Patmore, his late works, enigmatic, inspired, authoritarian, and prophetic, create for us a speaker who clearly sees himself as the would-be hierophant of a new religious truth.

Patmore the man emerges vividly from his works; but he does not give us his own interpretation of his life. He wrote no *Prelude* or

Praeterita, no *Autobiography of Coventry Patmore*. We must seek our own plot in his life, even if certain great events are rather firmly pre-inscribed. More than with most people, these are mainly about love and marriage, so that they create markers which follow the sexual preoccupations of the works. There might even be a temptation to lump them together and read Patmore's as simply a life of love mirroring a career in writing about love. However, a plot is not merely the sum of presences but a series of spacings between events, whether spaces of mere time elapsed, of radical change, or of discontinuity and loss. In Patmore's life, these seem most often to be times of confrontation with discontinuities, losses, or lapses and, as in his work, they seem finally the most prominent elements. Patmore's life-long urge to assert the saving and unifying power of desire paradoxically finds its home not so much in desire fulfilled as in confronting the failures of fulfillment.

As this study has been showing for each of the authors, the century of Victoria that has become so generally associated with prudery, bowdlerizing, and sexual repression was also one, as observers as different as Michel Foucault and Peter Gay have remarked, greatly preoccupied with sexual issues. Even the excesses of anti-sexual activity in some historical moments testify to a massive focus on sexuality; a focus, as Foucault would say, that essentially creates a large discourse on sexuality – a culture of sexuality – out of a few biological facts present in all ages and cultures. If we look at Patmore's family circumstances from this point of view it is not hard to see him very much immersed in this culture of sexual discussion from early in life. Indeed one is tempted to read an allegory in the odd circumstances of his father. Patmore's father, Peter George Patmore, a minor literary figure, carried into the Victorian period two scandalous associations from his wilder early manhood in the Regency period. He had been seriously criticized for his handling of a duel, in which he was second to a man named Scott who was killed; he had been one of the friends of Hazlitt to whom Hazlitt addressed his exceedingly revealing letters documenting his hopeless passion for the maidservant/landlord's daughter in the house where he lived. These Hazlitt published as *Liber Amoris*. If the father had sympathy for Hazlitt's so-expressive sexual passion in his own dandiacal youth, he was half-sorry (but only half-sorry) for such candor and association in his maturity and even blotted out some passages in the letters he possessed.

Young Patmore, embarking on a literary career himself, didn't care about the dueling association – indeed had the fierceness of a dueler about him into an age when dueling was slowly being eliminated – but he was perplexed by a literary heritage that made his family's major claim to fame to be a connection with Hazlitt's work. On the one hand, it encouraged him and empowered him to enter into the contemporary discussion of sexual experience as a kind of family right. On the other, it drove him to work out his own position in his embarrassment at the association. Although the father remained a friend and public supporter of Hazlitt until his death, the son would become critical of Hazlitt; when he found the originals of the *Liber Amoris* letters he sent them to Hazlitt's own son implying that they should be destroyed. Later, when the letters, still extant, were being proposed for sale and publication, he wrote a letter to *The Times* in his high-handed late manner, branding the works as "that wretched book the 'Liber Amoris'" and the letters themselves as "morbid trash" fit only for burning en masse.[1]

This filial response to the family literary heritage can be read, and probably was read by the son, in a twofold manner. There is the desire, obvious enough, to dissociate himself from the adulterous longing, the loose talk of sexual "liberties" of a time before distinctly Victorian values prevailed for reticence in public statements about one's private life. Patmore is typical of his age, not his father's, in considering details of sexual experience to be strictly of a "*confidential*" nature, as he wrote to Hazlitt's son. Yet Coventry, who was fond of his father, even after he suddenly left his son in embarrassed circumstances – this time, business ones as he flew abroad on the wings of a disastrous investment – quickly developed an ambition to justify the family by, so to speak, re-writing the book of love in an acceptable mode that would testify to his parents' very unscandalous marriage and to his own meticulously respectable sexual conduct.

The irony, of course, is that Patmore's life and writings still seem far more shocking to even a later twentieth-century sensibility than anything done or said by the merely infatuated Hazlitt. And that may be because fundamentally he was true to the tradition of honesty about sexual experiences as he found it. That was, of course, the best that could be said of Hazlitt and Patmore's father. The one amorous event of Patmore's boyhood is certainly most ordinary and unsensational; we are only aware of it because Patmore himself puts such an emphasis upon it. He was sent to Paris by his father at age sixteen and there fell in love with a Miss Gore, the daughter of the novelist Catherine Gore, an English friend of his father's who kept a literary salon. Documentation of Patmore's early life is almost non-existent, so that this incident looms out at us with preternatural clarity, but it would do so also for Patmore in later life. We know that sexuality, precisely that provoked by the relatively full discussions by the Romantics, had been on his boyhood mind; he had been reading Byron's *Don Juan* and received a letter from his now Victorian father warning him of the danger of the book and generally of the "harm" unselective reading can do.[2] Such presence in him of strong adolescent sexual curiosity led, apparently, not to the sexual experiment of many young men in Paris – though it doubtlessly developed the sexual experimentation we will find in his earliest work – but merely to a hopeless love for a girl two years older than he and soon to be married. This incident of passion unfulfilled seems to have written itself on his awareness with a heavy stylus, the more heavy perhaps just because of its total failure to be realized. Miss Gore, who isn't even given a first name in Patmore's recollection, is nonetheless the prime begetter of all that follows. Later in life, settled with his first wife, Patmore still kept a picture of a woman who looked like Miss Gore and spoke of her to friends as the "very first 'Angel'".[3]

In his writing he refers to an early experience of love as a central fact in life that opens a person's eyes to an essential reality. "Men of genius," he quotes approvingly, "spend their lives in teaching the world what they themselves learned before they were twenty." Oddly, he is quoting from Hazlitt. More explicitly, the introductory poem to Part II of *The Unknown Eros* speaks of the wild, fleeting dreams of love of a boy as a path back to the central reality of the sexual nature of the universe – dreams of intimations that a later poem in the series will call, strikingly, "auras of delight." His prose essay on dreams ultimately speaks of "the realities of spiritual perception" as a kind of sexual Wordsworthian remembrance: the man recalling "The heaven which 'lies about us in our infancy,'" which transfigured soul and sense in the time of his howsoever 'foolish' first-love." Those "poignant rays" then renew their splendor in unconscious adult experience, as also in sleep, or in mythic art forms. Such specifically unconsummated "virginal love" orients the sexual and religious experiences that follow.[4]

Having been touched deeply and permanently by the unfulfillment of virginal sexual love, Patmore began in his early poems his lifelong exploration of the complications of sexual experience, often with very candid admission of perplexity. In his life, however, with characteristic unpredictability, Patmore moved speedily not to a monastery or to a series of hopeless passions for Lauras and Beatrices far above him but to the placid, continuous, and easy gratification of a Victorian marriage of love. At twenty-two Patmore had been thrown from a life of study and writing poetry into hack journalism by his father's financial disaster. He was rescued by a position at the British Museum obtained through the patronage of Monckton Milnes, and was able to propose marriage a year later, in 1847, to Emily Andrews, one year his junior. She was something of a bluestocking, the daughter of a well-educated Congregational minister, who had kept an intellectual and well-heeled upper-middle-class church in the London suburb of Walworth. In *The Angel in the House*, where the hero also married the daughter of a churchman, the class affiliations are shifted upwards to a setting among the gentry and a daughter of an Anglican dean. Emily Andrews's father had died years before Coventry met her and her adult milieu was essentially a middle-class, intellectual and slightly Bohemian world of mid-century London. In the terms of that world she was an ideal choice, beautiful (Browning wrote "A Face" on her beauty; Woolner did a lovely medallion of that face; Millais painted her), well educated with a one-time governess's knowledge of Latin, French, and even Greek, and inclined to writing. She was, however, neither George Sand nor Elizabeth Barrett, but confined her efforts to lively stories for children, and a book on servants' behavior.[5] Patmore was no Rochester; she was a perky Jane the governess, without Jane's vaunted plainness, and ready to join with Patmore in a storybook ending of domestic happiness. Nor is there the long period of settling the balance of power between them. Patmore, inclined throughout life to a rather haughty patriarchal manner, and Emily both seem to have been relatively content with formal patriarchal authority somewhat balanced by Patmore's high regard for her domestic competence and authority and her frequent leadership in religious matters.[6]

Patmore says a good deal in *The Angel in the House* about such a relation as an idealized marriage; very little in the poem or his biographical materials gives us much sense of what the reality of their sexual relation or their marriage may have been. There is a sentimental remembrance of buying sand-shoes for the new wife, both in reality and in the poem, but this is almost a celebration of his taking on the role of the domestic husband. We also have a picture of her playing the role of domesticated wife, sewing and throwing in astute remarks as Patmore and friends, such as Tennyson or the Pre-Raphaelites, talk literature. Certainly life was not an idyll, with a growing Victorian-size family (and increasing conflict between Coventry and his oldest son, Milnes), Patmore's parents living and dying with them in the 1850s, and the sickness of Emily in the later part of the decade that forced the family to split up for long periods of time. The work and pain of all this seems not to register strongly, as if the idea of love fulfilled converts all such dross to the norm of a domestic idyll in some almost compulsive way. Like Kingsley, he seems to be living out an ideology in which sexual passion, middle-class marriage and domesticity, and religious values will all be harmonized by the happy believer, whatever irrelevant complications reality may pose.

Curiously, the only threat to this religious, sexual marriage (or religion of sexual marriage) that surfaces as anxiety in Patmore himself is the danger of excess sexual passion. (The danger of patriarchal marriage that may yell out to us in this relation never bothered Patmore.) To a friend he wrote of his wish to "mortify the lusts of the flesh," perhaps reminding us of Kingsley's much more elaborate efforts against his own sexual gratification. In a private memo by Patmore to himself in 1861, in which he recites the norms he hopes to realize in his marriage, it is notable which comes first. "That in my conduct to my wife I may become more and more chaste, affectionate, tender, just, courtly, and actively pleasing and benevolent."[7] Michel Foucault speaks of the sexualization of the Victorian family as sexuality is created and confined there – as it is with something of a vengeance in Patmore's idealistic idyll of marriage in his home. Unlike Kingsley, Patmore does not attempt to create any systematic program for controlling and channeling sexual expression into the narrow path of married sex that his idealization at this period in his life, like Kingsley's throughout his mature life, alone authorized. But it is not surprising to find this advocate and model of sexual marriage also joining the mania of some parents, some religious writers, and some doctors of the age for controlling children's sexuality by getting embarrassingly involved in it. Coventry writes to his son Tennyson, away at school, to tell the truth, "and to be *pure* (you know what I mean) . . . When the other boys say and do dirty things (as many boys at all great schools will) remember these words of Jesus Christ, 'The pure in heart shall see God.'" This is glossed as "they will go to heaven" but characteristically redirected to the family by a rather dreadful threat that " If you are not pure, you will not only not see God, but you will not see your dear Mama any more when she is once gone."[8]

The tensions between the exemplary sexual role he chooses to lead (and force wife and family into) and the sexual energies released by this new focus create an almost unavoidable double bind, or at least double think, for himself, much like that involved in Kingsley's sexual *via media*. As we will see, the conflict is expressed publicly in that epic of chastely passionate marriage, *The Angel in the House*, which both tries to force sexuality into an exemplary and religiously sanctioned mold and also, by its single-minded focus on sexuality and its simple, sensuous manner, promotes a kind of hothouse sensuality. It also allows, probably promotes, as with Kingsley, expression of sadistic impulses that don't seem well understood, impulses that also recur when he imagines sexual relations too directly in his major works. In his private writing he creates a diary of his love with Emily, including abstracts of letters, that he titles Liber Amoris: his first attempt at rewriting Hazlitt's book, converting – somewhat too compulsively – uncontrolled, illicit passion into married sexual love.[9]

Despite the tensions created by his determination to embody an exemplary controlled sexuality, there is no real evidence to indicate that he would have turned away from the Victorian family life created with Emily. In his work, the successor to *The Angel in the House*, *The Victories of Love*, does show Patmore's creative interest already moving, despite the great popularity of the idyll, to problematize the sexual vision of the earlier work by a study of love unfulfilled, love forced to accept second best. But it was the death of Emily in July 1862 from tuberculosis that was the shattering, if not unexpected, occasion that moved Patmore far more decisively to a personal and imaginative life very different from the Kingsleyan one of his young adult years and earlier career. The inner ferment that created the stunning redirection of his art in the odes from this period, eventually published in *The Unknown Eros*, appears in his life as a series of radical shifts of direction. The family man temporarily allows his family to remain rather scattered among friends and relations. The Protestant mid-Victorian, responding to the climate of division in the religion of the day that sent so many either toward agnosticism or Tractarian or Catholic conservativism, journeys to Rome and converts to Catholicism. He would claim that his wife had suspected him of wishing to convert and predicted that he would do so after her death; the conversion perhaps testifies more directly to her strength within the Victorian patriarchal structure of their marriage; he needed to reach out after her death for firmer support from a religious structure.

Next, the advocate and model of sexual marriage seems to have made a virgin marriage, or, at any rate, one that seemed so cool physically as to appear to contemporaries and later observers as unconsummated. That the marriage was, in effect if not in intention, one that set him up most comfortably for life as the member of the gentry and estate-owner he had imagined his hero to be in *The Angel* only complicates the history. Finally, there is the somewhat penumbrous story of his special relation with his eldest daughter, in whose later life as a nun Patmore would seem in some sense to function even as a participant.

If the unifying idea in Patmore's life in the 1850s was presence, having relations, love, sex, family, on certain restrictive terms, the 1860s have a unity only in loss, distance, or postponement. As we saw, it was desire unfulfilled that originally touched Patmore, and to some extent one could say inspired him; it is not surprising that the sad and strange conditions of the sixties should have been most fertile ground for his work as a poet. The loss of Emily should have central attention here. Despite the remarriage and rather total redirection of his life, the failure of earthly happiness before mortality remained the central event. His most personal poems, "The Azalea" – the famous ode about dreaming his lover had died, waking with relief from the bad dream, then discovering once again that she *had* died – "Departure," on the death itself, "Eurydice," a dream of endless searching for his lost love, "The Toys," based on an anecdote about his widower's sharpness with his child and the ensuing remorse, "Tired Memory," on the loss of memory and feeling themselves, all obtain their surprising emotional force (bordering sometimes on bathos) from the inner process of adjustment to loss. Emily, doubtless the muse of *The Angel*, becomes a far stronger influence in her absence than she ever was in her presence.

In a sense his new wife, Marianne, or Mary, Byles, seconded rather than controverted that effect. She offered the strength and security of a wealthy wife to a widower perplexed by a large family while fitting the mood of sexual absence and distance. She was, indeed, mistaken by Patmore originally for a kind of nun. She had been close to the future Cardinal Manning, possibly even betrothed to him, before he converted; she followed him two years later into Catholicism and also took a vow of chastity. Patmore, in his ignorance, assumed this would make it impossible for her to marry. It isn't clear how much she had been emotionally involved with Manning and thus came to Patmore, as he to her, with a preoccupied heart. Certainly Patmore had a raging dislike for Manning that suggests jealousy at his continued influence.[10] Patmore was attracted by her preoccupation, at least as an inaccessible semi-religious, if not by the money – of which he claimed he knew nothing. She in turn admired him for the "purity" of his work (on marriage) that would not "make a child's innocence wonder."[11] Her influence probably helped move Patmore to a final decision to convert to Catholicism. Her large fortune allowed her to retire Patmore to a country seat, to maintain his children, and to continue her other-worldly ways. She appears in all accounts more as nun in residence, reserved, scarcely beautiful, uncomfortable with children and animals, devoted to her set hours of prayer, con-templation, and good works, than as wife. She wrote on the rosary and began a translation of St. Bernard of Clairvaux that Patmore ultimately completed. Her private writings celebrate not her earthly happiness in marriage but her dreams of a day when Eternal Beauty will look on the soul "in love which makes the present time an eager prayer to be made fit to comprehend the joy of which she had a taste."[12] What kind of taste of love she had with Patmore will probably remain uncertain. The most authoritative testimony, by a close friend of the family, suggests that she may have kept her vow of chastity in marriage.[13]

If the new wife offered a present absence to complement the memory of the first, Patmore's favorite daughter stood in for her mother as a very present and intimate angel, only, of course, with a perpetual prohibition to actual physical relations. The father who had inquired too closely about his son's young sexuality also tended to create a nineteenth-century sexual hothouse in his closer relations with his eldest daughter Emily, who unfortunately even shared her mother's first name. Her second name, Honoria, identifies her with the imaginary beloved of *The Angel in the House*, and in some ways she seems to have served similarly as a vehicle for Patmore's imagination as it developed in physical abstinence in the 1860s and 1870s. The special intimacy between the two is clear enough. Patmore fell in love with his daughter at first sight of her infant blue eyes, declaring he would never consent to her marrying "if she looks so handsome."[14] The casual threat became more of a psychological one after the mother's death as Patmore allowed her to play little mother, burdened her with intimate letters such as he might have written to a wife, and insisted on her companionship on his regular long walks.

As a result of this pressure, or the loss of her mother, or both, the girl grew up nervous and withdrawn, with bouts of occasional willfulness. Visions of her dead mother focussed on a figure in white taking her hand or inviting her to join her.[15] Her escape from both her father and young men, one of whom pursued her seriously, was later into a convent boarding school kept at St. Leonards by The Society of The Holy Child Jesus – and ultimately into the convent itself. At a dance at home she ran sobbing to the chapel altar, preferring to go back to school. She nonetheless was conscious of having to subdue her will. With her father she was euphorically happy, "so *very* happy."[16] Her father's "continued anxious scrutiny" of her both oppressed her and was too dear. Eventually, a nun in the convent, she gave up his company during a very troubled and dark period shortly before her death; she was preyed upon by the fear that she "had loved her father too much and been too proud of him," that he stood (like Rochester to Jane Eyre) between her and God.[17]

Both before and after she took the veil and became betrothed of Christ, she provided not only a constant companion but, even more, a focus for Patmore's creative energies. (Patmore moved near her convent and visited her regularly except during the period, very distressing to him, when she resolved not to see him.) At the estate, Heron's Ghyll, she, not her stepmother, was the model for one of the window lights of great heroines/muses from Eve to Laura and Beatrice. Patmore, who had taken over her education for a period in her teens, shared with her his poems and reflections. With her close and sympathetic reading of the odes, which were not published (except for a few privately) for many years, she became in many ways his muse and his audience. She writes to him of her appreciation, even speaks of how odes, known by heart, "say themselves to me, whether I like it or not."[18] She wrote poems herself, not striking as expressions of religious feeling but repeatedly celebrating or expressing her hopes to meet her Lord.[19] A friend could speak of her closeness in spirit with her father as of "one mind in two bodies" but they led symbiotic rather than identical existences. Like the dead wife behind him and the chaste wife beside him, she was a figure of love heightened by distance, an influence potent just because the force of romantic desire generated by a forbidden relation was largely hidden, indeed revealed itself only in the tension and excitement that drove her to distance herself. Far more than the sainted late spouse or the religious current one, she also offered a positive image of sexuality recast in religious terms. Dead to the world, she was, by her vows and the diamond ring her father bought her, a bride of Christ. The symbolic marriage was sufficiently real for her that she could write innocently of a dream of religious fulfillment from which she woke "with a throb of ecstasy."[20] As a religious she was reverenced, and perhaps feared, as one who had "seen our Lord," as a nun who especially scorned this world in her devotions to the glories of the next.

She was thus a figure for her worshipping father of mankind's potential for redirecting physical passion toward a religious ecstasy that he was not afraid to define as essentially sexual. As we will see, most of his greatest odes, following the opening series on the strength of desire produced by loss, celebrated the new fulfillment of desire in communion with Christ. In this, he gives a central place to the ritual of virginity as the fulfillment of one extreme of desire: inflamed precisely by the closing of earthly channels, those vowed to virginity arrive most easily and burningly at the broader expression of desire in the union with Christ. His excessive involvement in his daughter's life, or indeed his creation of her in his imagination, allowed the poet of married love, who had written out of his marriage, now to imagine himself in a life devoted to virginity. Sexual feeling in the newly virgin Patmore, coming from the diverse unattainable women he loved – dead wife, virgin wife, and nun daughter – almost guaranteed that he would bring a strong imagination of sexual fulfillment to the religious system he developed. His daughter, pressured and deeply troubled toward her end by her closeness to her father, impressed by his celebrations of desire in virginity, mortifying herself "extremely" with hope only to die and be received by her Lord, perhaps confirmed the father's ecstatic picture of a man's relation to Christ by dying, as it was reported, in a kind of ecstasy, welcoming, with more than natural radiance on her face, both Jesus and Mary and exclaiming on their beauty. She was only twenty-nine; as she waited two hours for Jesus to return and take her – as she pleaded for him to do when she had her deathbed vision – her father joined her in prayer, then kissed her forehead and closed her eyes; at her burial he carried one tall white lily and threw it on the coffin impressively.[21]

Sister Christina Maria had complimented her father on his ability to understand completely the "real happiness of religious life," including the nun's joy in virginity. But she also told him she especially thought of him on the Feast of the Espousals of the Blessed Virgin and was herself struck by God's special courtesy to woman in exalting Mary so highly "that enough cannot be said of her dignity."[22] It isn't clear how much this is the daughter returning the father's ideas or an indication of her influence. Gosse underlines Patmore's personal discovery of the power of the Virgin as a kind of second conversion consummated in 1877 when he made a trip to Lourdes, subsequently, as Gosse says, "the key of his life."[23] The Virgin's special kind of virginity, as specially interpreted by Patmore, became an even more central focus to his sexual and religious thinking in his later poetry – which he effectively ceased writing in 1882 after his daughter's death – and his late prose writing. The subject is itself a kind of absent presence in Patmore's work: central to the two major works he planned but never completed/published. The plans for a major poetic song on the marriage of Mary, a "majestic song in praise of the Blessed Virgin," issued only in one fine poem, "The Child's Purchase" in *The Unknown Eros*, though as we shall see this poem occupies a major end-point in that series.[24] A prose "Sponsa Dei" was apparently completed, but then burned, in a complicated reaction to questions Gerard Manley Hopkins raised about its possibly controversial subject, "the significance of physical love in religion."[25] Most of the ideas are clear from "The Child's Purchase," the passages on the virgin in *The Rod, the Root, and the Flower* – Patmore's prose restatement and expansion of themes in the odes – as well as in articles, and in writing left unpublished at his death. If in nuns Patmore found humans who especially anticipated the fulfillment of their betrothal to Christ after death, in Mary he realized the ideal of a human linked in this life to both human and divine. Her actual relation as spouse of God epitomizes and exemplifies every human's relation to divinity, without abrogating her position in the normal human community. All Patmore's emphasis is on the Virgin as exemplum for others, indeed as model of ordinary human humility despite her exalted position, rather than on her traditional role as powerful intercessor: we shall all be spouses of

God, "the very same 'great things' are done to all that fear Him that were done to the Blessed Virgin"; "the relation of the soul to Christ *as his betrothed wife*" lies at "the *burning heart of the universe.*"[26]

Patmore's idealization of Mary as a person intimately related to divinity while very much part of human life, like his similar focus in later works on the intimacy with Christ in the transubstantiation (in the mass of *this* world), suggests that his personal need was not merely for renunciation and longing for consummation after death – much as his imagination joined with, or projected his daughter, in this aim. He sought an ideal that would allow him to have it both ways, or all ways: what he would eventually call in his prose work after the odes (confusing to modern ears) that of the homo – man seen fully as masculine lover and husband, and also as a feminine spouse to Christ.

In his life such an aim led to his trying to have it all in a more literal way. Even as he was developing the intense ideal of passionate sexuality in religion out of the configuration of absences in his personal life, Patmore was probably preparing the way emotionally for a rather different accommodation. In 1869 the family made a trip abroad. A slightly older friend of the daughter Emily came along as companion. Harriet Robson was a poor Catholic girl of gentle background; she served on the trip sufficiently in the role of governess to lead to complaints by Patmore's boys of Becky Sharpism.[27] On the return she stayed as governess and companion. Doubtless more Jane Eyre than Becky, she offered Patmore someone close to his beloved daughter with whom prohibitions of incest did not stymie his emotions. There is no evidence that the relation was more than familial until Mary died in 1880, though letters printed in the authorized biography as to an intimate and sympathetic friend show that a warm and easy friendship had grown up in which Patmore bared his inmost thoughts about his work.[28] Certainly it at least grew quickly thereafter, for he married her the year after the second wife's death and proceeded to have a son by her. If Patmore had a secret life, other than in his religious thinking, we don't know of it. Derek Patmore alleges that he hid a collection of pornography behind his book-shelves;[29] yet his works are filled with apparently most sincere exhortations to purity – which is not to say to sexual ignorance.

Probably he simply controlled a warm response to the pretty young woman, young enough to be in fact his daughter's friend, until his distant and invalid wife died. Then he felt free both to marry the *de facto* mother of his younger children and to throw a fortune from his second wife's estate into building a church in her and the Virgin's honor at Hastings. His extant letters to her also do not seem to suggest that his relation was more than ordinarily warm sexually, though certainly it was that. His descendant and biographer speaks sensationally of this third-time husband, as revealed in his letters to Harriet, as "the sensualist, the Eastern lover who demands complete surrender, a being who shocks by his almost unnatural exultation in the delights of the marriage bed."[30] This hardly squares with the letters we have, unless some code of reticence has held back family shockers even in a twentieth-century biography purporting to set the earlier authorized record straight. Patmore speaks of kissing "all such perverse feelings out of you" when he returns home.[31] The letters, if anything, are less warm, personal, and aware of his correspondent than those written to her before marriage when she was less easily available.[32] He seems, as another commentator has suggested, rather like his own older lover in the poem "Amelia" (1878), who treats his young choice with understanding brought on by a certain distance in maturity: just another wife, in a universe filled with sexual connections, not, as the young man might feel, the triumph of his life. The lover in the poem is warm but patronizing. Patmore himself spoke of Harriet as "a thoroughly good and sweet little wife." At his death he put his arms around Harriet and said, "I love you dear, but the Lord is my Life and my Light."[33] Such expressions speak loudly of patriarchal attitudes but not pasha-like desires.

And there is good reason to believe that Patmore was not able to content himself with the present *nourritures terrestres* of an attractive, intelligent, responsive wife when they were placed directly at his table. For in the last years of his life he fell in love with an aristocratic Catholic of literary brilliance, Alice Meynell, whom he could admire as a remarkable star. Moreover, she was not only elevated but married. The relation has puzzled and divided biographers just because it was so clearly not a clandestine adulterous affair and because it so clearly took center place in Patmore's life from about 1891 until his death. He let everyone know of his devotion to the young, intelligent, and captivating aristocratic poet. He left his country home to pursue her at her Palace Court London residence; he praised her in his writing and nominated her for the Poet Laureateship; he told friends quite openly of his devotion; he printed her good-bye poem to him, when the affair was over, in the *Saturday*

Review;[34] above all, he made her husband, editor and man of letters Wilfrid Meynell, his special confidant!

Yet his involvement seems to have commanded very strong emotions, which are hardly those of sincere admiration for what he considered her genius and gratitude for her public praise of his own achievement (they had first met as a result of a very positive review by her in Henley's *National Observer* in 1891). Sweet wife Harriet was apparently deeply disturbed by his interest.[35] Patmore's close friend and biographer Champneys, who does not discuss the incident in his official biography, wrote privately of the "bitterness" Harriet "had to endure in later years" and speaks of a gift of a jewel, or jewels, to Meynell that seriously impaired Harriet's estate. His conclusion, that "all, I thank God, came right at the last," implies that the troubles "nobly borne" by Harriet might have led to some kind of permanent breach had not Meynell broken with Patmore.[36] Patmore, almost seventy when the relation began, became deeply involved: not only publicly admiring and doting, but privately obsessed with her well-being, offering constant advice on her health and asking to be allowed to help her in any way possible. When Meynell put an end to their intimacy about 1895 and encouraged George Meredith instead, Patmore reacted with jealousy and hurt. He told *her husband* of his pain: "my primacy in her friendship has been superseded," and he spoke bitterly to Wilfrid of "the interest your wife's name is creating in London especially in connection with her great new friendship."[37] Meynell may simply have preferred Meredith to him, but her poem, "Why wilt thou chide," which she published and he republished praising her and calling it her "Belle Dame Sans Merci," suggests there had been some crisis. Whether there was a bid for physical love (the poem was about a kiss) or for some other commitment, her answer is, as he himself explained it, a compliment to the "one lover who has come so close as to be denied."[38]

It is probably beside the point to argue over whether this was a physical or a platonic passion. Patmore found in the situation exactly the strength of attraction in remove that he desired. It was characteristic of Patmore, from his first adolescent love to his most exalted religious reveries, to be most fully stimulated to sexual attraction by such a context of desire. Patmore told Francis Thompson, after the break, that "*Dieu et ma Dame*, is the legend of both of us. But at present Ma Dame is too much for the balance, peace and purity of my religion. There is too much heartache in it."[39]

Patmore was alluding to his own essay on the two loves of man but also, more broadly, to a tradition of humble devotion to a *dame* in which he seems to have cast his desire. Perhaps the way of conceiving the relation was Meynell's herself, since she moved easily from one literary servant to another while writing home affectionately, as she did from Patmore's house, to "my poor boy," Wilfrid. Yet Patmore's own recent essay had also reasserted the tradition of service based on "a mysterious longing for corporeal and spiritual captivity to the beloved."[40] Like a courtly lover, he saw himself indeed as in service: "For the past four and a half years I have devoted myself exclusively to her service and would have gladly done so during the rest of my life."[41] For Meynell the service of this aging, soon visibly declining knight of passion brought a black moment when she heard of his death in 1896 and a bitter memory of her own unworthiness in such cases: she felt she had not been able to respond as she would have wished to those who loved her. Yet this was hardly a failure for Patmore, who took her rejection, like a quixotic lover in a Browning monologue, as a challenge for the next world. His final word to her was a stern, hortatory note to take her own best moods seriously, as he did his: "Our meeting again in Heaven depends on your fidelity to the highest things you have known."[42]

Was this a glorious ending for a man whose central concern had been with sexuality throughout his career? Was it a scandalous one? We can easily imagine, and even perhaps for a moment enjoy, the Protestant scorn Kingsley would bring to this tale of Catholic loves, lovers, husbands, and wives. An aging patriarch, not content with the serial devotions of three wives and a virgin daughter ending with a public chase after an unattainable object? Was it also merely human? Why should not old men, especially poets, carry passionate hearts in aging frames? Certainly, it is entirely consistent with the experience of sexual desire that he had pursued in his life and kept exploring in so much of his work that his last personal relation should specifically follow, and allude to, the great tradition in the Western world of desire promoted by unavailability, that of adulterous service. The poet who is still perhaps best known as the advocate of Victorian domestic happiness was above all a man and writer who explored the power of sexual desire in itself, a power that needed an object to be realized at all, yet grew in strength in not apprehending the object. The year 1895, when his relation with Meynell came to its final crisis, was also the year in which he published his fine essay, *The*

Rod, the Root, and the Flower, where he elaborated the brilliantly
expressed insights of his masterwork, the odes of *The Unknown Eros*, in
a series of highly polished and penetrating aphorisms. There he
reflected over the odd working of desire that he had experienced
again and again in his life as further steps in the exploration of a
general mystery – "a dark, conspicuous, and insoluble enigma" –
that was for him, as his works proclaim with increasing directness, the
center of existence, the "source of all love, and of the celestial
decorum of the universe."[43]

THE UNKNOWN EARLY POEMS

Behind his work the inspiration in Patmore's life, from first to last
love, seems thus rather continuous and consistent. But the issue of
whether Patmore's works themselves are all of a piece or show a
distinct change with Emily's death and his conversion has been
almost ritually debated by his commentators from Gosse on.[44]
Stemming perhaps from extra-literary concerns about establishing
Patmore's position as an English rather than half-Anglican, half-
Catholic writer, the compulsion to assert a unity seeks and finds
evidence of Patmore's early concerns with the manifest sexual themes
of his odes and later prose work. Like Clough and Kingsley, Patmore
was precociously and then persistently fascinated with sexual
relations and, as much or more than they, he instinctively searches,
as he follows his experience, for logical or rhetorical strategies by
which he can relate sexual themes to broad ways of conceiving of
experience, especially religious ones. In terms of ideology one can
read Patmore's works almost as an emerging text, in which shadows
and types of ideas that will later be fully articulated haunt his text
from the beginning. And the commentators who work in an
ecumenical spirit are not wrong to insist on continuity from
Protestant to Catholic ideology, with new elaborations rather than
total reversal of his thoughts. Of course, these new ideas are central
Catholic concerns, ones that no Kingsley could glide over easily, with
the uses of virginity and celibate religious orders, with the Virgin
Mary herself, and with the nature of Communion. But his focal
interest in bridging the worlds of sexuality and religion is continuous;
far from sacrificing his private opinions on the rock of Church
authority, he found increased justification for his own esoteric and

eccentric religious spirit within the Catholic Church so that, if anything, conversion offered him more latitude to pursue his prior speculations to more extreme conclusions.

I think it is important, really essential, to make a case nonetheless for the radical difference between Patmore's earlier and later works, most especially between the two works we know, *The Angel in the House* of his early middle career and his mature masterwork, *The Unknown Eros*. This issue is finally not so much one of changing opinions in the work but of quality and recognition of an important voice in English literature now almost totally neglected. We open the Oxford edition of the poems, if we can find it (there is no Patmore in print at this writing), or worse, we turn to the first of the older two-volume poetical works, and find hundreds of pages of competent writing before we come to achievements of genius. The case would be the same if was had Wordsworth presented to us in reverse chronology, with all that competent work of his later Romantic and Victorian careers before his major earlier work. For Patmore was one of those Modern or Yeatsian, rather than Romantic, writers who greatly improved with the years. Though some individual odes are abysmal, *The Unknown Eros* as a whole is a stunning, resplendent work, certainly the most important group of odes by an English writer after Keats. His later prose, especially *The Rod, the Root, and the Flower*, which I will not try to look at here in detail, offers exceedingly lively aphoristic reflections that force us to stretch and revaluate habitual modes of thinking as Sir Thomas Browne's, Blake's, Carlyle's, or Nietzsche's writings do. They are permanently interesting works of literature, if not quite among the half-dozen masterpieces of Victorian literature.

It isn't a matter of a sprouting of new talent with replaced brain cells, any more than one can really believe in a diagnosis for Wordsworth's decline as a matter of subsiding abilities. Patmore's abundant talents were apparent from the first: his early publication, at age twenty-one, of a volume of *Poems*. Critical appraisal of such an early work was naturally mixed.[45] But there seemed little question of the talent demonstrated by the son of the tarnished but also clearly talented father. Tennyson would befriend him, Milnes would offer patronage, the Pre-Raphaelites and Ruskin found a fellow spirit and possible fellow-traveler. No one denied that this was a major new force in Victorian poetry. Browning, facing the wreck of his reputation as a rising star occasioned by the brilliant but very poorly received *Sordello*, looked on Patmore, with perhaps some nervousness, as a fresher rising star. His generous recollection, forty years later, was of that very positive impression – "of the genius which came on us all by surprise in your first volume."[46]

The modern reader, perhaps a woman moved to find out what the angel in *The Angel in the House* really is about, will wonder about such talk. She, or he, will find much talent in Patmore's first poems in the collections, but it won't be in those early poems, which have been virtually edited away by the author, who kept restlessly revising, deleting, and excluding them in later editions; now they are available only in a few major libraries or rare book collections. Certainly the talent is apparent in the long two-part story of Felix and his bride Honoria that forms the first two books of *The Angel in the House*. The reader may even come away with a better idea of Patmore: the angel, after all, is not a woman on a pedestal but the spirit of love; Patmore has some good things to say about the mutual respect and independence that makes a good marriage; he has some acute psychological insights and shares with Kingsley a generally positive attitude toward sex in marriage; this is finally not middle-class but aristocratic marriage, a marriage of true minds and comfortable financial independence, that mutes the patriarchal power structure in his traditional vision. There may even be some interest in the cameo social view of the whole, a pretty little period piece of the Anglican gentry of England as seen by the idealizing eye of a British Museum librarian hungry for the traditional promised land of landed culture. Like all antiques this Biedermeier vision, as Mario Praz typed it, will doubtless be subject to revival and renewed curiosity, despite its present disgrace as the chauvinist work chosen by feminist critics of all persuasions for a ritual jet-plane humiliation. We find in the verse itself moments of a more interesting revival, a return to some of the brilliance of metaphor and conceit, the witty conjunction of seemingly unrelated qualities by a line of argument, that charac- terizes English poetry of the seventeenth-century.[47]

The potential is there, but where is the genius? Close the book, let the dust settle again, Patmore has had his chance – unless the volume should open in the back pages to the very different order of expression in *The Unknown Eros*!

The difference has something to do not with finding new talents, not with a change in focus or theme, but in the poet's relation to his work. There is some kind of block in the work, right up to the writing of the odes, that keeps Patmore's full strengths from coming into play. It is certainly not a writer's block of the common sort. Blessed and cursed with the honorific title of minor poet Patmore may be; but his output is nothing of the sort. If he weren't also so prolific as a rewriter, editor, and shrinker of his own canon he would have left us in the collected works many hundred more pages of verse to work through before we came to the odes. Patmore's ruthless cutting and recasting of his earliest work in fact presents an additional obstacle to understanding properly the failure of the first half of his career. His editing, mostly done in the early 1850s when he was planning and writing *The Angel in the House*, as we shall see, in effect imposed the values of that period on his earlier work; it left very little at all. The later Patmore cut even more determinedly, leaving only a meager remnant in his collected poems that barely suggests an earlier career to the reader of the later edition. For a while he even turned on the entire four books of *The Angel* and *The Victories of Love* and tried to repress them, though he relented ultimately and left them as the formidably sized dragons at the gates for anyone beginning his poetry. If the earlier work had been left too, as perhaps it will be some day in a much needed historical edition of his works, the modern reader might actually have been more encouraged than she is today as she first confronts *The Angel*. Both states of his early career, as he rightly judged, show a problem of abundance. But the excess of his earliest work is in many ways, if not better in ultimate quality, at least more interesting and more promising.

If we bother, as I and, I think, very few other readers have, to go back to those rare early volumes and read Patmore's abundant earlier works as they actually appeared, we find that those early poems, especially those in the first volume of 1844, are surprisingly direct, even outspoken in the subjects they treat and range of interests they offer; they are also remarkably diffuse and experimental in attitudes and viewpoint, going far beyond mere dialogics to the point of incoherence. By contrast, *The Angel* poems of the 1850s, though abundantly long, show far more conscious control, even to the point of suppressing much of what makes the early poems exciting or fun in the interest of promoting one point of view; there the abundance seems repetitive more than incoherent, as if Patmore were trying to persuade himself as well as his reader.

In the earliest published work, that easy abundance of talents, the rich fountain of language and especially imagery that were often identified with romantic genius was certainly the young Patmore's. He emerged in a poetic milieu of the late 1830s and 1840s that still could authorize and encourage such a notion of genius as a direct outpouring of verbal gifts. His father, preoccupied with his own relations to men of genius of the Romantic age, the subject of his still-interesting memoirs, *My Friends and Acquaintance*, made contact with immortals seem easy. As lightly, he bestowed the laurel of genius on his son before any race had been run. His frame tale for the retold stories of *Chatsworth* brings together representative literary spirits of his age and adds a young man "The Boy Poet," down with his father and preparing for university. The experienced literary man in some sense sets his son up for literary failure, as his business speculations would soon betray the young Patmore's hopes to go to university. The boy poet is more poetry than maker of poems: "lithe," "Fragile" in form with a "small exquisitely modelled head" like young Coventry himself, he is lost in his own thoughts (which are for him feelings), lost in other literature (Milton just now), lost in the "poetry born of his dreams," which he rates even above Milton. He thinks of poetry not as a written text but as "the great poetical archetype existing in his own mind." The paternal friend of poets then quotes Wordsworth's Immortality Ode to explicate the boy's idea of clouds of glory still trailing within that is alike the poet and his poetry. He then proposes an even more appropriate image of the boy's psychic state, that of an "immortal *infancy* – the *face* alone of a sleeping infant – sleeping, – but dreaming; – an infant's face in the sky, dreaming, amidst those 'clouds of glory' which its Creator had breathed about it, and which the first touch of earth would melt and dissipate."[48] It is an attractive image, despite the too-literary language, one indeed that the son, by reminiscence or coincidence, would use in the fine ode "Winter."[49] The father's undercutting praise puts heavenly poetic insight on the side of inexpression as well as ineffability. The boy poet dreams of an infant poet who can have no productive contact with the outer world. Genius has nothing to say.

But of course young genius has been reading intensively, Milton most recently. Young genius writes intensively too, and when he does he tends to trail the glories of his reading; the archetype he first discovers is more nearly the types of the literary past than, to follow Browning's language in his Essay on Shelley, the "Ideas of Plato, seeds of creation lying burningly on the Divine Hand." The brief but fascinating picture of literary father and son suggests the precariousness of the son's endeavor. He may aspire to the role of seer and the father will applaud him as he did his own Romantic "friends." But as the father would in fact leave him without a university education or patrimony, he also leaves him in his portrait without an occupation, poet without a clear role or a plan for writing. He leaves him to display his genius by abundant language, echoes of abundant reading, but a lack of deliberate personal intention.

In approaching the resulting abundant early poems before *The Angel* it is hard not to focus more on how much Patmore later obliterated than on what and how much he wrote. Poem after poem of the 1844 volume is thrown out, rewritten, or torn in pieces for later volumes, beginning with the 1853 and 1854 *Tamerton Church-Tower and Other Poems*, only of course to be much further purged for the final edition. One senses not just an instinct for revision and improvement but a tremendous discontent and frustration with his own productions. His Saturnian rage against his own efforts suggests some extreme sense of failure, as if he was aware of the lack of coherence and thought that he might revise and excise into better shape.

It also seems likely that he came to understand the reasons for his failure in the very vitality and unresolved nature of his perceptions: a creative chaos, arising from his first instinct merely to explore experimentally sexual feelings and attitudes, that initially scared him by its abundance and lack of control. There is even a sense, in the usually constraining, sometimes reductive or bowdlerizing nature of his revisions, that he was sufficiently distressed by his early insights to wish to try to conceal his knowledge from both readers and himself. For when we bother to unearth the original poems of 1844 we find there, if not major art, at least freshness and boldness that Browning and others who greeted the very young poet might rightly have taken, along with the fluency, as signs of genius. There is a decided bravery in presenting sexual issues that may have caused Browning, for the first time in his bold young career, to have imagined a new generation on his heels. Indeed, we can more easily imagine this experimental young Victorian poet developing into the astonishing boldness of the author of *The Unknown Eros* than we can the young middle-aged poet who wrote *The Angel in the House*.

His first poems also show some of the openness to varied interpretation that Browning was beginning to obtain so effectively in his dramatic monologues. The difference is that Patmore's uncertainty seems not so much a matter of his deliberately exploiting a certain kind of poetry for its multivalent or dialogic qualities as his eschewing any attempt at authorial control.[50] Patmore tends to create not clear dramatic voices to represent the viewpoint of others but vague narrative presences for which, as author, he seems to take no responsibility. Coleridge is an obvious early influence: the dubiously antique, unclearly placed ballad voice of *Christabel* rather than the dramatic speaker of "Frost at Midnight." Where there is a more specific speaker, as in the poem "Lilian," Patmore distinguishes himself by refusing to take responsibility for the story he presents, the ranting and first-person history of a distraught friend. The strategy may indicate the immaturity of a poet's utterances before he had found his voice. But it is used not as a way of avoiding statement, rather as a device to allow easy and seemingly unpremeditated contact with whatever voices he might find within. There even seems a hope in his speaking an earlier voice of ballad that some "artless" expression could be given to a happy and simple truth of human nature.

As in the young Clough, and in some sense in Kingsley's entire career, this especially takes the form of a hope to speak a paradisaical sexuality, to find that he trails, all unawares, clouds of glory from an unfallen Adam within. As we have seen, it was a tenet throughout Patmore's life that there were such "auras of delight" that could be found within, generally by going back to the moment of awakening to love in childhood.[51] His first poems are a kind of experiment in an artless art that might make the latest and least-directed voice also the clearest testimony to the truths of human nature. In a kind of sexual rewriting of Wordsworth's "The Tables Turned" ("One impulse from a vernal wood"), Patmore's "Sonnet III" proclaims that he had been "love's wilting page" at age nine but had estranged love by using his "prodigal pen"; only the better artist, pretty village girl without art, could bring back love.[52] An artless narrator of the longer poem "Sir Hubert" (republished, much revised, under the title "The Falcon") also offers himself as love's poet, who has seen his soul as love's priestess, his body as her "pure fane." More, love is for him religious in ultimate implication, "the way, the truth, the life" (p. 106). At the moment, like the Romantic poets he follows, he has left boyhood exaltation and found not God but dejection. He suffers from darkness now and a taste of death. Nor can he find the inner resources to pray to love to restore his former state. In this predicament

Coleridge turned to the violence of a coming storm to inspirit himself to some passion. Patmore's speaker turns, he says, to "hot thoughts"; what he means, he shows us, is passion in a form that will restore his early simple faith in love as the blessed rule of earth and heaven. So he calls for a song of "some passion sane and strong" which is declared to be a matter of a song of "steady love well guerdon'd," a testimony to "God's earthly perfect plan, / The melody of woman / Making harmony with man" (pp. 107-8).

One is left staring at the tale of Sir Hubert, by love possessed, that is then offered as if in answer to these prayers. Sir Hubert, wealthy and pure of heart, loves the lovely Mabel. With his handsome looks and more handsome estates he can hardly fail to obtain happiness, we imagine. The narrator intrudes, however, to warn us that another fiction is brewing: "God holds such men worthy / To be glorified by grief" (p. 110). Mabel prefers another; Sir Hubert loses all his possessions as well – except a small holding and fine falcon, which provides him food and gives him, with its large lovely eyes like Mabel's, loving companionship. The poor man bears up until, on a day, Mabel visits and asks for dinner. Sir Hubert, still in love, finds his cupboard bare and in desperation slaughters the beloved falcon and serves it up roasted. Patmore might as well have had an English gentleman serve up his dog! After this outrageous display of masochistic indulgence, it is hardly surprising to find that the path of true love also runs crookedly over Mabel's husband and her child – both put out of the way so that, falcon sacrificed, Sir Hubert can finally win dear Mabel.

They end with a hot embrace – "Vigorous lips for answer press! / Feasting the hungry silence" (p. 151) – and the narrator, as if oblivious to the implications of his story (for instance, that "feasting"), proclaims the restorative power of such a "sober song" (p. 152). He goes on to reassert the power of love as a heaven-sent instrument for the soul's redemption. Does he recognize the incongruity between his use of his material and the clear story of the material itself? Perhaps, but only very obliquely. A secondary word of the prologue is of the danger of turning love into an idol: "The man that loves a woman / Loves his passion more than half" (p. 153) – certainly a conclusion better fitted for the material.

"Sir Hubert" is a naive but not a stupid or dully presented poem. Without the presence of the narrator, we would be less egregiously surprised by the masochistic indulgence in Hubert's odd version of a sane and strong love. Other poems exhibit the same conflict between idealistic hopes and more realistic perceptions, but, with less obtrusive narrators, the poems allow more direct negative statements. Some poems speak, like Wordsworth's ballads, from the pathos of common human experience, rendered as a sad folk wisdom. "Dear Mother Do Not Blame Me" lets speak the young woman who could not "say him nay" when she met her lover by moonlight: "why do you say it was not right?" (p. 19). Another ("I Knew a Soft-Eyed Lady") renews a man's grief over the death of his lover when he hears a voice like hers in the street (pp. 21–22). Such voices, not quite fully realized dramatic monologues, allowed Patmore to release feelings about the anxieties or loss involved in sexual experience that his narrative voice might have disallowed.

In a longer precociously imitative poem, "The River," the sexually threatening and mysterious gothic aura of Coleridge's "Christabel" is converted to a more direct ballad of loss. The plot also parodies and subverts that of Keats's "The Eve of St. Agnes"; here a true lover fails to act, leaving his true lady to marry the wrong person. The surprising power of the poem stems from its discovery of the potent feelings associated with sexual denial and loss. The poem presents itself as literally aghast at the proceedings it authors. It is specifically the soul – of the deprived lover, of the narrator, of the reader – which is made aghast by the tale. In a story of marriage we are asked to see only the reverse side of what would normally be expected: we see only failed fulfillment. We look at the fainthearted lover rather than the couple in the marriage bed in the old castle that he looks at. Posed by a lightning-cleft tree, the symbol of constant/ ruptured love that Charlotte Brontë would soon inscribe permanently in English literature, he exists in a natural scene of corresponding deprivation, wan, cold, and jagged moon, trembling willows, fast-flowing deep river. In the original (1844) version, the lover's death seems almost a sexual consummation, a merging in loss with the universe that mimics, as Georges Bataille would insist it must, the little death beyond human boundaries of sex:[53]

> A plunge! – a thin hand through the froth –
> A stifled gurgling sound: –
> The circlets dance, with lurid glance
> Like witches, round and round;
> Big bubbles rise, like demons' eyes;
> The wavelets skip and bound. (p. 12)

His suicide touches his lover in her bridal bed as nothing that night has. In her sleep she groans and, pale herself, seems also to roll "down a frightful tide" (p. 12). This imaginative mutual consummation *is* the marriage night celebrated by the tale. It finds an appropriate symbolic projection in Patmore's first (of many) emblems of religious virginity. He associates with the suicide lover an oriel in the old hall still portraying the Catholic English world of "nun and saint devout." In this perpetual virgin isolation – both as cold artworks and as professed religious – they enshrine the "aghast-ness" that Patmore intends the reader to share with the narrator. "Faded nuns stare through the gloom / Askaunt, and wan, and blear"; "wither'd cheeks of watchful saints / Start from their purple gear." The intense feeling released by sexual loss finds a correlative in Catholic virginity, a precocious and striking adaption of the gothic apparatus with which the young Protestant happened to work. Virginity is already a highly charged issue: not a mere blank set beside the hope of consummation but an intense feeling that dominates the entire being and ultimately the entire poem. Patmore would attempt to explain the potency of sexual loss that his remarkable poem discovers, for instance providing in 1853–54 a more ordinary economic motive for the true lovers' estrangement. Eventually his finest art would take him back to the constellation of religious virginity and sexual loss that he happened upon so early.

In these early poems sexual knowledge seems to appear as a discovery to the author himself. A rather nasty poem, not reprinted by Patmore, "'Tis fine, I vow, to see you now," a meditation on a flirty beauty, eventually discloses with sadistic iteration the speaker's rather violent antipathy. After acknowledging her present charms, he pictures her "finer much" when she is in "Time's full clutch," dead to all former joys, dead indeed to "everything but death" (pp. 48–49). Two longer poems not only evidence their surprise in the experiences they discover; they also trace the source of sexual problematics to the nature of the writing that brings them to us. They lead him to the verge of the difficult discovery of his later work: how sexual disappointment or failure allow access to the power of desire by freeing it from any particular context. Patmore came close to this realization in his very probing early work, only to evade the logical sequence to his line of thinking for many years during his *Angel in the House* period. "Lilian" in 1844 is a poem unclear about it status: comedy or serious story of loss? Patmore allows a comic flexibility by creating a narrator who presents, without endorsing it, the ranting tale of a friend who lost his love Lilian to a Frenchified and treacherous friend Winton. The actual story, framed as narration, is also thematically secondary: broken-hearted Percy rants primarily about the dangers of the written word, only secondarily about the betrayal that he sees as its necessary consequence. It is not just a Frenchified rival but his cursed French novels that have ruined his life. Patmore took out most of this theme in his total rewriting ("The Yew-Berry," 1853–54), perhaps rightly, but there is an adolescent abundance and fun in the earlier work just because the narrator need take no responsibility for his friend's excessive language. Unfortunately for the narrator, Percy finds him reading a "brilliant French romance" (p. 52). Percy dashes the novel to the ground and generally lashes out at "These literary panders / Of that mighty brothel, France." The story that follows this condemnation and justifies it is literally one of seduction by the book. Winton has returned from France laden with them – French books, "essay, poem, and romance." They have aroused him: "his blood might boil and gush / Over scenes which set his visage glowing crimson" (p. 71). He has easily succeeded in stealing Lilian away from Percy by letting his books do the work for him. Percy, merely browsing through one volume, stops in horror, fearful that such rancid writing will "petrify" his soul.

Percy's tale cleverly untells its own simple story of chauvinistic censorship. Percy has been deceived, then is put on track by an accidental revelation. In order to understand what has been going on he adopts the author's stance, writes out his own history as he now believes it to have been, and confronts the unhappy Lilian. In doing so he solves his personal dilemma but, of course, writes a very French tale, a triangle of seduction, betrayal, and innocence let into experience. His own experienced view thus gives him the insight of those French novels he still wishes to condemn. After explaining how he unriddled the riddle and fathomed how the French drugs worked a "flood" of passion in Lilian's virgin blood, he gives way to his own passion in pages of heavy rant. In a word, we see him as not only the teller of a sexual tale, but as the bearer of those strong passions that are the stuff of the French novel that he excoriates. In case the point isn't sufficiently clear, Patmore has also allowed us to see two sides of even the Frenchified Winton: he has appealed to Percy as a friend just because he speaks so well of love, including elegant praise of Lilian.

The point is really one about writing sex: knowledge of sex necessarily comes as a discourse on sexuality, one that finds its natural home in written language. Percy's tale, with its heavy attitudinizing carefully placed under suspicion by the framing narrator, who himself sees some use in education of the passions, states a universal problem of sexual experience: since the Fall, language has brought awareness of sexuality, with all its potential for intense bad – or good. Much as Percy may wish – perhaps like young Patmore himself – to avoid the painful side, even potential desolations, of knowledge of sexuality, understanding itself comes with a full baggage of good and evil: to have understanding at all is to accept the full awareness that Patmore himself offers rather painedly.

This is the realization structured into another tale, good enough that Patmore preserved it for his final works, though with changes that muted its implications. The woodman's daughter, of the poem of that name, befriends the squire's son. In this prefiguration of the *Adam Bede* story, both are true innocents who nonetheless fall into a tragic history. In Percy's hysteria over French fictions he sees a threat to his entire society. In this tale, society seems already eliminated as an organizing or restraining influence in sexual experience. The woodman allows an inappropriate relation to flower beneath his nose. After the fact he brings his daughter's guilt into focus and dies (or by dying). The broader society comes in only vaguely as a kind of chorus that wonders at the daughter's final plight yet cannot know the entire story as we come to know it. The children's seduction is not merely a matter of nature's triumph, however. They are corrupted, as Eve by Satan in the Garden, by words. Only, again, it is the written word and in fact it is the Adam figure, Merton, rather than the daughter Maud who first succumbs. He tires of their Edenic idyll of friendship in nature and begins to talk to Maud about his reading. She initially resists such book knowledge, which in her innocence she turns back into oral fable and romance (p. 28). Yet love poems especially are sweet to her and do their work. Patmore handles nicely the dawning self-consciousness and embarrassment that awaken in the children along with their desire. As Maud begins to ask difficult questions, Merton makes it clear that they should be referred to the primary source of awakening, the books themselves. "If, Sweet" – he answers her – "if poets fail to explain this to you, how shall I?" The past delivers its burden of embarrassment to them and after such awareness comes passion. In a powerful and, for the 1840s, relatively direct scene of initiation, they rush off, faster and faster, into the woods. Full sexual arousal comes with completed and isolating self-consciousness. He wears "cheeks ridged with a strong smile"; her face has a "serious cast." They no longer talk or see anything in their beloved natural world.

The sex itself appears in the text, appropriately enough, as a very pregnant set of printer's marks:

$$* \quad * \quad * \quad *$$
$$* \quad * \quad * \quad *$$

It has been a classic case of seduction by the text. Patmore wastes little time on the subsequent guilt, birth of an illegitimate child, death of the father, murder of the child, and Maud's final state of crazed grief. She is a figure out of Wordsworth's ballads, with a difference; her fall is explicitly mediated by past words. Her awareness of guilt comes only when she confronts her father's adult knowledge. The final picture we have of her comes back to books themselves. Feeling her guilt in every ray of sunshine and every bell that rings, she goes daily to the scene of her crime; there, as if to indicate the source of the force that has worked through her, she goes back to the word: "Maud, with her books, comes day by day, / Fantastically clad, / To read them near the pool" (p. 44).

In this tale of tragic sexual initiation Patmore creates a version of sexuality as something which is virtually imposed upon consciousness through the texts of the past. The resentment of textuality in both this tale and in "Lilian," often excessive or a bit absurd, suggests that the young Patmore still harbored an opposing view of an Edenic realm of unconscious sexual gratification. As in almost all these tales, sexuality appears, however, almost entirely as a phenomenon of consciousness; and most often that consciousness is of fall, loss, or pain, of an Eden lost, not of a lost Eden. As in "Lilian" there is a salient irony in finding this message in a written tale: young Patmore, as an author venturing boldly into a broad discussion of sexual issues in his first published volume, becomes another link in a chain of inherited written texts about sex. Because his own work is still obviously dependent on past language, and often shows an unsure authorial presence, it seems, more especially than many works – certainly more than Patmore's own later works – written by a tradition of discourse in which it takes its place. Of course, the tradition itself is, as generally in the nineteenth century, a mixed discussion of varied points of view, not one master position. Patmore plays his prescribed part in inscribing the sexual heritage even as one of his major themes begins to emerge as that of the tyranny of past sexual language.

Were he to have faced this irony head-on he might have drawn out the important, and to a large extent freeing, awareness that stares at us from this work: that he has discovered the independence of sexual discourse – sexuality – from the physical reality of the experience itself – sex. If sexuality is a creation of words, then the author might free himself from the burden of past modes of conceiving of sex, even possibly relieve the heavy or tragic perceptions presented in most of these tales and poems, by creating other language or restructuring the entire enterprise. But the most important implication, which Patmore by and large evades until his great odes, is that language about sex creates its own, different, world of sexuality. If sexuality is language, then there is always the possibility that language itself can constitute an area of sexual experience with its own compelling force. The simple label we have become used to using for this phenomenon in general is of course sublimation, the diversion of sexual energies into a cultural activity, of which language would be an egregious example. Although we may, albeit usually sloppily, speak of some kinds of verbal activity as sublimation, we do not usually apply this conception to language that speaks directly about sex. Pornography, for instance, even in its root meaning of writing about prostitutes, proclaims its divorce – as writing – from the physical experience of prostitutes (though it may then use every verbal art to try to evade the word and present the exciting thing, the body sex part). Yet generations of arguments over what pornography is and what it does have agreed perhaps on only one thing: that it is a form of sex in itself, therefore subject or therefore not subject to social controls. Are you sublimating reading this? Or I in writing it? Do we think of Freud and his successors in their writings as indulging in one of the most massive campaigns of sublimation the world has even known?[54] The experience of sex is too tied up in its varied representations in image and language for us to think of language about sex as sublimation of sex.

By the same token, there remains something shocking in the recognition we necessarily have when we become self-aware about our words about sex, that our conceptions of sexuality are necessarily language, not physical or even psychological reality. Sexuality is sex in the head, of its very nature. Patmore's early and persistent interest in the relation between language and sexual experience at least prepared the way for a literature in his later work that accepted this middle position of sexual writing between sex itself as a physical activity and cultural activities sufficiently far from description of sex acts to seem diversions or sublimations of sexual energies.

It has seemed worth this full a look at the early stage of Patmore's poetic work in order to see more clearly the dynamics of his later career. There is precocious facility and fluidity in verse, which continues in his work of the 1850s. But his first appearance shows an equally precocious awareness of the variety and force of sexual experience, with a surprising openness to the dangers and pain that are often also involved. His position seems to be that of a poet virtually surprised by the discoveries of his own pen; and he tends more often to blame the heritage of literature and language that allows him such disturbing expressions than to face their full implications. To do so is to admit his own excessive state of being written by his culture. Perhaps more accurately, he is written by feelings – for which he consciously refuses to take full responsibility – in the language of the past.

The severe self-criticism involved in the subsequent dismemberment, excision, and finally suppression of most of these works doesn't lead him to take responsibility for his striking perceptions or to cast them in a language less burdened by literary paraphernalia of the past. Further, he consciously acts to evade responsibility, to cover the tracks of his uneasy perceptions. "The Woodman's Daughter" is revised, first in *Tamerton Church-Tower and Other Poems* (1853–54) to reduce, later fully to eliminate, the scene of self-seduction; it is shrunk to fit the form of mere Victorian melodrama. "Lilian" is dismembered to create the more artful but far less interesting "The Yew-Berry," where there is again a melodramatic focus: the bittersweet berry of love found and lost – with most of the playful rant at French novels removed. Some of the perplexity of "Sir Hubert" is retained in the tale itself but Patmore drops the frame, which reveals too much of his own uncertainty and dismay over the realities of love. Other poems are simply quietly dropped. As he virtually suppressed these works Patmore seems to have also recognized his failure to shape his early works to express a conscious intention. His new writing of the 1850s moves toward much more directed work, until, in *The Angel in the House*, it reaches the opposite extreme of excessive control. The new poems of his 1853–54 volumes, the first harvest of the years of family crisis, marriage, and increasing critical judgment from a good deal of excellent work in reviews, show Patmore creating a new kind of poetry while still struggling interestingly with some of the troubling issues raised in the first volume. Poems such as "The Golden Age" – a sentimental tribute to youth by one not much beyond it – "Night and Sleep" (1854) – a poem aimed at evacuating night of its anxiety and mystery – or "Reprobate" – a sermonic diatribe against a stereotype of a bad man – attain rhetorical coherence at the expense of emotional interest or imaginative force. A two-part poem on "Little Edith" displays its own determination to avoid wayward or troubling thoughts by its self-injunctions to "think of" the innocent qualities of little Edith as a device for maintaining rectitude. Even so, we begin to feel the poem unraveling its own conflation of innocence and morality as the second part suggests that the speaker is not a fatherly figure with a daughter but a November husband leaning on his April wife for guidance. The unacknowledged sexuality of their relation threatens the entire construct.

The conflict between insight and control is especially clearly displayed in the long title poem, "Tamerton Church-Tower," the last of Patmore's pre-*Angel* narrative poems. This is modeled more on Tennysonian domestic idylls, with its realistic social context, than the romantic storybook types of the earlier poems. However, Patmore gives the narration to his central character, a young man of uncertain self-understanding, who indeed provides the poem's primary interest by his vacillating and unsteady perspective. And the subjectivity of his view is foregrounded by the ballad stanza from the intensely inward *The Rime of the Ancient Mariner*. The tale is of an ordinary journey with friend Frank, who is marrying. The journey soon assumes symbolic resonance as a kind of brief but emphatic expedition into sexual awakening – and out again. In a kind of dreamy compliance with his friend's direction, the speaker also falls in love with a maid named Blanche, marries her, enjoys a brief idyll, especially in a rowing trip on a placid ocean, loses his wife in a sudden storm on the same ocean, and eventually makes a return trip to the starting beacon of Tamerton church-tower. We know he is a sadder man; he believes he is wiser. The poem seems to split into two perspectives: the dreamlike but emotionally credible account of the sudden movement into passion and sexual exposure; and the subsequent, not entirely persuasive, moralizing on the value of his loss as an experience that builds character. He confesses himself at the opening living in a "land of dreams" where nothing seems to thrive.[55] The new dreams that come with sudden immersion in love and marriage seem overwhelming. His friend hastened him on by light talk of female bosom and waist; the narrator clearly wants "all that" only as a kind of inner need that he doesn't much comprehend; he finds his very veins filled with "love like Ichor." The rich imagery, drawn from Arthurian tales that the couples tell in their row-boat expedition, suggests a high anxiety that accompanies love fulfilled. They travel in a hot summer prime when "the wasp / lay gorged within the peach" (p. 24). This sense of a danger in excess is then repeated in a story of Sir Lob who, drunk, succeeds in getting himself drowned. Blanche is the speaker's idol, goddess and saint, yet the story that more sensible Frank tells is of how Pelles finally turned light Ettarde from his heart. The speaker feels a foreboding terror that undoes the joy of his idyll; soon the plot of his tale confirms this anxiety in the objective terms of storm and drowning.

In these scenes, the poem's openness, especially to readings of the speaker's insecurity, even terror, at the sudden experience that seems so little under his control, follows the best of Patmore's 1844 work, and in a more impressive diction with richer metaphorical and allusive resonance. As with those poems there is even a feeling of uncontrol, which here nicely fits the narrator's own failure of self-understanding. The poem is then taken into aesthetic and emotional custody and pulled rather violently toward a single meaning. The speaker's grief is not faced but whirled away in a flutter of years, as in a 1930s film. His own unconvincing moralizing on the use of grief, which tends to seal away any real feeling from both his consciousness and ours, is unfortunately confirmed by the story and the external commentators placed by the author in the story. What could have been a further interesting look at the way grief is deliberately not faced is nullified by the complicity of the author in closing off the tale. The speaker reads purpose and hope in the workers, ore works, and railroad train he passes as he journeys out of the world of sex, summer, and sea. He returns to friend Frank, father, and religion – in the person of a vicar. All agree in offering a new world of sage saws and pithy morals to replace that of frantic passion. The vicar preaches the use of griefs that raise the "sacred faculty of tears" (p.

47). We end with the speaker mounted on a "patient nag" beyond the world of "wild joys of the noontide" and hopeful of a new love – deliberately left vague and essentially lifeless.

The conflict apparent in "Tamerton Church-Tower," between Patmore's rather intuitive rewriting of sexuality as a location of vitality and danger and his desire to obtain control, at whatever cost, both of these forces and of his text, is also present in some other poems in this volume. The good poem, never reprinted by Patmore, "Bertha," sets the joy of love against the endless pain of its loss, almost a premonition of Patmore's major theme in his mature poetry. "Eros," a poem that was reprinted by Patmore, is a celebration of spring and love that also sounds lightly one of Patmore's major late chords: the sense of a greater erotic reality behind even our most lyrical ordinary springtime experience. The poem swerves suddenly at its end from celebrating nature to evoking a pre-lapsarian essence of eros evoked by such experiences but beyond it: "Ah, but the glory, found in no story, / Radiance of Eden unquench'd by the Fall; Few may remember, none may reveal it. / This is the first First-love, the first love of all!"

The few working drafts of *The Angel in the House* published in the 1853–54 volumes – "passages or sketches of passages for a long poem" – are significantly more turned to the sexual center of marriage than the final poem will be. Relative to the number of lines published, there is also a great deal more questioning than celebration of marriage. The poem that most immediately catches the modern reader's attention is "The Eve of the Wedding," a troubled and disturbing pair of night thoughts by future bride and groom. Had Patmore worked continuously at this level of psychological penetration and general realism, *The Angel* might have survived into this century to sit beside *Jane Eyre* as a work newly interesting to each generation of readers. As kinds of narrator/reader voyeurs we snoop on bride and groom on the nervous evening before marriage. At the prospect of the coming day, the bride suffers some of that feeling of "aghast-ness," alienation of spirit, that haunted Patmore's earlier marriage scene. All seems "strange" to her, covered in shadows, breeding giddy fears, a swooning feeling, thoughts of death. She feels oddly guilty at the coming sexual festival, imagines herself accused by her parents, soon to be betrayed by her lover. The disastrously simple verse form and meter that Patmore had already chosen for *The Angel*, one reason for its quick popularity and lasting critical failure, do work against the insight they carry; they allow Patmore to modulate to a "mere bride's fears" mode as he describes her turning to the support of prayer. We end the section uncomfortably drawn into a satanic position of viewing another man's bride undress and regarding her pure breast and "fragrant body" (pp. 133–38). She is returned to a "simple maid" sleeping with "unkiss'd lids" turned up like lilies to the moon; but Patmore can't evade the uncomfortable sexual awareness he has forced on us.

Meanwhile the groom is having a much harder night, exactly because he fully shares the sexual awareness of narrator and reader. Instead of sleeping, he gloats over his coming position; it is the Victorian power of bridegroom as perpetual and definitive lord. Power over the bride corrupts him sexually as it did us and the narrator in the prior section. He wants his desire satisfied now! The narrator sees the prospect of sexual control extending to Luciferian (or Othello-like) proportions, threatening "To pluck the chaste moon from the sky, / And tread out all the stars" (p. 140). Such conception breeds, in Patmore's nice conceit, like salamanders in "Love's unslacken'd flame," increasing unrest. The groom fears he may blend too much into one with his bride, may find she is not what he has hoped. Above all, he is troubled at his own troubled mood: the reality of possession and sexual fulfillment seem nothing like "That peace and gratitude, / The sanction and the soul of joy" for which he looked. He is instead in a chaos, "fire-mists of a world unform'd" (p. 142), throbbing pulse, burning temples. Clock and restless cockerel keep him from sleeping as the night wears on – both male enough to suggest the physical origin of his unrest. Dawn finds himself, in the striking image on which the sections ends, confronting a sun that glows like a carbuncle. The poetic sense of a glowing stone or ember suggests his unquenched and troubling fire. The more common sense of nasty sore, certainly present, suggests how much even this most legitimate of sexual initiations is infected by conflicting feelings – both for the groom and the narrator.

"Amy's Marriage," an apparent sequel (with the same name for the bride), perhaps also an early sketch towards *The Angel in the House* but never used, portrays the consummation itself with a similar refusal to sentimentalize or idealize. There is an attractive sense of the haste, flutter, and general confusion of a wedding. The outer confusion emblems that inside; only "thoughtless" hearts make a "merry wedding-day." All here are only too sicklied over by thought.

Amy is anxious; the lovers' eyes meet coldly among gossips at church. The wedding itself is nervous, hasty, trembling. We see the bride leave with faint heart, the groom with a suspect "high conceit / Of his superior joy" (p. 215). Focus then turns to the beehive of other people, all of whom hide troubled and complex reflections beneath their apparent gaiety, from troubled father, trying to be sociable, to mother going off to weep and pray alone, to the guests recalling regrets, crossed purposes in love, or merely the slow loss of feeling. The ending is brilliant, and also the most disturbing part of the poem: all know that "Upon the bridal bed / Where love to-day confirms his throne, / Sweet Hope lies crown'd and dead" (p. 217). The cadence and psychomachiac imagery, rather suggestive of that which James Thomson would adopt in *The City of Dreadful Night*, turn a statement about the natural end of hope in marriage into a dirge over the marriage-bed. Again it is the narrator's complex and uncertain feelings about the sexual consummation that marks this interesting approach to Victorian marriage.

KINGLSEYAN POPULARITY: *THE ANGEL* AND *THE VICTORIES*

The quarrel in these volumes between difficult expression and idealization, most obvious in the eventual suppression of most of the more penetrating poems, seems ruthlessly resolved in the notorious Victorian epic of domestic love that followed. The two books of *The Angel in the House* that were published separately in 1854 and 1856 were those that gave Patmore public fame as a poet. They also began, even in the Victorian heyday, to undermine his serious reputation, so much so that later in life he actually considered suppressing them and would think of them almost as cans tied to his tail. The two books, originally sub-titled *The Betrothal* and *Espousals* following the traditional two parts of the wedding rite, also have eclipsed the second two books, not published until the 1860s (and later treated as a separate poem, *The Victories of Love*), in many ways more probing and interesting volumes. Spoken of as the entire work (and eventually printed as a single work called *The Angel in the House*) the first two books have also virtually totally sunk Patmore's general critical reputation in the twentieth century. If Praz elegantly damned them to the closure of respect as period pieces – a bit of Biedermeier bourgeois art in verse – feminist reexamination of the nineteenth century has at the moment totally shut up the covers of the poem by taking even its title as nemesis for all that was wrong in the Victorian love system. When we are done explaining, with all specialized criticism of Patmore, that it is all a great mistake based on a misreading, the angel in question not being an epitome of Victorian womanhood but the spirit of love in a fine relationship, there is still a great deal wrong here. Far from the epic and definitive statement on love and sexual psychology that Patmore hoped for and his friendly critics briefly applauded, this work is really a large swerve, or lurch, from the interesting but highly unstable work of his earlier career. Despite the polished excellence of some of the verses and the broad reworking of major poetic traditions that mark a major poetic talent,[56] this is in many ways a *faux pas*. In view of the experimental thinking and writing in his earlier work it also seems in many ways a capitulation to the narrower spirit of his times – one for which he earned a short popular reputation and generally lost his critical due, perhaps permanently.

The suppression, by evasion and omission, of the two working drafts just looked at is roundly indicative of the censoring, idealizing spirit in which Patmore worked in these two books. As he began writing a wedding poem, the poet who had been preoccupied with issues of sexuality in most of his earlier work naturally homed in on the initiating ceremony itself with the awareness of psychological anxiety and disturbance that we have seen. It is just this hard-to-speak center that Patmore virtually eliminates in the final version, while he writes at epic length all around the event. Only a part of the vivid poem on the groom's experience is used in the 1856 poem as first printed, and this is largely muted by moralizing on love's duty that attempts to offer an easy program for perfect marriage: After the groom has relieved all sexual anxieties by resolving that "to serve seem'd more than to possess," he prepares for his wedding by enjoying a "soft sleep" rather than harriedly facing a carbuncular sun.[57] Subsequent revisions, beginning in 1858, reduced even further the original exploration of the groom's psychology. The voyeuristic section on the bride going to bed was omitted in the revision of 1856 and the entire section was reduced in later revisions, then totally eliminated. The troubled description of the wedding was dropped entirely in even the first edition in favor of wise, useful, distancing advice from the genial father of the bride. There is nowhere a reference to the marriage-bed itself – an extraordinary omission even in the terms of Patmore's time and certainly in light of his sexual focus in earlier work.

Homey bride Amy becomes idealized Honoria, her husband the happy man (with a touch of mystical inspiration recalling the metaphysical poet?) Felix Vaughan. Although the poem, doubtless intended as a tribute to his wife, is often read as a version of Patmore's domestic relations, even a perfunctory comparison of the real Emily Andrews Patmore and Honoria suggests how great has been the polishing away of all mere complexities. As noted above, we move immediately far up in class from the struggling young daughter of a deceased minister married to a clerk at the British Museum with poetic ambitions inherited from a rather disreputable Grub Street father. Felix, wealthy unworking gentleman of the Victorian middle-class imagination woos the placid daughter of a Church of England dean. All is hushed, reverent, unreal as only projected desire for a life of leisure – a very spacious room at the top – can make it. Honoria has no occupation; Emily raised a large family in hard circumstances, eking out family income by a respectable writing career of her own. Emily had to deal with an overworked, rather nervous, peremptory, and high strung, if adoring, husband; Honoria has as husband the flower of British gentry, unbothered by any worry except her comfort and preparing a fitting tribute to their ideal marriage. Emily faced the loss of parents in her early life, and was soon to face a long illness, the dispersion of her family, and death; Honoria moves from happy, sheltered deanery to the neighborhood great house, where she presides in lawned leisure over the play of her children. If we find in the beautiful Emily's life a story of character and endurance, we find in Honoria almost no drama in character, no core of self; and her presentation by her husband renders her essentially second-hand, a woman seen through the eyes of a character/husband/poet himself created as an idealized self-projection by the husband/poet Patmore. Surely the opportunities, and incentives, for filtering out the realities of marriage and idealizing what is left are enormous! And Patmore, with his personal life centred in his love for his strong, lovely wife, seeing himself, unlike his father, as a model of the Victorian writer as respectable family man, yielded to the temptation to try to close up for a while the disturbing insights of his earlier work.

Felix, the poet-squire, is lucky in life and wife (if too-comfortable but insipid situations could be called fortunate), but less fortunate as a poet. His frequent comparisons between himself and Petrarch are, on reflection, ludicrous, a comparison one hopes Patmore would have had the good sense not to dare in his own person. The great poet of love at distance, even because of distance, passionately devoted to another man's wife while fathering his own children on casual liaisons that he held in guilty contempt, hardly offers a fitting model for a Victorian lover of his wife of indefatigable probity. His poetic claims to be going back to the real springs of life and poetry in celebrating sexual union – a program Patmore of course took very seriously – are rendered equally silly by the very failure to probe the source rather than the surrounding social context. "Marry her and take her home" (p. 130),[58] Felix explains, is the tropeless center of poetry that otherwise exists as nothing but troping differences. But it is precisely this still center of sexual discussion which his poem refused to occupy, indeed, even in its use of the off-centred euphemism of "take her home" for the wedding-night's sex.

Most apparent, there is none of Petrarch's or Patmore's own usual deliberate psychological probing. There is a general stultification by idealization. A model Victorian married lover has no room for other than straight paths in his single-minded pursuit of Honor(ia) – Patmore's own insistent play between the woman and her not very different allegorical valuation. In place of the perceptive observations on family pressures and childhood sexuality in his earlier poems, we are given lovers virtually cut loose from any hint of Oedipal tensions. The bride's dad, the old dean, is mature understanding almost literally personified. The groom has neither father nor mother left to trouble him. His mother exists as a memory of her room, preserved as a perpetual shrine in his great house and linked by association with an historic visit of a real queen. Felix makes an easy identification between mother, queen, and his poetic muse. Unlike so many real bridegrooms who find some difficult meshing of gears in merging mother-queen and wife into one inspiring mass, he easily introduces his bride into mom's room, which she much admires. Similarly, stereotypes are offered without reflection by this isolated aristocratic poet Felix: a single reference to fallen women is of the sort Clough mocked so easily and well: "Behold the worst! Light from above / On the black rain writes 'Forbear!' / Her first crime was unguarded love, / And all the rest, perhaps, despair" (p. 65). The tensions and anxieties produced by sexual excitement in the earlier poems are here reduced to some very general observations on the value of un-platonic love over platonic (pp. 33–34), and analysis of a crisis provoked by touching a hand (p. 68) – a part that could have stood for the whole adequately as a way of getting around Victorian codes of reticence (as such synecdoches do, say, in Charlotte Brontë or, as we shall see, egregiously in Hardy); in this static world, however, a hand is only a hand.

The restless, sometimes extremely troubling energies that find direct expression in the earlier poems are formally excluded but nonetheless find their subversive, textually deconstructing outlets. To even the casual reader the figure of the chase must have an odd prominence in this poem set in a world of deanery, great lawns, geraniums, and children playing peaceably with pet hedgehogs. Whereas the real aristocracy – those unspeakables not much like gentleman Felix – let their savage energies loose from those so-mannered country houses in an actual chase, Patmore seems to have recast the poor beloved as the pursued inedible. At the allegorical level the metaphor is dead enough: the happy man's pursuit of Honor in a love relation. But it comes alive with surprising and rather Frankensteinian, monster independence when it is put into play. The climactic section in Felix's winning of Honoria – displacing the scene of actual climax for which we look in vain – is formally titled "The Abdication." But the chase, the title of the long section, is the dominating trope for love triumphant. An interesting and disturbing passage, closer to rendering a sense of Honoria as a living being than elsewhere in the poem, describes her at length sighing, restless, upset, as she slowly yields to feelings of love. The decorum of Victorian courtship fades away before a strong, more primitive image of bold youth and maiden fleeing. It ends in the language of an actual chase: "She's chased to death, undone. / Surprised, and violently caught" (p. 72). The end of the canto is even more explicit: Felix has her soul burying "its face within my breast, / Like a pet fawn by hunters hurt" (p. 76). For all the elaborate courtesy Felix has displayed in his upper-class courting, one feels a gloat here.

Patmore's own unease with what is released is registered by a brief poem interjected in the middle of this canto, first added in the 1860 revision. In four lines it tells us that the churl is he who, having won his love, finds the grace was "not in the woman, but the chace [*sic*]" (p. 73).[59] Unfortunately, offering the moral only alerts the reader to the possibility that it might fit the author's own stress on the chase itself. Later we find Patmore's hero accepting the churlish premise as he explains that continued married love calls for an endless renewal of the chase: "her spirit's vestal grace / Provokes me always to pursue" (p. 138).[60] Submerged in all this, but always floating deconstructively to the surface is the good old strong meaning of a woman's honor: virginity and maidenhead. The pursuit of honor must be a pursuit of dishonor, or, as he more exactly presents it, a desire to have her honor and have honor too. Marriage has long been the English solution: but Patmore's love of the chase, the pursuit of dishonoring, keeps threatening to unsettle what could have been avoided entirely in the tradition of married love he ostensibly rehabilitates. He himself calls the chase after an unending chase "Love's Perversity" (p. 108), and we sense especially in the violence of the language a degree of unacknowledged sadism that undoes the ostensible ultra-civility of the book of model courtship. When Patmore has his poet conjure up a sexual state of nature it is hardly surprising to find that it exposes what the poem has been in any case revealing to us all along: beneath the elaborate language and codes of civility human nature reveals a sexuality as problematic as that explored in the earlier poems: "Lo, how the woman once was woo'd: / Forth leapt the savage from his lair, / And fell'd her, and to nuptials rude / He dragg'd her, bleeding, by the hair" (p. 124).[61] Such an un-Rousseauian instinct in a vernal wood indeed suggests that the experimental approach to the problems of sexual experience has become only too rigidly structured. As he tries to provide a model for a sexual life that avoids all the complexities of his own experience he also begins to see sexuality in a simple polarity. A complex map of sexual anxiety and difficulty in the earlier poem yields to a duality in which civility in love is opposed everywhere to a subverting sadism and brutality. No wonder the sadism keeps erupting into the pattern of civility when it has come to signify the sexual in this reduced and binary world.

Although with age Patmore would come to value the trappings of patriarchy and he did subscribe to an ideology of male authority, his poetic insights are rarely dominated by issues of sexuality as power. Idealization here, as so often, seems to create the brutality it begins by opposing. That Patmore's most famous (but far from best) poem, in his day and ours, should offer his extreme focus on sadism helps explain its permanent blot on his serious reputation. He wrote artfully and gracefully in this polished poem; but his sensibility seems virtually out of control in its rigidities of conception. If his early work was in some sense written by the sexual confusions of his inheritance, this one seems deliberately inscribed into a newer tradition, very close to Kingsley's, of very controlled sexual assertion: one that created a text of marital satisfaction – which it formally advocated – surrounded by danger. Not surprisingly, this was the one popular work of this highly experimental, individualistic, and deeply unpopular poet. Like Kingsley's career-long production, which, as we have seen, also contained a good deal of only partially submerged sadism, it seems to have met a certain need in a large readership, in effect to state a positive view of sexual marriage while directly or subliminally registering and defending against the fears of excess that this liberal view opened up.

With Patmore, unlike the case of Kingsley, the situation is not static; he is exploring this position but already moving to another. There are signs in these first two books of *The Angel in the House* that Patmore was still alive to other issues of sexuality, explored in his early work and to be a major subject of his finest work in the odes. The death of the beloved, only imagined by the fortunate Felix, has nonetheless an emotional weight hardly felt in the social descriptions of most of the poem. The poem "The Revulsion" (1856) even pre-states the main external stages of Patmore's future real loss: the waking to loss, remembrance, dealing with the children. Here Felix wakes to find Honoria *is* alive; but the section is a strong intrusion suggesting that loss preoccupied the author more than his theme would normally require. Too, there is that theme, obsessive in Kingsley and important to Patmore in this period, of love's survival, including physical survival, after death (p. 130).[62]

Anxiety over loss is also figured marginally in these first two books of *The Angel in the House* in the person of the rejected lover. In this poem of successful love, the rejected lover, another suitor to Honoria, named Frederick Graham, puts in only a cameo appearance. Yet Patmore gives him surprising prominence. As Felix is happy winner, Frederick is presented as the unfortunate loser. Patmore renders his failure to arouse more than friendly family interest in his beautiful (and rich) cousin Honoria through the painful device of Felix's narration – that is, the rival not only bests him with Honoria but has entire control of the incident: a version of history being written by the victors. Felix portrays the two in front of Honoria barely controlling their annoyance at each other's presence; he happily describes her clear choice against Frederick. He then even allows himself mag-nanimity of pity for poor Frederick, who is figured now as dead hope "in his voice and eye" (p. 22). Felix's dream that night, which is of a chivalric fight in which he vanquishes "all I saw / Of her unnumber'd cousin-kind, / In Navy, Army, Church, and Law" (p. 23) unmasks the pity and suggests the way in which loss is imaged as aggression/defeat. In this it merely repeats the terms of aggression against the female. The theme is repeated some pages later where Patmore allows Felix to dwell more abstractly on the idea of rejection as a form of "martyrdom in love." Here Felix briefly imagines himself in the masochistic rather than sadistic part. Love often is not returned, he worries, because of poverty, trifling shades of temperament, a false appearance of manners, faintness of expression, fate, etcetera, etcetera (p. 34).

Felix has his moment of agony, then goes on to arrant success in the chase. But Patmore comes back emphatically to this theme in the second two books of the original *Angel*, later separately titled *The Victories of Love*. These are indeed Frederick's books and though always eclipsed by the fame and then notoriety of the first two, they are far closer to Patmore's more habitual themes, also more convenable to his temperament, of the problems and uncertainties of love and sexuality. With their almost obsessive focus on loss and its compensations, they show Patmore already turning back in the late 1850s and early 1860s to the major themes of absence and loss, prominent in his early work and central to the great odes to come. Indeed the books retain interest, though they have hardly retained any readers, just because they exhibit a spirit of experimentalism, even confusion and uncertainty, in matters of sexuality, much as the earlier poems did. In contrast to the clear central theme of the two *Angel* books, where other issues arise mainly subversively, there is a multiplicity of issues, with a general avoidance of predisposition. This is reinforced by the formal structure, which is now one of the long poem in epistolary form, setting letter against letter in dialogue, rather than offering primarily monologic display of Felix's view of a life by love possessed. Patmore was pressed by family troubles, especially the illness of his wife, during some period of the books' creation. He later, as almost always in his poetry, very substantially revised the poem, dropping out entire letters, adding others, reorganizing the whole and doing much incidental rewriting.[63] The final version still has an air of works and thought in progress.

The issue of love as failure and hurt is now exposed directly as a central concern; and now Patmore seems no longer afraid to let its force stand out clearly. If there is a similar playing with sadistic and masochistic themes, they now flow easily into other issues of sexuality rather than stand out starkly as perverse alternatives to Felix's commonwealth of high-toned love. Indeed, the only point of view that seems out of place is Felix's own, represented by his letters and Honoria's: their aristocratic love, though still an ideal for Frederick, seems to pale before the stronger, more unsettled feelings of other characters, most particularly Frederick himself.

Frederick, in his milieu and uncertain life much more like Patmore himself than is Felix, is also given experiences much closer to Patmore's own. While in one version Felix was provided with Patmore's rather wooden conservative political opinions (opposing the Reform Act),[64] Frederick is allowed to recall Patmore's own intense and biographically central experience of childhood rejection in love. We hear from Frederick at the opening of the two books as he assumes his duties on a warship after his unsuccessful wooing visit to Honoria. He and his mother exchange opinions that are more direct and psychologically acute than anything in the first two books. Frederick's gunboat passion, expressed with some Byronic force and vigor in the imagery of his strong ship exposed to the elements, gives a direct voice to the theme of passion in loss that was more like a submerged iceberg than a prowling fighting boat in the first two books. In response to his mother's fears for his mental health he assures her that this is not a new experience for him; it whelms him over again but won't overwhelm him.

When he bares his soul back to childhood origins, it is a primal scene of lost love that he offers his mother (her possible role as the primal object of lost passion is nowhere explored, though her presence as confidante is suggestive of such origins: he returns his loss to her). He fell in love with one of two sisters in his childhood. He recounts this almost as a pathology of the passion of love's loss. It hardly mattered which sister of two rather alike; yet, once in love, the experience itself was fundamental. In the "bright apocalyptic sky" of "O'erarching childhood" he still sees the central experience of his conscious life. And its form is strongly masochistic: "I seem'd to be / Whirl'd round, and bound with showers of threads / As when the furious spider sheds his captivity upon the fly / To still his buzzing 'til he die." His only desire, fly that he found himself, bound by his intense inner responses, was "to dream myself her slave" (p. 151). Patmore lets Frederick give free, direct expression to his sense of loss,

which is now revived by Honoria's polite rejection of his suit. In a
Victorian social context, the one established so solidly in the first two
books, he is an outsider (prowling out there, defending his country)
and clearly a loser. He emphatically lacks the two tokens needed for
entrée in the upper-class society of the Honorias and Felixes – Greek
and money. In an especially cruel turn we even find the old dean
assuming that he knows the gentleman's Greek he so badly lacks (p.
154).[65]

Mother warns that Frederick, sailor on the rebound, may seek safe
harbor with any woman in this emotional storm. The letter crosses
with Frederick's announcing his involvement with a plain Jane: she
is no beauty; but then again she is far below Frederick in class and
even further below his aspirations. The modern reader finds this
painful, even embarrassing material, just because it is so honest about
the class anxieties Victorians actually felt (and we perhaps only hide
better from ourselves). Only in the Victorian novel of Dickens,
Thackeray, or Trollope does one find similar honesty. Here again,
Frederick seems written from the kind of first-hand experience that
betrays Patmore's own distance from a happy Felix. With Patmore's
usual awareness of the obverse of masochism in sadism, he portrays
Frederick, humiliating himself in this ricochet choice, passing along
all his own pain to poor Jane. Like another Frederick, she seems to
love him more for his being so clear that he preferred Honoria; she is
entirely in accord with his assessment of her vulgarity and *déclassement*.
Like the worst embodiment of the stereotyped angel in the house that
Honoria certainly isn't, she even seems happy, when she comes to die,
to know that her death will allow Frederick and Honoria to be in
closer rapport. In the earlier version Patmore had even included
letters about her rich uncle John that more painfully underlined her
vulgar origins.[66] Frederick seems to incorporate the pain that he
causes her in his own: both agree that all men abuse their wives, he
in shame, she almost in pleasure.

Such a chain of pain in love, Honoria, to Frederick, to Jane, is a
painful subject, clearly not likely to please the audience captured by
the first two books. The explicitness of Patmore's presentation follows
his experimental look at love's problematics in his earlier work. Here,
too, the painful issues of masochism in love broaden easily to more
universal, less pathological themes. The larger theme is indeed that of
loss and absence of love rather than rejection. Those childhood
memories, while colored by Frederick's pleasure in emotional pain,

are easily generalized, as they were for Patmore personally. When the little experience is over, what is left is a Wordsworth-like intimation: characteristically recast by Patmore as a sexual one. The "rapture and the grace / Ineffable" of young love pass when the "sunset dies to dark" leaving an unquenched taste for something beyond even such earthly passion: a "patient, poignant appetite / For pleasures that exceed so much / The poor things which the world calls such" (p. 152).

If Felix bravely claimed the mantle of Petrarch, the more prosaic Frederick is actually closer to the original inspiration of that fountainhead of Western thinking on love. Like Petrarch, Frederick in some sense remains devoted to his honorary lover even as, somewhat like Petrarch, he takes a woman from a lower class than his own and produces children by her. Patmore's confused attempts to reconcile this tradition of a split psyche, ideal love taking the lover to heaven, desire still demanding everyday food, seems at least far more honest here than in Felix's version of the traditional English solution of married lovers.[67] On the one hand the high aspirations released in erotic experience create lives based on pain, rejection, distance; on the other, they bring humans closer to ultimates that lead into essentially religious experience. Frederick vows to pray for Honoria for a lifetime, as a saint would (p. 162), turning sexual passion into religious aspiration. His mother, a voice of sympathetic everyday good sense, warns of the alienation that can invade such religious cultivation of desire in absence. He who "too nearly hears the music of forfended spheres / Is thenceforth lonely, and for all his days like one who treads the Wall / Of China, and, on this hand, sees / Cities and their civilities, / And, on the other, lions" (p. 155). Frederick himself, in an equally striking image, feels God as a present reality but too distant for comfort, "a tower without a stair, / And His perfection, love's despair" (p. 168). Despair in love brings people back to the origin of love but seems to do so too painfully and impersonally.

As he begins to create a system linking experience of love's loss with religion, Patmore seems at first to falter into a multitude of solutions for the intrinsic intolerability of the hopeless Petrarchan lover's position. All lead ultimately to heaven but some also provide some comfort here. So we have a major counter-theme of sexual marriage. Frederick and Jane have come together under the worst circumstances. But whereas Petrarch eventually renounces sex and his casual alternatives to Laura, Frederick ultimately finds a consolation in his faithful/cruel marriage to little Jane. As with the Clough of *Amours de Voyage*, there is an intense awareness of the apparent absurdity of building a life around what is usually a happenstance connection. Frederick and Jane, not idealized Felix and Honoria, are the usual couple; Patmore works hard to show both coming to a marriage of spirits through a permanent sexual liaison. Before she dies Jane triumphs in her naiveté, even with the folk at the great house; Frederick will honor her in memory with a passion parallel to hers for Honoria. Life is a sexual gymnasium in which we exercise our spiritual muscles with whomever we end up, or a nursery where we learn to tend our gardens in preparation for the transplantation to heaven. Themes familiar from Kingsley, of interest to Patmore before, have full statement here. Jane herself is given language assuring her husband that there will be marriage in heaven as here. A death letter from her (in the popular Victorian tradition of pre-written letters from the grave) follows closely the passionate belief, such as we have seen in Kingsley, in a marital paradise regained after death where "'tis / In the flesh we rise."[68]

This Kingsleyan doctrine sits a little uneasily with more radical sexual/paradisaical assumptions that ultimately lead more directly to Patmore's mature work. In the original versions the type of Leah and Rachel, so dear also to Clough, had been emphasized by sub-chapter headings suggesting that Frederick's long odyssey ends with possession of Rachel. Rachel is somehow to be both Honoria and the ostensible Leah, Jane. Not only did her death bring Frederick and Honoria together in sympathy in this world; she also hopes, as does he, that somehow in heaven all Leahs become the Rachels of their husband's intuitive and more than earthly sexual aspirations. The concept was embodied in a long, interesting dream, deleted from the final version, reported by Jane in one of her (too many) death letters. There she finds herself in anticipation among the resurrected virgins; her story is of the universality of sexual experience: in heaven the virgins have one nature and one response to their suitors.[69] Jane finds herself a universal woman: "And lo, within the crystal drawn, / I laughed the laugh of Mrs. Vaughan!" Frederick likewise expects to find in heaven his earthly love. But he is moving, in a way that Kingsley would find absolutely upsetting, to a kind of marriage to all womankind, beginning with a joint Honoria/Jane: "he whose daily life / Adjusts itself to one true wife / Grows to a nuptial, near degree / With all that's fair and womanly "(p. 219).

Patmore allows Frederick to begin to develop what he himself will attempt so boldly in the odes, a mythology of sexuality. Like central Victorian poets, Patmore's admirer Browning and sometime friend Tennyson, he looks in the human heart for an ultimate authority over the unclarities or disputes in the religious text. His "I have felt" has however the significant sexual intrusion, "fleshly": "On fleshly tables of the Heart / He penn'd truth's feeling counterpart / In hopes that come to all" (p. 227). What Frederick finds he knows in the flesh of his heart is that heaven is a place of unattainable desire's full realization, not merely of Kingsleyan continuation of sexual wedded content. "I'm utterly imbued / With faith of all Earth's hope renew'd / In realms where no short-coming pains / Expectance, and dear love disdains / Time's treason" (p. 185). The theme is not so much the Kinglseyan one of sex in heaven as the more universal Western question of desire and its lack or absence, as it has been varyingly posed from Petrarch to post-structuralists. If his story begins with the special theme of the masochism of losing in love, it ends on the even more universal, less pathological one of the death of a lover. Having pursued Honoria in Jane, Frederick finds after Jane's death that she was also an Honoria. Her loss, like the archetypal Western loss of Petrarch's Laura, becomes occasion to find in his heart faith in the power of death to strengthen love into a mythic power of undying desire. She becomes parallel to the idealized Laura figure, Honoria, by her death ("What distance for another did / That death has done for her!" p. 220). The love raised by the absence of death then justifies the leap of faith of the fleshly heart to create a mythic realm of desire's fulfillment.

The two books end in the final version with a fairly good poem called "The Wedding Sermon," the wisdom of Honoria's old father the dean on the union of Frederick and Honoria's offspring in marriage. The sermon, somewhat too long but fitted with lines of fine reflective verse, balances somewhat uneasily between Polonian advice and the often splendid abstract statement of the later odes. Like the two books themselves, it is diffuse because it puts together almost a kind of miscellany of speculations on love and sexuality. Generally it recapitulates the themes of the two books in more abstract terms. Patmore's decision to give a final statement of the issues raised in these books to a voice of explicitly religious authority suggests that his experimental thinking had taken him to the point where he saw fundamental liaisons between sexual issues and religious ones.

In an easier, more genial tone the dean restates some of the major points presented through Frederick's experience. Married love, based often on a seemingly rather casual choice ("blind election of life's chance," p. 259), often developed by bitter adversity or painful final loss, is nonetheless a great (the great?) earthly proving ground. Even passionate young love that is not fulfilled – "Eschol grapes" to travellers in the wilderness – has its ultimately comedic force in developing the individual. Unlike Clough's Claude, the dean's awareness of the problematics of sexuality does not disturb his strong advocacy of sex itself. Contrary to Augustinian Church tradition, the dean affirms that love, not procreation, is the business of marital sex: "Love's self the noblest offspring is, / And sanction of the nuptial kiss" (p. 260). He further counsels couples to follow the authoritative direction of nature, rather than any narrow rules of sexual conduct, in expressing their intimacy. The advice, presented in somewhat coded, decorous form, would seem not too different from the modern sex manual's advocacy of sexual experimentation: "So let your Grace with Nature chime. / Her primal forces burst, like straws, / The bonds of uncongenial law." "This I may" is the rule in married sex, "seeking delight, / Esteem success true test of right." The dean's metaphor of happy children exercising "exuberant liberty" at play "In their own free and childish way" even suggests a general openness to what our manuals would call polymorphous sexual experimentation: "Take in love's innocent gladness part / With infantine, untroubled heart" (p. 256).

His apology for, and celebration of, earthly love always has a larger religious rationale. Our love life is a moral farm growing us for transplanting above. Congenial married love indeed works to erase the "primal curse" (p. 260) of original sin.[70] Adversity in love, such as Frederick experienced, opens us to our need for a heaven fully to realize our nature: "The heaven of heavens is symbol'd where / The torch of Psyche flash'd despair" (p. 254). Even in its fulfillment love has an inner lack that drives us beyond earth: its home "is not here: / The pathos of eternity / Does in it fullest pleasure sigh" (p. 262). As he insists on man's religious life beneath his sexual one, at the same time the dean begins to recast religious experience in sexual terms. Heaven is a place *à la* Kingsley, where sex survives; as Patmore will in the odes, the dean stresses the physicality of spiritual things. He also implies, as the discussion of heavenly sex in the two books had, that heaven not only preserves marriage but celebrates a more universal sexuality, a kind of hierarchy of angels, "of active and recipient / Affections" (p. 262). The unclarity speaks loudly here, and the dean drops the speculation without much more explanation than that there will be some more unisexual sharing. One senses a movement toward a broad vision of sexuality in mythic terms, here developed only fragmentarily, as it was also in Jane's dream. There is also some tendency in the Anglican dean created by this still-Anglican writer nonetheless to create sexual myths by building on special readings of Church tradition. For instance, he reconverts the standard rationalization of sexual passages in the Bible, most notably the Song of Solomon as about the marriage of Christ and Israel or the Church, back to a sexual meaning. "Christ's marriage with the Church is more, / My children than a metaphor" (p. 254) both dignifies the marriage at hand and headily suggests that our experience of physical marriage may offer terms for understanding a mystery of the Church in mythic, sexual terms. Similarly in a poem on marriage the old Anglican pauses surprisingly long to praise, albeit in Miltonic phrase, "the doctrine of virginity" (pp. 254–55). The deferring of fulfillment demanded by pre-nuptial virginity creates far more directly the inner force of unrealized desire than the major themes of love's defeat or loss emphasized in the second two books. The experience is powerful, an "ineffable delight" (p. 255), though the dean also warns of the danger of a "virgin will."

THE UNKNOWN EROS

Patmore announced at the end of his original edition of the fourth, concluding book that his personal loss, the death of Emily, had led him to abandon plans for further elaboration of this long novelistic poem, including the Kingsleyan project already somewhat achieved and to a large extent outgrown, of examining the "hope which remains for individual love in death."[71] Whether he was in any case tired of the poem and ready to find an excuse for ending hardly matters.[72] Certainly he had written beyond the conformist, limiting, and narrowly ambitious drives which had led him into the too-popular poem on a too-popular and narrow theme in the first two books of *The Angel in the House*. He had worked his way indeed back to the more open, questioning, eccentric, and interesting obsessions with themes of sexuality and love which had greatly occupied his early work. With their virtual miscellany of sex problems and questions the final two books had brought him back to his central concerns with love's problematics. They had also moved him, in their many stabs at explanations through broader visions or even mythologies of sexuality, to the border of his final career as a difficult odist and myth-maker of sexuality. The astonishing new direction and accomplishment of this later work is perhaps less surprising when seen through this history. Faced with both an intuitive and cultural awareness of sexuality as a locus of problems in human experience, Patmore had attempted many early statements of his difficulties, all troublesome to him in their implications. He then tried what proved a false start in restricting his vision to successful married sexuality – his most Kingsleyan moment – and writing for the broad audience that his difficult early works couldn't reach. He then worked back to a restatement of the earlier issues in broader terms of various forms of absence and desire. At this point he was ready for the far more consolidated and knotty expression of his insights in the difficult, mystery-bearing, exceptionally flexible, even erratic medium of the ode.

As a passage to this final statement of his life's works, a passage that reappears as such in the odes themselves, he went through those totally reordering personal experiences: the death of his wife, his conversion to Catholicism, and remarriage to a woman imbued with a religious spirit of virginity. The Kingsleyan center of mid-Victorian married sexuality and middle-class responsibility had not held for his imagination; it did not hold any longer for him personally. Henceforth he emphatically followed his own unpopular and more challenging course. The awareness of an obverse loss that had occupied him in even his first works on love and sexuality now found overwhelming confirmation in his life. Instead of turning his attention from the loss of his first wife, the second marriage seems to have created a life permanently centered on absence. Marianne Byles's ample means put the aristocratic ease of a Felix at Patmore's disposal; he welcomed the freedom and security but established a life otherwise more like that in a convent than a great house. Whatever the facts of the sexual relation with his second wife, there seems certainly to have been an understanding that this would not be a new start with new children but the completion of unfinished business:

they would join in raising his children; and they would share a life of serious thinking about the facts of mortality as he had now experienced them. In the nun-like and religiously preoccupied Marianne Byles he had chosen a most appropriate partner for this new life. She seems to have been content with the freedom to continue her withdrawn meditative life; he could allow his emotions to continue to dwell on the awareness of absence that still preoccupied him from his first marriage.

If Kingsley hoped really to have to face no separation by the simultaneous deaths and sexual translations to heaven of himself and his wife, Patmore had to face a long life after the mortal end of his first relationship. The final version of *The Unknown Eros* organizes this process of grief in a roughly biographical chronology. But it isn't clear that Patmore wrote in this order; indeed what evidence there is suggests that he came to many of the most direct statements of his loss only after a number of years. In 1868, six years after his first wife's death, he published nine *Odes* privately. Only two are among the poems immediately on his loss.[73] Possibly some were withheld as unfinished or about experience still too raw to expose. His emotional confusion, and the degree to which the new relation mainly permitted focus on the loss of the first are clear in the early version of "Tired Memory," where a long section, later not printed, characteristically explains with almost too much candor his wooing of the second wife by talk of the first and vague hopes for a Kingsleyan meeting in heaven – as a kind of very un-Kingsleyan threesome (themes returned to with much more control in the too coy, separate late poem, "Amelia").

The general impression we have of the 1860s in Patmore's life is of very little creative activity (certainly as compared to his earlier production), a quiet and dark period of brooding, caring for his family and his new wife's property, and above all of isolation and alienation. This is the one period of his grown life, indeed, when he virtually disconnected himself from a lively additional career as an active (and very acute) reviewer and man of letters; and of course he gave up, in his squirish country isolation, the manifold literary contacts of his work at the British Museum. His little preface to these privately printed poems speaks of being discouraged in plans for a greater series and assumes that he, formerly a poetic household word approaching Tennyson in general fame, speaks really to no one. Poems stress not only "Pain" but his distance from his age and even from his muse. The very poor and angry ode on the second Reform Act, "1867," is distempered and entirely out of tune with his age. Disraeli, viciously attacked there, is said to have commented when the poem was shown to him that he was in England, Patmore in Patmos. Patmore was in his own purgatory rather, and his personal detachment bred the political satires that disfigure the final *Unknown Eros*. Other poems of 1868 show him thinking of himself as both cut off and voiceless, perhaps one of the prophets who cannot sing in the poem of that name or the singer at the end of a now unheeded great tradition, the theme of the ode "Dead Language."

The subject of virginity as a focus for the conjoint themes of sexuality and presence was already before him, perhaps in a virgin marriage, certainly in the religious preoccupation of his new wife and his own interest in the subject within his new Catholic faith. By 1868 he had already written one of the great odes on the subject, "Deliciae Sapientiae de Amore," probably the greatest of these early odes. His daughter Emily loved the poem; and her increasing involvement after 1873 in the Order in which she would eventually become a nun herself turned Patmore's attention even further to the subject of virginity. By the mid-1870s Patmore seems to have worked his way through this long period of reflection on loss in isolation. Even as he identified with his daughter's entry into the convent (or she acted out his desire), he began to live a more sociable life, developed the friendship with Harriet Robson that would later lead to his third marriage, and began to seek publication. Even his increasing involvement in Catholic thinking took the form of a holiday-like visit to Lourdes in 1877, where he came the year before the publication of the full group of odes, to share in the historical tradition and community of Mariology. He began to publish poems publicly, in periodicals, albeit at first anonymously, and would take up his old habits of reviewing and writing feature articles.[74] The additional odes at first appeared, in 1877, in no particular order.[75] Perhaps now only was he able to face writing (or rewriting) the poems of personal pain. More mythological or philosophical odes followed an increasing ease with the tragicomic vision of life that he had finally come to accept in the 1860s. It was, then, only in the last separate publication of odes in 1878 and the editing and pruning for the final version opted in *Poems* of 1879 that Patmore created an order, from personal anxiety and loss to larger vision, that reflected symbolically, if not in actual biographical chronology, the painful development of these years.[76]

There were some other good poems also published in 1878 and some odes eventually excluded from the final *Unknown Eros*. Thereafter Patmore would write a great deal, but all in prose. Presumably he had finally expressed, as best he could in his central form of poetry, the full vision of sexuality and love that had possessed him and largely perplexed and even thwarted his obviously great talents until then – thwarted them because he had not been able to say fully what he intuited and to make his contribution to the complicated tradition of writing about sexuality, a tradition filled with insights but also – as Clough showed so well – with manifold confusions.

I hope this perspective on Patmore's career, from early un-controlled, troubled, exploratory work, through the attempt to force himself into a Kingsleyan celebration of one approach to sexuality, to its breakdown and transformation in *Faithful for Ever* and *The Victories of Love* and in the painful and isolated work after his first wife's death, will make the odes of *The Unknown Eros* themselves seem less surprising, if not less artistically astonishing, than they normally appear in his work or in the literature of the period. The new art of the odes seems like an incredibly great break from the popular and conformist verse of *The Angel*. In fact, it is a radical but very comprehensible solution to the broader set of problems he had been facing in his poems from the beginning. In the odes the power of sexuality, but also the force of its disturbance, of its vagaries, above all of its loss and absence, are given full play. Patmore allows himself to write more directly from his own experience than in any of his earlier work and to present, in largely uncensored form, not regulated by any set of orthodox norms, his difficult experience of loss. At the same time he gives his strong imagination, so apparently provoked by sexual issues in his early work and trammeled into unintended, subversive expression in *The Angel*, freedom to soar: to create from the experience of loss a visionary expression of humans' sexual nature.

Patmore's poetic career began with idiosyncratic rewritings of his particular Romantic heritage; it then moved to the popular but very limited achievement in the verse novel form distinctive to the mid-Victorian age and its attempt to write for a broader audience (there are the obvious parallels with Clough's *Bothie*, Elizabeth Barrett's *Aurora Leigh*, and Tennyson's *Enoch Arden*; or the finer works of Meredith's *Modern Love*, or even Tennyson's *Maud*, and Browning's later *The Ring and the Book*). Patmore now moved simultaneously in two directions to strengthen his poetic voice. First, like the major Tennyson of *In Memoriam*, he chose to use something close to a personal voice based on personal experience. This choice followed the direction of his thinking in *The Victories of Love*, where he argued, in a dramatic epistolary poem, that our understanding of both sexual and religious truths must come from within. Now he would allow that personal perspective by the form of his poem.

Second, just as in his religious life Patmore reached toward the broader, more inclusive traditions of the Catholic Church, he now sought to model his poetry on traditions that extended back before Romantic and Victorian ones. The seemingly odd and eccentric new work actually puts Patmore's poetry far more in a mainstream of writing of Western and even world literature, than his more approachable early work. As often, the quest for an authentic personal voice went hand in hand with the adoption of more powerful, broadly traditional voices of authorship. The early Patmore wrote of sexual matters through the inherited language and forms of Romanticism, and he often seemed not fully aware of the strains that passed through his pen. The mature Patmore of *The Unknown Eros* allows for more universal voices and language to flow through his work but, except in the few ranting political odes, he seems the competent magician who can wield as effectively as is feasible the strong traditions he invokes.

We have seen that the odes were written over a period of possibly ten to fifteen years, apparently in no particular order. They were then reshaped into a narration that moves roughly from introductory poems, to a personal story, to broader mythical or philosophical statements. Obviously there can be no question of a tight plot or imposed pattern such as Patmore tried in *The Angel* books. At the same time there is an overall coherence of situation – a man making sense of sex and religion after facing the major loss of his life – and evidently there was an informing intention. The 1868 preface speaks of an "idea" he wanted to express. The successive additions to, and subtractions from, the series, and its final restructuring suggest an overall plan being discovered by an author. Patmore was a fusser, a rewriter and reshaper of earlier work. When he finally left the odes to stand in their finished order he presumably had completed a larger poem of poems. The same sense of a work being put together from independent parts, much as Tennyson shaped *In Memoriam*, is apparent in form and title. Patmore calls his works "odes" from the first, trial, publication of nine odes in 1868. Eventually the title *The Unknown Eros*, applied in 1877 only to the poem of that name as a title poem, was adopted as a proper title for the whole. By and large, there is enough coherence to talk of a poem made of the collection of odes or at least to think of it as a structured collection.[77] There was also enough freedom in the composition of individual odes to allow Patmore to express the varied and complicated perspectives on love, sexuality, and religion that had been so hard to articulate in his earlier works and that he had been moving toward in the many epistolary voices of *Faithful for Ever* and *The Victories of Love*. Now he approached these subjects in the varied voices of a lyric poet speaking at different times and from different points of view, sometimes as an individual talking quite simply to others of his grief, sometimes as a poet with the singing robes of tradition wrapped around him.

In the roles in which Patmore offers himself in the odes there is both a larger coherence – parallel and compatible voices of a poet in a series of poems – and also exploratory attempts to find and try out the appropriate role for the difficult insights he wishes to articulate. We thus have something like the deliberately personal/impersonal voice of a great modern writer such as Yeats: a passionate, very individual attempt to find a role and voice to express universal truths. Taking on roles of poetic tradition with individual passion, the poet most often speaks through the strengths of an entire culture in giving shape to an adequate vision of sexuality.

At the lowest, or most everyday, level of his register, there is the voice of the ordinary person, albeit of education and sensibility, who reports his experience, who speaks of visiting the bed of one of his children whom he has punished too harshly, especially now that his mother is dead ("The Toys," I.x), or tells the story of his wife's sudden alienation at death – "With huddled, unintelligible phrase, / And frighten'd eye" ("Departure," I.viii), or wakes thinking, wrongly, that he has only dreamed of her death – "It *was* the azalea's breath, and she *was* dead!" ("The Azalea," I.vii). His voice is the one we may hear sometimes in Wordsworth when he shares ordinary personal experiences in *The Prelude*, or in Coleridge in the quiet, intimate voice of the conversational poems; or we hear it more steadily in the Victorian novel as the voices, say, of Jane Eyre or Esther Summerson, who dare to create an intimate dialogue with their readers about their personal experience and even more individual feelings. That voice is still heard everywhere in our fiction and poetry so that it seems still, in the most general sense, the note of modern literature. We discover it in *The Unknown Eros* as in other major Victorian poetry; for example, in Meredith's *Modern Love*, in the opening of Arnold's "Dover Beach," in Browning's uniquely personal "One Word More," or, very rarely in *In Memoriam*, always with a certain surprise. It is by far the most intimate voice in Patmore, speaking to us strangers of his problems with his motherless child, the terribly alienating moment of his wife's death, the widower's sexually disturbed and disappointed sleep.

Again, like Yeats, however, who can also give us such moments of sudden intimacy, the Patmore of *The Unknown Eros* never presents himself as merely sharing personal experience for its own sake. To the modernity of that voice Patmore usually adds at least a voice of wisdom, trying to find meaning in the experience. The epigraph Patmore finally chose for the entire poem was from Proverbs – "And my delight was with the sons of men" (Proverbs viii.31, King James; Patmore uses the Latin "Deliciae meae esse cum filiis hominum"). The speaker is the spirit of wisdom, there with God as he created the universe. Wisdom is sometimes seen as a type of the Virgin in Catholic tradition and sometimes explained in modern commentary as a pagan female goddess irrupting into the Old Testament.[78] Modest as it sounds, the epigraph states Patmore's rather bold aspirations: to claim for himself the language of God's own wisdom on the view that God took joy in a communion of wisdom with man, made the more intimate if we image the figure as in some sense female.

Occasionally the voice of wisdom in *The Unknown Eros* approaches too closely to the distinctly Victorian voice of the dean of the Wedding Sermon at the end of *The Victories of Love*. For instance, the personal father's story of "The Toys" must be reread by Patmore at the end almost as a kind of modern type of God's sympathy for all his children. More often, however, there is not this kind of reading of a moral to his tale so much as the wisdom of careful reflection on experience structured into the very way it is presented. "Departure" is framed with the painful observation that "It was not like your great and gracious ways!" Between this opening and the conclusion that restates it with greater finality – "'Twas all unlike . . ." – the "it" that was "unlike" is filled with a meaning from his personal experience of the strangeness that death brings as it cancels all human fine tone and civility. His understanding is exactly of this difference, which has undone not only her civilized ways but their attempt to bring a ritual and dignity to her departure, as they sat at sunset sharing parting love and praise. As he now sees it, the experience has been not the anticipated human one of grief, but the radical one of lost humanity: "all at once to leave me at the last, / More at the wonder than the loss aghast, / With huddled, unintelligible phrase, / And frighten'd eye, / And go your journey of all days / With not one kiss, or a good-bye, / And the only loveless look the look with which you pass'd." The wisdom here, at the bleak center of loss in the poem, is one that begins in personal experience, yet which impresses us as that of a mind that goes further in accepting even difficult realities and following their consequences than most persons would who might have the same experience. Elsewhere Patmore assumes more formal voices of wisdom, for instance, the voice finally accepting comfortably personal and general fate, as in "Magna Est Veritas" (I.xii), where he literally sits down and accepts a world bound to go on without him in the faith that truth will prevail independent of our individual desire for it. Or there is the more forceful voice of "'Let be!'" (I.xx) who, in a series of penetrating paradoxes, discerns the good beneath apparent ill, evil beneath apparent good.

The too-popular poet of *The Angel* even conceives of himself now as a deliberately and necessarily unpopular voice of special understanding. At the highest point in his register, he presents himself, as he indeed would be presented in Sargent's stylized portrait of him as Ezekiel in the painting for the Boston Public Library, as a prophet offering unpalatable truths to his unhearing generation. As in the portrait, the pose itself is in many ways the most impressive thing. Patmore offers himself, in an anticipation of the alienated and haughty figures of modern literature – Joyce, for example – as writing for future generations, who might better appreciate his insights. The change heard in the opening "Proem," especially by contrast to the first two books of *The Angel*, is radical and irreversible. He writes out of a settled sense of limits and acceptance of failed hopes. Personal hope and grief are alike "surely vain" to his matured reflection. And their hopelessness is involved in the larger failure of a civilization. Instead of the period-piece idyll of middle-class aspiration for a place among the gentry, Patmore now reads only the dissolution and exhaustion of his time. Like the biblical prophets, he finds himself presiding over the demise of a great civilization; like Joyce, he must write for times to come – his poems "chants" of a lonely thrush "at latest eve." Oddly Patmore is remarkably prescient in seeing that the English language will survive to speak to "nations yet unborn" when Victorian British civilization, deep in winter, already a "corpse," is entirely extinct. Of course, while Joyce has played a substantial part in creating the unborn conscience of his and other modern races, Patmore has had almost no place in the emergence of the English-language world literature he forecasted. But Patmore is hard to defeat in the odes, even when we have the huge benefit of hindsight. The failure of *his* civilization has been that he no longer can expect an audience for serious poetry with a radically different perspective, as opposed to the popular *Angels* of his time. Serious literature has become classical, an "imperial tongue," as he says in "Dead Language" (II.xviii), to the future, as the classics have been to his culture: and therefore guaranteed some immortality in an English-language world – at the expense of any real readership who might take the message to heart. That the odes are recognized in anthologies as poems of interest and merit yet are never read today – continue to be a "dead language" – because of prejudice against his earlier poem and because they are very difficult poems rather continues Patmore's point.

Patmore will sing "of forgotten things to far-off times to come" ("Vesica Piscis," I.xxiv) – presumably times not yet arrived. The pose of unhonored prophet with an ancient, still unheeded message is an appealing one; so too is the stance in some odes of tough-minded seer who faces boldly a vision of the worst. In "Crest and Gulf" (I.xix) the prophet is one of the stony-faced ones who can see steadily the mismatches of intention and result, of apparent progress and real failure, that make man's history a matter of waves up and down, crest and gulf, rather than meaningful advance. His gnomic wisdom rides above the waves, tough, paradoxical, aware even of unintentional successes as well as failures, calling the "nought" he sees in history the nought it is. From this tough view he claims also the prophet's view of greater harmonies not in man's control: a listener "at the doors of destiny," he hears above the din of the waves, in Patmore's great image, the "fly-wheel swift and still" of God's larger will.

Such a magnificent conceit establishes Patmore's prophetic claims as at least a persuasive attitude; but this status is threatened by the misuse that he, perhaps not so unlike those very unpopular and usually self-righteous and ranting biblical prophet predecessors, sometimes makes of his new vocation. After the fly-wheel image we

are sorry to hear "Crest and Gulf" end with the line "The amorous
and vehement drift of man's herd to hell." We are suddenly moving
from a great stance to a strong hint of mere invective. Where in other
odes he tries really to play the prophet against his times, he descends
into mere high-toned bombast: "1867" (I.xiii), against democracy,
"Peace" (I.xv), in favor of war, and "1880–85" (I.xvii), against
democracy again. Like the ultra-Tory of the landowning class that he
had joined, he evenhandedly condemns to perdition both Disraeli
and Gladstone, one for the 1867 Reform Act and the other for the
Third Reform Act, of 1884, and admires Prussian activism. We can
understand such unappealing attitudes, which Patmore shared with
Carlyle and many other intellectuals of his day, in an historical
context. But we are not called on to appreciate the very weak poetry
of abuse that such immediate political concerns permit him. His
future editor of any reader's text should quietly consign these poems
to an appendix for the merely curious.

If he needed authorization for such a bold move of friendly concern
for both Patmore's reader and the poet himself, he could find it in the
charming poem, "Prophets Who Cannot Sing" (II.xvi). Between
David and Dante, he admits, the poetry of prophecy was a poetic
failure; and the same has been true since. These "Poor Seraphim,"
among whom he evidently would include most of the shrill biblical
prophets, and we must include himself as Tory Jeremiah, are merely
"harsh and stammering." They "screw the pitch too high" and
sound like nails dragged over slate. In the poem these criticisms are
ascribed to critics (I would be among them), but they are not
gainsaid by the voice of the poet. Rather than be "hoarse as frogs,"
he admits in comic desperation, "Far better be dumb dogs." But the
problem is more than merely the prophet's tendency to turn in
tuneless harsh judgments of his age. And the poem, placed near the
end of the final series, directs us to the larger problem in the role of
prophet-poet. Others, the critic points out, sing well of lesser subjects:
hedge-flower, water, or wandering cloud all have songs and seers.
Even when not venting their spleen on their age, the prophets have
a special difficulty. Attempting to render the greatest truths, "Views
of the unveil'd heavens," prophets find they can't sing, only croak.
Their songs, if successful in their aims, Patmore admits to the critics,
would be too much, would "burst an organ-pipe."

Of course, it can be done without such rupturing straining. The
names of David, presumed author of Psalms, and Dante are inscribed

in his genial poem to guarantee there is an answer to those critics. But the answer is also clearly in a mode other than the merely prophetical-satirical. David's songs are of love to God, not the power or scorn of prophecy; Dante marvelously managed to work all vengeance on his enemies, in a poem that keeps its central focus on God's plan and, led by his human love, ultimately also on God's love. The strategy allows Patmore to make the comparison between his work and theirs in an engaging, far from arrogant prophetic way. Accepting the criticism of his tendency to prophet's rant, he also gains credit for his better intentions in assuming a high role as poet.

Much of the same happens in the series as a whole, where Patmore picks up and works with poetic traditions that allow him to speak, indeed, with some of the sense of special understanding that the ranting prophet, in the Bible or in himself, has more trouble communicating. Most obvious is the enormously rich and influential tradition of Western love poetry, one that in part springs from Dante's own writings on Beatrice in the *Vita nuova* and *Divine Comedy*. Patmore's Felix had already claimed him as model along with the other great taproot of this tradition, Petrarch, in his aspirations to the role of laureate of happy Victorian marriage. Long before our contemporary fascination with the interdependence of apparent opposites of absence and desire, that tradition had been founded not on fulfilled love but on the passion inspired by the absence of the beloved. In the courtly tradition out of which Petrarch emerged, desire was for the unavailable person.[79] Dante and Petrarch founded their poems on distance and unavailability, then on the far more profound and universal absence of death. Patmore had come closer to the strength of this tradition in exploring the imagined feeling of unfortunate Frederick. Now truly *infelix* himself after the death of his wife, he is far more able to adapt Petrarch to English marriage than his happy narrator could in the idealized celebration of married presence.

Patmore situates his poems on love squarely in the realm of loss, beginning with a poem, "Saint Valentine's Day" (I.i) that finds love's feast in the mid-winter where desire wakens, only to die at the end of the short day. His opening poems tell a very brief tale of love, focussed on the beatitude of a divine thing come to earth ("Beata," I.iv), a kind of condensation of the trope in the tradition of the lady as heavenly creature that also reminds us that her home is not here, and a poem on the lover's joy in anticipation ("The Day After To-

Morrow," I.v), also a condensation, in this case of the theme of desire in absence. But the series of love poems only begins with this hesitant assertion of love's presence and it soon finds its center in anticipation of death, the loss itself, and, above all, accommodation to loss by mourning. In turn, as in Dante or Petrarch, loss, once fully realized, drives Patmore to fill the void he feels with some presence seemingly less vulnerable to mortality, while it also facilitates the sexualization of religious mythological traditions.

Patmore could have followed the formal models of Dante or Petrarch, as he broadly followed their poetics of desire and absence. In a sense he had followed both in *The Angel*, by explicitly claiming Petrarch as model and writing many brief songs, if not actual sonnets, on love; by creating in the entire poem the modern epic of domestic love in scrambled order from Dante, starting with Felix and Honoria's little paradise and proceeding to the internal pain of Frederick and his domestic purgation. If he thought of the parallels Patmore may well have often wished, as indeed he for a while tried, to suppress that little epic entirely. His new intention was to reach out to a far larger universe of ideas, images, and myth, while he allowed himself to expose much more deeply his pain and desire. At the same time he sought not length and apparent impressiveness – the domestic epic dear to his middle work and to his age – but the intense resonance of succinct, compressed, utterance. He needed a form that would allow him to bring together and weld into a few lines the multifold experience he was uniting: starting with the center of things as he found them, the gain and loss of love, he wished to try to state some vision of man's place in the universe and in relation to God. Like Petrarch, he would wish to write the love poem as a form of elegy; like Dante he would move from love to epic, mythic, statement of the universe; and like both, in his loss his poems to his love became also hymns to God.

One poetic form especially was appropriate for concentrating so many different poetic aims and consequently so many forms into one poem. It was in many ways the freest of traditional forms, certainly the best adapted to mutate from form to form while maintaining its own intrinsic character. And it was a form entirely suited in its elevation and seriousness to Patmore's aims – though also perhaps the easiest in which to fail completely.

This was, of course, the ode; Patmore seems to have been clear that it was his right vehicle from very early in his writing. After the verse

novels, epistle verses, and many light if also often intricate forms of
The Angel and *The Victories of Love*, Patmore chose the difficult,
austere, generally also obscure ode as both form and title for his first
trial publication in 1868 of nine *Odes*. That miscellany of odes, few on
personal issues and only a few central to the later work that would be
organized in the full series of forty-three poems, could be said to be
ordered and conceptualized only by the genre of ode. Before he knew
all that he wished to write, he knew that what he wanted to achieve
was in some sense the form of the ode itself: like other complex,
combinatory genres – the Shakespearean romance for instance – its
complex melding of voices, points of view, and forms could set a goal
for the attainment of mature wisdom.[80] The genre tag was used again
in the title in two later publications as he moved toward the final
version and title of *The Unknown Eros*, where it was finally dropped;
it is by then clearly a collection of odes.

Suppleness and flexibility, especially in the form of rapid change
and repeated turns, had of course been a fundamental quality of the
ode since the startling, bold, and so motile performances of Pindar
with their dramatic shifts of view from strophe to antistrophe to
epode, well Englished by Ben Johnson in his own odes as turn,
counterturn, and stand.[81] Horace's odes had not reached as high, nor
were the turns as dramatic; but he had brought to the form a
different kind of changeability, the suppleness of quick changes of
tone of voice and subtle shifts in attitude. In the most common
English form, the so-called "irregular ode" first fully established in
the seventeenth century by Cowley, the facility of the ode for sudden
changes was, if anything, extended by eliminating a formal stanzaic
pattern. With essentially variable line length, unpredictable use of
rhyme and expandable overall length, the ode allowed English
writers to move rapidly from one poetic form and mode of feeling to
another. Like modern free verse, the form put heavy demands on the
poet to create his or her own new form with each poem. Unlike free
verse, it allowed the poet easily to incorporate various formal
traditions of poetry in the new creation. As he or she melded forms
together in the ode the poet also found useful kinds of unity in this
loose but not casual form of poetry. By its frequent ceremonial and
public nature the ode allowed elevated or abstract language: for
Patmore an opportunity to take risks with broad statements on
human destiny or, more often, to create a metaphysical poetry,
provoking and thoughtful, in which bold, unusual ideas or knotty

paradoxes might emerge from new conjunctions of perception or argument. Similarly, irregular rhyme, and use of alliteration within and between lines as another kind of rhyming,[82] allowed Patmore to suggest the connections between seemingly unlike things. The irregular flow of the ode keeps being stopped by unexpected instants of recognition when relations are suddenly glimpsed beneath the surface of phenomena.

If the protean form of the ode offered to Patmore a vehicle for articulating, in one set of poems, and often within the fast-changing course of a single poem, the broad range of experience – of love, of loss, of history, of religion and myth – that he now wished to connect and interpret, it also offered certain more specific traditions of its own, both of subject and presentation, that were rather precisely attuned to Patmore's preoccupations. As he explored the potential of his new chosen form he in effect found already formulated in the nature of the ode as it had come down to him many of his own insights. Tradition thus still spoke through him as Romantic traditions of sexual discussion in poetry had in his early poems of the 1840s; but he was now a much more conscious utilizer of tradition. He gives everywhere a sense of working every rift of the ode's great potential for what gold of complex expression he could extract; we rarely find him merely borne along by the force of the tradition itself, except in those few cases of noble prophetic rant, a mode of excess unfortunately only too much a part of the tradition of the ode, especially in its frequent abuse in the eighteenth century.

Paul Fry has usefully, if also rather curiously, defined the ode by what it fails to be – an appropriate mode of definition for a tradition that has been about reaching for what is beyond its grasp. The ode is in some sense a failed prayer or hymn to a god or mythic power. Instead of, as in a hymn, celebrating a public belief in the presence of a god, who is only to be properly summoned in the ritual of the poem, the ode speaks for the poet's private sense of distance from sacred presence, whether god-creature or supernal or superlative quality (as in Coleridge's absence from imagination in "Dejection"). There is a sleight of hand in such a definition that should be registered; for, like the ode it defines, the definition creates a kind of imaginary presence in the hymn that it contrasts to the ode, a shamanistic work entirely sure of a deity's presence. And this is probably a mistake. As E. M. Forster's Godbole in *A Passage to India* explains, even where traditional faith persists in a public, mythic belief, mortal control over deity is not be counted on: "I say to Him, Come, come, come, come, come, come. He neglects to come." Whatever their rhetoric, all works about religious assurance are about the wish and quest, as all love poems, no matter how seemingly assured, are also about the fear of love's loss. But, like T. S. Eliot's similar ideal notion of an age of unified sensibility, the abstract idea of a hymn of public possession of a god is useful in defining a continuum of modern absence from a postulated felicity. In its history the ode, then, is preoccupied with attempting a kind of myth-making or magic with words. It would like to create a god or power by addressing it or describing it. That done, it would like to command the power it has summoned to replenish the human author's self and world. If hymns were truly hymns in Fry's ideal sense, they would not need to exist. For the ode, like any kind of prayer, is motivated by a sense of absence, need, failure of fulfillment. It would restore by its speaking voice, and indeed by any poetic means it can draw into its desperate attempt, a sense of plenum and presence.

Certainly doing such magic with words becomes progressively harder – a large human loss and large gain in artistic possibility – when belief becomes more individual than communal. From the Psalms, to Pindar, to Milton's Nativity Ode, to Wordsworth's "Intimations of Immortality" there is increasing pressure on the odist to fill the vacuum he experiences by the terrible business of exploring that vacuum itself for some hint of presence. As the odist seeks his god within, he also naturally becomes more aware of the poem as a poem about his powers – a poem such as Coleridge's "Dejection" or Shelley's "Ode to the West Wind." The figure of invocation, as Jonathan Culler has remarked, is really one of the vocation of the poet; or, as Fry puts it, the ode becomes a "deliberately rhetorical test of originary strength."[83] The result is that the modern ode is especially far from the imaginary ideal of simple assertion of presence. It is situated immediately in the author's sense of loss in life, inadequacy in himself, or both at once. It puts him to a sudden ultimate test: can he, with whatever poetic powers and traditions of language he can muster, bring meaning and assurance out of the insecurity and loss of ordinary experience? And this is, of course, exactly what Patmore set out to do.

Fry attempts to explain the genesis of the ode in a compulsion-repetition complex in the author, which leads him or her to seek to escape the realities of sex and death by the effort of the ode to call down a god; he sees the ode's necessary failure in the poet's inability to keep back recognition of the realities he seeks to avoid, so that the ode is really set not in a world of bright gods but in a twilight, too-human world of repeated loss. Like so many interpretations by translation into psychological tales, this one assumes that the author must remain unconscious of what is, therefore, neurotic behavior. Patmore, unlike Wordsworth, Coleridge, or Keats before him, is not betrayed in his odes into recognition of loss and death; he is conscious that this is the center of his subject. More than the Romantics (one thinks of Coleridge's half-recognition of a sexual defeat in the imaginative failure engaged with in "Dejection," or of the central but unexplained figures of an angry, dying, or departing lover in Keats's "Ode on Melancholy"), Patmore is always already consciously focussed on the sexual problem of human life. The clear sexualization of the ode in the movement from the Romantics to Patmore suggests how quickly thinking generally was already becoming Freudianized in the century that brought forth Freud. Dejection and melancholy are now *about* sexual loss; the quest for the presence of a god will be, as clearly as in Eliot's *The Waste Land*, also a quest for a figure of sexual potency. (Indeed, as I suggested in the Introduction, rather than stumbling upon sexuality, as in Fry's model, religious aspiration is generally very often directly connected to sexual aspiration.) In Fry's formulation the ode goes nowhere, merely confronts limits as it performs itself. But the form actually demands a maturity of reflection on its subject that settled understanding, rather than new discovery, properly provides. To the extent that the writer, as Patmore often does in the odes, can build his poem on awareness of the limits to his aspirations for a higher presence in the loss and unfulfilled desire of his normal experience, he doesn't display a compulsion but embodies conscious self-understanding. Only when Patmore seeks to create from his loss too firm a vision of plenitude, a new, complete, sexual myth of man's relation with God, does he reveal in a very few poems his own failure to understand the desires he displays. For the most part the odes, not the least in their careful ordering as a group in the final version, suggest an author rather unusually aware of his own response to his experience, showing us the motivations for his search for a replenishing relation to God at the same time that he exhibits and shares the search itself.

In the following two sections I invite the reader to join me in a more specific look at the two books of odes that make up Patmore's masterpiece. I also beg indulgence for what may seem a rather extended critical enterprise on a little-recognized poem. As will be quickly obvious, these are extremely compact and often extremely difficult poems and, if not all worth the kind of detailed attention we give to accepted classics, a great number in the two long books are. In addition, as a series they can only be fully understood in relation to the poetic plot, so to speak, of the whole – and as will also be soon apparent, it is a rather subtle and difficult plot. But the most important incentive to myself in writing, as I trust to my reader in reading, is the quite rare pleasure of exploring works of major importance that are virtually unknown to serious lovers of poetry or serious scholarship and criticism. In making up for the lack of the latter in the service of the former, I have also had to undertake more explanation than would be necessary if I could refer readers to an established set of opinions and critical information – though here, as is usual in such cases, a longer route through rather full explanations of the many difficulties in these hard works may prove for Patmore's readers the shortest way home.

BOOK I: THE LOSS

The area occupied by the series of odes is both subtly and beautifully laid out in the opening poem. "Saint Valentine's Day" (I.i), many of whose themes are repeated in the equally lovely poem "Winter" (I.iii).[84] In the "Proem" Patmore had spoken in his more public voice of the failure of his hopes for his country, which he found in its "last lethargy"; he hoped only that his own work might have the calm joy of a clear song at evening. "Saint Valentine's Day" and "Winter" expand the terrain of this winter's tale considerably. The time of "Saint Valentine's Day" is explicitly a season out of season for love. Love's feast is in winter, not in "some rosy day" of May. Love is most honored, paradoxically, out of its normal natural time. And it is associated with its opposite, virginity. Love's holiday is in "vestal February"; its image is not the usual rose but the snow-drop, which is itself related to an oath of virginity, "first-love's first cry." We are thus immediately placed in relation to both terms of love. There is the winter world of the speaker, imaged here by the "Thrush" – the lonely bird singing at eve of the "Proem" – who speaks from full experience of love. And there is the seeming opposite of ignorant virginity. Both are versions of love at the extreme of its apparent absence. Along with "Winter," this poem comes closest in the odes to offering a restatement of the Romantic poem of meditation on a landscape. Though very different in texture – it offers a series of tableaux of winter activity – it is no less than Stevens's "The Snow Man" a poem of nature as absence. The most positive presence of love is the snowdrop, an image of pure wintry absence. The rest of nature, a blackbird that "breaks the young Day's heart," a hill that smiles to the setting sun, the "drooping skiff" of a fisherman, children playing as the sun sets, all join in the speaker's awareness of winter as a time of loss, when the sun's certain and rapid setting dominates the day.

Images of brief happiness, cries of the children, calls of the birds, like the momentary appearance of the snowdrop, only sharpen the speaker and our awareness of what is missing. As in a Romantic poem in which the failure of nature fully to satisfy the poet heightens his or her sense of power of imagination, Patmore's winter landscape of unfulfillment raises absent powers of love. The feelings evoked are odd ones of powers elicited that we normally ignore: "peaceful poignancy," "joy contrite," "remorse." The entire landscape is seen as sighing over the loss – and the potential – felt in the winter day. The "pang" of absence is a "cherish'd pang" because it opens up feelings not otherwise available. The dominating image of the entire description, when we look again, is of pregnancy. The entire scene, ourselves included, is a womb from which the "Baby Spring," promise of full bloom of love, will eventually come forth. Absence, virginity of February, makes us pregnant to give forth love. The free-floating, easy transitions of the ode form allow Patmore quickly to jump from the descriptive scene of love's potential in absence to a more general statement. The experience is not merely the special, transient one of old age or virgin youth. His mistress, happy in love, nonetheless averts her lips from his kiss; in this mood she asks from "Love's bounty" "much more than bliss!" Even mature lovers for whom love's feast is, in fact, celebrated, find in it a power of love that goes beyond nature itself.

Patmore is then quick to insist that he is *not* celebrating a platonic power of unsexual love. Two rhetorical questions subtly expose rather the interrelation of love's absence and its presence in desire. "Is't the sequester'd and exceeding sweet / Of dear Desire electing his defeat?" Desire conceived as choosing not to fulfill itself is seen not as defeated but as therefore made even stronger, "exceeding sweet." Is "Earth," the next lines ask, "Vainly renouncing, with a seraph's sigh, / Love's natural hope?" The rapid oppositions and abstract images available in the ode allow Patmore to pack a great deal together, the renunciation – theme of the poem – its impossibility, the parallel with love on a celestial level (the seraph sighs just as the entire landscape of the poem has), and the double meaning of natural: both the way of the Earth and the inevitable way. Renunciation is not opposed to natural desire; it only enhances it.

The conclusion of the poem is, then, a total triumph of amorous life. It is inevitable, as the entire structure of the poem has created it. We have been learning about the power of love in its absence, but we have been sighing over the infant spring whose birth is the fruit of winter love. The rosy May announced as the other pole of love in the opening now necessarily has her day, not in opposition to winter's desire but as its inevitable fulfillment. Earth's vows of virginity were "foredoom'd to perjury." May "all-amorous" with warm bosom and roses heaped on "laughing brows" comes as an irresistible force to void the void: "Avoids thee of thy vows!" The triumphal car-like quality of this rush of sexual fulfillment, however, also has its casualties. The "sharpness of the Seraph's sphere," in which we cannot always live, is now avoided; yet Earth brings a heart now less aware than in winter. In Patmore's striking image it is filled with dead "Innocencies," as a nest of birds when the hawk has killed the old ones. In some sense love needs the old ones and young ones, those aware of loss and those still unaware of fulfillment, to preserve its intensity. May's fulfillment, in the profit-and-loss equations so natural to the ode, is also a sad loss. The poem then ends with a brief return to February, reasserting the value of a different winter, "noon of . . . soft ecstasy," which is caught between fears of loss ("Or e'er it be too late") and loss of the anticipation ("Or e'er the Snowdrop die").

"Winter," a lovely meditation as well, stresses the fruition itself found in the season of unfruitfulness. Patmore insists on two simultaneous truths. First, the odd truth made familiar to us by modern philosophical criticism, of the opposite generated by statement of its opposite. Winter, season of absence, reminds us everywhere of the fullness of summer presence. Winter's pallor that seems of death is really a sign of its opposite, "warmth and light asleep."

Lily shafts "Stand full – arry'd . . . perfect for the Summer, less the flower." But also winter's absence is everywhere turning into its summer fullness. The poem asks us to join the speaker in "duly" looking into things, reading rightly the present "characters of dark and cold." This is a repeated gesture of the odes, leading us to a wisdom that sees beyond accepted barriers and oppositions. Honeysuckle puts out a "little, wandering spray," in "sheltered brakes." "Primrose or violet bewilder'd wakes" and tries to flower; the buried bulb "hails far Summer with his lifted spear"; gorse field becomes a magical golden fleece. The meditation begins and ends on more self-reflexive signs of summer in winter, summer itself sleeping as a hidden "infant harvest" beneath the snow, the "ghostly chrysalis" that "stirs in its dream dark." The dream, as the poet's, is of summer known by and in winter; he again appears figured casually as a bird singing in winter, here "the flush'd Robin," who, "in the evenings hoar, / Does of Love's Day, as if he saw it, sing." That figure alone makes explicit the erotic issue between winter and summer that is far more muted here than in the parallel earlier poem.

The delicacy of the poem, interrupted only by the robins and the poet's momentary flush of enthusiasm for love, is retained in the conclusion, a lovely figure of winter herself as an infant thing. She is lovable and innocent rather than amorous, smiling with "wandering, languorous gaze" on the "elemental, chill adversity" of the absence around her. Her sigh is one that speaks of her sense of exile from a place suited to her loveliness, a sphere like that of ether in the old system of the heavens or "something still more tranquil." The focus is on the lovable repose of winter's pure virginity, which we have seen is only a side of summer's fulfillment. Rather than the triumphal figure of May that predominates at the end of "Saint Valentine's Day" we have only hints of the grown love to which infant winter is nonetheless connected, the phallic "lifted spear" of the bulbs, the lilies who quickly slip "their gowns" in Autumn, the dangerous love story evoked by the allusion to Jason's fleece. The power and necessary pain and loss of fulfillment is written gently and peripherally into the poem; the power of what moves him "singularly," the full potential of all fruition seen in the lovely vacant gaze of infant winter, is central. Again, we are taught to find the passion of growth and love as finally located in ourselves; we love winter not because it is virginal but because we can write on her absence, and find in her mere traces the fullness of our own desire for love's presence in summer. It is thus in some sense in the "dream dark" in the chrysalis of our own minds that we find the power of passion.

Patmore's final title was *The Unknown Eros*; early scholars quoted Robert Waring's seventeenth-century *Amoris Effigies*, known to Patmore earlier, which stated that Cupid had the property of a god, that is, to be unknown; or they reverted to Patmore's claims for *The Angel*, that wedded love was a theme largely unknown to the poets (a rather dubious claim to make, by the way, any time after Spenser).[85] The experience of the opening poems rather suggests a more direct meaning; as those poems have, the series as a whole will try to lead us into a different experience of love from the common one of summer fulfillment. That looks on the end of love; Patmore has been exploring rather its origins in the need of the psyche facing vacancy and absence. Patmore seems to suggest that what is unknown about love is love itself as opposed to its manifestations in its fulfillment. Even in these unusually descriptive odes he has, in effect, been calling upon a god to come to him, finding the power of the god through his own experience. Only after he has created this radical perspective on love as an independent power found in one's individual self does he then move to the usually central subject of love poetry, the love story of a couple.

The opening poem in the long story of his love that occupies the center of the first of the two books of *The Unknown Eros* approaches a love relation very much from this unusual perspective. Instead of the kind of personal detail that so occupies the four books of the entire *Angel in the House*, we begin with only the most general, even universal situation. "Beata" (I.iv) is nonetheless a lovely brief poem, a line longer than a sonnet and consisting of one long sentence leading through "toil and weariness" to a caress of the spirit and sense of delight. The oppositions of darkness – his painful "cavern black" – and light – heavenly light strikes her as a "diamond stalactite" creating a "rainbow's blaze" in his dark – gives a powerful sense of love's force within a Petrarchan tradition that also reaches back to Platonic images of cave and light. Yet the experience is very much presented as a generic, if a very powerful, one. The diamond blaze of the loved one is also blessed, *beata*, because it puts her lover in touch with more than her, with the rays of "infinite" heaven.[86] The power of heaven, seen as mere absolutes of "Reason, Power, and Love" only tired him with "deadening might" and "undistinguishable stress / Of withering white" until he could experience them in a personal way through her. Thus the complimentary wit of the end – "Nothing of Heaven in thee showing infinite / Save the delight" – is that her great, infinite in the common sense, delight to him is that she disguises her connection with infinity. Yet the burden of the whole is certainly that a love relation brings into play powers far beyond those of the merely individual. The individual seems rather the necessary vehicle of a contact for the lover – and we should stress that it is, of course, for both lovers – with a force of love more than individual.

The second love poem is much more of a passionate statement of love; indeed it stands in the entire series for the recognized and totally accepted power of ordinary lovers' sexual passion. It is a love poem about mature lovers almost unique in its century and certainly still rare in ours in that it awakens neither scorn nor embarrassment in grown-up readers. It, too, is nonetheless presented from the point of view of absence established by the poems we have looked at in the beginning of the series. The title, "The Day After To-Morrow" (i.v), tells us already that it is about love deferred and the power of absence to awaken love. But unlike the poems on winter's more general season of absence it is almost totally located in the intense summer world of personal passion at its strongest; and it is spoken by the lover directly out of his passion. The speaker waits for his lover by the sea, which offers, as in the little poem "Wind and Wave" (i.ii), elemental images for love's power. The lover speaks to his lover in a kind of odic dramatic monologue: it is almost certainly the most expressive and sensual love poem Patmore ever wrote. He addresses her indirectly, through odic calling to the clouds, winds, and waves, who are to speak to her of their deferred but passionate meeting in two days. In his invocation he is able to assume the power of the elements to express his and his lover's feelings, beginning with a deliberate confusion in the opening between the real ocean waves and "the great wave of coming pleasure." That wave draws a "hollow gulf" of absence which his utterance now fills. His description of their coming meeting then becomes the filling wave of passion that, in an obvious but powerful symbol built into the poem, fills her gulf.

That she and we are given language about that meeting rather than the thing itself – which is, in the fundamental structure of the utterance, deferred – is not apparent as we read, because the description is both sensuous and passionate, much more so than anything in *The Angel*, if still under the controlling decorum of Patmore's age for over-counter writing about sex. The key phrase is the essential opposite of deferral or absence, almost a universal lover's code for everything we want: "Our lives shall be fulfill'd!" The description emphasizes the failure of words and signs in the presence of physical contact; that contact is imaged as a complex intermingling of what still remains individual, threads and meshes, the mingling of hands and the awareness of the alien pulse in one's touch. The ode assumes lyric, even operatic, form as the speaker describes their bliss. And the repeated invocations, the series of rather slow, often half-end-stopped lines, each with its own central beat focussing on the physical presence – "sweet hands . . . The pulse . . . each long finger . . . palm . . . wrist" – gives his speech an hypnotic quality, as if it has come under the control of the rhythm of the passion itself.

Repetition, apparent throughout in the repeated "Ands" that begin lines, and in the parallel structures, eventually slows the lines, and the passion, to a stop:

> And yet our lives shall now be first fulfill'd,
> And into their summ'd sweetness fall distill'd
> One sweet drop more;
> One sweet drop more, in absolute increase
> Of unrelapsing peace.

The poem as a whole then repeats, with a second address to the sea, second reminder of the present distance – enhancing desire – that lies between them, a second description of fulfillment. As Patmore explicitly states, the difference is in the awareness of repetition. Even in the first description, though they look forward to what seems ultimate fulfillment, yet they also will have nothing *new* to say: "It all has been before." From the apparent immediate rendering of passion of the poem's first half we are driven to realize the opposite: that his words offered two days before love are about a lifetime's experience, in that sense the "sweet drop more" that is really the essence of all love's distilling.

In the second telling we are, then, clearly dealing with the psychological distillate of their relation, what it has always already been: in this one poem of fulfilled passion Patmore thus succeeds in representing the power of the experience, then in summarizing the inner impact of the experience itself. It is a subtle, deft management of the problem of recreating sexual experience, as it necessarily is in a poem, as language. Patmore has given central place to the actual occasion of passion, which he places at the center of the experience of sexuality. At the same time, in the second half of the poem, he focuses again, as in the opening winter poems of passion in absence, on the inner experience.

It is not surprising to find him then fully returned to some of the disturbing psychological insights that had emerged in his earlier work but had been largely suppressed in *The Angel*. Here the counters are more abstract, as they can be in the ode, and the oppositions and connections more sudden and striking. First we see even more clearly how distance and deferral create passion; here, in the second half, the speaker virtually celebrates the postponement of meeting – really the subject of this central love poem of the series. He now invokes the elemental powers of nature not to call them down but to stay their power, already equated with the power of love, for a while. The strategy only increases his sense, and ours, of the established power of the passion. He calls upon the sea to keep them apart, though in the very request he admits they are already together, though their hearts that beat together still beat "too far apart." He calls on love to make it appear that their love is passive, calm in her breast as if it were not. Yet again he admits he can already see her smile despite the distance; the language, as throughout the poem, is rich and sensual: "folded to her breast . . . years and years of rest."

Second, he now displays the force of sexual passion in a kind of psychomachia that makes clear its strong, even almost overwhelming effect on him. The language, as the ode easily permits, now rises to grand phrases that embody the complexity of his response. Such language that has, as often in the odes, a Miltonic ring, used to be called, in the high moments of Modernism, Parnassian – with contempt. (Ironically, it was a term especially dear to Patmore's friend and admirer Hopkins.) But the issue is, of course, whether the language works effectively to communicate something or whether it merely puts a derivative screen between author and reader. Except in the poems of political rant, Patmore generally uses abstract language to great effect, usually to suggest psychological depths. Here the screens become "oceans of intolerable delight" and the passionate reunion "The blazing photosphere of central Night" ("photosphere" is the luminous surface of a sun or other sphere, so we have an intense sense of a more than planetary brilliance in the dead of night).

The image suggests a danger of overexposure, only too much brightness in the dark chamber of love or the psyche. The plea is that their experience may be forgotten for a while: obviously it can't be. In writing and in revising *The Angel*, as we have seen, Patmore suppressed earlier lines powerfully revealing the groom's and bride's anxiety over the wedding night. Here, in this mature and repeated relation, "Terror" is freely acknowledged as the "swarthy Groom of Bride-bliss." Strongest fulfillment, represented here by the trope of marital union, brings with it strongest fear. Death follows close behind, as bringing a "hope intense / Of kisses close beyond conceit of sense." The phrase may look forward to themes of love beyond death, but these are not, in fact, very prominent in the series as a whole. More important is the traditional identification of death and sexual consummation, another version of the intensity experienced as high danger in the postponed meeting. And finally, life is called upon to hold back its liberality, since even holding her hand overwhelms his heart with joy. These figures of danger, invoked to hold back their power, have thereby been nonetheless actually invoked; that is, as always in the ode, description of their attributes has served to present them before us in their power. Now, almost as in a ritual, reciting the protecting days which obviously can't stave off the force of desire, he releases the lot:

> One day's controlled hope, and one again,
> And then the third, and ye shall have the rein,
> O Life, Death, Terror, Love!

He can do so because he knows their strength – and their limits. After "flaming Ethers," after the "rapture" will come new "abiding sweetness"' and the poem ends with a focus on the image of a distillate drop of "honied peace."

We have experienced both peace and terror as cycles of love, literally a peace already anticipated as part of lovemaking that is also anticipated; peace expected at the end thus still serves to control the anxiety of the coming together; more generally, the peace after the storm is part of the larger cycle of recurrence. "Has all not been before?" and therefore the desire springs again necessarily from the peace. Sexual desire, the season of summer, follows the same pattern of absence-desire-fulfillment that we have seen in winter but, running far more into fulfillment, it includes the manifold passions in the full experience of sexuality. It is a mature vision of sexual experience, experience never to be taken for granted, never to be without complicated, even conflicting, certainly tempestuous feelings. At the same time it offers a broader pattern of sexuality as a way of talking of intense experience generally, the plenitude of summer at the other end of winter absence. The speaker seems able to accept every aspect of an intense sexual relationship including its necessary variations; as writer, Patmore creates a vision of human nature centered on a necessary alternation of sexual absence and presence, each in effect begetting the other in the speaker's mind.

To suspend or postpone love's intense encounter is a way of defending against our exposure; it is also a way of defending against loss by seeming to have some control over absence – as in Freud's famous observation in *Beyond the Pleasure Principle* of the good little boy's throwing away and pulling back his toy – "*fort/da*" – as a way of learning to deal with his mother's absence. The last poem of fulfilled love in the series of odes, "Tristitia" (I.vi), is spoken in full union with his lover; but it now – perhaps we should say therefore – begins to face the possibility (inevitability) of loss more directly. The poem opens warmly with the opening address, "Darling." Thus hearts are at the still moment of union hoped for in the previous poem: "conjoin'd in such a peace." But in Patmore's matured view this necessarily calls up its opposite. Hope, he tells her, must gaze back upon the "happy track" of their love – "so not to cease." Of course, he then looks not back in peace but forward, not as a mistake or a trick of his anxiety but as the acknowledged necessary complement of the achieved fulfillment. The poem, a fanciful rather than intense one, then plays with the future of their love beyond death. We have the first clear sense of the new, Catholic Patmore, who raises questions of different levels of hell and asks his lover to promise not to look back if she ends up in happy heaven, he in limbo. The mythic system here lightly played with (even to Hopkins's dissatisfaction)[87] enables Patmore to accept the limits of love as part of the necessities of a larger world where God's love, unlike in Kingsley's mythology, comes first. But of course he speaks from the momentary security of love present and fulfilled. His limbo is a place of absence and regret, where love and desire, never to be fulfilled, make a half-heaven, half-hell of nurtured loss. The description of these lost ones, the center of the poem for its very attractive images of beautiful sorrow, in some sense stands for his present mood as it faces the ordinary certainty of losing love: the lost wander as "pale spirits among willow'd leas, / Lost beyond measure, sadden'd without end." Unlike those damned in hell, their punishment is exactly their imagination of love fulfilled. They are like "spurned Lovers" who prefer the "weal" of their loss to the "world's delight"; or they are poets moved to tears by sunset: "when they mark / In the clouds dun / A loitering flush of the long sunken sun, / And turn away with tears into the dark."

This description of how lovers and poets feel about loss in a love poem about loss by a poet/lover is obviously a rather sideways approach to a fundamental issue. It prepares us as much as the speaker for the much tougher realities, not fancies, that follow immediately. A major cycle of love poems, numbers seven through eleven, at the emotional and imaginative center of Book I, enters fully into the domain of radical absence, the loss of the lover in death – that central subject of love poetry since at least Dante and Petrarch. Petrarch's own poems have been seen as parallel in form to the ode. But whereas his poems and Dante's call to the presence of the lover as a version of a god or saintly power, Patmore's poems on death more directly call to, invoke, the negative force of the absence itself. Patmore recognizes that she, or he, or it, is a very powerful, dangerous god indeed, the more so because so unknown and perhaps most so because it is a god found especially within ourselves. The quest for the unknown power of eros that will be more formally pursued in Book II begins here as a search into vacancy within. The poems are the most personal and individual of the entire series and have, for that reason, become best known as anthology pieces. The directness and simplicity allow him both to record the personal nature of his so-painful discovery of the power of absence and also to keep under control, at this stage, the generative power of the discovery, which will in some sense propel the intensely imaginative poems of Book II.

The first, "The Azalea" (I.vii), approaches the power even with enormous caution, caution which we learn, when we finish, has been deliberate. Here it is not dangerous fulfillment that is being deferred but more dangerous loss. The narrator knows better, knows the ending of this reticent, even coy, poem, about loss before he begins, but insists upon repeating, and asking us to join with him in, the process of delayed discovery. This allows him, for almost the entire poem, to preserve the appearance of fulfilled love as a kind of ritual barrier created against facing loss. The poem begins with warm celebration of the sensuous fulfillment of love, indeed a good deal more directly sexual and immediate in its qualities than anything in the poems preceding it. Sun, gold-azalea, and its perfume all fill a marital room – "our room." His lover is present as the trainer of the azalea and in a deliberately confused line, in which "she" can mean her or the azalea, as the spring-like dispenser of breathing grace. First reading assumes it is she, not merely the azalea, that causes the perfume of the plant to pervade the room. The ode would seem to welcome her presence as a kind of goddess of spring.

The other power directly invoked in the poem is the Christian God himself, twice named as the speaker recounts a terrible dream he had even at the moment when azalea buds were opening to "burst" under her nursing. He "dream'd, O God, that she was dead"; then "waked, ah, God, and did not waken her." We seem to have a version of the anxious poems of presence we have just been reading. The nearness of such intense sensual fulfillment, imaged in the room and bursting azaleas, brings on anxious dreams of destruction against which the poem invokes God for protection. But of course just when this seems to be working and he lies assured of her presence – "bless'd in the delicious sphere / By which I knew so well that she was near" – a hole opens up that will not properly close, which we now realize was there all along, which he had been trying desperately, as character and as creator of the poem, to bridge over: "It *was* the azalea's breath, and she *was* dead!" The recognition, or re-recognition as we immediately realize it to be, comes as a different kind of experience, deregulating and physical, "'gan to stir / A dizzy somewhat in my troubled head." The "somewhat" names the unnamed power of contingency, uncontrollable loss, that is invoked by this ode despite itself.

The poem then ends with a rather desperate attempt to return to the apparently filled space of the opening. We are again reminded of the fullness of the buds, spreading their perfume; and the lover is restored by her own words: four warm, even sentimental love lines to him. Physical and verbal presence are to no avail, of course, because they only serve to explain the illusion, not to restore it. The repetitive nature of the love lines, with their echoing phrasing and "sweet . . . Sweet . . . sweet" flip-flop from their original expressive warmth to the coldness of what now seems a ritual and meaningless assertion of closeness against the present fact. Above all, those "Spring-like" azalea buds spilling their perfume into the room now operate pathetically in reverse. Empty tokens of the meaning that her presence put into them and their odor, they now are signs of absence as they undergo a total deconstruction or stripping of their former values. The eponymous flower, on second reading, thus becomes the ironic attribute of the real god invoked here, the absence and loss found in all appearances of her presence now that she is dead. And of course the central location of these is the poet's imagination itself, which kept trying to read former values into the appearances of presence; reversing the speaker of the winter poems, who found signs of summer in apparent absence, he must now see the more than winter absence at the center of the marital chamber and its perfuming azaleas.

"Azalea" uses considerable ingenuity in showing the process of avoidance, and its necessary failure, by reenacting it with us as its participants. Indeed, we are the only ones fooled in this reiteration of self-deceit about loss. "Departure" (i.viii) faces the vacant god of loss far more directly. The power seemingly invoked is the loved one herself to whom this poem, in second person, is addressed. Yet her presence only as an absent counter, similar to the azaleas, is acknowledged in the first line and brought home strongly in the course of the poem: "It was not like your great and gracious ways!" She is what it was *not*. What it *was* is not suspended but soon told: the contingent event, uncontrollable by love or any human feeling or need, that opens up a vortex of meaningless event. The warmth of the lover's speech strikes up against the blunt facts of the case, presented without decoration. You died: "You went, / With sudden, un-intelligible phrase, / And frighten'd eye . . . / Without a single kiss, or a good-bye?" The power of its very unintelligibility is what defines the parting and dominates the poem. Despite the intimate warmth of the scene and in his voice, despite her true courtesy in working to take his thoughts away from her sickness, despite even the sensuality in her "luminous pathetic lash," their afternoon is heavily shadowed by foreknowledge of its finality. His own attempt at warmth – "Well, it was well" – has a hollow sound to it; and the love scene seems too weak to sustain its aura of connection. The sun's rays are weak and so is her voice, which he can barely hear. It is entirely canceled with her repeated "huddled unintelligible phrase" which ends all attempt at meaning and restores the hollow void. In the restatement of the opening line all former meaning in her "great and gracious ways" seems wiped away or at least brought to a definite close. In its place is only the void of something else, something whose meaning is only its unintelligibility.

The repeated "frighten'd eye" in "Departure" suggests also the scared seeing that the acknowledgment of loss actually is. He is "aghast," frightened to his soil as by a ghost, not so much by the loss itself as by its disordering strangeness, its "wonder." The three remaining poems in the cycle show him, in effect, running scared, trying to understand and perhaps control the unsettled emotions and imaginations that keep generating new feelings and new images to try to fill the void opened by unintelligibility and total absence. The variations of mood and level of voice possible in an ode sequence allow Patmore to write here much closer to the bone than in the intimate, but far less personal, certainly less immediately revealing, poems on winter or on the perils of love unfulfilled.

The most immediately appealing is the simplest, "The Toys" (i.x). Here the patriarch Patmore dramatizes himself as out of control, striking his thoughtful little son and sending him away angrily. The verbal clause that ends the little story, "His Mother, who was patient, being dead," makes its widower's appeal for our understanding. But it also speaks of his spiritual difficulties, especially an obsession with the finality of her death – "being dead" as a continuous present state to him – that not only explains his problems in bringing up children alone but also his emotional failure. In contrition he visits his son's bedroom, finds the boy has cried himself to sleep after taking comfort in creating a kind of artwork out of various counters, stone, shells, bluebells, and French coins. The reader in our century may prefer to stop there, though Patmore, in a manner a little reminiscent of his popular *The Angel* poetry, moralizes: so God may forgive us also when he sees what toys we made our own joys from. It awkwardly restores Patmore's patriarchal moral authority, one father under God the father, when we have just seen his injustice and might be better prepared, as in Hardy's poems, to move up to question the justice of the universe. But if the poem's failure of logic shows a speaker out of moral control, it does so in a rare moment of inadvertent division; the norm is rather a controlled understanding of necessary duality (except, again, in the political odes). What seems more important is the identification with the child's activity in relieving his grief, literally filling the void with the work of imagination, if only by making artistic counters out of mere counters.

In two, far more impressive, poems (which, perhaps for that reason have never made it into the anthologies) Patmore reports the imaginative work by which he himself sought to avoid the hollowness of loss. "Eurydice" (1.ix), as the title suggests, is a descent into hell in an ill-fated attempt to recover his lost lover. But the hell is entirely within and both its sordid images and that of his forever lost lover are manifestly generated by his troubled imagination. The poem indeed begins not with the account of his dream but with questions about the origin of dreams that places the act of his imagination before us consciously. Are dreams in effect decaying sense from our lives, merely products of a "restless grave" of things past? Or are they little waves from a great world of spirit for a moment in touch with ours (as in Yeats's Spiritus Mundi)? The answer seems to be, neither. He has been dreaming with his own aim and motivation. As in "The Toys" he foregrounds his own emotional confusion. He admits he has already (quite unlike faithful Orpheus) found another love in reality to fill the void left by the first's death; yet is troubled, doubtless doubly guilty, because he still loves the first extremely: "more than Heaven." In his dream his spirit actively pursues her through a tawdry hell that probably takes some of its qualities from his guilt. Unlike others he encounters in the dream, he feels his grief deeply and is jeered at because the others resent his true grief showing up their malicious pretense at mourning.

Seeking to see her, he first finds instead a Victorian hell of mean streets and worse dwellings, a kind of scene out of *Oliver Twist*, where one goes through tortured ways filled with malicious, uncaring people. This hell, cast from the universal Victorian middle-class hell of lower-class East End London (or poor Birmingham or Liverpool), is only too human, degraded in its merde-like browns and yellows:

> I, dreaming, night by night, seek now to see,
> And, in a mortal sorrow, still pursue
> Thro' sordid streets and lanes
> And houses brown and bare
> And many a haggard stair
> Ochrous with ancient stains,
> And infamous doors, opening on hapless rooms,
> In whose unhaunted glooms
> Dead pauper generations, witless of the sun,
> Their course have run.

The consciousness that of course creates these alien habitations through which it then runs reminds us of at least two kinds of intruder, the Victorian charitable visitor, often bent on reclaiming fallen women, as Dickens and Gladstone were, or, perhaps with interests not so different as Victorians imagined, the more ordinary gentleman visitor. The speaker, who seems to project his own guilt on the world he creates, finds the woman he seeks, in as terrible a condition as he could, and does, imagine. She lies "On pallet poor" and her hopeless patience is "Ingrain'd in fretted cheek and lips that pine." It is a troubled and troubling image. It provokes in his dreaming self a release of tears and a sense of sweetness at having found, "After exceeding ill, a little good."

As in the myth, this provides no lasting reunion; in fact, far from singing beautifully to win her back to life, he seems to be there only to stare at her and release his feelings of loss and guilt. As in the myth, his need to stare seems to bear a relation to her consignment to die again. His neglect, the dream tells him, more than the entire world's, has placed her where she is. If the dream seems to take him to a discovery and a relief, the case is actually just the opposite. We are told it is a repeated, compulsive dream, so that nightly he places her in sordid circumstances, finds her finally, weeps at the relief only to realize the necessary repetition of his loss. His imagination, burdened with grief, with guilt that even seems to project back on their love relation as one that caused her death, invokes only a renewal of the moment of loss, so that the void is filled only with an image of the void itself. In the process sexual feeling is replaced by guilt alone; one could even say she has become in his imagination a victim-virgin figure over whom he then has his cry. The poem is at the dead center of loss in the sequence, not winter absence that can quicken the imagination but absence finding only itself repeated. Such a painful compulsion of the imagination is also a necessary one: facing again and again her return to life only as a person sick and dying once again, he also comes to accept the fact of the loss itself.

The companion dream poem, "Tired Memory" (I.xi), begins with full acceptance of the negative reality of death. It is imaged in the first line as anti-imaginative matter, unintelligible, mere brute reality as contingency: "The stony rock of death's insensibility." For a while the rock gave honey, but, as in "Eurydice," it was only the dying image of her love and even that finally went dry. No effort of imagination or deliberate meditation can restore her image. The mention of love letters reminds us how far we now are from the apparent presence of "The Azalea." Even a directly sexual prompt, "The band which really spann'd the body chaste and warm," does nothing – unless remind us that Patmore always assumed the sexual and sensual in his images of love, no matter how "Victorian" the "picture," "empty glove," or "long letters" may seem to us. With this death of imagination, he proclaims her really dead, a correlative of the rock itself. The honesty of these poems, if not to the actual details of Patmore's own reaction to his wife's death (and they may be this) then certainly to the turmoil and futility in a psyche trying to accept the void of death, is nowhere more striking than in the natural term he admits to grief. It compares most favorably to the sense of dutiful working up of dulled grief we have at some moments in his friend Tennyson's poem on Hallam. And the acceptance of his natural need for life with the living after, or even during, his grief, seems exceptionally honest in contrast to his friend Browning's agonized indecisions and aborted courtships after Elizabeth's death. The speaker here honestly and disarmingly admits that he kept up the work of mourning "daily," with "many a fond, unfeeling prayer" and "wilful faith, which has no joy or pain." Finally, he let go and returned her to heaven.

And now, imagination, which had seemed only able to repeat his loss, suddenly is restored to the generative power it has in the opening landscape odes:

> the same night, in slumber lying,
> I, who had dream'd of thee as sad and sick and dying,
> And only so, nightly for all one year,
> Did thee, my own most Dear,
> Possess,
> In gay, celestial beauty nothing coy,
> And felt thy soft caress
> With heretofore unknown reality of joy.

With tremendously effective use of the varied line lengths of his odes, pitting the long tale of "sad and sick and dying" against the single word line, "Possess," Patmore shows imagination returning all that has been lost. The meaning of "possess" is perfectly clear, even under the restraints of Victorian decorum. At this lowest point in his loss, when he has accepted the rock or void entirely, he attains the strongest, clearest image of sexual union. She is no way coy in her caress; the reality of joy in imagination surpasses the anxiety-filled unions of ordinary reality as they were presented in "The Day After To-Morrow." As the poems on winter had predicted, imagination can fill the vacancy of pure loss with the strongest projection of sexual desire and fulfillment.

The poem goes on from this epiphany, aware of the short life "in our mortal air" of even "the happiest dream," to tell us briefly the end of the speaker's personal tale. Again the attitude and tone is interestingly problematizing rather than justifying. He eventually accepted the possibility of happiness without his lover. On the one hand, this is a further sacrifice of what he had and what might again bring relief; on the other, he again must admit that he had in any case come to the natural subsiding of his feelings: "My heart was dead, / Dead of devotion and tired memory." At that point his love was given back to him again, in an even more perplexing form, as new love for a woman who reminds him of her – "a strange grace of thee" – and who in turn loves him through sensing his devotion to his first lover. The poem is written in the second person to his first lover so that it has the form of intimate confession. She had encouraged him to remarry after her death; yet he still is troubled at having allowed "Nature's long suspended breath of flame" to burn again. The poem ends on a question of treason: "But (treason was't?) for thee and also her."[88]

The cycle of personal love, thus concluded on a deliberately incomplete and uncertain note, serves in many ways as a powerful prelude to the further subjects of the odes. Prelude is an appropriate term, because the true subject has been the poet's discovery of the power of imagination even more than the ostensible story of a strong love relation and then a harrowing loss. Imagination in its connection with sexual desire has been shown to have a life of its own, by which absence may be filled with plenitude, loss at least momentarily restored. The Orphic powers to charm desire away from the dead, so signally failing in "Eurydice," have been ultimately asserted. The ode can, in effect, call from absence the presence of sexual fulfillment.

Looked at from a different perspective, one with which we have become familiar through Foucault's thinking about the construction of sexuality as a discourse, or cultural phenomenon, out of the mere, literally unspeakable, acts of sex in bodies and pleasures, Patmore can be said to be discovering the power of language to fabricate sexuality. The intellectual historian might wish then to emphasize the restatement of views of sexuality in Patmore as ideas flow through language from author to author. We have seen how much Patmore was aware in the early poems, where he played freely with inherited

ways of writing about sex, of how greatly language about sex seemed
to have its own life; and in the odes he deliberately works in known
traditions of expression, including the liaisons to Petrarchanism we
have already observed, as well as the revisitings to religious
discussions or rituals that we will find in the odes of Book II. But
Patmore also insists on the personal inspiration involved. The ode
form indeed is a tradition that allows for, even calls for, new
inspiration with each worker in the tradition, who should attempt to
call down his or her *own* god. His discovery of the power of
imagination to create in words a presence of sexuality even in the face
of winter or love's loss reasserts this belief in repeated inspiration. If
his account of love's loss has been generalized and given mythic
overlays, it remains a personal testimony, as, say, does Wordsworth's
Prelude or Tennyson's *In Memoriam*. Truth, found perhaps in the
language of a tradition, is nonetheless found within, as a process of
desire working with imagination.

Patmore's instinct in organizing the odes, indeed like Tennyson's
in *In Memoriam*, was to suggest that personal experience led to the
more general assertions of understanding or wisdom of the less
personal poems. Like Wordsworth or Tennyson, Patmore establishes
his credentials with us by sharing his personal history and his
discovery of a source of insight, then offering his other, more general,
poems for our approval. I have already indicated my own failure of
sympathy with one area in which Patmore now claimed to speak with
inspiration, the prophetical-satirical poems on the politics of his age.
Of at least one of these, when pressed by Hopkins, Patmore himself
was willing to admit that "the expression of the feeling is not for
verse."[89] By contrast, the less specific poems stating general views of
man's place in the universe have endured and deserve the reader's
attention, though I cannot look at them in detail here. The first,
"Magna Est Veritas" (I.xii), follows "Tired Memory" and should
properly be seen as ending the cycle of personal love and loss. He
sits by the ocean, seeing its daily coming and going as happy
but nonetheless essentially meaningless. Accepting easily now the
essential lack of value in nature's cycles, he can be comfortable
with himself, removed both from nature's activity and from the
lives of other people (the nearby town): "I sit me down." He
can accept without bitterness his distance from both worlds of
nature and people. He has a skeptical but not pessimistic faith
which can be welcomed by the reader as a personal wisdom of

acceptance, where the political poems seem merely over-emotional rant:

> For want of me the world's course will not fail:
> When all its work is done, the lie shall rot;
> The truth is great, and shall prevail,
> When none cares whether it prevail or not.

Other, similar, poems, for instance "Crest and Gulf" (i.xix) and "'Let Be!'" (i.xx), mentioned above, or "'Faint Yet Pursuing'" (i.xxi), "Victory in Defeat" (i.xxii), or "Remembered Grace" (i.xxiii), interestingly find ways to assert his faith in a larger order – "The fly-wheel swift and still" of God's will – seen athwart, or despite, the manifold deceptions and disillusionments of ordinary experience.

The consolation is in each case finally religious, allowing him faith beyond the world as well as in the ultimate destiny of the world. But Patmore in no way abandons his lifelong preoccupation with sexual experience for a new otherworldly focus. If Petrarch could renounce his early concerns with love, Patmore by contrast took up the challenge to integrate his interests in sexual desire and religious aspiration. His work in *The Angel* had tried to sanctify sexual relations as Kingsley did, with religious approval on certain terms, and it had also gone beyond Kingsley in hinting, as in the dean's Wedding Sermon at the end of *The Victories of Love*, that there would be a new place for man's sexual nature in the world of religious experience. Now the ode form gave him a way to explore and speculate far more broadly on the place of sexual desire in religion. The personal poems already embody his claim to a special knowledge of the force of sexual love within the self. In Book II of the odes he grouped poems that experimented with building on this inner experience a broader, mythic and religious view of man's nature and place in the universe. Such an enterprise obviously smacks of humanism, even of inspiration and mysticism. Patmore is outspoken about his humanism in the fine poem "The Two Deserts" (i.xviii), where he looks at the worlds of very big and very small that science has shown man. With playful sophistication, he lists the horrors of the macro-universe that the telescope shows us and the more friendly, but equally unaccommodatable world of the very small – "A torment of innumerable tails" in the microscope. He chooses rather "A mind not much to pry / Beyond our royal-fair estate / Betwixt these deserts blank of small and great." Wonder and beauty are the proper concerns that should catch man's attention, not such abstractions. It is a fine poem of deliberate anti-scientific obscurantism – rather rare in a century much threatened by science but rarely so lucid both in seeing what science can do and in circumscribing the limits of its interest to the private individual.

Such clearly stated humanism, in an ode that only mildly summons spirits of wonder and beauty against its clever depiction of scientific new views, one can take or leave, or take some days and leave on others. Patmore's odes in Book II are more often focussed on asking us to join with him in summoning major powers, God himself or representations of him, through our own inner capacities for wonder and beauty, the royal-fair estate of imagination. Some talk elegantly about the experience, some may take us with them, some fall flat. None can be treated with indifference; they explore seriously an aspect of experience that he has already convincingly made real to us in the personal odes of Book I. As in those odes, the fundamental appeal is subjective and experiential, but here the claim being made by the poet is of a certain kind of inspiration bringing to the odist special knowledge of mysteries not unveiled to most persons. As with the poems of human love, Patmore works with traditions of expression and ritual, but the source of understanding is finally within. "Vesica Piscis" (I.xxiv), concluding Book I, tells a fable of his poetry. As a poet of love he has fished for *nourritures terrestres*, "the quick, shining harvest of the Sea," but has caught something quite different. The poem speaks to God in the second person, less as prayer than as some of the love poems had to his lover. What he caught was "Thee," whom he has found within himself, "As hid was Simon's coin within the fish." In this peculiarly intimate image (the title means "bladder of a fish") God is something very close within. And God's instruction to him from the belly of the odist is to speak mysteries that have been hidden, "Speak but of forgotten things." It is Patmore's immediate transition to his book of mysteries, discovered within, in Book II. The Catholic convert finds, in this idea of God as coin within, an image that can easily be read as one of the Mass, coin as wafer. Yet it is a very personal kind of experience that Patmore locates in the mystery of his own version of the Mass. And Book II, with many more allusions to, and whole poems about, Catholic tradition and ritual, maintains a rather Protestant spirit very much in tune with the religious approach of Patmore's Protestant sometime friends, Browning and

Tennyson, though not out of touch with the inspiration of his Catholic friend, Hopkins, either.

BOOK II: THE SEARCH

The bold project of Book II, based on finding inspiration to forgotten mysteries by feeling the coin of God within, can hardly leave us contentedly indifferent in the way that Patmore's humanist wisdom in Book I can. In Book II he in effect attempts a kind of reversal of the skeptical reductive concept of sublimation. While sublimation claims to unmask religious phenomena and reveal the sexual realities below, Patmore openly seeks to find religious experience through the sexual. Skeptical readers thus have a direct and easy route back, that of deconstruction through the concept of sublimation, to mere sexuality. Yet "mere sexuality," as both Patmore and Foucault would agree, is itself already a creation of words in which most of us in some degree normally believe. To the extent that Patmore's poems have power they tend to pull us, even against our native skepticism, up the route of increasing articulation of sexuality toward his tentative mythic formulations. And they also have power just because they admit the necessary tentativeness in the attainment of such mythic sexual–religious discourses and risk – eventually even experience, as we shall see – their potential to collapse into fallen card-houses of language.

The power Patmore works with is not the ecstatic summer one of love fulfilled. His sexual religion is not one of orgy and frenzy at the height of which the god is seen or invoked. Rather, he builds on the power whose force he has already demonstrated in Book I, that of imaginative desire working on absence.

Book II opens with what is perhaps the most direct invocation of the entire series of odes, "To the Unknown Eros" (II.i). It was well chosen as an introductory poem to Book II because it strongly focusses our attention back to the issue raised by the title of the entire series. Nor does it so much tell us what this Eros is as give us a preview of the special kind of erotic attractions to come. Having summoned this power only indirectly, through his personal experience of the season out of season or his anxiety or loss in love, he now suggests how we may approach it more directly. The poet is still very much present in this introduction to a myth, but now less as an individual lover than as a privileged poetic, even vatic or clairvoyant, sensor of deity. The poem literally places him in a position of inspiration/invocation; he is exposed to great forces which he specially senses, almost as a poetic lightning-rod in a storm of supernal forces. The language of the poem consists of his dramatic utterances, great sweeping questions reaching out to try to define the forces he feels working about him. What seems a shocking arrogance in this inspired stance is, of course, also the oldest poetic stage business, the odist's traditional attempt to call down a force by defining its attributes.

Other than the careful way he has prepared throughout Book I to take up the age-old role of the odist in Book II, what is most striking in Patmore's version of mythic invocation is the insistent strangeness – unknownness – of the force he invokes. The sense is that it is the one serious force that we still can invoke, because it still remains a mystery while all other gods have already been only too often invoked and too easily tamed and humanized. Its power is in its continual uncertainty and absence. As we have been prepared to, we understand it as just that power found through the force of our own unfulfilled desire. The poem formally defines the god by what it is not: neither Amor, god of merely fulfilled earthly love, nor Diana, "mooned Queen of maids," mere chastity: neither simple presence nor abstinence, but the great force of desire in the face of absence.

To convey this positive power the personification offers powerful images of sensual closeness, all preserved as a kind of teasing nearness/distance. The poet feels as in a night scene a brushing "breeze / Of sudden wings," momentarily fanning his face, then speeding off soundlessly through incredible distance back to "delicatest ether" of "interstellar space" from which they came. What they leave is literally their verbal absence, no "trace / To speak of whence they came, or whither they depart." The source of what seems external seduction is really within; the images have focussed not on the god's approach so much as on the stir created inside him. He then moves to his own direct signs, a kind of vital statistics of his *Sehnsucht*: "Palpitating heart," "blind and unrelated joy," "meaningless desire." An extended comparison to a child in a frenzy of pre-pubertal anticipation vividly suggests a kind of unfolding chrysalis of powers of desire going on within him. The child is troubled in the "flushing darkness" inventing prophecies; his heart is on fire with "dreams that turn him red and pale." The boy will find wilder dreams fulfilled as fantasy yields to the sensed/unexpected reality of sex that "bashful Love, in his own way and hour" shall bring. The comparison is a strong and obviously potent one, and Patmore turns deliberately from this ordinary, most extraordinary experience of finding that there is a bliss beyond troubled imagination to the new promise of an Eros still unknown. The void of the very unknown to be offered by this "sire of awful bliss" leaves us panting for language for what we can't put in words. Like a snake charming a bird, the unknown "portent" and "Delphic word" lures us to express our desire. As the grown odist repeats at his level the boy's attempt to define what he doesn't know, images of potent absence abound: what "eddies" in the flood of his life? Planetary images take up and review the themes of enormous space of the opening; here the huge power of a "perturbed moon of Uranus" lifts the blood like a tremendous tidal force toward "some great world in ungauged darkness hid" (the moon was indeed the planet Neptune, discovered by the gravitational irregularities it exerted on Uranus). It is, finally, a pulling absence felt, as the boy felt his, with sensual force. Whence is the "rapture of the sense" that reveres the unknown – un-languaged itself – by "obscure rite and sacramental sign"?

For an instant Patmore hazards an image of absence overcome, of being united to "my unguess'd want." As we will find whenever he does so in Book II, it is an exceptionally sexy one: not only is there an overtone of specialized (kinky) sexual activities (albeit in a lofty tone) – "This subject loyalty which longs / For chains and thongs / Woven of gossamer and adamant, / To bind me to my unguess'd want" – but there is even a description of total sexual consummation, less as metaphor than as mythic description, man in union with god: "And so to lie, / Between those quivering plumes that thro' fine ether pant, / For hopeless, sweet eternity?" This is suddenly as literal and as astonishing as Kingsley's picture of sex with his wife on a cross floating up to heaven. But this is no human wife but desire itself.

As Patmore begins to strip this god to find out who it is we may well become increasingly uncomfortable. He risks this because he wants to insist on the sexual nature of our unknown desire for this unknown force. Patmore might say in some moods that it was simply union with God himself, a sexual theology he would put forward directly in his later prose. Or, following the poem's own logic we can read it as a personification of that desire within that we know by its force but to which we cannot easily give a name. What we should not do here is jump to an allegorical reading away of the force, for instance as the love of the soul for God or other such abstraction. Desire in absence has been brought to an exceptionally high pitch; Patmore wants us to see that it necessarily seeks language and an image of fulfillment that satisfies the sexual nature of humans thus strongly wakened. What that satisfaction will be, of course, he doesn't know: its nature is to be unknown, hence the difficulty with images of fulfillment, which necessarily reduce the idea as well as the sexual/spiritual tumescence Patmore has aroused: a problem, as we will see, that will recur in a more fundamental way in some later odes in the series. Words are indeed bound to be inadequate to celebrate this full union of the soul with God.

The ode, thus rendered problematic but unmistakably about sex, concludes with a return to questions and mysteries. As if to cover his tracks, Patmore now resorts to full enigmas rather than teasing questions. The unknown love is both vestal and consummated; it feeds on accepting the "Nought" which is, word of negation and denial which is nonetheless a focus and furnace (Patmore becomes metaphysically obscure and abstract here, an alternate embarrassment to the too-explicit lines before). The crown that cures all longing is won by shunning it: "Refuse it, till refusing be despair; / And thou shalt feel the phantom in thy hair." We have retreated, in this at least attractive ending, to the surer place of the opening: absence does breed longing; all may experience the sense of an oncoming god that the poet presents so strongly at the opening. Yet the attempt to read enigmatic lessons leads only to this retreat. Patmore seems comfortable and sure in his astonishing sexual premonitions of godly contact; when he attempts to go beyond what he thus knows personally, whether to envision ecstatic union with God or to read a lesson or litany of a new cult, he embarrasses us because he is himself perplexed.

"To the Unknown Eros" promises us a direct, and, whatever the shock of it, explicitly sexual relation to God while it also forecasts the difficulty of a poet – even an odist – adequately making good on this promise. But the greater power of the poem, as we have seen, is derived from desire working on deferral and anticipation, much as it did in the realm of human heterosexual love in "The Day After To-Morrow." Drawing indeed on this analogy between the elusiveness and difficulty of consummation in the human realm and in the religious experience introduced by this poem, Patmore, as almost always in the odes, convincingly suggests that his understanding arises from personal experience, though it has, of course, a long history in Christianity as a whole, and especially in Catholic writers known to Patmore.[90]

The union with the unknown god that is so strongly suggested in the first poem in some sense echoes this process of desire deferred in the structure of Book II itself. Having been told about, and given a glimpse of such an astounding union, we are then prepared not so much for the union as for poems that ask us to understand the tremendous desire of the psyche for such a great and deferred union. The direction of the odes in Book II obviously is away from the immediate life of this world on which Patmore focussed even in poems of nature's absence, or love's anxieties or loss, or indeed in poems accepting his relation to the world as he has found it. He moves now toward a celebration of absence even more uncompromising than that in the poems of winter. There he focussed on the desire raised by the promise in absence of the seeds and buds of spring. Now his subject will be deliberate and total deferral from earthly gratification, in a word, the word so horrid to a modern ear, or perhaps even postmodern ears, virginity. How horrid it was to Kingsley – in part because of its seductiveness as a coherent alternative – we have already seen; and we can gauge Patmore's distance now from his Kingsleyan moment at the time of *The Angel*. Kingsley had insisted, to Fanny in his private life as in his works, that a choice had to be made between two incompatible systems of sexuality, virginity and married love.

By contrast, Patmore stresses close relation between the two. He is careful, and we should be too, to be clear that he in no way intends to disparage human sexual love; his commitment in the odes and in his earlier work and his life has been obvious. He writes the odes, as we saw, at a time when he may have been living with a woman sworn to virginity; he watched the daughter with whom he was closest affiliate herself with a religious order; and he eventually encouraged her as she resolved to become a nun. There is no question that there are biographical connections between this heavy involvement in the vows of virginity of daughter and probably wife and his focus on the subject of virginity in the odes, written during this period. In some sense he celebrates the choice that one or both of them made by odes on virginity, even as he himself would choose a third decidedly sexual marriage and a final infatuation with a married woman of genius. Rather than force him to separate sex from religious virginity in the usual sense, his close relationships to those vowed to virginity allowed him to think of virginity as closely bedded to sexual experience. To the isolated but lusty Patmore, on his second wife's country estate as almost in a religious institution, there would have been no more attractively warm, living, and loving women than virgin or virgin-like wife and virgin daughter. A virgin would have been clearly not a sexless person but one attractive but untouchable. Virginity could thus seem, both personally and theologically, exactly the quality best suited to provoke or to embody the extreme of sexual desire deferred that he wished to explore in religious experience.

That this is a focussing of life's own forces rather than a denial of life is made especially clear in a poem called, in fact, "To the Body" (II.vii) set, probably deliberately, among poems celebrating virginity. It is an ode in form but calls down nothing; rather it celebrates what is most immediately before the odist, the human body. The poem defines the importance of the body in the humanist terms of "The Two Deserts." The body, as the human measure and center of all things, is indeed the prime "Wall of infinitude" that keeps our focus on the humanly relevant and away from the deserts of the infinitely small or remote. Writing now clearly as a Catholic, Patmore can gracefully pull out the old stops of a traditional Christian humanism: the body is the center and last great work of physical creation, its harmony the music of creation against the discord of chaos. But he also insists on a more intimate description, moving from the grace of the hair to the "tingling, sweet / Soles" of the feet, from heart to skin. Far from turning from the body in his tribute to virginity, he somewhat embarrasses his verse as he emphasizes the beauty and importance of "every least part." In the religious perspective of Book II the body is, if anything, more important than in Book I. Patmore's ode celebrates the body as, above all, the central source of pleasures both in this life and in a future heaven. The speaker judges the joy to come by "the pleasures" he has already known in his body: mere "first-fruits" of the coming "quintessential, keen, ethereal bliss." Far from being banished through virginity, the body only comes to heaven better ready for its greatest pleasure, "Quick, tender, virginal, and unprofaned!"

The ode enacts a kind of miniature *Paradise Lost* in its few lines, showing the body as the live trophy quarreled over by heaven and hell, its destiny a higher one than merely to be restored to the human sexual companionship of the original garden. Such a broad perspective on the destiny of the body allows Patmore to make a case for virginity that does not oppose it, rightly seen, to the pleasures of the body. Virginity is in effect a tremendous deferral of a pleasure of the body, not its antagonist. "The Contract" (ii.ii) is another little *Paradise Lost*, the ode by its high reach and swift transitions once again permitting a kind of epic in shorthand. It tells a different myth than Milton's, in which sexual indulgence might at first glance seem to be the cause of the Fall. But the Victorian father of many children, patriarch husband of many wives, was not trying to settle the vexed theological issue of the relation of sex to the Fall in a repressive radical displacement of the sin of pride by that of carnality.[91] Rather, he creates a drama of the human need for sex now, with a partner, and the other desire to defer full bodily pleasure for heaven. Adam and Eve, speaking in obviously aroused language, pledge to each other, in effect, not to go all the way – which is not to avoid sexual feeling but to husband it. The poem pits all odds against the couple: they are deeply in love, totally alone and unchaperoned; the season is of course perfect; Venus has risen and a bed of roses awaits them (not to mention their lovely nakedness and their ever-more intimate and warm embraces as the poem proceeds). Patmore exploits all these readily available prompts to love to create, in effect, a sex-drenched moment for father Adam and mother Eve to make what were obviously pre-perjured pledges of virgin marriage.

Their contract, which, Patmore underlines, was their idea, a contract freely entered into, is inspired by something like the intimation the poet felt in "To the Unknown Eros." Adam speaks of finding within his breast "something bright, / Not named, not known, and yet more manifest / Than is the morn, / The sun being just at point then to be born?" That this greater desire comes to Adam as he first begins to feel desire suggests the two are related, not opposed. As he and Eve draw ever closer, his enthusiasm for the virginal contract takes on climactic proportions: "Yea, with my joyful heart my body rocks, / And joy comes down from Heaven in floods and shocks, / As from Mount Abora comes the avalanche." We are left to conclude that this virgin contract leaves out very little of the physical or/and that these vows are already breaking down, as we, of course, find they have. Patmore's ending is effectively dramatic, a sudden opening up of perspective that puts the little dialogue of seduction in a Christian epic picture. Mankind has other pleasures – "fiery throes, and upturn'd eyeballs blind" – and is sick at heart – desire breeding more desire, as we have seen in Book i. His only hope is not in fact to abandon sexual desire, so obvious a part of human nature, as we have just seen, from the beginning, but to look to greater espousals, namely the new virgin ones of the "Glad Saint" Joseph and Mary that bring forth "The Son of God and Man."

It is a hard ending to swallow whole. For the first time in the odes we are asked to accept a religious mythology already full-blown, rather than in process of creation in the poem.[92] Patmore also risks our focussing on the appearance of the Fall being caused by sex in his boldly stated comparisons between sex in the fallen world and the original virginal marriage. The use to him of these risks is in the bodiliness and sexuality thus ascribed to virgin sex. "Sick-at-heart Mankind," as Patmore has shown him through his own experience, reaches to something greater for "succour" from a sexual life that feels insufficient. The poem ends not by opposing the body but, once again, by asserting a greater bodiliness. Mary's fruit comes not as ordinary humanity – "No numb, chill-hearted, shaken-witted thing, / 'Plaining his little span" – but as something greater. As in "To the Unknown Eros" we are asked to fill in this greater human: the words are "proud" and "joy," and we can provide what else is "appropriate": something that fits the strong beats and triumph of the last line's presentation of Christ as archetype of that better man: "The Son of God and Man."

On the whole, and while taking some risks, this very sexy poem manages to suggest that virginity is sexier. Two of the finest poems of Book II that follow in the earlier series of ten or eleven odes are even more directly celebrations of virginity. They are also among the most impassioned, as well as most successful, odes of the entire poem. "To the Body," as we have seen, ends with a sudden glorification of virginity from a speaker who is clearly no virgin himself: if his pleasure in his body here is any gauge, what even greater pleasures await those who go with virgin bodies to heaven! It is precisely the seeming of oddness of the comparison that Patmore wishes to break down. Virgin experience and that of most people is different in degree, not kind. Virgin experience is sexually more intense, not anti-sexual. And, finally, Patmore wishes to include himself, indeed all of us, in the potential joys of virgin experience in "death's sweet chrism" ("To the Body"). That is, virgin experience is the special privilege of a few yet it is open imaginatively to all. The two splendid master poems, "Legam Tuam Dilexi" and "Deliciae Sapientiae de Amore" are similarly laudations of virginity as a mystery reserved for a few, yet available as experience to all. Spoken by one who is, like most of us, an outsider, they ask us to recognize in their peculiar path the expressed essence of our own sexual experience.

This remains sufficiently astonishing as a concept that we perhaps need to remind ourselves of Patmore's premises, as established especially in Book I. Sexual desire is created by an absence or lack; even in moments of apparent earthly fulfillment, anxiety or the prospect of loss makes desire a thing essentially impossible to satisfy. The ravages of normal human loss quickly restore desire as a force feasting on absence. The further premise of Book II has been that desire, forced thus to be deferred in life, has still an ultimate home, with God. The primacy suddenly given to virginity by Patmore then becomes apparent. By accepting a condition of total absence in life, essentially accepting the ultimate life-long winter experience, the religious virgin chooses not to deny desire but to accept its greatest and unmitigated (because unmediated) force. Turning away from life, he or she is totally consumed with only desire. Control in the sense of abstinence thus lives with the strongest imaginable force of passion. And, rather than dying inside, the religious virgin dies only to life as he or she defers until after death the great fulfillment of all desire in God. For Patmore there is no equivocation with the name of desire as there usually is in such discussions at this point: sex is what is essentially denied in life and sexual pleasure is what will be given to postponed desire at the end. As Katherine Stockton has emphasized, the essential Christian metaphor is that of eventual marriage with the bridegroom Christ. Of course, the ceremony of the female religious as she takes final vows says just this: she is married with a ring to Christ, foreswearing all lesser gratification.

Certainly this seems such a different side of the story that it does not easily co-exist with the better-known tale of asceticism that emphasizes dying to this life by control of the body and its pleasures. And it hardly squares with our more everyday view of the realities of repressed or possibly hypocritical religious virgins. It is, after all, a great tradition of *the central* anti-clerical and/or Protestant line in English and American culture, shared by Protestant and Catholic alike, to expose failures of this strategy. (And it was also, of course, one of Luther's great thrusts against the Catholicism of his time.) Failure was marked as scandalous escapes of nature (for instance, the nativist American tradition that portrayed religious houses as gothic castles of terrible sins, or Chaucer's portrayal of the sexualized prioress even in Catholic England – not to mention the Continental tradition represented egregiously by Diderot). Or it might take the form of mere sexless and joyless repression, life- *and* spirit-denying (as in Brontë's nuns in *Villette* or the religious in the Catholic world described in Joyce's *Portrait of the Artist*). How deeply this tradition has pre-interpreted religious virginity as hypocrisy and/or repression can be gauged by our surprise that Patmore should actually have spent his retreats at an English monastery in talking enthusiastically with the brothers about "the greatest of natural delights": "nuptial love" and the "marriage embrace."[93] It catches us off-guard because it defeats our normal categories in which religious virginity and sexuality have been separated as binary opposites.

This author, who is not Catholic, not even a practicing believer in any creed, may perhaps be permitted to step before his reader for a second here – in a paragraph that he or she may easily jump over – and indicate his own reservations. I can follow Patmore's logic, I can learn and sympathize from his passion, I can even join imaginatively in his celebration of total deferral as an experience that presents the strength of human desire in an unadulterated and extremely clarifying way. To do so I don't have to believe that there is a place where deferral is rewarded. I can agree with Lacan that one has to accept the overweighting of desire, which is to accept the necessity of a lack on earth, without being assured that the hole becomes whole (as our current wits like to pun) beyond death. I can certainly see, as Protestant and Catholic critics of religious virginity have for so long, a danger in playing with the fire of pure desire. And I can even affirm that, however much sexual experience may show me my vulnerabilities, my ultimate lack in face of all desire for fulfillment, that experience is in itself desirable (is the usual object of desire rather than total deferral) and is even part of my usual idea of a life fully lived.

In a practical way the much-married Patmore obviously agreed. In *The Unknown Eros* he used his new interest in religious virginity as one path to God as a kind of hypothetics of sexuality. Knowing the possible misuses of religious virginity as well as we, he defined, by praise, a special, extreme, sexual experience that he believed put humans not only in touch with intense desire as the pure product of pure absence but, thereby, in touch with God. The odes on religious virginity define an experience at its best. As odes they speak of man's relation to God by calling not so much to any god as to humans in possession of a special experience that is not normally available to most of us; nor was it indeed to Patmore, nor even to his speaker, for whom this is also unknown territory – an unknown kind of sexuality, as his title and title poem proclaim. The point is that these are poems about cults hard for non-cultists to understand, but they are not cult poems. The experience that most of us have, of being led into something new, as we also were in the winter poems of absent desire and perhaps also in the poems of loss, is what the author expects. The exceptional reader, such as his own daughter the nun, is the one for whom the poems do not seem to introduce mysteries.

"Legem Tuam Dilexi" (ii.vi) skillfully invites us into a rapturous celebration of religious virginity, which is to say conscious and chosen virginity, by leading us through a set of contrasts familiar to us from the fine ode in Book i, "The Two Deserts." Once again and with similar sophisticated playfulness, Patmore creates a religious humanist picture of the universe in which the human is pitted against the infinite. Here we are concerned less with a human measure of things than with the play of forces that creates or threatens to destroy a human scale. And God's sustaining and controlling force, working against those of disintegration – not man's sufficiency – is his theme. The heathen feared God was only infinity; but God announces himself as a kind of model of control, "One / Confined in Three"; devils take infinity as their destructive blazon but are so upset by their own endless vistas that they prefer God's gift of some confine in the "shores of pain" of hell, which they can at least dash themselves against. In this view, even in the ordinary world, things threaten literally to fall apart: "But for compulsion of strong grace, / The pebble in the road / Would straight explode, / And fill the ghastly boundlessness of space" (a problem of the mystery of gravity and dispersion of matter in the universe that our science still finds a mystery). The world has a strong force of its own, "furious power" or "Seditious flame," in no way to be underrated even in the smallest things, that must be constrained or beaten "backward" to produce leaf, flower, or worm. From this bold definition of the universe the ode moves on brilliantly to man. Man's centering on the human imitates God in control: the just man "does on himself affirm God's limits" and in his small way joins with God in building "bulwarks 'gainst the Infinite." More, God creates control in humans as the centerpiece of his constant care.

The title of the ode affirms the speaker's love for law (I took pleasure in your law) but the poem celebrates first God's delight in bringing order to man in the warmest way. Hopkins especially liked this poem among the odes and it is indeed dazzling, especially in rendering the impression of huge swoops of space and activity, often completed formally by one or two short lines, some hitting us with a sudden, chime-like echoing rhyme.[94] One half-believes Patmore literally has God's combined mastery of infinity and tender, gentle care for man in his sights:

> For, ah, who can express
> How full of bonds and simpleness
> Is God,
> How narrow is He,
> And how the wide, waste field of possibility
> Is only trod
> Straight to His homestead in the human heart,
> And all His art
> Is as the babe's that wins his Mother to repeat
> Her little song so sweet!
> What is the chief news of the Night?
> Lo, iron and salt, heat, weight and light
> In every star that drifts on the great breeze!
> And these
> Mean Man,
> Darling of God, Whose thoughts but live and move
> Round him; Who woos his will
> To wedlock with His own, and does distil
> To that drop's span
> The attar of all rose-fields of all love![95]

The intimacy of the final description of God's nuptial care for man prepares us emotionally for another rapid transition, still following the theme of control, to the vows of the religious that "select" souls, following God's "own style," impose on themselves voluntarily. The speaker praises poverty and obedience in rather conventional, graceful ways: paradoxically they bring plenitude and freedom. But like a sudden solo section in a violin concerto, the praise of chastity takes off astonishingly. The joy of love's form of obedience authorizes a brilliant flow of imagery that is, again paradoxically, the most direct and forceful celebration of sexual energy in the series. It is especially effective because it captures the two powers that have been at play in imagery throughout the poem: the force of dissipation (in both senses) which as a force of life in devils or clod or leaf has had its

Dionysiac attraction (God works to restrain it, not eliminate it) and the opposing force of control. The genial laws of "natural sense" are portrayed as a great "self-dissipating wave" whose force sweeps across the description and is in effect enhanced as it is controlled by an imagery system of "artful dykes." The effect is one of power being driven orgasmically out of control as it is confined in a system that releases all its energy in a climax, and at that moment the system becomes suddenly and startlingly the human body itself, thrilling with the waves' energy in each part up to the brain:

> the genial laws of natural sense,
> Whose wide, self-dissipating wave,
> Prison'd in artful dykes,
> Trembling returns and strikes
> Thence to its source again,
> In backward billows fleet,
> Crest crossing crest ecstatic as they greet,
> Thrilling each vein,
> Exploring each chasm and cove
> Of the full heart with floods of honied love,
> And every principal street
> And obscure alley and lane
> Of the intricate brain
> With brimming rivers of light and breezes sweet
> Of the primordial heat;

Patmore's mastery of the suddenness available in the ode is nowhere better displayed than in his swift escape just as the ecstasy peaks and would, if extended, merely cloy. We have seen what is going on in those virgin cells and have had to believe the plenitude of such embracing of absence. Desire pure and simple is sex at its most intense.

Suddenly we recall our outsider position. Because of our necessary distance, "unto view of me and thee," what is going on so passionately in those cells appears no such thing. All the "intense life" of the religious virgin's inner experience is lost to us or seems merely ludicrous, as a "soaring eagle, or a horse" seems mere rag or stone from far off. And the poem ends abruptly in a recessional from a mystery that is, in effect, not really for us. We may have seen intensely for a moment; but we are also those anti-religious or skeptical forces that have joined in wild asses' bray or, worse, destructive hooves – hooves that have attacked this mystery of sexual intensification through denial and control. The poem ends with the "religious walls" now put up between us and what we have glimpsed for a moment: an extremely effective frame and return to ordinary life which is, in fact, part of the rhetoric by which Patmore suggests the unique experience inside. Closed out from God's love and the waves of ecstasy, we begin to replicate the production of desire in absence of the religious virgins themselves.

It is remarkable – worthy of remark and quite surprising – that Patmore writes intimately and rather explicitly about the physical experience of sex only now when his topic is total deferral of earthly sex. When he wished to speak of lovers' sex in Book I he did so only indirectly, by putting us in the position of their longing or loss, a position that directed us toward absent fulfillment. Now, even as an onlooker at the cultivation of pure desire, he can risk physical celebration because, during the course of the ode, he shares the safe position of the religious virgins he evokes: they can open themselves to a desire that will not suffer anxiety, distancing, or loss; sexual imagination can be given free play to fly toward ultimate fulfillment in as sexy a language as desired – and desire is, under such control, able to express its unlimited force. And of course Patmore needs a way to write desire; he could write of earthly sex effectively by evoking its promise and its limits, images of hope (as in the winter odes) or of pain (as in the odes on loss). Here he needs to make the god he has conjured, that of huge virgin desire, credible in words. And so he begins to risk the more direct description of sex – the risk of course being that he necessarily must use words taken from our world and from another kind of sexual experience. At first, the risk seems well worth it; it does the job Patmore wishes above all to do, to jolt us, his audience, of mainly non religious-virgins into a shock of recognition: this *is* our sexuality, only writ larger. And indeed Patmore, who has just celebrated the body, our physical body, as the same vehicle of delights here and hereafter does not find the representation of religious sexuality as a version of ordinary sexuality in itself problematic.

In his most ambitious poem celebrating religious virgin sexuality, indeed probably the finest poem of the entire series, Patmore throughout uses the framing device that he discovered at the end of "Legem Tuam Dilexi" to guard the direct celebration, the sexy language, from too direct, and thus too quickly deconstructive or reductive, examination by us. It is tempting to classify "Deliciae Sapientiae de Amore" (II.ix) in Fry's distinction as a hymn of settled faith rather than an ode reaching after some new god or his quality. Its magnificent ease and control of the ode medium at almost a continuous pitch of exalted celebration does suggest some kind of hymn-like ritual. But if it alludes to former religious modes, especially the rites in Revelation, it presents an essentially original concept of celebration; and the eye of the artist is especially keenly focussed on his odic task of trying to bring a special god down to us while he simultaneously finds a way to lift us up.

Even the title performs the complex double-act of inviting us in/teasing us as necessarily outsiders that is repeated again and again in the rhetorical structure of the ode. The reader may recognize an allusion to Swedenborg's own sensual account of a heaven of loving human marriage – *Deliciae sapientiae de amore conjugiale* (1768) – which Patmore knew. More present and more important for most readers is the allusion back to the epigraph from Proverbs to the entire *Unknown Eros* – "Deliciae meae esse cum filiis hominum" ("And my delight was with the sons of men"). By its intricate cluster of associations linking God's feminine counterpart, the figure of Wisdom, to his joy in intimacy with man, we are given something intrinsically and immediately attractive, "Deliciae," delights, allurements, of love, but then pushed back by the high requirement for entrance: wisdom. The poem itself begins with a command to love – "Love, light for me / Thy ruddiest blazing torch" – that would suit *Antony and Cleopatra*; and the setting, palace, not temple of Revelation, roses not lilies, is anything but austere and forbidding. Then it withdraws again; he is only a "beggar by the Porch" of the palace of virginity. He places us, with him, in a voyeuristic relation to the sexual festival within: we are free to enjoy by overseeing, or later by overhearing, the celebration within. The position makes the audience, not part of the cult, comfortable with their outsider's relation to this material; here it also wakens his or her desire for what is kept at a distance.

Nonetheless, in the course of the poem there is a slow process of entry, allowing us increasing access as we also make an increasing commitment. In the poem's progress we pass through a series of definitions and tests of our belonging; as readers we work to follow a difficult and relatively long ode. The first cut warns us away if we have no idea of "the shining wall," the first of a number of direct allusions to Revelation, here to the wall of jasper in the vision of the New Jerusalem. The effect is, of course, to bring us to claim some vision and hope we belong. We are pleased to hear there is no room for what we may have thought that religious virgins were, those who, "most vile," try to exalt merely a spirit of denial, "The charnel spectre drear / Of utterly dishallow'd nothingness." From warning off those who don't belong, the speaker makes a rapid odic shift to bidding in – "Bring . . . anear." Worrying about our qualifications for entrance, we may be surprised to find we are acceptable as virgins because we are true young lovers, or "wedded Spouse, if virginal of thought." Presumably this last doesn't mean only those who, possibly like Patmore himself in his second marriage, choose virgin marriage; or if we don't find ourselves strictly included, we may take advantage of the latitudinarian spirit toward access to virginity to draw closer in any case.

As if to encourage us further, the speaker turns from the festival itself to try to define for us the state in which we understand virgin desire. He has already shown us the pomps of virginity as attractively warm, a ruddy blazing torch, a festival which is that of love and whose celebrants wear the nuptial roses of summer fulfillment. The Unknown Eros is thus in one form unmasked as virgin love in sexual celebration. The danger is, of course, that we take this merely for a love feast and Patmore's digression thus reminds us of origins in absence, not ordinary sexual fulfillment. The ode form allows him to jump to a series of rather metaphysical images, as usual handled well by Patmore. The first set is splendid. The consummation of sex in the natural world, projected on the grandest scale, is contrasted to unfulfilled desire's much greater power. Images set in logical opposition serve also to augment the sense of great desire, which is also thus greatly passionate and sensual, in virgin deferral:

> The magnet calls the steel;
> Answers the iron to the magnet's breath;
> What do they feel
> But death!
> The clouds of summer kiss in flame and rain,
> And are not found again;
> But the heavens themselves eternal are with fire
> Of unapproach'd desire.

A second long conceit moves rapidly and wonderfully from an appeal to our own experiences (an inclusive gesture) to an arcane and difficult conceit naming our true desire (a hard action for us to follow). We all recall the great yearning that we felt in childhood which left us at first unsatisfied at the mere facts of life and love. As in "To the Unknown Eros" intimations of desire in childhood help define the greater intimations now. The conceit, a hard but rosy, sexy, one is of a "star," evidently a planet that looks on his "Mistress," another planet, all his long year without ever touching. His pace, like that of a bridegroom rejoicing on his course, hastens him one time in his long year "Nearer, though never near" his "Love" and "Home." Patmore's stress on the light of space allows him to make such certainly withheld fulfillment a thing of enticing beauty, stressed in the rhyming words: gaze, rays; throughout his ellipse there is no eclipse in her light, whose source is an ardent secret clothed in night. The approach brings doubling of light (double is repeated, "doubly," "doubled" in two lines). Like human lovers in Patmore, the bridegroom planet feels the "delicious" approach as one of both ecstasy and fear, suffering even in his sphere, in a cute coinage, "praeternuptial" anxiety (more than regular nuptials with hints of preternaturalism, if not dangers of celestial pretermission or even pre-emission). The odd, half-fanciful, half-serious image of love writ large continues to augment and inspire our sense of love's force even as it offers a celestial tease, or even *caelestia interrupta*, as an image of desire provoked by deferral. Patmore wittily *and* mystically suggests the secondariness of all desire by reminding us that all this lovelight burns from a greater source, that mysterious "ardent secret."

Having explored our awareness of the power of desire, as indeed in so many odes before this, we are now welcomed in further by a poet who has clearly assumed singing robes finer than those of a mere beggar at the porch. Now we may "gaze bold" and we should hear. What we see and hear in the celebration is now at a visionary level, a "dainty and unsating Marriage-Feast," the "Husband of the Heavens" (which has here at least planetary force), and the Lamb. They sing "Cor meum et caro mea," an allusion to Psalms lxxxiv.2, where heart and flesh sing to the living God. Virgin love is seen for a moment fulfilled, indeed taking its fill, in all senses, of God himself, "The 'I am.'" The language and imagery from biblical texts of man in relation to Maker (the virgins and the Lamb, Revelation xiv.1–5, the marriage supper of the Lamb, xix.9, God as husband, Isaiah lv.5,[96] the "I am" of Exodus iii.14), presented as a palimpsest of quotation and allusion, tell us we are on mythic grounds; we find that they are places especially where opposites meet, where dyads dissolve in each other. Even in the planet conceit desire grows on absence, though this is placed in stasis in a way it couldn't be in the real world of Book 1. In the mythic Palace, now also revealed as Revelation's temple, there is no gap between desire and fulfillment, yet each is also maintained fully, desire entirely potent, fulfillment ever plenteous. The ode's language revels in opposites reconciled, a "dainty" (thus virginal) but also "unsating" Marriage-Feast (at the festival of virginity!). The singing choir of virgins (as also in Revelation) are both "shining" and "sacrificial." They give up – offer – their "dearest hearts' desires," but, unlike with lovers in the earthly world, loss of desire only promotes its increase and fulfillment: desire comes back "to their hearts . . . beatified." Desire begets desire; it is blessed, in that sense fulfilled, and returns even stronger. Patmore plays the fundamental oxymoron, not for irony but ecstasy, again and again: a "nuptial song" for virgins; Mary hailed as "Virgin in Virginity a Spouse!" (Patmore's own rhetorical embroidery on the angel's simpler greeting in Luke), a place where virgins wear roses, not lilies, and indulge rather than hold back.

Patmore's tact and timing is marvelous here. Having offered the full paradoxical mythical spectacle for our gaze and ear, a vision of a land of heart's desire all fulfilled, he leaves it before – as certainly his earthly language would have had to – he actually pulls the God down after calling it up. Instead, he snatches away the scene of a sexual Revelation and returns us to the desiring ones: the cry of virgin spouse was heard in the human world in Nazareth; it is heard in nunneries, where paradise is still hidden and sought amid absence. The lines, combining winter absence and a sense of intense hidden sexual joy, are splendid, and master whatever hesitations we have as non-religious virgins, non-Catholics, or non-religious, non-virgins.

> Heard yet in many a cell where brides of Christ
> Lie hid, emparadised,
> And where, although
> By the hour 'tis night,
> There's light
> The Day still lingering in the lap of snow.

Having pulled us away, forced us to focus on cloistered, very interior scenes where most of us normally don't belong, the poem now ends in satisfying our readers' hearts' desire by a series of ever more inclusive invitations again to "Gaze and be not afraid," "Gaze without blame," "Gaze without doubt or fear." Repetition breaks down our resistance, whereas direct description would tire and repel. The ending builds a sense of sexual celebration that, if not orgasmic (such an easy literary effect to claim!), at least ends in something of a lyric crescendo. Wedded folk are "highly styled" among Revelation's "thousands twelve times twelve of undefiled" (xiv.1). Patmore repeats an entire line from early in the poem, "Young Lover true and love-foreboding Maid," with a similar rhyme on "not afraid"; he repeats words or sounds at beginnings of lines, "Gaze" or "There"; he uses alliteration similar to that he had found in Anglo-Saxon poetry ("There where in *c*ourts afar, all un*c*onfused, they *c*rowd") to give both strongly marked meanings and a chant-like effect. Young lovers find their true Hymen in the Palace, with total sexual fulfillment as on earth – "No spark minute of Nature's keen delight" being omitted. In this full noon the lovers already at the festival find their early intimations of something better than earthly love are now fulfilled: "each to the other, well-content, / Sighs oft, / ''Twas this we meant!'" The recall of "'Twas" not only brings back the discussion earlier in the poem but the entire experience of Book 1.

Finally, Patmore makes his most inclusive gesture: "of pure Virgins none" – other than Mary herself – "Is fairer seen" than . . . whom? Mary Magdalene, of course. Patmore splendidly recaptures old Church truths – the sanctification of the Magdalene – as striking new truth: yes, even the prostitutes (whom Victorians called magdalenes) are not only at the rite of virginity but stand fair, sexually attractive, there. The concluding line of this section is almost breath-taking: "Gaze without doubt or fear / Ye to whom generous Love, by any name, is dear." The embrace of that "generous Love," really God as love at the center, not only welcomes the reformed magdalenes but even all the names and name-callings at their misplaced generosity. From nuns to prostitutes: we have now come to a virgin love so expansive and inclusive that it welcomes the daintiest and ruddiest of human lovers. To say, but they must now all vow virginity, means little as explanation: in the Palace (not mere temple) to which our full and open gaze is now drawn, sexual fulfillment is the *donné*: what isn't there is the stinted life of ungenerous love – perhaps we think of those mean halls and habitations of "Eurydice" with their sense of deprivation and guilt, where he found his love, to his shame, beyond all hope from love.

Patmore concludes this extraordinary ode with a shower of images and namings of generous love, a phrase repeated itself for ample measure: virginity is a perpetual fountain; by all names the virgins affect God; and he in return is "Husband of the Heavens." His lovers come in potence; they are all heirs; they are all clad in bridal robes "of ardour virginal." The plenitude above all is the repetition of opposites reconciled or oppositions walked over; names no longer matter; signs, the creations of absence, are canceled out and we are left with language fading to an appearance of presence. Patmore's ode moves from inviting us to gaze to the momentary magic of "For, lo," vision achieved at the point where language self-destructs. But he is still careful with his terms: this is an experience of the elect, and we hope we may be among them; they "affect / Nothing but God" (a fine phrase in itself) but this is either "mediate or direct": there is some place for other loves in this most generous love.

Of course it is only an appearance of plenitude, a system for suggesting presence created out of our awareness of its distance from our approaching gaze. Patmore's boldest attempt in the odes of Book II takes the next step he approaches at the warmest parts of "Deliciae Sapientiae de Amore": to try to find some way to describe God's love-making with humans. Patmore's late Victorian and early twentieth-century commentators regularly dismissed this attempt as a kind of vulgarity, as if Patmore had merely hit on the wrong trope – that of sexual experience – to describe God's care for the soul and the soul's aspiration toward God. But in the tradition of many Christian mystics, many of whom he read and one, St. Bernard of Clairvaux, he and his second wife translated, Patmore was entirely in earnest in thinking of God's relation to mankind as that of lover.[97] And this was not merely a conception designed to shock the philistine, or indeed the poet himself, into realizing the passion of religious belief (as for instance Donne's famous "except you ravish me"); as we have seen, Patmore found his way directly to passionate religion by his logical solution to the problem of sexual absence and desire.

He also was well aware that, at the least, vulgarity would be the accusation. Indeed, he was on his way to another, really quite stunning, gesture of contempt for his popularity that would do a great deal to submerge the exceptional achievement of his best odes. Shocking poems about God could hardly be expected to please most religious persons of his own time, in or out of Catholicism. Love poems with God would also not be much on the program of the next generation, the Modernists, whatever sympathy they might feel with the wasteland of the odes of Book I. Patmore approaches this problem in "To the Body" where, hinting at the final dignity for which the body is destined, he also notes that the prophets hinted darkly too, "Lest shameless men cry 'shame'." In "The Cry at Midnight" (II.x), a poem that picks up some of the thrust of rough eighteenth-century stage satire that Yeats would also use so effectively, he defends himself against those who would respond to the cry "Our Bridegroom's near" by bawling out "'Blasphemy!'"

He includes some poems on Catholicism, one, "'Sing us One of the Songs of Sion'" (II.viii) a warm and elegant tribute to Newman, another, "The Standards" (II.iv) a defense of the declaration of Papal Infallibility of 1870, which had been extremely unpopular in both Protestant and free-thinking England. Patmore, like most English converts, like Newman himself, takes comfort in the authority of the Church. Yet, as often, certainly with Newman too, the strategy seems to hide an attitude more Protestant than Catholic: the Church, with its enormous variety and ever-changing historical articulation, provides even more freedom for the inquiring religious spirit than the more precise formulations of authority, interpretation, and theology that define various Protestant creeds. So in "The Standards" Patmore is careful to link obedience to the Church with his most controversial theme:

> Come who have felt, in soul and heart and sense,
> The entire obedience
> Which opens the bosom, like a blissful wife,
> To the Husband of all life!

In fact, the same conservative forces in the Church that led to the proclamation of Papal Infallibility were working in the British and American context to dampen or extinguish the rather rich accumulation of moderate and realistic practical sexual discussion, guided by the moral formulas of St. Alphonsus Liguori for pastoral counseling; and they would also tend to suppress the richer tradition in mystics such as St. Bernard of Clairvaux, St. John of the Cross, or St. Francis of Sales, defining man's relation to God in sexual terms.[98] Responding to accusations of encouraging licentiousness or to charges of outright sexual scandal, the Church, a much-criticized minority in both England and the United States, began to adopt the strictly conservative or even anti-sexual policies that have been its main contribution to sexual discussions of the twentieth century. Nor was it likely that Newman, "without superfluousness, without defect," as Patmore portrayed him, was likely to endorse his venture in pushing to the extreme traditional limits suggestions of the sexual nature of man's relation to God. Father Hopkins, in whom repressed sexuality but not a sexual discourse has been detected by some critics, showed appreciation for Patmore's poetic achievement, but his nervousness about the doctrinal aspects of Patmore's sexual speculations was made painfully clear in those comments on the prose "Sponsa Dei" that Patmore destroyed.[99]

Whatever troubled him enough in that later manuscript to lead him to seek Hopkins's opinion, and that of his spiritual advisors, did not bother the rich Catholic layman sufficiently in his odes to bring him to follow any other advice than his own. And whatever the direction of Catholic thinking in his day, he had no trouble finding a precedent in the Bible and in some Church Fathers and some mystics for the vision of man's sexual relation to God that he wished to explore – a complex terrain that I mapped out in broad lines in the Introduction. In Revelation Christ is the Bridegroom of the Church, as Patmore's allusions to this "blasphemy" in "Deliciae Sapientiae de Amore" remind us. In the tradition of St. Bernard, the Song of Solomon (Douay Canticle of Canticles), probably love poems dating much later than Solomon, was interpreted as a sensuous celebration of God's love for the soul. Even Augustine speaks of Christ's passion as the mounting of the cross by a bridegroom, thereby consummating marriage to humankind.[100] And the mystics such as St. Bernard or St. John of the Cross showed that such ideas could be made the center of a devotional practice. Perhaps even more important, the Catholic Mass, unlike the many Protestant revisions of the Lord's Supper, retained faith that God was not only physically with mankind at the end of time but intimately present, in the believer's body, during his or her lifetime. While Protestant belief came to insist upon a gap, ultimate bodily union with God as a consummation as devoutly to be deferred as it was desired, Catholic practice retained the form of immediate relation that Patmore could recover. He would represent himself in his late prose writings as digging again "the wells which the Philistines have filled."[101] In Catholic tradition and practice his very personal archaeology was able to find sufficient precedent to justify the bold and idiosyncratic move he makes in this final development of the odes.

The difficult subject of a human's personal, sexual relation to God is introduced lightly and charmingly in the ode "Sponsa Dei" (II.v), which leads its reader seductively from sophisticated and casual comments on our universal love-yearning to the brilliant and stunning reversal of the end, an *éclaircissement* lurking in the title all along. The ode leaves us finely unclear about its initial action. Like "To the Unknown Eros," it presents a series of questions about an unidentified power of love. Here it is a "Maiden fair" rather than the apparently masculine force of the first poem, an object of love from the male speaker's view rather than a god visiting him. We are left uncertain whether this is a power being called down by the ode, as in the earlier one, or merely a generic maiden standing for all those maidens loved by different individuals. The power of her laughing eye, the gleams that play around her, a glimpse of her gazing in the glass to set her hair, her gentle step, her dancing, the desolation she exacts when she refuses to smile – all these quick touches, attractively of Patmore's period without cloying in the way of many descriptions in *The Angel*, suggest a medley of real loves and real lovers. Yet the effect – as we have already experienced it in the speaker's own history in Book i – is always to lead the lover beyond that normal encounter. The laughing eye of his love doesn't merely bewitch man but provokes "renew'd virginity," as always in Patmore a state of extreme passion rather than its extinction. It frees a desire for some marriage beyond imagining: "With hope of utter binding, and of loosing endless dear despair." Her shining seems transient divinity, her look in the glass makes him fall "humbled at her feet" – appropriate if this were his own love language, but the odist's somewhat distanced report reminds us how excessive it is. It is as if he reports the language lovers might use with a kind of friendly understanding of how they speak and at the same time underlines the madness in such love behavior. Her dancing makes him ready to die for her. Oddest of all, it opens a "heaven of heavens" to him that makes him now her rival in glory.

The general question, "who is this?" is repeated in the easy epic language Patmore masters so well in some of the odes. It is a larger affair than that of some mere individual in love: each has seen the Fair in this "bewailed dell" unless he is damned to hell; she is identified as precisely the one too good for this world, "Too fair for man to kiss." Indeed the whole process is fatuous, a deception created in desperation. The particular mistress – Patmore uses the Victorian ordinary names, now charmingly of his time, as in an Oscar Wilde comedy, of Margaret, Maude, or Cecily – is given absurd praise and attributes "by a frantic flight of courtesy" which is actually "Born of despair / Of better lodging for his Spirit fair." Patmore wittily captures the anomalous procedure with the common, always misused, "adore" for love: "He adores as Margaret, Maude, or Cecily." From this almost quaint statement of a major problem Patmore shifts to a larger perspective and takes on a more prophetic voice. What is this sigh for incongruities, "Heaven high" and "Earth's last lowlihead" locked in the lover's mind "in dateless bridal-bed."[102]

What, in effect, are we doing with our desire in this crazy business of love-longing that Patmore shows so genially as such a universal folly: "Are all, then, mad, or is it prophecy?" The shifting up of tone that Patmore accomplishes so well in these odes here actually moves him to prophecy, and a very bold one. "'Sons now we are of God,' as we have heard, / But what we shall be hath not yet appear'd." The tone is biblical, actually an adaptation from Christ in St. John. Patmore's context makes it clear that he believes he knows the answer that Christ left unanswered.[103] As always, his mode of hinting at great consummations to come is imaginatively effective and sexually suggestive, just because it invites us to imagine and desire in a vacuum. The answering revelation adds to, rather than destroys, this effect because it is kept brief, oracular, and shocking in subject and dramatic reversal. With a gesture, which Yeats often sounds again in the twentieth century, of passionate introspection – "O, Heart, remember thee" – he totally recasts the mystery. The gesture itself first demands notice. Patmore's ode has called down a kind of a god: some image of its passion (in this poem the maiden fair each man dreams of); now it calls directly to the author's self. This might seem an ultra-romantic gesture of imaginative self-sufficiency and control. In fact, it is the reverse. Man finds his aspiration in a radical discovery about himself. "Man is none, / Save One" means a man is in God but also that his apparent division into desiring self and desired lover, or image, disguises his unity. His soul *is* the Lady that he created in his desire, nothing else. The move might seem an anticipation of the Jungian concept of the anima, but instead of offering a healing of self-division it actually evacuates the self. "Man is none," *only* God. Passion, once the possession of the apparently helpless lover, is now taken from him and he finds his true absence. "Not thou, but God" will "enjoy" the beauty. Man's fire is "sick"; more than that, it is not true fire but a "female vanity." Man's passion is only a "reflex heat" from God's passion, from "His immense desire." Man becomes specular only, "a Bride, viewing her mirror'd charms," which are no longer hers but "for his arms." All power, in the brief and splendid conclusion, is now God's which is the power of God's passion crowding in to fill the vacuum by man's self-recognition:

> A reflex heat
> Flash'd on thy cheek from His immense desire,
> Which waits to crown, beyond thy brain's conceit,
> Thy nameless, secret, hopeless longing sweet,
> Not by-and-by, but now,
> Unless deny him thou!

The helpless soul, reading his true absence, can hardly deny the passion which finally solves the problem of his unknown love, his quest for an ideal lady love – a love generated not by his supposed fullness of passion but by his real sense of lack. Patmore now sees God almost as the necessary invention, opposite presence, to his own recognition of absence.

The recognition here goes one step further than Patmore's other, frequent meditations on desire stimulated by absence. Desire was still in the human speaker as a consequence of his consciousness of winter or his experience of loss. The model, one that came easily to the author of *The Angel in the House*, the patriarch *par eminence* in the feminist gallery, is one based on a gender difference: someone (male) perceives absence and desires someone (female). The male speaker of Book I endures the loss of love but maintains his personal orientation as the male desiring a female. In the odes of Book II on virgin desire the model is the same, except that the desiring figure can be equally female or male. Indeed the type is the nun, formally betrothed to God by the ring she puts on as she accepts the veil of fulfillment's deferral. But hidden in that paradigm is the reversal in the vector of desire that becomes obvious when Patmore looks directly at the relation between humans and God. Now, in Patmore's explanation of *man's* search for ideal woman, God becomes the desirer (male) possessing the human (male explained as female to God). The paradigm is itself familiar enough in the Christian tradition of God as lover of man's soul. Unfortunately, it offers greater problems to Patmore than to writers using it metaphorically or allegorically. From a myth of desire's general activation in "Deliciae Sapientiae de Amore," where issues of male and female were suspended before the universal human relation to God, he was now thrown back, as he tried to describe the individual's situation, into a strongly gendered poetic discourse. Gendered: he, lover of Maude or Cecily, is suddenly (with an effective shock in this poem) reversed into the lady beloved of God. Thrown back, because it forced him closer to the stereotypes of male and female sexual roles – highly polarized – that he had first questioned in his early poems, then by-and-large accepted and asserted in *The Angel*.

BOOK II: EROS FOUND AND RENOUNCED

The problem is typical of those he now encountered with less success in poems that tried to take the logical next step and portray in more detail God's love-making with humans: the danger, in effect, of rendering the relation so comprehensible and human that it became merely a poetry of love. The poet whose instinct not to describe human love as in any simple sense fulfilled was unwavering throughout Book I, here risked falling into a tension-free, too-human poetry in reaching for the ecstasy of divine relation. As Paul Fry has pointed out, the ode that seems fully to succeed in bringing a god to earth may inadvertently find itself back where it began, merely describing the ordinary.

Such a barely avoidable and reductive return largely dogs Patmore's boldest attempt to find language for his heart's desire in three poems that conclude this section of Book II. The falling off is registered immediately in the fact that these three poems, known as the Eros and Psyche poems, are about a secret love rather than an unknown Eros. Indeed, Eros as merely that Greek god again is only too familiar, as was the story of his love with Psyche.[104] In his fine "Ode to Psyche" Keats had taken the late myth from Apuleius of the god of love's passion for a human as a story that he could recast into a way of speaking of internal feelings. Patmore, having so far used most effectively the concept of a divine love obscurely seeking the human through the human's response to absence and loss, now chooses to re-objectify the myth. The change here is also registered in form: instead of the ode form, so useful to Patmore in providing a sense of great sweeping movements of desire into the unknown, we have the achieved world of ordinary dialogue.

In the first poem of the series, "Eros and Psyche" (II.xii), Psyche has already – to her amazement and concern – had complete success in calling down a god. She has him in her bed; they have made love; she is already quick with child. We may try to repress our own response, especially if we began with commentators telling us of Patmore's belief in divine truth found in pagan tales, but it will come out: quite a night's work! The myth itself, in its general outline, suited Patmore's aims, as the effective vague reference in "To the Unknown Eros" suggested. Eros, Love, hence easily God, loves Psyche, the human soul; their love is deferred after Psyche becomes too curious (a kind of Fall) but they are ultimately reunited after Psyche undergoes much pain and privation. But the problem is, of course, that Patmore takes little interest in such an allegory of the soul. What attracted him was just the part of the myth that could not be represented without a very literal effect, the actual sexual unity with God. Commentators may dwell on the allegory (Patmore's devoted orthodox editor, Connolly, warns that chaste ears must come to the reading) but the redeeming quality of the poems is actually the bluntness that also makes them failures. There is the same refusal to think about religion beyond the human scale, even in pillow-talk of God and man, that is so attractive in the poems on infinity. Certainly better create a God of routine sex and ordinary sexy talk than a God of fear or power used to bully or diminish other humans – though our Western traditions may have so often preferred the latter that a God modelled on our pleasure rather than fear may still seem mainly shocking. Patmore writes his most risqué poetry since that of his youth. He dares to describe lovers in bed, hearts joined, his arms around her bosom, linked in "pure pleasure" as "the cocoon is with the butterfly." It is not a passage that twentieth-century readers will run to for titillation, but it is sexy, affectionate, and direct, three qualities we used to be told couldn't be found together in Victorian literature.

The relation of humans to God portrayed as a warm Sunday in bed could have a kind of naive attraction, as in medieval poems that present religious mysteries in the terms of simple ordinary folk: we might have here a kind of weak but warm center to the much more complicated odes that lead up to it. But Patmore is in these matters not naive; and the complications of ordinary sexual experience come back into these realistic descriptions of a theophanic liaison with almost a vengeance. Most obviously, questions of gender and social disparity naturally raised by the allegory, as they are even in Kingsley's far less developed use of the myth in his drawing of himself with great wings sweeping a naked Fanny up to heaven (see Illustration 2, following page 100), provide an entry at the realist level for almost comic versions of patriarchy in sex.[105] God takes a decidedly patronizing tone to his mignonne (the title indeed of an ode he excluded from the series), keeps her in the dark (literally, as well), and justifies his love for her by the story of King Cophetua and the gypsy maid, the point of which seems to be that the king knows best why he finds a special attraction in her nothingness – "the charm for which he loves her most."

Two aspects of the Christian allegory fall especially flat in the realist context. God's love for all becomes something like the Victorian gentleman's secret life. Imagine God as an even bigger-than-life Walter! Psyche, visited tonight and then left to wait, contents herself that this impossibly promiscuous lover has reassured her, "'Tis all to know there's not in air or land / Another for thy Darling quite like me!" Of course we remind ourselves that this is no ordinary bed-hopper; but Patmore's extreme myth of sexuality fails here where it could still succeed in the distant, veiled view of a multitude of rose-crowned Virgins with the Lamb.

Similarly, God's trials for man get re-rendered here as an unfortunate celebration, by both God and human, of sadism in love. Patmore's susceptibility to this most common of sexual perversions was clear in the rather uncontrolled passages in *The Angel*. There is the same impression here of forces in *his* psyche not entirely under control that find an outlet through the enabling allegory. Psyche's lines of devotion to her lover would have made, indeed, a far better anthem for feminist postmortem attacks on Victorian patriarchy than anything in *The Angel in the House*, including the title: "do with me as thou wilt, / And use me as a chattel that is thine! / Kiss, tread me underfoot, cherish or beat, / Sheathe in my heart sharp pain up to the hilt." Apologists for Patmore could explain until Patmore's sexual kingdom come that this is the soul speaking to God, as they have tried to remind us that the angel is the spirit of love between married lovers. The damage is done. And here we do feel we come closer than we wish to the man Patmore, who at some point in, or more likely after, his probably virgin marriage to the second Mrs. Patmore took up with the young governess who would become number three. The reversal of gender in some sense only confirms the pathology. Patmore seems to enjoy both creating God's playful sadistic dominance and identifying as human with the masochistic

Psyche. Masochism and sadism are of course flip-sides of a psychological coin. Both are rather let out of the bag by the myth and allegory. That Patmore chose this vehicle and worked it for these effects as his way of presenting fulfilled sexuality gives the biographer a good reason to consider this a real tendency in his psyche (even to find hidden meaning in his creation of his Psyche as a troubled figure), though doubtless a tendency finding outlet mainly in such open fantasy – no one has suggested that any of Patmore's wives wore stiletto heels and brandished cruel instruments of joyful pain. Meanwhile, the poems are pulled down from the odic explorations of universal experience to what seem impressions of sex valid only for a specific age or an individual, somewhat distorted, personality: from art to individual pathology. In *The Angel*, where Patmore's similar tendency to sadism was concealed from himself, the damage was broader – into a general falsity of perception. Here we experience this tendency as an unattractive intrusion allowed in suddenly by the bold turn to sex description. We hear the sex kinks of his personal peculiarity and probably also, to some degree, of his period, when male power over females might have seemed a more fitting attribute of deity than it does today. But, like the failures of intrusive rant in the political odes, these invasions do not undermine the broader poetic program. Nonetheless, in themselves they are to be regretted – the more so because they attract reductive criticism that can use them to avoid confronting the quality and difficult discourse of the larger series.

No need to follow the same process at work in Patmore in two other poems, "De Natura Deorum" (ii.xiii), where Psyche has some girl-talk with a mother-figure about how to handle a God-lover, and "Psyche's Discontent" (ii.xiv) – except to acknowledge that Patmore both allows Psyche to voice for womankind/humankind the sense that sexual delight is not everything in life or in a relation, and allows the winged boy/God Almighty to reaffirm the value of such delight as the central fact of the universe it was to his author. Interestingly, Psyche is even allowed to use the language of absence and desire that is so prevalent and powerful in the rest of the odes. Constant delight is too much – "Enough, enough," the poem begins. Psyche needs distance, is overwhelmed by "this infatuating flame." She would feel closer, as Patmore himself argued in "The Day After To-Morrow," if they stayed apart and yearned after each other. The image even recalls Patmore's own powerful planetary ones of great desire at huge distance: "I should feel thee nearer to my heart / If thou and I / Shone each to each respondently apart, / Like stars which one the other trembling spy, / Distinct and lucid in extremes of air."

We can even credit Patmore with being of the humans' party here without knowing it and giving poor Psyche, oppressed by her sexual fulfillment, the more powerful lines despite her ultimate submission to god/God's patronizing, but firm, explanation of his necessarily God-like level of gratification.[106] Patmore in any case must have sensed that his pursuit of his system of redirecting desire to God to its abstract completion had somehow short-circuited the human energies of his poems, creating a sexual paradise that even he could not dwell in long without blanching or sickening. We almost feel Patmore's own pathologies coming out in the form and subjects of the poems as he imagines himself into the ultimately pressured sexual situation. After all, he had been especially aware of the dangers of too much fulfillment, as well as the pain of absence, in even a puny human affair! In "De Natura Deorum," where Psyche and a Pythoness (oracle) talk while Cupid is out on business, we are given a series of too-cute human parallels for human–divine interaction. Psyche fears she will lose him now she has found him; she finds his love for her unmerited and is told that gods, like men, are mysteries. The Pythoness assures her that great ones must pay properly for their mistresses. His liking for rough treatment – "a whip / Of deathless scorpions at my slightest slip" and a penchant for calling her "Gypsy" and for love "wounds" – are explained as "Happiness at play." At best, human intimacy that maintains Patmore's disdain for infinity is realized at the expense of the dignity of this ultimate union with God; human quirks of sexual feeling take the place of any very direct attempt to render the force of a divine orgasm. As always when Patmore represses his sexual excitement, presumably because he too, like his image in Psyche, can't face the ultimate intimacy that he conceptualizes, it is released in an *échappée* of sadomasochism that embarrasses us and should have embarrassed him as well.

In his "Ode to Psyche" Keats had turned the ode from its traditional quest after an external god to a Romantic search for authentic power of imagination within; and the myth of Psyche had allowed him to identify and locate the source of imagination in the universal power of love and sex. Patmore's choice of myth was unimpugnable. Even in Apuleius the myth was allegorized as man's union with God; and Patmore could draw upon the power of Keats's invention to unite the formal meaning to the inner force of sexual imagination discovered in the course of *The Unknown Eros*. In his concept, Patmore failed neither in taste, as has often been suggested, nor in culture, where his broad and just use of tradition is present as always. Nor should the problems he encountered in realizing his extreme aim in terms familiar and commonly human be blamed intolerantly on his use of sexual union as a center for religion. Psyche voices the question of whether the entire affair isn't a mere heathen fable; the Pythoness warns her not to talk like a Protestant. The convert's little joke reminds us that we must approach someone else's religious vision with religious minds at least temporarily open, not as Protestant, Catholic, or agnostic censors. Patmore's difficulties arise fairly from an attempt, intelligently and honestly undertaken, to complete the myth of sexual yearning he had so well taken from a personal to a general need. That he ended in a descent into problems of human sex that he may have imagined for a moment that he had left behind suggests the fragility of all such attempts to build a general vision on the experience of sex. It also reconfirms Patmore's own central insistence on the ordinary sexual origins of religious ecstasy.

Poems before and after the Eros and Psyche triad appear to stress the origins of myth and its human limits as if to suggest that Patmore was aware of the odds against his one further step. Immediately preceding the triad, "Auras of Delight" (II.xi) stretches back, not forward, to insist on the intimations of sexual plenitude from earliest childhood. Envisioned rather beautifully as a place of latency and sublimation, those "Beautiful Habitations" of childhood are also places of danger, even forbidding: "crags and bitter foam / And angry sword-blades flashing left and right." The swords suggest tabooed sexual experience, as if ultimates were bound to be unapproachable. Its virginity – "ne'er-profaned snow" – is both its sexual power and prohibition, a pattern now familiar in Patmore. About to do so in the succeeding poems, he here asks whether we would indeed wish to profane – "foot" – those snows to recover their full power. The imagery of conflict and desecration, more powerful than anything in the Psyche poems, is explained as the types of unrealized knowledge, good that is known but not willed. But the image of a serpent and dove "in frightful nuptials" –

> The tortured knot,
> Now like a kite scant-weighted, flung bewitch'd
> Sunwards, now pitch'd,

> Tail over head, down, but with no taste got
> Eternally
> Of rest in either ruin or the sky,
> But bird and vermin each incessant strives,
> With vain dilaceration of both lives,
> 'Gainst its abhorred bond insoluble,
> Coveting fiercer any separate hell
> Than the most weary Soul in Purgatory
> On God's sweet breast to lie

– speaks even more powerfully of sexual union as necessary trauma and discord, the possibly antithetical relation of sexual virginity and experience, sexual desire and fulfillment. Patmore ends the poem by beautifully celebrating the foundational experience of those auras to his being – "I *did* respire the lonely auras sweet, / I *did* the blest abodes behold, and, at the mountains' feet, / Bathed in the holy Stream by Hermon's thymy hill." But the overall effect is more problematic. He has essentially lost (forgotten) the knowledge once possessed; and it is a necessary loss of innocence lest he reject fulfilled desire itself – "refuse God to His face." That the desire of desire and the desire of its fulfillment are incompatible is a paradox clear enough throughout the odes up to this point. It might have suggested that the mystery of a burning bush of desired, consumed, never extinguished, is better left to the Almighty Lover himself.

Man's relation to God on a more ordinary level is the subject of the flanking poem on the other side of the Psyche odes: "Pain" (ii.xv). Instead of the fantasy pain of sexual indulgence we come – with some relief, we may be willing to admit – to the subject of the usual dreary human necessities. Again, by placing the poem here, Patmore almost seems to admit that it is on a more usual human level, which will include much pain, not the level of union attained, that he must normally operate. He returns us to the various and so strongly rendered themes of loss of Book i of the odes. No need to repeat the specific cycle of his own pain; he works, as always in Book ii, on a general level. But the power called down from God is not a form of ultimate to which he must stand in troubled relation if realized: it is God's gift within. He praises it for bringing him to the full force of desire and in this sense he accepts the place of pain in the cycle of absence, desire, fulfillment that he has tried to follow. But it is now to be accepted as a good in itself that cannot merely be experienced, overcome, and left behind.

The topics are general, purging and burnishing of the being through the necessary experience of pain, whether in this world or some purgatory. The voice is extremely intimate, an "I" that speaks directly for the poet who created the odes. Pain is the mysterious next of kin through which he finds love. And if perverse pleasure in sex is explicitly mentioned, it is not the poet's own perversity and is brought up only as a case to dismiss: they who "pursue / Pleasure with hell's whole gust" find they must "Perversely woo" pain. The perspective is generally broader than any form of sexuality – the moral and psychological sharpening of the self in life's pains. Here Patmore accepts more explicitly the kind of paradoxical truth that "Auras of Delight" approached. Pain leads to the joy of "assured desire" in fulfillment with God. Yet we experience its negative force as a positive thing in itself, the negative experience whose presence orients us and polishes us for God's love. In that sense we feel the love present in absence as God's pain, "the clear heat of Love irate" which brings its own "fire of bliss" that, "pangful, purging . . . / Shall furiously burn / With joy."

The poem is a striking *tour de force* that clarifies the series as a whole by contrast, as a negative among positive prints. Here God woos in the more usual way, with suffering and absence that makes any touch of fulfillment, even the mere lull in the experience of pain, entirely precious. The poet even presents himself as a different young maid, now loved by the "fierce kiss" of God's pain and finding the value of this love only as she is forced to experience it. The poem brings him not to a sanguine celebration of pain but essentially to the position that his entire personal journey in the odes has developed. He knows what to desire at least, a "learned spirit . . . / That does not faint, / But knows both how to have thee and to lack." The phrase could stand as a motto for the series, though the usual subject is reversed: how to live with the pain of desire absent and how to accept its presence, lack fulfilled. The negative ends positively, on the normal human experience of pain in love that has been his subject from the beginning, not its ultimate defeat in a mythic world of desire fulfilled.

Accepting the necessity of lack, which so much goes against Patmore's life-long commitment to exploring sexual passion as far as desire will take him, is a definition of psychological maturity Lacan offered; and in some sense Patmore's journey of exploration into the unknown of Eros brings him to the unexpected goal not of passionate intercourse with God but of a fuller acceptance of limits. What he had

learned in human love, the unavoidability of absence and the
ultimate necessity of loss, he found in the compensating divine love as
necessary distance and deferral: he could imagine an ecstatic union
with God but perhaps not reach it here and now. More importantly,
he had to accept the gap and lack of his own failure: he could not
actually put that which was, for him, ultimate reality into words that
would bring it before himself and his reader as an immediate
presence. The final major poem in the series, penultimate to the
valedictory "Dead Language," also has a maturity of accepted
limits. Like "Pain" it is crisp, witty, filled with bright paradoxes. It
obtains astonishing range in a poem of only about 170 lines by
abandoning the attempt at passionate realization. It restates the
Christian epic from the viewpoint of a Catholic poem focussed on the
role of Mary (again, Catholics, much as Protestants and atheists, will
have to check in their firearms before entering Patmore's elegant but
very personally decorated establishment). The poem was purportedly
written as a prologue to a never-completed poem, or possibly the
prose work Patmore destroyed, on Mary. As such it serves here
appropriately as prologue for epilogue. The view of Mary connects
nicely to the premonition of a redeeming Eve in the early poem in
Book II, "The Contract," as well as to the implication that we are all
Marys to God in the title of the ode, "Sponsa Dei." The new attitude
of fine control and resignation ends the series appropriately by
accepting the force of what has been discovered in the ecstatic quest
for union with an unknown Eros. And it now demonstrates how to
create the only kind of art possible under the new conditions of failure
in that quest. As we shall see, the new poem thus necessarily looks at
its own art with a self-consciousness new to the series, despite
Patmore's earlier reflections on the need for, and difficulties of,
creating prophetic art.

If Patmore still claims the right to write his own, very idiosyncratic,
version of the Christian myth, he now plays within that format rather
than essentially creating his own. Rather than wash out his concerns
in the prior odes, the attempt to write a more orthodox myth
essentially translates the tale of absence, desire, virgin passion, and
fulfilled love with God into new terms. Patmore may be abandoning
his ultimate aim for the ode – really to represent sexual union with
God – but he in no way abdicates his way of thinking about religion.
His witty achievement in "The Child's Purchase" (II.xvii) is to write
a poem that could be read in itself as a series of well-honed traditional

Catholic platitudes about Mary (his Ave Maria) but which, taken in the series or in a careful reading, opens up Patmore's entire sexual system. The poem presents itself as a gift back to Mary of the powers which she, as a kind of religious power of love, inspired in her poet throughout his long career as poet of love and of religion. May she accept the gift of his understanding of sexual love! Whether the Church, or his religious readers, really wish to receive it or not is, as always with Patmore, no issue. The gift is to celebrate Mary's relation to God as a master version of the relation of each human to God that Patmore attempted to present in the Psyche poems. In Patmore's view Mary is the central consort of God, the model spouse of God for all of us to imitate in the role of "sponsa Dei" assigned to us all, whether in his anticipation of her before her birth (it was not good that God, any more than man – Adam – "should be alone"), or in the conception of Christ, or in her present position as "Queen-Wife" beside Him in heaven. Patmore defines her relation to God in remarkably direct terms. As the stalwart historian of religion and literature, H. N. Fairchild, complains, God is made to sound like a real lover, a kind of "gallant infatuated nobleman."[107]

Like Psyche, she is the small, finite, human which attracts the God by her limits, as God her by his greatness: "absolute delight / His Infinite reposed in thy Finite." Because the stress is on Mary as human (her traditional weakness as a woman in a gendered society used as a unisexual symbol of all humans' weakness), not in the first instance female stand-in for every man/woman, she does not lead Patmore into embarrassing comparisons to unequal relations between powerful males and their younger, poorer, mistresses. Trying less hard to make the passion of God and human visible, Patmore finds more resonant language that is also more effective because it points to the mystery without hoping to capture it: Mary is the "Desire of Him whom all things else desire! / Bush aye with Him as He with thee on fire!" The conversion of burning bush from God's majesty in Moses' encounter with Him to a figure of mutual passion is shocking, striking, impressively bold.

More shocking is the deliberately witty focus on the nest of incestuous relations hidden not very deeply in the God–Mary relation as Patmore mythologizes it. Again he is content to state the relations and give them a general tone through metaphor without attempting to make them come alive before us. Mary shines as a "Rainbow complex" of "all beams of sex": her different colors are those of different sexual relations defined by her gender roles. She shines "To One, thy Husband, Father, Son, and Brother, / Spouse blissful, Daughter, Sister, milk-sweet Mother." If Patmore had dramatized this all-in-the-family romance it would have made Milton's Sin and Death look like a mere domestic interlude by comparison. But the rehearsal of names has the abstract quality of some other tribe's kinship diagram. Patmore points to a world of total sexual realization, in which all relations are merely versions of a central intimacy. What would normally be transgressive, tabooed activities are accepted in that ultimate relation of human and God, as we accept that parallel lines meet at infinity.[108] They would not easily be if Patmore had tried to realize them.

Even in this most intense statement of Patmore's sexual theme, what we have in this poem is not an attempt at realization but naming: naming in effect acknowledged by the author as no more than a set of signs for things he no longer hopes to body forth imaginatively. Our deconstructionist friends will here rush in with the ultimate word, laid down by Saussure for all time, that this is of course true of all language. But there is a great difference between a poet trying to use words, whatever their slippage and straining, to make us see the thing itself with some force and a poet making it clear that all he chooses to give is names pointing toward absent realities. In this case, the continuous naming is an acknowledgment, after the earlier attempts at realization, that we must mainly content ourselves with language as a version of our distance from what we desire. Justifying to Hopkins the repeated interjected lines, adapted from the traditional Ave Maria, "*Ora pro me!*" Patmore said, "The Ode consists of a somewhat inconsequent sequence of exclamatory sentences, and the strong break, caused by the Latin, helps to hide this from the reader."[109] The poem attempts no more than to name Mary by naming her attributes. The poet speaks of his own ability, given by Mary, as a kind of golden talents, "golden speech," which he renders back to her in his naming praise. In this he follows her, because she is, in stark comparison to his little language, the giver forth of the Word itself: "Thou Speaker of all wisdom in a Word, / Thy Lord!" But in relation to this Word, which is the sign that is truly a thing, word as flesh itself, absolute presence of God, his position, like hers, is that of a negative or reverse mold. She speaks the Word, but is herself silent after her first splendid acceptance of her role – "Speaker who thus could'st well afford / Thence to be silent;

– ah, what silence that / Which had for prologue thy 'Magnificat?'" Patmore's eloquence in praise of her silence doesn't obscure the fact that he too, in giving word to her, accepts absence from the word become flesh up to which he had tried to screw the power of the ode in prior poems.[110] Indeed, her prime attribute in the poem is essentially not anything she was or did but her essential absence. As *the* Virgin she possesses those non-traits in the extreme that characterized virginity in Patmore's odes on virginity.

It is significant that he ends with an ode that focusses not on the sexual potency of God but on a quintessence of human need and absence in the Virgin of virgins. Mary is a "Vast Nothingness of Self, fair female Twin / Of Fulness, sucking all God's glory in!" The form is still that of the ode calling down a special power by describing it. But Patmore calls to the epitome of his human sense of nothingness, not to a power of fullness. He immediately offers himself as parallel, only less than she because less purely without attribute: "(Ah, Mistress mine, / To nothing I have added only sin, / And yet would shine!)." Joseph, to whom even Matthew allows normal human suspicions of his whitely married spouse, is here only a kind of stand-in for our universal relation to Mary: he experiences a similarly virgin desire from his position of absence. He feels a very "rapture of refusal" and, despite his sainthood, he is held in a permanent position of distance from his passion: "whose good singular eternally / 'Tis now, with nameless peace and vehemence, / To enjoy thy married smile, / That mystery of innocence." This is a remarkably human role to be eternized in Patmore: as a model for the poet and all of us other mere humans, it suggests acceptance of absence in the religious realm, as in Book I Patmore previously accepted it in human love. His lovely praise of the very virgin Mary – "Sunshiny Peak of human personality; / The world's sad aspirations' one Success; / Bright Blush, that sav'st our shame from shamelessness" – doesn't obscure the fact that she too is only human in her lack, indeed her prime virtue being that she even lacks reason for shame.

Patmore prays to her, in those Latin refrains that T. S. Eliot imitated in the much more obscurantist "Ash Wednesday." He prays to her because she is a type of all our relation to God: we hope that our desire, created by our sense of emptiness and lack, can be answered by a plenitude that chooses us, as it chose Mary. Patmore prays to Mary to pray for him, not as to another deity, as the Protestant critique always claims, but, in his case anyway, to another lacking person with whom he can identify. She is indeed his mother, human mother of human, as well as the bride of Christ that he too hopes to be – but can now no longer imagine, only name.

The lofty odist, whose powers might call down a god/God has here become a little boy, praying to mother to pray for him. In Fry's definitions of the ode this is really a hymn, a ritual of received religion rather than an attempt at individual discovery. Rather than reach out to the planetary forces and the brush of great wings, Patmore settles for elegant rehearsal of the names of his faith. What needs to be added is that this is not so much a public and assured affirmation of a living myth as a retreat to a less ambitious, less perilous position for the singer. Patmore ends by celebrating the persistent sense of absence and lack that he had hoped to overcome but now essentially admits he cannot. Like Yeats's late descent from myth into the rag-and-bone shop of the heart, it is an admission of limits that also embodies a considerable insight into the nature of his art. Mary is the "Chief Stone of stumbling" (stumbling-block), a "sign built in the way / To set the foolish everywhere a-bray," not because she is a hard bit of new mythology to add to the already considerable Christian confusion (the orthodox view of her as a test of faith), but because she is a figure of the merely human that our arrogance wishes to overrun, as Patmore's own did in earlier poems. Of his love poems Patmore can now say, "little guess'd I 'twas of thee I sang" not because he really wished to write of the Virgin but because she is just that human need of which he wrote. The poem thus defers from the quest for Eros, still in some sense unknown because found unwritable, to take possession of human need in the figure of Mary. From the opening odes on the winter of human passion unfulfilled we come full circle to the blue vacancy of Mary.

The poem concludes its tableaux of her with death conjoined to sex: we watch Mary in her *stabat mater* role at the foot of the cross at Christ's passion. He too is now the human side of God, suffering, passive, feminine; his death is presented as devagination by the soldier's spear. His experience is identical with hers as she co-experiences it:

> In season due, on His sweet-fearful bed,
> Rock'd by an earthquake, curtain'd with eclipse,
> Thou shar'd'st the rapture of the sharp spear's head,
> And thy bliss pale
> Wrought for our boon what Eve's did for our bale.

The thing to say here is not the obvious one of how very sexual and voyeuristic this makes the crucifixion; rather it is how very painful is this sex; it is the climax of sex as the need of our only too-human selves. God here is brought down to the level of the suffering human lover of Book I of the odes – rather than being reached up to by the aspiring odist. The human Christ, like Mary, suffers absence and loss as sexuality, a pale bliss far more traumatic than Eve's; is pierced and left literally gaping with lack and gap.[111]

The rest is pretty but unreal by comparison. Mary dies graciously and easily ("holding a little thy soft breath, / Thou underwent'st the ceremony of death"), undergoes Assumption, and is installed as "Queen-Wife," a name for a total translation that Patmore won't try to show us imaginatively. The poet addresses her in the end only as her human self, "mother." That humanity is his humility; following the pain of sexual need he has been led and is led "by unknown ways." The prologue for a work that we know, by its presence in the odes, will never be completed (or was destroyed, if it was the prose work), ends speaking of the odist's "many wasted days" and doubting its own aim: Mary's smiles seem dubious; he spells from them mainly the limits of words: "Humility and greatness grace the task / Which he who does it deems impossible!" The poem is followed by the chiming words of "Dead Language" (II.xviii). There a voice addresses the poet as a singer, "Bard," and warns him to stick to themes of virtue and tenderness, not high matters of Church and religion. "Heaven's liberty," which he has celebrated, may call down violent abuse. His answer is merely a modest disclaimer as to the readership he may obtain: his language, the hard language of these uneven but often truly splendid odes, is not likely to reach anyone in this time: it is a "dead language" of and for other ages. The issue of fame and criticism, interesting as it is, really evades the problem faced in "The Child's Purchase." The task is in fact "impossible" if taken as the *gradus ad coelum* that the second book of the odes originally proposes. He has found that he must end on the level of yearning desire and absence, in the religious sexual life as in the life of human lovers. While some odes in Book II excitingly suggest the fulfillment of sexual need in ultimate relation to God, the odes as a group take their strength from their honesty and force in describing the experience of sexual desire as a function of absence and loss. What may seem at points like a too-sanguine or even jejune attempt to wash away the very human pains of love faced in Book 1 is revealed, to us as to Patmore, as a larger exploration of need.

I will not prevail on the reader's interest to continue this history in Patmore where it naturally leads, to the often striking and polished aphorisms and paradoxes of the prose *The Rod, the Root, and the Flower*. His position there essentially follows that of "The Child's Purchase." Patmore names, plays with elegantly, the mysteries of man's sexual relation to God that he believed he discovered as he dug the sand out of wells filled by the prudish philistines. But he remains a namer and pointer at mysteries rather than the odist who, in trying to bring them for a time into being, engaged us in his struggle, partial success, ultimate abandonment of the attempt. Let me merely recommend this striking little wisdom book for what it is: the finely polished elaborations and reiterations of the insights about sexuality and religion to which he had come with great pain and great imaginative passion in his master work, *The Unknown Eros*. *The Rod, the Root, and the Flower* shows the serenity of a writer who has found his own way of looking at issues central to him. Published in the year that his final, and painful, unfulfilled desire for Alice Meynell received its quietus, this prose anthem elaborated the thoughts of a lifetime about the power of sexual desire. Patmore's little sexual *summa* offered to the modern mind, troubled by scientific thinking and social change, a new religious world system to replace the old great chain of being. Sexual desire was again proclaimed, as in his poems but here even more bluntly, to be the center of all things, the force in the heart of man that joins him simultaneously to other people and to God.

It is *The Unknown Eros*, however, a work still, and most unfortunately, much too unknown, that is the enacted culmination of Patmore's long experimental, often troubled or self-repressed attempt to put in somewhat adequate words his sense of the confusions and pains of sexual experience. For the self-chosen poet of sexual love in an age fascinated but afraid of what he might have to say, his success entailed the necessary failure to reach an audience in his day and, pretty much, since. What he found he had to say was not so much obscure or mysterious as painful and troubling. The odes certainly deserve to be read, as the Victorians and our contemporaries both say, by a mature audience – not of those who can handle hot topics like sex with God but of those who can face the bleakness and pain, unremittingly coupled with great desire and yearning, of Patmore's ultimate vision.

CHAPTER 5

Conclusion: Hardy's Jude: Disassembling Sexuality and Religion

I would like to end this enquiry into one culture's preoccupation with the conjunction of sexuality and religion with a brief look at a greater writer than the three very talented special cases I have been considering. This is Thomas Hardy, specifically the Thomas Hardy of the novel – *Jude the Obscure* – that effectively finished his career as a popular Victorian novelist and opened the way to his second writer's self as a modern poet. Hardy is by no means the only or the inevitable choice to extend an examination of how some Victorians related the two most elaborated discourses by which humans attempt to describe/define their human natures. In our century, where it is religion, not sexuality, that has been repressed, it still seems shocking or eccentric to link the two, and my choices for major focus might seem to aim at promoting the view that this is another production of that age and nation of eccentric shopkeepers – to be set beside the exotic travel literature of a Sir Richard Burton or the other-Victorianly bibliographical researches of a Henry Spencer Ashbee ("Pisanus Fraxi"). But if the development of thinking and articulation of expression in Clough, Kingsley, and Patmore is in each case certainly individual to the point of near-genius – at the least the preoccupation of genius – the instinct to relate sexuality and religion is not. As Foucault has rightly observed, Victorians often *are* unusual in their dual obsession with a discourse of sexuality and their need to seem to repress it. On the other hand, they are closer to the general history of human culture than Western people in the twentieth century have been in feeling and instinctively expressing a kinship between sexual theories and myths and religious ones. Indeed, Victorians' awareness of the liaisons that seem naturally to develop between these two areas of discourse (as opposed to willingness to appear in print on the sexual issues) seems to have been so common that the problem would be in not finding such connections.[1] As we have seen in different ways in Clough, Kingsley, and Patmore, Victorian writers still thought within a great tradition that had almost from its origins combined religious and sexual discourses. If there was no agreement over the nature of each, or of their relation – indeed a tradition of disagreement – there was still a common context for thinking about the two. By contrast, for twentieth-century writers it has often seemed necessary to find a new context – in other times and other cultures – to recover such a discussion.

Browning, for instance, did not generally deal explicitly with a sexual discourse in his work, as he wished not to add obscenity to obscurity as reasons for his unpopularity. Yet his ventures into this area, in the guarded language of *Pippa Passes* or *The Ring and the Book*, or in the unique case of the obscure *and* obscene Don Juan poem, *Fifine at the Fair*, always seem to bring religion directly into play. The extreme sexual exploiter of "Porphyria's Lover" quite naturally looks over his shoulder to see if God has anything to say of his new-fangled discourse on romantic possession. Bad Church figures, whether in Pippa's Asolo or at Saint Praxed's at Rome, reveal the disfigurement of their religious thinking by their sexual criminality or lasciviousness. The human, and inevitably sexual, call of distress of Pompilia in *The Ring and the Book* damns the lackadaisical Church administrator but electrifies and regenerates the saved priest: a tawdry tale of adulterous passion to the dull and worldly; to the pious, a history of salvation working its miracle out of the dung-heap of sexual abuse and intrigue; to the central participants, Pompilia and her priest rescuer Caponsacchi, a conflict between sexual and religious desires and beliefs, working in each of them side by side, irreconcilable in this life but perhaps just manageable – in some Kingsleyan way – in heaven. For the modern Don Juan, the lure that draws him through the guilt of betrayal to the pneumatic charms of the sexually ubiquitous woman of the fair, Fifine, is none other than the realization of connection: an electric spark that joins him to her in the dark also illuminates the construction of religious culture – the modern graceful spire at provincial Pornic – on the overthrown but not overmastered, obviously phallic, impulse of Europe's primitive forebears. Religion and sexuality have one intertwined discourse at the now hidden root, one great way that humans find their cultural relation to each other.

Or take the generally more chaste Tennyson, a poet in any case less able to hide in obscurity, yet in the hard poem "Lucretius" concerned also rather directly with the sexual bases of philosophical or cultural discourse. Secretly given an aphrodisiac by his jealous wife, the calm and logical originator of a new, rational, religious dispensation, a kind of Comte before his time, is obsessed by violent sexual dreams that drive him ultimately to suicide. But they also drive him far closer to the common discourses of humanity, where the image of Helen of Troy brings him, as it brought Greek civilization, to a far more tumultuous and passionate vision of religion. Tennyson's radical story, like Browning's in *Fifine*, tells us that the religious tales we tell, whether passionless and rationalistic or passionate and mythic, are intrinsically fused with our sexual stories in their very origin. The point could be easily extended into Tennyson's tales of religious and sexual aspiration and confusion in *The Idylls of the King*. And it could be similarly explored among the other important Victorian poets, few of whom focussed as explicitly and repeatedly as Clough or Patmore on sexual issues but almost all of whom naturally joined sexuality with religion when they discussed either one.

The near-exceptions, whose works on sexuality are sufficiently considerable to be subjects of separate studies, Swinburne, Meredith, Dante Gabriel Rossetti, perhaps Christina Rossetti, reach instinctively for religious connections. In "Laus Veneris" and "Hymn to Proserpine" Swinburne pits Venus and the pagan pantheon against the conquering pale Galilean as a debate (or war), between Christian puritanism and pagan sexual joy, creating in their conflict the angst, perversity, and isolation of modern life. Dante Rossetti, like Kingsley, would colonize heaven for sexuality, but his method is a kind of deliberate crossing and confusion of terms so that religious poems are sensualized, love poems textured in a language of devotion, blessed damozels holy and sensually warm-bosomed alike. His work seems to attempt to unify at the level of sensibility and resonating, echoing language the worlds of sexuality and religion that Kingsley and Patmore insisted upon uniting first with conceptual structures. Much the same can be said of the nonetheless very different, and also very fine, poetry of his sister. Christina Rossetti's wonderful and forever debatable "Goblin Market" is clearly all about sensual temptation – those luscious fruits that Laura *must* have – and relations between men and women – those dreadful and only too-alive goblin men. And it is also clearly about the opposing need for a system of control. As in so much of her work, or in that of her American counterpart Emily Dickinson, there is a sense of religious reference, a sense of a traditional conflict between religious values (is Rossetti's Lizzie doing Christ's work in exposing herself to the ordeal of the flesh for love of her sister?), with deliberate avoidance of a full discourse clarifying the conflicts she so vividly raises. More explicitly, Meredith, somewhat like D. H. Lawrence, who would largely displace him in fame as a prophet of a new mythic order, made some steps toward defining a new, more nature-centered religion based on open respect for the body and passions, the blood of Westermain's woods. But even a writer little concerned with sexual issues, such as Matthew Arnold, seems naturally to expand out from sexual discourse to a perspective on religion when he does bring up sex. "Dover Beach" strikes us as powerful, strange, and parody-able in its central shifts of register back and forth from amorous to philosophical or religious speculation; it was *only* powerful to his contemporaries – indeed bringing together quite naturally two great subjects at a central initiatory moment in an individual's life.

The major novelists, as popular and as public as, say, television programs have been in our age, were subject to far more restraint in discussions of sex, as Thackeray's well-known observations about the need for a "conventional simper" in the portrayal of man in the novel in his Preface to *Pendennis*, quoted above, make clear. Censorship of novelists, he adds, has been direct and effective: "Many ladies have remonstrated and subscribers left me, because in the course of the story, I described a young man resisting and affected by temptation . . . You will not hear – it is best to know it – what moves in the real world, what passes in society, in the clubs, colleges, mess-rooms, – what is the life and talk of your sons." Yet he himself not only finds ways to at least drive his readers' imaginations to follow Becky, where he can't in her mermaid activities underwater or in the demimonde; he also creates a world that implicitly renders problematic the conventional social categories of valorization, religious virtue or vice. Lady Jane Sheepshanks or Amelia herself are so pious, so properly religious: and so enervated and dull! What are we to do with Becky's own good end, a pious lady of Bath, regular church-goer (with a footman), friend of the distressed muffin-man and ornament to every charity list: a conforming hypocrisy made possible by sufficient returns on consols that subvert even the respectability of religion. To laugh with Becky's final prank at the end is to be of the devil's party: sexual vitality may seem best; but then society's religious system will need major overhauling. Or in Trollope's similarly realistic social world, focussed on practical politics and practical psychology, a good man like Mr. Arabin is confirmed in his near-escape from a potentially dangerous abstract religion – the Oxford tendencies and temptation to Rome he had absorbed while a celibate don "at the feet of the great Newman" – by a healthy marriage; an untrustworthy religious opportunist, the Evangelical and greasy Mr. Slope, proves naturally a bounder and cad in his sexual adventurism. In the novel's social world, as in the imagined worlds of poetry, sexual issues seem to imply religious ones.

Dickens and Charlotte Brontë might seem exceptions, for opposite reasons. Dickens avoids sexual explicitness and opens little space for romantic passion. When, hesitantly and usually in coded language suitable for family reading, he does deal with erotic themes, the underlying associations with religion, which he also avoids discussing directly, are nonetheless clear. The good fallen woman, Nancy, in *Oliver Twist* is not only a magdalene in the connected meanings the word had for Victorians, but also takes on some characteristics of Christ himself as sacrificial lamb and redeemer of the lost lamb Oliver. The discussion of Esther's engendering, that mystery that turns all those fine gears and clockworks of the enormous plot engine in *Bleak House*, raises the other great Christian issue – of sexual original sin. Is Esther tainted by her parents fall? Is such a sexual act further corrupting this already very fallen world? Or does the corruption come, as their names must suggest, from the puritanical Miss Barbarys and the perverse and envious Tulkinghorns and Smallweeds who convert sexual passion into sin to enrich themselves at others' expense? The background discussion to the events of the novel in effect reestablishes for this modern world the long and central Christian debate over the moral status of sexuality as it had been focussed since at least the time of Augustine on diverse interpretations of the meaning of the Fall. *Great Expectations*, more concerned with the origins of myth-making than with the full mythic systems of organized religions, more interested in the genesis of romantic idealization than in the full cycle of sexuality, views Pip's desire for a sustaining myth as intrinsically connected to the sexual desire that finds in Estella the false pole star on which all his personal myth-making is centered.

Brontë offers, by contrast, the fullest sexual discourse of any major Victorian writer and does so largely and quite unusually in the secular spirit of twentieth-century sexual psychology that follows her interest in family relations and the perils of adolescent sexual integration. Yet the cold, repressive misuse of sexual energies for their religious aims by sex-powered zealots like St. John Rivers in *Jane Eyre* is a persistent sub-theme in her work, an acknowledgment of how often religion seemed to her tied up with sexuality: generally, as in twentieth-century explorations of religious hypocrisy – for instance, in Strachey's biographical portraits – in a negative way. In *Villette*, a work in which the sexual history of the shy heroine, Lucy Snow, is spelled out in biblical typology, Brontë moves closer to a more positive view of the role of religion in sexuality. As Katherine Stockton has argued, Lucy's sexual liberator, Paul, also functions as a Christian sacrificial figure, Emanuel, and Lucy's ambivalent ending, which I have read as sexual maturity and mature resignation, can also be read as a version of Patmore's projections of desire out of this world.[2] Certainly, the relations between sexuality and religion were occupying Brontë more, not less, in her later career – as they also did Freud, who also began by separating them, as so many twentieth-century thinkers on sex have done, in order to try to see sex more clearly.[3]

Or, to take one final example, George Eliot, of course, subtly and beautifully explores the motions of sexuality and piety that are inextricably intertwined in her most sympathetic heroines, Maggie Tulliver in *The Mill on the Floss* and Dorothea Brooke in *Middlemarch*. Maggie vacillates perplexedly between sexual exploration and ascetic, religious retreat; without finding a solution that will unite her sexual growth and her religious aspirations, she also demonstrates, somewhat in the manner of Clough's treatment of his similar perplexities, how impossible it seems to her author to separate the two. The later portrait, of Dorothea, reaches back to a myth of heroic sublimation, the life of St. Theresa, to suggest a possible reconciliation of the conjoined, religious and sexual instincts that we see at play, and often at war, in her nineteenth-century heroine, beginning with the brilliant opening scene, where Dorothea inspects the family jewels and attempts to give religious meaning to what first appears to us as only sensual feelings. If Dorothea's experimental search eventually brings her to some sense of meaning in her life and offers some sexual gratification, a solution that might harness religious and sexual instincts to one great work seems necessarily unavailable to modern humanity, tortured and teased as it is by the need/impossibility of fully reconciling sexual and religious, sensual and altruistic, desires.

George Eliot's linking of sexuality and religion in *Middlemarch* is especially impressive because she handles so tactfully and subtly the burden that a commingled desire places on her heroine's life: her sexual desire is first sacrificed before the unlit lamp, ungirt loin, of Mr. Casaubon, not just because she misjudges him, but because she seeks to satisfy her religious nature through her sexual choice; later her sensual nature finds its gratification in young, romantic Will Ladislaw, but now at the expense of her religious idealism. Coming relatively late to the nineteenth-century discussion and coming with a need to master by historicizing, George Eliot begins to frame and question the essential nature of the discussion. She implicitly asks us to consider the problematics of a system in which two kinds of desire, religious and sexual, are supposed to seek unitary and simultaneous gratification. Kingsley and Patmore had proposed ever more complicated systems of relation between the two as their rather individual solutions to the problems of dissonance between the religious and sexual discourses that they had inherited. Clough had sensed a dilemma, as he found himself unable – despite all his skepticism about his society's ways of thinking about both – to separate sexuality and religion. But he had not become conscious of it as a problem that could be in itself directly analyzed and discussed.

Two further evasions of the problem were possible, and they have perhaps been the usual paths taken by thinking about religion and sexuality in the modern period. One follows the direction suggested by Brontë's tendency to separate off a sexual discussion from a religious one. Twentieth-century thinkers, whether creative writers or professional specialists on sex, often have wished to see sex as in itself it really is. And, unlike the scientists-as-priests who put themselves forward as sex-experts in the nineteenth century, generally only to disguise religious orthodoxies in pseudo-scientific language or to manufacture their own, mythic–moral discourses of sexuality, some twentieth-century sexologists have succeeded in isolating relatively independent scientific discussions of sex. The difficulty has been that in cutting sex off from a traditional broader discourse their work threatens to fall into physiognomy, or pornography, in effect a mere naming of the body parts or acts.[4] If this seems a useful task in itself not only for professionals such as Kinsey or Masters and Johnson but also for a Victorian author of *My Secret Life*, or for (in some phases of his work) a twentieth-century Henry Miller, for many writers it has seemed a trap. No sooner do they look at sex

in itself than they begin again the process, inscribed in the history of
their culture before them, to connect it to other ways of conceptualizing human existence. As with Brontë herself in *Villette*, or the later
Freud, their attempts to establish an independent discourse of sex
may bring them around eventually to renewed interest in the broader
discussion that involves religion.

The other evasion of the problem takes the form of affirming in
some other religious context the easy connection of religion and
sexuality. This essentially arcadian process involves a radical
restatement of the history of the West as a unique, unsexual
development of religion; thus space is opened for a new discourse
under the aegis of a different religion, in which there are no problems
in relating sexual and religious conceptions. We see the beginnings of
such thinking in a writer like Swinburne, where Christianity is
revised into a conquering, totally anti-sexual force. In Swinburne,
still loaded psychologically and intellectually with the unresolved
issues of his inherited Christian religion, the revival of paganism, a
consummation of religious and sexual life in theory greatly to be
desired, can only be conceived as a Proserpine wine for the already-
dead or a killing and sadistic rite of Venus.

In a modern writer such as D. H. Lawrence there is a more vital
attempt to replace the Christian system with a new way of relating
humans to each other sexually and to the universe mythically
conceived. And, of course, after him there is no end of writers who,
boldly or timidly, attempt to revive old gods and old rites (often on
a quick reading of Frazer or Margaret Mead), or presage a new
religion to match their new sexual dispensation. Well may they! As
my reader is doubtless tired, at this point, of hearing me reiterate, the
development of a discussion uniting the symbolic structures by which
humans give meaning to sexual and religious experiences seems an
inevitable and necessary cultural activity: though this is no guarantee
that all efforts achieve happy conjunctions. Far from it. And there is
an historian's proper objection to the tendency of modern myth-
makers, which this study attempts to correct for the nineteenth
century, to obscure or white-out the tremendous traditional ab-
sorption of Western culture in these issues.

I will want to return briefly to both these directions of later
thinking in conclusion. But I have chosen to focus here on Hardy,
rather than moving on to look in detail at either of these more typical,
but more evasive, moves of twentieth-century thinking on sexuality

and religion, because I find that his thinking, which emerges quite directly from a very unevasive and clear-eyed look at the nineteenth-century traditions of discussion, is in some ways more deeply original. Hardy follows George Eliot in focussing on the relation between the two areas of desire as a difficulty in itself. He thus takes the occasion of a review of the long and agonized, and extremely interesting nineteenth-century discussions of the relation of sexuality and religion to try to obtain a perspective on the universal relation of the two. By the time he came to write *Jude the Obscure* (1895), Hardy was able, even a good deal more able than George Eliot, to attain a historical perspective on the persistent, if varied, discourse joining sexuality and religion in the century that he was about to usher, so grimly, out. More than George Eliot, more than the many other Victorian major writers who dealt in some way with sexuality and religion, Hardy was akin to Clough, Kingsley, and Patmore in their special insistence on giving these issues clear and controversial centrality – regardless of whatever double affront this procedure might offer to respectable middle-class standards of propriety. He especially follows Kingsley (though also Charlotte Brontë), and of course precedes Lawrence – who notoriously wrestled with him as a potently impotent forefather – in daring to bring both subjects into the most public and popular Victorian writing, the novel. Kingsley succeeded in avoiding excessive opprobrium by offering just the advanced views that a considerable segment of the Victorian public wished to have boldly put forward, with just the moral pronouncements against libertinism (of any sort) on the one side and just the outraged condemnation of the Catholic religious–sexual system (or of the threat of it in the Tractarian movement) on the other that would put a lid on errant imagination. And, as with the modern fantasy cultures of violence, much of the gratification was hidden in sadistic but censored form.

Hardy, as is well known, looked for no easy acceptance by the time he wrote *Jude* – "There is something the world ought to be shown, and I am the one to show it to them," he wrote in his Notebook – and offered no easeful accommodations. In his earlier work, especially in the modern version of pastoral, *Far from the Madding Crowd*, he had seemed for a time, like Clough in *The Bothie*, to attain a comfortable vision of natural sexual force. There it can be destructive, as in the famous scene of flashing phallic swordplay in which we see the overruling force of Troy's unguided missile of sexual domination. But it can also seem a force, as in shepherd Gabriel Oak (the very name suggesting an easy union of heaven and earth) and ultimately in an educated Bathsheba, that joins humans to traditional rituals of form and nature – thus offering a cultural definition of sexuality that for a while can appear to be almost a thing of nature in the young novelist. But even in that arcadia, farmer Boldwood, the poor bachelor driven finally to suicide by the unsatisfied fantasy of fulfillment raised by Bathsheba's little prank valentine, also exists. And quite persuasive revisionist readings can uncode the comradely union of Oak and his Bathsheba as a troubling type of gender and sexual conflict (the oak-like male shepherd and his bathed – even fleeced – sheep).[5] In that lesser tableau of this work, desire itself, as in Patmore, is already the problem; even in this optimistic early consideration, Hardy, unlike Patmore, can see no easy redirecting solution.

Chance: the letter that goes under the door and under the rug; misprision of others: the jaded sophisticate finding his idea of rural innocence in a woman who is herself looking only for adventure and glamour; uncontrolled impulse: the sodden, sudden sale of a wife; sexual puritanism: a pure wife lost to silly, sordid scruples – all such topics of sexual failure in Hardy's later fiction leave the poor human suddenly thrown back alone on his or her desire. Ungratified desire, with no place to go, seems to alienate Hardy's characters, cutting them off from other people, first from sexual fulfillment with the person loved, but ultimately from every ordering system of existence, whether the near world of nature, which seemed almost a possible religion in the early work, or more formal religious beliefs. By the time of *Jude the Obscure*, Hardy wanted to approach this problem more directly, not merely as one of casualty or contingency – the accidents, coincidences, even little accident-like flaws in character that lead to frustration – but as a problem of desire. And this attempt at a more direct attack on the problem behind the problems led him even more directly into the territory occupied by Clough, Kingsley, or Patmore. That is, he would look more explicitly at sexuality itself: what in fact can we say of it? And he would look at the nexus of desire in the connections between religious and sexual aspirations.

Jude then fittingly caps the discussion of this book. But it does so by offering the most radical and destructive version of sexuality, religion, and their relations that we have looked at. Its clarity is the clarity of one who sees all cultural discourse as just that, mere talk, and who tries, paradoxically enough, to create a discourse that looks through words to the nature of human desire itself: first as an hypothesis of mere sex: un unnameable play of the body parts outside of discourse; then as language: sexual or religious desires seen as versions of a comprehensive human tendency to create discourse out of its own need for meaning, for discourse itself. The enterprise, of course, is not so different from Patmore's own, not so different even in its arrogance. The difference is that Patmore finds in personal pain something in desire to celebrate, and through that celebration a connection with a cultural order. For Hardy, the interrogation of desire also opens up painful feelings; but it yields a negative vision, of the relation, but essentially valueless relation, of sex parts/acts, sexual discourse, and religious discourse.

Hardy writes a simple tale; he is not afraid of representing "squalid real life" in the new tradition of realism for which he had already given two cheers in his essay "Candour in English Fiction," while also reserving the right to exercise "the Daedalian faculty for selection and cunning." It is a story about the culturally and socially limited, if complicated, personal lives of his two "simpletons," Jude Fawley and Sue Bridehead. He gives it historical dimension, not by the creaky apparatus of the worn-out historical novel of his day, where great affairs were arranged to intrude on simple lives, but by historical reference and allusion. These, whether the voices of the past, Keble, Pusey, Newman, and the rest, who speak to Jude from his pious reading and from the very stones of Christminster, or the "modern" reading on which Sue modelled her new woman's mind, are intensely focussed not so much on sixty years back as on the preceding sixty or seventy years. They give this century-end, solemn novel a sense of brooding over the meaning of an era, and they speak especially of the collective aspirations of the century.

The nineteenth century had some "blessed hopes" that Hardy holds up to somber critical inspection. One was in the direction of piety and religion, rather specifically related to the ascetic renewal of the Oxford movement of the century, the potent spiritual development back to traditional Christianity that had tempted both Clough and Kingsley toward a kind of Anglo-Catholic monasticism, and that in more general ways lay behind Patmore's initial embrace of Catholicism itself – though he himself then moved in a mystic direction that more directly expressed sexual desire in ascetic Christianity.[6] These voices, like the stone-renovating business by which Jude makes his living, tell of a desire to renew religion, to establish belief publicly and firmly, and covertly they carry the traditional conservative Christian view of sexuality in its most attractive form.

This has been one desire of the century. The other has seemed opposite: it has been toward freedom, individual fulfillment. Sue has listened to the voices of Shelley or John Stuart Mill. But Hardy associates this impulse with a broader force of desire. From reading in Pater it pleases Sue to think of herself, like the Mona Lisa, as the renewal and embodiment of an older religion, "more ancient than medievalism." She sees the Song of Solomon, that central taking-off point for the projection of desire out of the world and on to God, as a pagan document about human love strangely subverted by long-faced bishops who wrote the chapter headings into the Bible (in this rather agreeing with Kingsley's sense of a healthy Old Testament celebration of human love). As in Swinburne, another favorite of hers, pagan liberty is associated with a hope for renewal of a pagan erotic religious impulse celebrating forces close to nature, love goddess Venus or great mother Demeter and her daughter Proserpine. We see her in her own small way paying her hesitant and clandestine homage to the naked and the Greek with her little statues of Venus and Apollo, which touch her with their pipe-clay dust. Like Jude's stone-work, which speaks of the restoration movement, not really of the medieval world, they embody an allusion not so much to the classical world itself as to the nineteenth-century neo-paganism that produced cheap "images" of one side of the century's desire.

Hardy thus writes the history of his century into the novel as a history of its desire, its apparently diverging and conflicting aspirations for religious fulfillment or personal liberty and sexual gratification. The little history of his characters then allows him to interpret, really to reinterpret, these hopeful desires. Even a cursory look at the plot suggests how radical a critique he intends of the conventional two worlds by which the century liked to mark out its hopes, whether with the intention of reviving the dead medieval world or hastening on the one struggling to be born. Young Jude is inspired no less strongly than Keble or Newman by reverence for the historical tradition of Christian religion; he is touched like them by a sense of a possible holiness as a calming and illuminating spiritual presence, an ascetic and unworldly vision that he and they found inscribed so firmly into the work of the Church Fathers. He creates from the far-off lights of Christminster a personal myth of fulfillment through religious learning and very much wishes to join that semimonastic university community that Clough finally put behind him.[7] He reads Newman, Keble, and Pusey, goes through what Sue calls specifically a "Tractarian stage"; early reading in an old copy of the Fathers is followed by systematic reading in Pusey's Library of the Fathers. He even finds in the saints what Sue calls his "demi-gods in your Pantheon." But aspiration to the religious life causes only repeated failure of the spirit. Instead of pursuing a career as a renewer of vital religion, he finds himself brutally forced to gain a cold subsistence by hardening the letter – literally, as an ecclesiastical stone cutter. He can only experience medieval religious life as a lifeless hulk, an architectural fossil. Eventually he burns his books, Fathers, Tractarians, and all. He dies in the town of his glowing dreams, realized for him only as a harsh modern industrial suburb in which the this-worldly realities of alcohol, prostitution,[8] and pneumonia alone prevail – Jude's "grind of stern reality." Hardy's apocryphal gospel of a Jude the obscure of modern life, a kind of ordinary brother to Jesus (as the martyred St. Jude was sometimes thought to be) who undergoes only an ordinary crucifixion, follows finally the resigned narrative path of Job rather than the exalting and glorious one of Christ – as Jude's own references to the suffering Job make clear.[9]

His cousin and alter-aspirant, Sue Bridehead, seeks a different fulfillment of the spirit, in personal freedom and innocent delight. But her dream of realizing a joyful secular future brings only repression and pain. She raises the forces of scandalized society against her, leading ultimately to the terrible loss of her children as Jude's boy solves her conflict for her. She succumbs repeatedly, ultimately permanently, to repressive forces within that oppose her own philosophy: fastidious and timid, she resists the sexual experience that would logically accompany her philosophy; like Jude, only with less awareness of what she is doing, she actually worships images and her desire is activated by their discourse of freedom, not by sensual life itself. She chooses rather to incarcerate herself in a deadly marriage of mere convention; later, after bearing children with Jude, she regresses further to a permanent state of latency in which she is a fully desexualized, un-Patmorean nun-like figure, even as she forces herself, "clenching her teeth," to consummate her return to Phillotson because any second marriage – as Kingsley and the Fathers would agree – is fornication.[10]

Hardy's characters enact his historical vision of the two failed aspirations of his age. This creates an effective form of historical novel, as well as novel of ideas, in which correspondences between individual and age make a simple fable also a complex and typical one. But Hardy's explication of this dual failure is not primarily presented in terms of social, historical causation. In some sense, the age prevents Jude from going to Christminster and it denies Sue her special claims to freedom. But their failure is seen equally as a betrayal from within, by Jude's conflicting sexual appetite, Sue's timorousness and conventionality, and their common self-destructiveness, symbolized in Hardy's tale of their mutual family romance, a depressive and destructive one. Hardy is far less concerned in this novel, even in contrast with the splendid predecessor *Tess of the d'Urbervilles*, with the effects of fatality and chance, far more with explication of psychology. This takes the form of a discourse on the nature of sexuality, especially in its relation to religion, that mimics but also greatly complicates the discussion implied in the historical framework and the plot of the novel.

What is most striking is the degree to which Hardy's vision is deconstructive in its approach to character. People are presented as highly unstable, without any unifying moral or humanistic core.[11] They can be in some sense understood by their motivating sexual or religious aspirations, but these in turn are seen as destabilizing and destructive. Jude attains only an increasingly profound comprehension of his hopelessness, ending with his final success in his repeated rounds of suicidal intention – an ultimate personal self-unmaking. Sue Bridehead is reduced from a very precarious whole to a mere part, the shattered, regressed intellect: the sexual partner and mother ending her days as penitent conventual wife.

When we look at the directly sexual content, deconstruction needs itself to move over for the most obvious term "dismemberment." Jude's first conscious knowledge of sexuality emerges, of course, when his world of scholarship is bluntly intruded upon by that "fragment of pig," or "missile" from "novel artillery" as Hardy re-rendered it in the revised text that responded to "shocked criticism" about his naming such country matters: the pig's pizzle or sexual part.[12] It is hurled as a dramatic entrance by the third character in Hardy's sexual dramatis personae, that pre-Masters-and-Johnson adept at sexual physicality: the pigwoman, Arabella Donn. Any reader who tries to see her as a *tertium quid* between the extremes of Jude and Sue, as a figure of healthy sexuality, is quickly disillusioned and disabused.

In the original book edition, Hardy focusses on the *partness* of the part she throws: he or his characters call it not only "fragment" but "slip of flesh," "the piece," "lump of offal," and "piece o' the pig," and he notes its provenance from the "bladder, from which she had obviously just cut it," as well as its physicality, clamminess, and its dangling and hanging. All this was removed in 1903 and later English editions, suggesting that Hardy sensed that the fragmentariness was intrinsic to the shock it had given. As her effective communication shows, Arabella is a master of synecdoche: Jude reads all that is on her mind from the one vivid segment. The simplest Freudian analysis of imagery will reveal that she is a dangerous woman – especially if we read this scene in Hardy's un-castrated text. But the author seems more intent on showing Arabella's own sexual fragmentation. She, like the pig, is not more nor less than a "substantial" "animal." She is a female animal; he (the pig) was a male. Like the pig, she seems already dismembered when we first see her: we remember her by her dimples that come and go like directional flashers. Like a good used automobile, she is fully loaded with optional features. And these can be disassembled: as Jude finds, when, married to her, he watches her hang up her lovely long tresses for the night. He also finds that her most mysterious sexual nature – the generation in her womb – has become instantly modular. Pregnant when he feels obliged to marry her, she somehow is *not* pregnant once they are married. This is a trick he might have been alerted to if he had noticed her similar trick with an egg – which she hides here and there in her body to encourage Jude in a treasure hunt. The narrative voice confirms this view of Arabella as a set of detachable sexual parts: "She had a round and prominent bosom, full lips, perfect teeth, and the rich complexion of a Cochin hen's egg." We know her not as a rounded character but just as rounded parts: a series of allurements that easily change to a series of sexual grotesqueries.

After she leaves Jude she seems almost like an odd part that pops up unexpectedly here and there, like her own egg. And we never have a sense of wholeness of character as she shifts unexpectedly from role to role. We often hear critical observations about Arabella as Jude's sensual (or sometimes carnal) nature. But, if we ask "what kind of sexuality we have here," this old body/spirit dichotomy – even Hardy's own, often cited "deadly war waged between flesh and spirit" – clearly isn't sufficient as an answer. This is not average sensual woman but the democracy of the sexual part. The pig is deconstructed at the opening; and his brother must be deconstructed as the final symbol of Jude and Arabella's relation. Arabella quickly puts an end to his last attempt to speak a coherent squeak before he is rendered into so many parts. Later Jude mercifully kills a rabbit being pulled apart by a trap. Arabella's sexuality is aggressive, vigorous, victorious. She might seem an emblem of mature genital sexuality as she lies out on a hill – "supine, and straight as an arrow" – trying to seduce Jude. But her sexuality is really an arrow that points only somewhere else – as most signs in this work are merely decentering, not truly indicative. She is important not for what she means but for the limits she places on a certain kind of meaning. She speaks mere sex and shows that, as in pornography generally, this is an unspeakable discourse: not only because it is reduced to the obscene naming of parts but because such play of the body parts – Foucault's "bodies and pleasures" – is essentially beyond language, a discourse outside of all discourse.

Hardy could grossly offend his late Victorian readers with the pig's sexuality business. But he has no positive picture of sexual fulfillment to give us with Jude and Arabella – only a scene that ends with a blank as Arabella rushes "up the stairs, whither Jude rushed at her heels." There are aroused parts, and arousals, but no coherence. And this is clear in the analysis of Arabella's motivation. The narrator or narrators tell us that she *must* have Jude for purely sexual reasons. *And also* that she drags him into marriage because he seems a good earner. Having married him by trickery, she proceeds to abandon him. Later she is all done with him and also wants him back. Her main decisions in life are as playful and painful as her sexual workings. In both cases she seems a collection of alternatively functioning parts rather than any unity.

What of Jude? We are told he hears, with Arabella, "conjunctive orders from headquarters, unconsciously received by unfortunate men when the last intention of their lives is to be occupied with the feminine." But the orders he receives throughout the novel are not so much conjunctive as disjunctive. And we wish he or we could identify any one central headquarter in him. He seems whirled around by his own disparate motivations far worse than any Farmer Troutham whirled him as a child for switching over to the birdies' side. He goes from idealistic student to crazed egghunter to hard-working family man back to student, and on to suicide in a few months time. Later he will move from place to place and from role to role – student, stone cutter, lay preacher, lover, father, drunk – as often, but not with as much ease, as Arabella. His sex life shows the classic incoherence of Freud's famous most common degradation in the sexual life. He moves from the apparent potency of Arabella's organ anarchy to his falsely idealistic and falsely coherent vision of angel Sue Bridehead.

With Sue, as with Arabella, the obvious Freudian explanations seem less significant than Hardy's articulation of disorganization. There is the incest material of cousin lovers; the partial fictive strand of a family curse; the epicene nature that makes sex with her also homoerotically charged. These are possible explanations and Hardy is not much interested in using them to explain away Sue. He concentrates on showing us her nature and sexual nature. Certainly she is anything but the sexless spiritual creature that Jude, viewing her through his own religious preoccupations, initially mistakes her for – a misprision continued by many critics. As much or more than Arabella, she is almost exclusively preoccupied with sex and the men in her life. Our first full vision of her – with those Greek statues she buys, then covers over with leaves (like museum-pieces), then hides – is of her persistent sexual interest. She identifies herself with strongly erotic, but highly idealized and intellectual traditions, especially with Shelley's Platonic aspirations in *Epipsychidion*; she insists she is in no way sexless, only self-controlled in her personal life, like "some of the most passionate erotic poets."

The difference, as D. H. Lawrence long ago pointed out, is in the location of her sexuality. Her part is the head – sex in the head – as her surname of course suggests. This is another synecdoche, here with the complicated allusion to another sexual part (namely maidenhead) that makes her thinking head seem even more like merely another sexual part. The odd vendor of naked statues calls out "Images" as if they were various foods at a market. Sue has, exactly, sexual images – so many disembodied parts of sexual experience – that she uses to tease her husband Phillotson and Jude. She is so many separate sexual role-playings, as Arabella was so many organs. Each part is a game. And Jude and Sue seem like two children playing sexual games. Sue is decidedly polymorphous, and equally perverse. She must have a man with her to play with. Far from sexually cold, she brings Jude to a state of continuous passion. Only, he must go to Arabella now and then – not to be a whole man, but to move from an image of the part to the part itself.

In fact, Sue and Arabella are not the classic antitheses they appear. Hardy brings Arabella back just to pair her and compare her with Sue. He forces us to see them as in some sense interchangeable sets of parts. Long after they have separated, Jude meets Arabella at a pub. She and other barmaids sport pink, flushed cheeks as the time of quitting and assignations with customers approaches. Jude and she take a train and have their married one-night stand in a hotel. The next day Jude returns, takes another train with Sue. The narrator must observe: "It seemed the same carriage." Later Jude will take Sue – coming to live with him – to the *same* hotel. Sue rejects Arabella's role that time and insists upon moving to another hotel.

But it is Arabella's presence, of course, that finally sends Sue into bed with Jude. And we have the odd scene of the two women confronting each other almost like lovers the day after. Arabella knows instinctively what has happened. This mating of Sue and Jude parallels that of Arabella and Jude. Both occur in the blank of the page – as notable absent moments of possible unity. Children appear to both Arabella and Sue, but we aren't told how or when. As oddly, they take themselves away. And Sue takes responsibility for Little Father Time's mass murder because she failed to provide him with the whole story – only a part – of the birds and the bees when he questioned her about life's organization.

Even more radical than this collapse of apparently different modes of sexuality into one disintegrated model of desire is Hardy's implosion of the two seemingly polar realms of desire, sexual and religious. As Sue and Arabella are ultimately displayed as two poles of one deconstructed, disintegrated sexual nature, as they are parallel studies in incoherent, disorganized personalities, so finally Jude's seemingly traditional war of flesh and spirit, body and soul is shown to be one confusion, not a confusion of two things. We see his "spiritual" longings rise from the rag-and-bone shop of Phillotson's school at Marygreen. The boy loves, idealizes the schoolmaster – as the full-time students, who know him better, do not. Such a puppy crush leads to great scholarly and religious aspirations, including that lover–mistress relation to the lights of distant Christminster. But, when these come crashing down at one shot from that "novel artillery," Hardy is at great pains to show us that we are not really dealing with a new side of Jude. Again and again he points out that the two are interchangeable, sexual desire and religious idealism: that they occupy literally the same ground and the same psychic ground. Jude is thinking of his studies when the pizzle hits him. He talks love with Arabella just at the "spot of his former fervid desires to behold Christminster." His love for Arabella is seen as just such an illusion – self-fed – as his belief in a Christian unity at Christminster will be. Sue he meets at Christminster and takes her – like the place – for a Christian ideal. Hardy pointedly has him formally exchange his Christian idealism for his idealistic love for Sue. Her intellectual erotic appeal proves indeed far more permanently destructive artillery to his religion than anything Arabella could mount. Sue, of course, proves only a series of illusions – a set of sexual images that don't hold together. She is seen as a marine deity at her nunnery-like school. Later she will be the mother who regresses back into the ritualistic nun-wife.

The apparently brutal regression from pagan Sue to nun should shock us into a recognition. Sue's paganism of the head is in fact not much different from the religion of a nun. Both nuns and pagans worship images; both paganism and Christianity create discourses of sexuality and religion, one directly manifesting the sexual forces of this universe, the other masking them in an other-worldly religious tradition. Sue's paganism is only apparently more sexy than her nun-role. Both are only discourses and at a similar distance from the anarchic play of the parts that, in Hardy's view, they only succeed in reiterating on the level of discourse. Hardy's central realization is of the interrelation of religious and sexual discourses. Again and again the book shows us that the same place can have a sexual or religious sign on it, but not two different signs at the same time. Religion and sexuality seem the ultimate interchangeable parts. Hardy abolishes the split in the Western psyche by reading sexuality and religion as two codes for one psychic location. They are alternate and mutually undercutting attempts to articulate a general desire which cannot be articulated, or long gratified, in the real world of body parts. In this Hardy provides a unified rather than dualistic vision of man that might seem to restore the traditional Christian connection between the two discourses – but only to show that that unity is itself hopelessly dismembered and incoherent, a set of parts when he tries to imagine sex in itself, or a set of images in the discourses of religion or sexuality that only pretend to give order to the play of the parts when in fact they mirror their incoherence. The only real coherence exists in the process of collapsing and exposing the nature of desire itself. Author and Jude collaborate to disintegrate and finally annihilate his agonized inarticulations.

This brief look at a very familiar text of the nineteenth century isn't offered as an endpoint or solution to the various Victorian discourses on sexuality and religion. Its radical, *fin-de-siècle*, *fin-de-glôbe* perspective is a useful foil, in absolute black, to the mixed pictures looked at in earlier writers. The significance of Hardy's presentation is not mainly in the satirical attacks on both sexuality and religion as forms of frauds that he indulges in passing. This made the book a sensation, and in some sense a book rightly seen as a kind of higher muckraking. No reader easily forgets the association of human sex and pigs' parts, material that could have come out of medieval misogynistic literature; nor do we forget the condescending letter to Jude from the Master of Bibliall College, which has the quality of a very barely concealed attack by a latter-day Tom Paine on the bastion of Victorian Oxford high culture, Balliol.

What is more significant is the radical quality of the vision of sexuality and religion alike. Far more than that of the young Freud of a few years later, Hardy's approach attempts to strip off all cultural norms to look clearly at what really happens in those two great cultural endeavors in which humans seek their happiness and generally realize so much distress. One is led easily to speak of Hardy's novel in terms of deconstruction – not as a mode of critical interpretation but as a way of speaking about Hardy's own thinking – because his view of both sexuality and religion so clearly reveals that they are constructed things, fabrications by culture out of words. In revealing how they are made, the pressure of his skepticism rather relentlessly breaks them down into a kind of diagram of parts and tends to leave them effectively in fragments, body parts seeking an organization into a system of pleasure or – what Hardy suggests is really the same thing – into a system of holiness. Somehow the architecture or adhesion has gone out of both cultural systems so that they seem to sit in ruins about the author. Yet, despite his repeated ridicule, he is far from being able to discard these traditionally great areas of experience as so many atavistic concerns that have finally atrophied. The loss of living systems, the disillusioning vision of their discourse as in many ways identical, only leaves him more aware of the need for both sexual and religious gratification. Hardy's implied author is both the extremely needy Jude, who goes to his death still yearning for Sue and Christminster (for whom and where he indeed dies), and the cynical distant narrator who will educate his character and readers to the bitter realities of cultural loss. The novel provided his most effective vehicle for the general vision of the universe he was working out in poems and personal reflections: a place in which the creature's desires, as they become articulated in fabricated discourses, bear almost no relation to the ability of the universe to satisfy them. In *Jude* desire is a kind of unitary currency of human need; it can be paid out equally to religious or sexual systems and it is convertible from one to the other. Only it is really a system of universal debt, not potency: human need that cries out for fulfillment but in the novel finds its only end in accepting the void of suicide.

The focus in this view is necessarily on the cultural creation, the making, of sexuality and religion and on their artificial construction of routes to fulfillment for a power of desire that can go either way. Hardy's radical skepticism gives his approach a clarity that no earlier writer we have looked at, not even the agnostic Clough, possessed. He raises their discussions, in effect, to a meta-level in which he can spell out the nature of the discussion; and he certainly provides a useful tool to help us understand the century that he comes from and reflects on. From another view, his discussion attempts premature closure to cultural concerns that his own system acknowledges as unending and universal. His predecessors can be seen not only as failing to attain his clarity but also as maintaining a necessary resistance. If sexuality and religion are cultural creations, as Hardy shows that they are, they are necessarily also cultural possessions, systems embodying values that can only be maintained by being cultivated and cherished. A comparison with the even more central cultural creation of language is at least helpful, if not exact. Linguistics can show us that language is a cultural creation and can display the parts from which it is constructed. But unless we take up and nurture our individual languages we have no means of expression at all. Clough, Kingsley and Patmore all display, in an especially strong degree, the concern of Victorian culture generally to preserve some language for the gratification, or at least articulation, of desire through sexual and religious systems.

Clough is, of course, closest to Hardy's own skepticism. But his is a spirit of questioning that displays the varieties of positions on sexuality and religion, and plays with their dogmatics and absurdities, while acknowledging all the while the need that they serve. If he finds no happy systematic answers, or even any unhappy ones, he also doesn't abandon the quest for a meaningful system. That each will be found, in the event, lacking only leads him to defer a conclusion as he explores the next. In his own experience he found in the "great sinful streets" of Naples, and later Venice, that religious certainties, the strict moral codes of a don planning to take orders, the transfer of sexual energies to the religious asceticism of an early Christian or St. Augustine, fell as the certainty of lust and temptation was revealed. But he doesn't take the next step, which Hardy will, of radically questioning a situation in which desires and reality are so out of sync with each other. Desire must be served, even at the expense of religious guilt; in the end skepticism moves Clough toward a moderate kind of worldliness in *Dipsychus* or the *Mari Magno* tales, where people must learn to accept the realities of sexual need and try as they best can also to please their religious beliefs and consciences. He will not abandon his sense of the human need, so clear in many of the ideologies he scrutinizes, for acceptable ways of conceptualizing sexuality, religion, and their relation. Excesses and absurdities certainly need criticism. Just as surely, the process of quest is necessary and will go on.

Kingsley and Patmore, of course, ignore Clough's liberal, skeptical dampening down of extreme discourses. In each writer, an intense personal involvement in establishing a system to guide his own sexual and religious needs leads to an elegant, elaborate, and rather eccentric formulation. Kingsley, parson in the Church of England, found his way to a lifetime system of sexual and religious beliefs that took distinctive shape from his vigorous, but perhaps somewhat emotionally perplexed, rejection of Christminster celibacy. Religion and nature were read strictly to yield a system in which married sexual love was at the center of this life and the next. As an historian he could see this as one of many systems possible in human culture; indeed, his is an early statement of the still-debated position that English Protestantism created and was created by a unique sexual culture. Yet he was an historian with a very unrelativistic bias for his own culture, as he saw it. He uses history, as he does novels, poems, theology, or social lectures, to promulgate his sexual–religious ideology. And this generally provides a very effective defense against a line of thought, such as Hardy's, that would inquire into the origins and justifications of such cultural systems. Instead he spends his abundant energies as thinker and writer in elaborating his system, justifying a strong sexual life within the privileged confines of married religious union while he attacks every other kind of sexual expression. Of course, he is as fierce, really fiercer, in defending Victorian married sex from the temptation to indulge sexual feeling and language in areas of experience that do not directly relate to the central life-renewing ritual of the marriage bed.

Kingsley's relatively greater difficulty here, for instance the manifest loss of control in attacking Church of England beguinage, the celibate Newman, or the Catholic priestly system in general, suggests he found it harder to distinguish his system from certain traditional religious formulations. The problem begins with his own need to meld sexual and religious beliefs. His religious desire obviously gives an added value and aura to his sexual ideal: the wedded couple who will copulate there as here implicitly have God joined to their consummation, at least as its blesser and sustainer. Married lovers are in some sense officiating priests or saints in that union. Whatever actually happened in the Kingsleyan double-bed – and perhaps not too much as the years went on – there was an ideal bed, projection of both sexual and religious desire, that formed the holy grail in his system. Kingsley liked to go back to healthy natural ideas of married sex in the Old Testament to answer the confused discourse on celibacy in the New. But, of course, those patriarchal beddings were completed when their owner descended into the earth after their long and fruitful lives were over. While Clough heard in the great streets of worldly lust the message that Christ had not risen from the realities of loving and dying flesh, Kingsley essentially preached a very new testament of resurrection for husband, wife, and nuptial bed.

The instability of this attractive formulation, in which we all can take "it" with us as long as we don't accumulate an embarrassing surplus of demanding angel partners here below, is especially clear in Patmore's career. Much more experimental in his early work, he began far closer to Clough than to Kingsley, a writer who dared let the various sexual confusions of his day find expression and outlet in his work. Yet he is like Kingsley, and unlike Clough, in not being able emotionally to live long in delightful complexity and intellectual confusion. As he tried to control the mixed expression on sexual issues that had been flowing through his pen, he moved first in a direction very similar to Kingsley's. The too-controlled *Angel in the House* soon made him even somewhat popular as he eclipsed Kingsley's position as chief spokesperson for the Victorian doctrine of married sexual love – that central dogma of so many Victorian writers that still seems so surprising to those who view Victorian culture through the distortions of fanciful histories of prudery rampant. But while Kingsley tried to engineer a successful nuptial embrace of mutual passion that would move him effortlessly from one married zone to another, Patmore's more restless talent insisted on imagining the psyches of the losers in love, both here and hereafter. And he soon experienced the death of all his Kingsleyan hopes with the early loss of his lovely first wife. Having given an aura of religion to his celebration of married love, he naturally moved in the direction that Kingsley most feared, toward a further projection of sexual desire and language into religion or, to put it another way, a further mingling of the two discourses that Kingsley had already bedded together. The result, in the often splendid odes of *The Unknown Eros*, is a poetry that goes further than either Clough or Kingsley's writing in examining the nature of desire itself.

In this he does come close to Hardy's more radical formulation, especially at moments in both the cycle of human love and the cycle of divine love in which he finds his projection failing, his deck of cards falling down to a simple but terrible human need for a reliable object of desire. Very unlike Kingsley in the freedom that he allows to his imagination in his sexual–religious discourse, also unlike him in his openness to failure and loss as central experiences, he is, however, like Kingsley in his resistance to abstract and analytical thinking. Both sexual and religious discussions are a bulwark against the kind of thinking, associated by Patmore with the natural sciences, that analyzes subjects into their parts in order to try to understand them. His intuitive sense of the working of desire through language remains a personal drama; his response to failure, as in "The Child's Purchase," is to accept his limits humbly in a faith that belief and understanding, gone today, will return tomorrow. What is natural to Hardy, to ask what all this tells us about the nature of human culture, ideals, religion, language, or the universe, and what we should or can do about it, is entirely alien to Patmore.

I would not be comfortable leaving Hardy with quite the last word – which he indeed wished to have – on the attempts of his century at a sexual and religious affirmation. Certainly his position seems naturally to expand and then decisively to end the skeptical but still quizzical formulations of possible systems for the age in the mid-century Clough. Certainly one feels in examining in their complexity the assertive systems of Kingsley and Patmore that these very different formulations share a certain strained and excessive quality. The job of relating two great areas of concern in this age, as it had been in different ways in past ages, was done, but it was also a somewhat hard job. Kingsley's repeated absurdities show the difficulties in upholding a fairly simple but necessarily rather limited and dogmatic formulation. Patmore's somewhat wild restatements of mystic traditions suggesting sexual relation with God and his intensely self-conscious and difficult poetic formulations show the opposite tendency, toward excessive development. Here is a full system, with great space for the reader to annotate and explore, as I hope he or she will wish to do after reading my discussion of the odes. But it is also a baroque palace working against its obvious grandeurs in its extreme assertions, intensely idiosyncratic structures, and many intellectual or emotional blind corners and useless splendors. Representative of a tendency of Victorian culture to create great syncretic structures that keep aloft sexual and religious beliefs by cementing them together, it is highly susceptible to Hardy's unbuilding realistic imagination. But strange and exotic as my Victorian samples may at first seem, their preoccupations with uniting sexual and religious issues are local manifestations of a recurrent, not finally unbuildable, human obsession.

It would be fatuous to try to provide a catalog of all the new buildings that our century has erected on the leveled surface prepared by Hardy's view of the worst. D. H. Lawrence is a name that obviously comes to mind, Hardy's self-chosen answerer and successor. Bernard Shaw rushed in before Lawrence with his own speculations on a new determining discourse, simultaneously sexual life-force and meaning of the universe. E. M. Forster's *A Passage to India* attempted a religious formulation in a non-Western context that might solve the sexual muddles of his characters' lives: one of the earlier of so many twentieth-century reformulations of Western problems in the terms of other religious and sexual cultures. T. S. Eliot drew on James Frazer's massive, if already outdated, compilation of sexual–religious mythology across many cultures to write the history of modern loss and express the need for a belief that could reaffirm both sexuality and religious meaning. Doubtless it is the skeptical side of Eliot's exploration that now seems most impressive and was most representative. Without Eliot's ultimate hope to return to faith in a traditional Christian religious and sexual formulation, Hemingway, like Eliot, wrote the tragedies of a world of sexual and metaphysical impotence – as did so many writers after these.

Whether as a new positive vision – occasionally drawn from a restatement of Western tradition, more often from a non-Western alternative – or as such a set of counters for the world that was lost, sexual and religious discussion was as often linked in the twentieth century as in the nineteenth. Indeed, as in the nineteenth century, the rarity is the writer who can keep them in fairly distinct categories. Joyce might be one, but his celebration of sex for itself is inscribed within his greater saga of the rejection of a Catholic sexual and religious myth. Even Freud himself increasingly moves, after the sexual science of *Three Contributions to the Theory of Sex*, to his own myth of the unitary origin of sexual and religious beliefs, seeming to explain religion as an outgrowth of sexual conflict but increasingly caught up, as religious disciples such as Jung would exemplify, in a language that represented itself by a religious mythology, whether that of transgressive Oedipus or of repressive Moses.

The interesting exception, suggested to some extent by both Joyce's *Ulysses* and Lawrence's *Lady Chatterley's Lover*, those two landmark legal classics, is of course the twentieth-century elevation of pornography to a serious art form. The enterprise follows Hardy's conceptualization. Where both religious and sexual discourses are dissolved in skepticism about mythic or other ultimate statements and rent through with doubt about the value of what begin to seem merely linguistic gratifications of desire, there is always the endless metonymic articulation of body parts to fall back on. No one doubts that these skin and bones live in some sense in their non-verbal experience. But the question is, can they live in verbal art? To write the body is a paradox, an impossibility. As in Hardy, one seems necessarily to dissect, to create a heap of spare parts, in trying to articulate bodies' satisfactions and connections. A goal for the moment may be, as it has often seemed to be in modern visual art's similar but broader movement away from statement, to limit articulation, to allow the physical thing of sex into the work on the condition that it trail no larger meanings with it; and the price for such conceptual purity in obscene art, that the work may not attempt to conjure any spirit out of the exposed flesh, may willingly be paid.

But even here, just as minimalist art creates a tension between the work's denial of meaning and the viewer's restless attempts to find significance in it, pornography exists as an art that invites the controversy of meaning. Its wisest enemies see its meaning precisely as a refusal of meaning.[13] More often it is seen and attacked as a covert sexual or religious discourse, a violent patriarchal (but why not matriarchal?) new faith. Its creators themselves keep being tempted beyond the limiting confines of their chosen form: the simple-minded to an easy faith in endless pleasure, what Marcus called pornotopia, heaven as the endless return of the endless kick or kink. The serious writer is forever tempted back into the world discourse in which sexual and religious meanings begin to frame the anarchy of the body part, body pleasure, body agony. The signal work in the opening up of the entire genre to over-counter art, *Lady Chatterley*, is of course a work that refuses to live in its own minimalist and controversial voicing of the four-letter word as the nearest thing in cold print to the hot sex object/event. Lawrence's physical detailing is intensely involved in a different project, canceling a conservative Christian discourse and inserting a neo-pagan vision of phallic and Eleusinian regeneration. Writer or critic may settle for the naked object, the part in itself. Once either reaches out for meaning, the discourse begins to fall back into the universal cultural discussion of sexuality and religion.

These tentatives on twentieth-century literature can only be suggestive. Another study would be needed to show adequately a tradition of discourse moving after Hardy in some radical new ways: to seek new meanings in other cultures or a broad world culture, to lament lost meanings, to try to live with the part and not to seek fullness of meaning. And it would show the broader Western tradition of discussion of sexuality and religion that was so present to the nineteenth-century writer continuing also, but often as a distorted misconception in the minds of its self-appointed enemies, sometimes as a tradition still strongly living in the minds of adherents ignorant of its past, often as the ghost of a major cultural preoccupation that can neither be brought back to life nor entirely exorcised. I will be content if the reader of this specialized study, focussed on the rather remarkable discussions of some serious Victorians, sees such an ongoing discourse more clearly as a continuation of Victorian preoccupations – and, more broadly, as part of a necessary and only somewhat cabbalistic discourse on central mysteries, in all cultures. Our own experience in handling – so often of mishandling – these penetralia should teach us to respect the seriousness and relative success of Victorians' approaches to such special discourses. If we think for a moment even more broadly of the various, often misshapen, but also deeply engaged attempts of our century to create its own sexual religious myths – cults of orgones or of mutual orgasms, priestly attempts to explain away AIDS or to scourge its victims, other priestly attempts to hold Catholics of a most unpatriarchal age to ages-old Augustinian myths, holy wars over abortion, very unholy sex scandals among the television evangelists, cults of sex gods and goddesses from the death and resurrection of Marilyn Monroe or Elvis Presley to the triumphant ascension of Madonna, Nazi sex nightmares or radical fringe pipe-dreams of new sexual communities, and on and on among the sex- and religion-charged phenomena of our days – we may readily acknowledge not only how inevitable but also how problematic and precarious these undertakings may be.

Notes

I INTRODUCTION: THE SUBJECT SOMEWHAT BROADLY CONCEIVED

1 Anthony Kenny, *God and Two Poets* (London: Sidgwick and Jackson, 1988). Kenny brings a philosopher's perspective to the variety of issues Clough attempts in his poems.

2 Seymour Chatman, *Story and Discourse: Narrative Structure in Fiction and Film* (Ithaca: Cornell University Press, 1978), made familiar the distinction between mere story and discourse as a mode of presenting: from Emile Benveniste's linguistic study of *récit* and *discours*, *Problèmes de linguistique générale* (Paris: Gallimard, 1966), pp. 237–50; similar ideas in Todorov and, with some variation, in Genette. In Foucault there is, of course, especially the implication of a world of language embodying the fundamental ways of thinking of an era, a discourse that underlies and underwrites all other discussions. In his thought such a discourse exerts a controlling social power on its age, though in Foucault's latest work – on sexuality – this power cannot be reduced to a system of authority of some classes or groups over others: it exerts its force and creates its oppositions throughout the society. Foucault's brilliant rethinking of the problem of sexuality and repression in the nineteenth century has been extremely important to my own conceptualization. At the same time, I have had to resist Foucault's totalizing tendency that often diminishes the importance of debate and disagreement in an age in order to define one central episteme. This may be a matter of whether one focusses on woods or individual trees (mine is a study of the thinking of a few individual writers of interest on one subject), but it is also especially a problem in approaching the eclectic and historically self-conscious thinking of the nineteenth and twentieth centuries. In my reservations I follow, as my remarks below suggest, the implied critique of Foucault in Diane MacDonell, *Theories of Discourse* (London: Basil Blackwell, 1986), who stresses the view that any broad modern discursive field should also be seen as a cluster of competing and contradicting discourses that may themselves be advanced or retarded by historical forces present in the culture. In the area of sexual discourses this more pluralistic and interactive approach has been well used lately by Linda Mahood, *The Magdalenes: Prostitution in the Nineteenth Century* (London: Routledge,

299

1990) – see her theoretical statement of this issue, p. 11 – and Frank Mort, *Dangerous Sexualities: Medico-Moral Politics in England Since 1830* (London: Routledge & Kegan Paul, 1987) – similar points, pp. 7–8. One of the most distinguished general historians of sexuality in the nineteenth century, Jeffrey Weeks, who generally follows Foucault's insights, nonetheless also has come increasingly to present his own project as a deconstruction of the discourse of the period since 1800, not just to show its constructed nature but to acknowledge its diversity: "sexuality has a history, or more realistically, many histories, each of which needs to be understood both in its uniqueness and as part of an intricate pattern": *Sexuality* (London: Tavistock, 1986), p. 25. In a manner that does not really falsify Foucault's own increasing tentativeness about the power organization in sexual discourse, Weeks sees a complex and also contradictory social effect: power operates "through complex and overlapping – and often contradictory – mechanisms which produce domination *and* oppositions, subordination *and* resistances": p. 37. Although she cites both Foucault and Weeks, Lynda Nead, *Myths of Sexuality: Representations of Women in Victorian Britain* (Oxford: Basil Blackwell, 1988), really moves in an opposite direction from both as she criticizes Foucault for unclearness in the definition of discourse and substitutes a Gramscian idea of hegemonic discourse as a mechanism by which a dominant group (in her case the bourgeoisie) exerts control and exercises power over others. Although this seems like a simple solution – how one group creates the discourse of an age and uses it to aggrandize themselves and weaken others – it actually creates (or reinvents) many problems that Foucault's much more complex approach rather well avoids: for instance, how hegemonic is hegemonic? What place can competing systems be said to occupy once one has been dubbed hegemonic? How much control does a hegemonic system of thought that is nonetheless not unchallenged exert? And there is, of course, the complicated issue of intention: is such hegemonic discourse the same or different from overt and deliberate forms of power such as police action? I think we need to know more about what competing discourses there were in the period before offering such totalizing explanatory systems; Nead's book itself provides useful information about the discourse in the world of art in relation to that of writing. As a very public world subject to much censorship and control (and occupied with highly publicized annual exhibits), Victorian art is perhaps a form of discourse less likely in any case to exhibit variety and dissent.

I also claim the right to use the word "discourse" in an untechnical manner as a way of talking about a subject. Cary long ago used it, indeed for love, in Dante's "Love that discourses in my thoughts."

3 Camille Paglia, "Sex and Violence, or Nature and Art," in her *Sexual Personae: Art and Decadence from Nefertiti to Emily Dickinson* (New Haven: Yale University Press, 1990), pp. 1–39; Paglia's reductionistic theme, which picks up many of the oppositions developed by some nineteenth-

century anthropological thinking about differing matriarchal (nature) and patriarchal (sky, eye) religions (see n. 7, below), leads her not only to understate the sexual element in Christianity but to overlook anti-sexual or ascetic traditions in classical paganism. Her book nonetheless offers a lively account of sexual types in art and literature, including those in a number of nineteenth-century writers.

4 This book will use the word sex for physical acts, sexuality for the remaining 99 percent, which is cultural construct, in language and symbol. The critique of essentializing thinking that offers cultural systems of sexuality as the products of nature, implied in Foucault's work on sexuality, is made fully by Jeffrey Weeks, especially in his two general works: *Sexuality*, esp. pp. 12–15 and the fuller *Sexuality and Its Discontents: Meanings, Myths, and Modern Sexualities* (London: Routledge & Kegan Paul, 1985), Introduction and pp. 61–123. See also the Introduction (by Caplan) and articles in Pat Caplan, ed., *The Cultural Construction of Sexuality* (London: Tavistock, 1987). Two articles in Kathy Peiss and Christina Simmons, eds., *Passion and Power: Sexuality in History* (Philadelphia: Temple University Press, 1989), the editors' "Passion and Power: Introduction," pp. 3–13, and Robert A. Padgug, "Sexual Matters: On Conceptualizing Sexuality in History," pp. 14–31, also state clearly the case against "essentialist ideas" of sexuality and in favor of an historical understanding of their nature. Padgug, p. 20: "We *become* human only in human society . . . Social reality cannot simply be 'picked off' to reveal 'natural man' lurking beneath." Barbara Johnson has also noted the danger of such essentializing thinking: that it may become a means of one sex oppressing the other – for instance, calling socially constructed qualities natural. Georges Bataille, *Erotism: Death and Sensuality*, trans. Mary Dalwood (earlier trans. 1962 as *Death and Sensuality: A Study of Eroticism and the Taboo* from the orig. French of 1957; San Francisco: City Lights, 1986), similarly compares the relation between the different terms "brain" (the physical thing) and "mind' (the phenomenon of thinking) to physical sex and what he calls "eroticism" – expanded to mean the equivalent of sexuality as I use it – though Bataille sometimes prefers to locate eroticism in a single psychological state rather than in its manifestation as cultural productions of sex. Perhaps the most manifest distinction between sex and sexuality as I use it is the famous Lacanian mystery of penis – the physical thing – and phallus – a word so weighted with meanings it would certainly fail if it were a mere physical object. See Jacques Lacan, "La Signification du Phallus," *Ecrits*, II (Paris: Editions de Seuil, 1971).

5 Geoffrey Parrinder, *Sex in the World's Religions* (New York: Oxford University Press, 1980), p. 1. I am indebted to Parrinder's useful and very broad survey of the interrelation of sex and religion.

6 From a notebook entry, quoted by Paddy Kitchen, *Gerard Manley Hopkins* (London: Hamilton, 1978), pp. 34–35.

7 See my fuller (still merely exploratory) discussion of this messy, central

concept in Freud, in n. 54, ch. 4. Ernest Jones's theory of the Virgin's
innocent conception through the ear as a displacement of a pleasurable
infantile fantasy of anal conception of which we are no longer aware is
a good example of the kind of obscured (and somewhat obscure)
redirection Freud has in mind. It is interesting to observe the degree to
which Freud's ideas of the development of religion from displaced and
unresolved sexual feelings about parents were set out on a framework of
religious history that matches the evolutionary anthropology of his day.
Although he is normally most concerned with the patriarchal Oedipal
God figure, he leaves room for the great mother "kindly Nature." He
sees religions progressing from open worship of sexual parts (his reading
in R. Payne Knight's work – "the laborious compilations of the student
of civilization" – from the turn of the nineteenth century was important:
A Discourse on the Worship of Priapus [1786]; *An Inquiry into the Symbolic
Language of Ancient Art and Mythology* [1818]) to increasingly hidden
sexuality, with the more repressive Western religions, more civilization
and more discontent, triumphing, seemingly necessarily as a massive
form of sublimation in an entire culture. Why the open worship of "the
genitals . . . the pride and hope of living beings" and their projection into
lustful gods should have been unrepressed for so long, or even still exist
unrepressed in other, presumably backward, cultures isn't, I think,
adequately explained: *Leonardo da Vinci and a Memory of His Childhood*, in
The Standard Edition of the Complete Psychological Works of Sigmund Freud,
trans. Alan Tyson (orig. London: Hogarth Press, 1955; rept. New York:
Norton, 1964), p. 47.

As in the common historical myths of progression from matriarchal to
patriarchal religion of his day (on which Freud works a rather original
variation), he sees patriarchal religion as a rather recent phenomenon,
with the most important version being the development of Judaism and
Christianity. In the full myth of the rambling account in the late *Moses
and Monotheism* – in *The Standard Edition of the Complete Psychological Works
of Freud*, trans. James Strachey (London: Hogarth Press, 1964), XXIII –
where Freud admits he was working from the by then superseded
anthropological ideas of Robertson Smith – Freud sees Moses bringing
from Egypt a monotheistic, patriarchal belief to replace the predominant
matriarchal polytheistic one. (That existing polytheistic society is the
muddled period in Freud's thinking where the incest taboo and Oedipal
complex somehow are and are not fully achieved, allowing unsublimated
pagan sexual religion.) Moses' death revives the guilt repressed through
the totem ceremonies that followed the mythic murder of the father by
the sons – as explored in the earlier *Totem and Taboo* (1913) – and leads
to a total suppression of the sexual element in religion that originally
generated religious belief, a suppression emblemed in the symbolic
castration of the circumcision ritual. In Judaism, and in the following
Christianity that relieves the guilt by having Christ take it on, there is
thus sublimation of sexual experience (a true sublimation in Freud's

sense in that the original sexual content is now unknown). Religion is thus a comforting "childhood neurosis" that should ultimately yield to the "education to reality" that Freud hoped for in *The Future of an Illusion – Works of Freud*, trans. Strachey, XXI, 53, 50. As I suggest below, Freud seems to leave no place in his idea of sublimation for a discourse of sexuality that is removed, but not totally removed, from sexual activity, e.g., his own discourse. On W. Robertson Smith, the important Scots nineteenth-century anthropological student of religion, esp. the Jewish Old Testament tradition, see Thomas O. Beidelman, *W. Robertson Smith and the Sociological Study of Religion* (Chicago: University of Chicago Press, 1974). Smith misled Freud into undue stress on religious evolution through totemism as a central and universal phenomenon; he remains important for his stress on ritual, rather than myth, which importantly influenced Durkheim.

The best general account of the broader history of sexual discourse in nineteenth-century anthropology is Rosalind Coward's *Patriarchal Precedents: Sexuality and Social Relations* (London: Routledge & Kegan Paul, 1983), which provides an excellent history of the debate over matriarchal/patriarchal theories of social origins. Writers such as the German J. J. Bachofen and, in England, J. F. McLennan and L. H. Morgan, offered evolutionary systems in which matriarchy (Bachofen's *Mutterrecht*) was replaced by patriarchy. On the other side, a writer such as E. B. Tylor constructed an argument from nature (primate organization) to argue universal patriarchy. Coward shows the tradition mired in confusions over whether sexuality is a natural or cultural construct and forced, as Freud would be, to invent origins in a void of real information. She sees most anthropological thinking on sexuality in the twentieth century, after Malinowski's break with Freudian thinking, as turning from both questions of origin and evolution and looking primarily at the social configurations of sexual practices in various cultures. Nor is there any longer an attempt to read "primitive" societies as antecedent to "modern" societies in some universal system of evolution. See also the generally parallel summaries of twentieth-century anthropological thinking on sexuality in Caplan's Introduction, pp. 13–17, and Weeks, *Sexuality and Its Discontents*, pp. 105–7; both identify residual essentialist ideas in anthropologists such as Malinowski or Mead.

On the parallel history of Victorian attitudes toward sexual issues in classical antiquity see n. 15, below.

8 E.g., in Erich Neumann's classic, *The Great Mother: An Analysis of the Archetype*, trans. Ralph Manheim, 2nd edn. (Princeton: Princeton University Press, 1972), where consciousness is presented as growing by developing a religious system that is simultaneously a set of sexual symbols. Though it is much less salient in Freud's thinking on anthropology, he too at least sometimes accepted an "archaic heritage" of unconscious symbols, in his case acquired symbols from the time of the

murder of the father that are thenceforth inherited: *Moses and Mon-otheism*, in *Works of Freud*, XXIII, 101.

9 Lee A. Stone, *The Story of Phallicism* (Chicago: Pascal Covici, 1927), pp. 3, 86.

10 Quoted in The United Church of Christ, *Human Sexuality* (New York: United Church Press, 1977), p. 80.

11 *The Book of J*, commentary to the translation by David Rosenberg (New York: Grove Weidenfeld, 1990). On God's problematic corporeality and sexuality see n. 25, below.

12 Pierre Gordon, *Sex and Religion*, trans. from the original French by R. and H. Spodheim (New York: Social Science Publishers, 1949), esp. pp. 1–48, in a universalistic reading that tries to find unity in all earlier religions of antiquity, summarizes information on real and symbolic sacred deflowerers. Stone, *The Story of Phallicism*, is an anthology of essays, by himself and earlier authors, collecting information on phallic worship, ritual defloration, and sacred prostitution. Thorkil Vanggaard, *Phallós: A Symbol and Its History in the Male World*, trans. by the author from the Danish original (New York: International Universities Press, 1972), is a somewhat more scholarly approach in a psychoanalytic framework; his focus, on homosexual phallic practices, leads him to look at the ritual initiation of pederastic intercourse – as a conveying of male qualities from the ritual deflowerer to the young male. On Hindi ritual, usually initiation of sacred prostitutes, see Parrinder, p. 27. Parrinder manages to review a great deal of material about sexual practices in many societies and in different ages without falling into the vaguely pornographic mode of the earlier anthologies. On religious prostitution see also Vern Bullough and Bonnie Bullough, *Women and Prostitution: A Social History* (Buffalo: Prometheus, 1987), pp. 5–7, 18–19, 23, 39–40. J. S. La Fontaine, *Initiation, Ritual, Drama and Secret Knowledge Across the World* (New York: Penguin, 1985), also a broad summary, here in a context of social anthropology, has the even greater advantage of being self-conscious about the problems of interpretation involved in des-cribing any ritual of initiation (summarized below, pp. 20–22). The linking of sexuality and religion in what La Fontaine describes broadly as maturity rituals is taken for granted by both the interpreters she studies and herself, though only Freudian interpretations seem to address the issue of why they appear together. La Fontaine rightly criticizes Frazer as well as Mircea Eliade for assuming an evolutionary movement toward monotheistic religion and a cross-cultural uniform pattern of development. Similar simple assumptions underlie and vitiate the generalizations of the older studies of initiation in antiquity cited above.

13 In his *Eroticism* (see n. 4, above). René Girard, *Violence and the Sacred*, trans. Patrick Gregory (Baltimore: Johns Hopkins University Press, 1977), constructs a more totalizing (and reductive) system of religious origins based on the need to control violence, itself often the result of

sexual drives that help encourage multiplying blood feuds. These can only be stopped by religious sacrifice (or modern systems of abstract justice where the law ends the feud). In Girard's primal horde, incest comes first, then father or king is sacrificed to control the resulting violence: yet another myth, of our time, of the relations of sexuality and religion.

14 On Japan and Africa see Parrinder, pp. 106–10, 131–34; Stone, pp. 256–325, includes earlier informed essays by Genchi Katô and Edmund Buckley on Japan. The classic studies were, of course, R. Payne Knight's (see n. 7, above); Knight liked to argue the primacy of sexuality in creating religion by making phallicism the original worship. Walter Kendrick brightly recounts the open secret of Pompeii's phallic treasures: *The Secret Museum: Pornography in Modern Culture* (New York: Viking, 1987), pp. 3–18.

15 Frank M. Turner, *The Greek Heritage in Victorian Britain* (New Haven: Yale University Press, 1981), pp. 77–134, summarizes British attempts to provide a theoretical explanation of Greek religion, e.g., George Grote, who saw the religion working out its sexual content as it developed, and the German emigré scholar Friedrich Max Müller, whose reversed but complementary theories traced the decline of a higher spiritual "solar" religion into vulgar sexualities. This tendency to deny the sexual content of Greek religion was counteracted by Symonds and Andrew Lang and, more systematically, by Frazer and by Jane Harrison, Francis Cornford, Gilbert Murray and others of the Cambridge school of ritualistic interpretation, though Frazer could still embrace a concept of evolution in religion. On the parallel history of anthropological ideas of matriarchal and patriarchal origins see n. 7, above.

16 On Browning's exploration of phallic objects of worship and his associations between this hidden history and an idea of an unconscious see Samuel B. Southwell, *Quest for Eros: Browning and 'Fifine'* (Lexington: University of Kentucky Press, 1980). Turner provides an excellent survey of R. Payne Knight's influence in the nineteenth century – Grote's more chaste reading of Greek myth-making was greatly preferred so that until late in the century Knight's discoveries had only occasional impact, as probably on Browning's poem.

17 Michel Foucault, *The History of Sexuality: Volume I: An Introduction*, trans. Robert Hurley (New York: Pantheon Books, 1978); the most interesting study of asceticism as a general anti-sexual power in discourse and language is Geoffrey G. Harpham, *The Ascetic Imperative in Philosophy, Art, and Criticism* (Chicago: University of Chicago Press, 1988).

18 Parrinder, p. 22. I don't intend to deny the weaker force of ascetic denial in the Hindu context: the stories of Hindu ascetics sometimes include their yielding to happy love-play. Hinduism in its capaciousness can even imagine the forces of sexuality and ascesis working through the same vehicle. Sudhir Kakar's study of the sexual psychology of modern Hindus based on his clinical practice, *Intimate Relations: Exploring Indian*

Sexuality (Chicago: University of Chicago Press, 1990), esp. pp. 19–20, finds a great deal of repression in contemporary Hindu marriages as a result of male incest fears. I note below the way in which Christianity, generally moving in an anti-sexual or ascetic direction in the first 500 years of its development, also seems to have spawned some aggressively pro-sexual fringe traditions. And even before the current very pro-sexual turn of most Protestant groups, such developments were always a possibility in its long history at moments of radical crisis of authority, as immediately following the English Civil War. As another example there is the Christian Jamaa sect in the Congo where the ascetic story of God and Mary has been logically reversed into a parallel, and in some sense templating, tale of divine/human copulation: Parrinder, p. 149.

19 R. C. Zaehner, *Mysticism Sacred and Profane* (New York: Oxford University Press, 1957), pp. 151–52. The case is even more clear in Hinduism, which in its capaciousness can easily imagine the forces of sexuality and ascesis working through the same vehicle: Shiva combines phallic desire (*kama*) and asceticism (*tapas*): Parrinder, p. 8, and the full monograph study by Wendy Doniger O'Flaherty, *Asceticism and Eroticism in the Mythology of Siva* (New York: Oxford University Press, 1973). Kakar explains this as a full and direct idea of sublimation where sexual forces are consciously acknowledged as the source of spiritual energy: male force can be released grossly in semen or be directed upward by continence as a "raising of the seeds upward": p. 120; Indian women similarly seek an ideal phallus in fantasy instead of physical sex: p. 145.

20 *Erotism*; Bataille generally writes to make rituals of non-ascetic religions credible to the Western reader; his focus, even bias, makes him unclear and even rather ambivalent on the incorporation of violation in ascetic systems, as in his discussion of mysticism (pp. 223–49); but he does see the clearer situation in Tantric cults. The earlier French writer, Pierre Gordon, similarly explained the difference between the usual dread of incest and certain cultures' practices allowing special cases of incest as a violation of a taboo for the purpose of religious intensification (also a part of Girard's argument).

21 For a well-organized brief description and display of Ranters' writing – for instance the work of Abiezer Coppe in which God is described as "UNIVERSAL Love, and whose service is perfect freedom, and pure Libertinisme" – see Nigel Smith's Introduction and edition, *A Collection of Ranter Writings from the 17th Century* (London: Junction Books, 1983). Peter Gardella, *Innocent Ecstasy: How Christianity Gave America an Ethic of Sexual Pleasure* (New York: Oxford University Press, 1985), looks broadly at the confused pattern of violation of taboo and celebration of sex in Christianity that creates such variations of license and puritanism in American religious history; Milton Rugoff, *Prudery and Passion* (New York: G. P. Putnam's Sons, 1971), gives a welter of social detail; see esp. pp. 190–213. More impressionistically one could add the Western witches' sabbath, which often had a sexual orgy; whatever its origin or

explanation, its explicit form, as in the name, is a parody by inversion into sexual activity of the apparent chastity of the mass. Carlo Ginzburg's interesting (and controversial) *Ecstasies*, trans. Raymond Rosenthal (New York: Pantheon, 1991), offers a useful prefatory summary of the welter of explanations and interpretations.

22 Parrinder, pp. 34–38, 49–53; Kakar, p. 122. In Japan the Tantric Tachikawa sect was eventually suppressed for having mass sex at its meetings.

23 *The Use of Pleasure*, trans. R. Hurley (New York: Pantheon, 1985); also his similar study of non-Christian Roman thinking, *The Care of the Self*, trans. R. Hurley (New York: Pantheon, 1985): both under the general title of *The History of Sexuality*.

24 Susan A. Handelman, *The Slayers of Moses: The Emergence of Rabbinic Interpretations in Modern Literary Theory* (Albany: State University Press of New York, 1983), p. 101, suggests that Judaism came to substitute God as text-giver for God as begetter of the universe.

25 Parrinder, p. 195, notes more generally the instability of this male monotheism: Jeremiah found Jewish women in Egypt worshipping Ishtar, Queen of Heaven, and there are numerous references to the need to prevent such straying. Papyri from Elephantiné, near Aswan, show Jews in a military colony worshipping other gods including one, Anathyahu, possibly a spouse of God. Wisdom in Proverbs (as in the later Christian Apocryphal Ecclesiasticus) seems a kind of veiled female deity with God from "the beginning." And, of course, in the Song of Solomon and elsewhere the relation of God to Israel could be interpreted as at least metaphorically a version of bridegroom and bride, though it was not until long after the Diaspora, in the same climate as Christian reinterpretation of the Song of Solomon, that Jewish Cabbalists could begin to imagine in other special cases some kind of personal, sexual relation of God and man.

On the issue of God's corporeality and possible sexuality see Howard Eilberg-Schwartz, " People of the Body: The Problem of the Body for the People of the Book," *Journal of the History of Sexuality*, 2 (July 1991), 1–24, a condensation of his work in *The Savage in Judaism: An Anthropology of Israelite Religion and Ancient Judaism* (Bloomington: Indiana University Press, 1990). He sees the body of God as a site of great conflict between priestly tendencies to celebrate procreation and a monotheistic idea of God, in whose image man is made, as beyond body or sex (or gender). The need to describe man in terms of God obviously cuts as easily the other way and tempts writers to find human qualities in the image of God. If we must speak of God's "loins," then even loins of fire can sound asexual or highly sexual to different readers. I find his explorations of a problematic area in the culture's discourse that keeps producing further discussion and disturbance more persuasive than the fairly static analysis of a societal ordering system – in which incest and adultery simply occupy different positions from holiness in a structure – of a writer such as Mary Douglas: *Purity and Danger: An Analysis of the Concepts of Pollution and Taboo* (1966; rpt. London: Routledge, 1989), p. 53.

26 Here perhaps sometimes helpfully keeping alive a tradition; it is surprising to find how few anthropologists seem aware, for instance, of the work of Freud's interesting anthropologist disciple, Géza Róheim. Coward, pp. 247–49, chronicles his exclusion from professional consideration (as the Freudian practical anthropologist trying to establish the universality of the Oedipal complex) in the aftermath of the debate between Malinowski and Ernest Jones on this issue. Morris at least mentions him in his summary of psychological approaches to anthropology (see next note).

27 Stanley R. Barrett, *The Rebirth of Anthropological Theory* (Toronto: University of Toronto Press, 1984), provides a clear and useful summary of the welter of competing explanatory systems, present and past, in anthropology, though he is still not without his own ax to grind. Brian Morris, *Anthropological Studies of Religion: An Introductory Text* (Cambridge: Cambridge University Press, 1987), gives full summaries and critiques of a smaller number of major systems that have predominated in studies of religion; his survey is especially useful in relating anthropological thought on religion to neighboring systems in social thinkers such as Herbert Spencer, Marx, Weber, or Freud and Jung. The same is true of the exemplary study by Coward of specific discussions of sexuality and social relations. See also the attractive briefer summary by M. E. Combs-Schilling in his *Sacred Performances: Islam, Sexuality, and Sacrifice* (New York: Columbia University Press, 1989), pp. 26–37.

28 See the fuller critiques of Frazer and Eliade in La Fontaine, pp. 19–23 and Morris, pp. 103–6, 174–81: La Fontaine is not without her own bias: she is, somewhat eclectically, in the British structural functionalist school, with its stress, *à la* Radcliffe-Brown, on social correlates to ritual activity: i.e., subordination of meaning to sociological function; Morris is more judicious but finds that both positions stress evolutionary systems and that Eliade creates a universal archetypal system that closes off other interpretations and perspectives. Douglas, pp. 22–28, is far more critical of Frazer. In such criticisms by anthropologists there is, of course, a frequent predilection, from Durkheim to British anthropologists such as La Fontaine, for social explanations of religion. More, there are few anthropologists who have taken an interest in the content of religion itself (that is the beliefs as the possible kinds of truth that believers find them; Lévi-Strauss analyzes content, of course, but only to reveal a universal structure of thought not directly available to the believer). With this, there has been a broad tendency to define the study of religion as a problem in explaining a more primitive (savage, or whatever the going term) mentality which has encouraged the tendency to evolutionary thought that contemporary anthropologists now deplore. As Morris notes, the reason for religion's power on the individual – the question of affect – has been left mainly to psychology students such as

Freud or Jung, just as the sexual experience of the individual, as Coward notes, has been left to psychologists or biologists. The interest in Geertz's work outside the world of professional anthropology doubtless does stem from his willingness to consider the question of meaning in the content of religion and religious symbolism as well as the issue of the motivations (threats of chaos in different areas of experience) for religious belief.

29 My critique of Campbell, as of Frazer or Eliade, is of methodological simplicities. I am much indebted to the detail and the adventurous spirit of all three writers.

30 P. 157; I am generally indebted to Foucault's distinction, pp. 150–59, between sexual discourse and an inarticulate physical process, sex.

31 I should note a general debt here to Bataille's discussion, in *Erotism*, of the emergence of human sexuality from animals' sex. He finds a two-stage process: first, the creation of taboos – unknown to animals – then their violation as a central sexual–religious event. See also Padgug, p. 19: "If we compare human sexuality with that of other species we are immediately struck by its richness, its vast scope, and the degree to which its potentialities can seemingly be built upon endlessly, implicating the entire world. Animal sexuality, by contrast, appears limited, constricted, and predefined to a narrow physical sphere."

32 The complex social discourse of animal breeding so wittily displayed by Harriet Ritvo in her *The Animal Estate: The English and Other Creatures in the Victorian Age* (Cambridge: Harvard University Press, 1987) strikes us as deliciously comic just because of the participants' desire to project their own sexual interests (theories of masculine dominance or concerns with female purity) into an arena where the brute facts are so obviously hard to talk around.

33 My subject is the interrelation of sexual and religious discourses. I would not wish to be misunderstood as implying that neither exists apart from the other. For instance, in many religions much of the ritual of death exists first as a way of ritualizing loss (or, as many anthropologists would prefer, mobilizing loss in support of the social structure), though it easily moves to a mingled discourse in which loss is repaired by sexuality as rebirth (into other world, in a return, in a renewal of social organization) or as fertilizing sacrifice (e.g., Frazer's favorite fertility myths of the death of a god). Similarly, while sexuality tends to exist as a mingled discourse of some sort, which reaches out for connections with other subjects, it often focuses on non-religious topics: for instance, sexuality as the site of power or gender relations (or both); as a place of joy and anarchy (the potential of Foucault's play of bodies and pleasures explored back in the 1950s, as Foucault knew, by Norman O. Brown's *Life Against Death* and *Love's Body* and his development of the concept of polymorphous perversity, and also revived by the attack on the Oedipal structure as authority in the work of Gilles Deleuze and Félix Guattari – all also sexual discourses); as a site of communication (among classes, sexes, ideologies); as a location for the production of difference (the

production from undifferentiated humanity of male and female, heterosexuals and homosexuals, of deviants, courtly lovers, bestials, prostitutes, ascetics, or hermits, etc.). As most of my examples can be made to suggest (gender and sexuality as the production of different versions of Christianity, sexual joy as religious release and ecstasy, sex as a site of holy inspiration or the production of saints), virtually all sexual topics can take a religious turn, but aren't therefore necessarily involved primarily in a religious discourse. My own *Charlotte Brontë and Sexuality* (Cambridge: Cambridge University Press, 1984) argued for a primarily secular perspective on Brontë's complicated sexual discourse despite the frequent use of religious typologies, symbols, and language in her work.

34 La Fontaine, p. 114.

35 La Fontaine, p. 115.

36 La Fontaine, p. 115.

37 See especially the discussion, pp. 255–71, with useful contrasts between all three systems and polytheistic sexual structures. It should be said that the idea of heaven in Judaism has been less consistent and persistent than in the other two traditions, with earlier views of Sheol offering little of the reward or consolation of the later notions of a heaven where God receives the dead.

38 *The Body and Society: Men, Women, and Sexual Renunciation in Early Christianity* (New York: Columbia University Press, 1988).

39 *Adam, Eve, and the Serpent* (New York: Random House, 1988). Pagels's stress on early Christianity's faith in the Christian's reason leads her to somewhat understate the sexual ideology developing its own life apart from the political situation of Christianity. Her discussion of Jerome seems embarrassed before his obvious commitment to virginity as a value in itself and not just as a site for testing the Christian's will.

In my necessarily brief summaries of a large and complex history of early Christianity below, as in the following surveys of later developments in Christianity I have also drawn freely, usually without specific reference, on the summary work of Parrinder and on two other earlier useful and scholarly surveys: William Graham Cole, *Sex in Christianity and Psychoanalysis* (New York: Oxford University Press, 1955) and Derrick Sherwin Bailey, *Sexual Relation in Christian Thought* (New York: Harper and Brothers, 1959). Their more survey work has been outpaced but not entirely replaced by the more recent summaries of important areas of sexual-religious history by major recent historians, Brown, Pagels, and others whom I cite.

40 Brown, p. 93, offers a specific example of disciples of Tatian who promulgated the myth of a Fall by sex, though this was a rare theological position.

41 Handelman, p. 119, offers a suggestive transposition of Augustine's thinking on language into contemporary terms of desire and language. The formulation implies that God is also the right focus of all sexual energy, a great corollary that some of Augustine's medieval successors, rather than he, would dare to explore.

42 See James A. Brundage's discussion of this long process of controversy, soon reawakened massively by Protestantism, in his *Law, Sex, and Christian Society in Medieval Europe* (Chicago: University of Chicago Press, 1987).

43 A small piece of his ongoing work is available in "The Battle for Chastity," in Philippe Ariès and André Béjin, eds., *Western Sexuality: Practice and Precept in Past and Present Times* (Oxford: Basil Blackwell, 1985), pp. 14–25. As readers of his *Introduction* would expect, he focusses on the development of a large subjective world by the discourse of self-interrogation in the battle against the self for chastity: the creation of a large new world of thinking that elaborates and transforms earlier sexual discourses rather than subdues them. See also the discussion with Richard Sennett, "Sexuality and Solitude," *Humanities in Review* (1982), p. 15; "after Augustine we experience our sex in the head."

44 Emmanuel Le Roy Ladurie, *Montaillou: The Promised Land of Error*, trans. Barbara Bray (New York: George Braziller, 1978).

45 See Noonan, *Contraception: A History of the Treatment by the Catholic Theologians and Canonists* (Cambridge: Harvard University Press, 1965), and Boswell, *Christianity, Social Tolerance, and Homosexuality: Gay People in Western Europe from the Beginning of the Christian Era to the Fourteenth Century* (Chicago: University of Chicago Press, 1980).

46 See Fuchs, *Sexual Desire and Love: Origins and History of the Christian Ethic of Sexuality and Marriage*, trans. Marsha Daigle (New York: Seabury, 1983); Flandrin, *Un Temps pour embrasser: Aux origines de la morale sexuelle occidentale (VIᵉ–XIᵉ siècle)* (Paris: Editions du Seuil, 1983): on penitentials' prohibitions of intercourse during large parts of the year; also Flandrin's broader study, *Families in Former Times: Kinship, Household, and Sexuality*, trans. Richard Southern (Cambridge: Cambridge University Press, 1979). Vern L. Bullough and James Brundage, *Sexual Practices and the Medieval Church* (Buffalo: Prometheus, 1982), is also a summary of the general subject.

47 Philippe Ariès, "The Indissoluble Marriage," in Ariès and Béjin, pp. 140–57, interestingly explores this uncertainty in the case of attitudes toward divorce.

48 Handelman, p. 89, formulates a contrast between religion as text and religion as body, which she parallels to the contrast between accepting the necessary alienation involved in interpretation and hoping for a direct presence. Her formulation, however, simplifies the Christian situation, which is normally not possession of presence but a quest for it, often indeed, as generally in Protestantism, through a text rather than a mystery of bodily presence. Cole, pp. 17–20, and Parrinder, pp. 207–11, review the few explicitly sexual statements attributed to Christ in the canonical gospels, which in their brevity and enigmatic formulation have been used to justify virtually every sexual practice: from asceticism (being eunuchs for the kingdom of heaven); to earthly naturalism to be followed by heavenly abstinence (the gospels' Jesus celebrated marriage in generous style but spoke of no marrying in heaven – a pronouncement

that, as we shall see, troubled both Kingsley and Patmore sufficiently to drive them to elaborate explanations); to rigid or highly exacting moralism (no remarriage and no adultery even in one's thoughts); to extreme liberalism (none should cast stones and the woman who wiped Jesus' feet with her hair – if indeed she even was a sexual sinner – was to be forgiven her sins because she loved much): to suggest only a few of the avenues that have been so amply explored in nearly two thousand years of explication.

49 Even Brown, p. 61, credits the possibility of such groups in the second century, whom we know of through orthodox polemics against them. Records of a possible Gnostic celebration of sex are reproduced in Marvin W. Meyer, ed., *The Ancient Mysteries: A Sourcebook* (San Francisco: Harper and Row, 1987), pp. 235–42. However, the text, of a bridechamber ceremony from the Gospel of Philip (from the Nag Hammadi Library, trans. W. W. Isenberg), has been subject to varied interpretation; neither Pagels nor Brown sees it as a text about sex activity (see Pagels, pp. 70, 164n, on differing views of the ceremony: some argue that it represents a sexual sacrament; others that it is a mere metaphor of the soul's relation to God). Jean-Louis Flandrin, *Le Sexe et l'Occident: Evolution des attitudes et des comportements* (Paris: Editions du Seuil, 1981), pp. 104–5, suggested Christian severity toward sexual activity might have developed from a reaction to Gnostic libertinism. But Pagels, and Brown (p. 112) see the Gnostic thinking of Valentius and his disciples as mainly concerned neither with sex nor asceticism, but with spiritual self-discovery, which would lead the knower away from involvement generally with this world. However, the interpretive system was itself very much occupied with a mythic version of sexual union, say of God and divine wisdom or of psyche and spirit, often read as Eve and Adam (or vice versa). Some Gnostics were explicitly opposed to sex.

Of course, the issue of Christianity's potential as a religion celebrating sex has been in question again and again in certain splinter groups in the history of Christianity and certainly, as Gardella and others have recorded, we have seen a massive shift to liberal, permissive sexual attitudes in many Christian churches in the last two centuries.

50 Brundage's study of the tortuous discussion of this issue in the increasingly rational and incisive discourse of lawyers and legal education in the canon law is most helpful; see also Flandrin's study of penitentials and his briefer survey, "Sex in Married Life in the Middle Ages: the Church's Teaching and Behavioural Reality," in Ariès and Béjin, pp. 114–29. Cole, pp. 66–91, explores Aquinas' important contribution in some detail, especially the modification of Augustinian thinking on concupiscence to see the effect of the Fall on sex as the weakening of man's reason in what otherwise would have been a natural and pleasant activity, and the ordering of forbidden activities by their relative violation of nature; his views of marriage follow the usual prescriptions of procreation and marital debt.

51 The metaphors of Christ as Bridegroom or of the marriage of the Lamb were of course present from earliest Christian times and always open to an interpretive turn that took them more seriously as definitions of humans' potential relation to Christ/God. Tatian, for instance, in the Syrian Church in the second century, was preoccupied with images of marriage and nurture in describing the soul's union with God; Origen wrote on the Song of Solomon and spoke of a spiritual pleasure, greater than any of the body, in the embrace of the Bridegroom (Brown, pp. 91–92, 172); Gnostics used similar imagery in their bridechamber sacrament (on the current debate over its meaning see n. 49, above).

52 *Love Declared: Essays on the Myths of Love,* trans. Richard Howard (Boston: Beacon Press, 1963): a split into passion without sex leading to death or the merely physical repetition of Don Juan.

53 From the question of its origins (de Rougemont's theories of Catharist heresies, others of Arabic, Byzantine, or even Celtic or classical influence – C. S. Lewis despaired of any one solution) to that of its very definition (Lewis's classic formulation of an adulterous relation has been widely questioned, along with the older assumption that desire had to remain unfulfilled – even to the point of seeing courtly love as the source of later, idealized married love), courtly love appears in its histories what it doubtless was: a highly diverse and variedly articulated development in Western psychic history. The unifying factor would seem to be the development of a subjective realm of love at least initially conceived of as different from bodily expression in sex, presumably (or is it possibly?) a reaction to the negative attitudes toward sex itself. For helpful surveys see Larry Benson, "Courtly Love and Chivalry in the Later Middle Ages," in Robert Yeager, ed., *Fifteenth Century Studies* (Hamden: Shoe String, 1984), pp. 237–57; E. Talbot Donaldson, "The Myth of Courtly Love," *Speaking of Chaucer* (New York: Norton, 1979), pp. 154–63; Bernard O'Donoghue, ed., *The Courtly Love Tradition* (Totowa: Barnes and Noble, 1982). De Rougemont's founding, but now highly controversial, history was *Love in the Western World,* trans. Montgomery Belgion (New York: Pantheon, 1956).

54 Brown's study of varieties of early ascetics is again very helpful here. The treatment of Irenaeus in Colleen McDannell and Bernhard Lang's survey, *Heaven: A History* (New York: Random House, 1988), pp. 47–68, gives a misleading impression that Christians before Augustine dreamed of a life to come fully like this. Their point on Augustine, that he relented from a purely spiritual view of the afterlife to a vision of a controlled body in his later work, brings him closer to prior thinking as Brown presents it.

55 See the summary in McDannell and Lang, pp. 94–110. For the broader context see Caroline Walker Bynum's fine *Jesus as Mother: Studies in the Spirituality of the High Middle Ages* (Berkeley: University of California Press, 1982), as well as her essays, *Fragmentation and Redemption: Essays on Gender and the Human Body in Medieval Religion* (New York: Zone Books,

1991). Bynum sees medieval religious women imagining very close relations with Christ, often imaged in female terms – drinking at his breast-like wounds or eating him in the Eucharist. Bynum acknowledges the release of erotic energy to God in their mystic trances (*Fragmentation*, p. 168) but needs perhaps to be more clear about the broadly sexual – sensual, bodily, oral – nature of the gratification found in the female Christ.

Leo Steinberg, *The Sexuality of Christ in Renaissance Art and in Modern Oblivion* (New York: Pantheon/October, 1983), looks in a study of visual representations at the later but somewhat parallel focus (despite Bynum's critique of his position from her emphasis on the female elements in Christ) on the sexualization of Christ, especially in pictures of the infant, of the circumcision, and their connections to versions of the crucifixion. Rather than imagine sexual desire transposed to God's world, Renaissance painters often insist on the incarnation of Christ as a totally human experience, including Christ's central participation in the sexual process of this world. Jesus is fully sexed, but not sexually active; he triumphs for us over lust as He later triumphs over death. Steinberg's very (even excessively) tactful discussion of subjects of painting that have been ignored or literally covered up (e.g., the exhibition of the infant Jesus' genitalia, the baby's erection, or even that of Christ on the cross) does not sufficiently explore the reasons for the earlier hesitancy of Christian artists to present a literal picture of Incarnation (he contrasts Renaissance to Byzantine stylized and hieratic treatments of Christ) and for the later veer away from such subjects. Isn't it that the subject is inherently scandalous, as D. H. Lawrence or Scorsese have understood, because, once broached, it always threatens to turn from Jesus as God-figure denying sex to God-figure participating in the sexual life of the creation he has made dependent on sex for its very continuation? Or, as Steinberg does note, at least to Christ as a fertility god in which the penis in the crucifixion acts as a symbol of triumph (see pp. 84–89 and p. 185, where Steinberg notes the ways in which a fully sexed Jesus can approximate Christ to earlier fertility gods)?

56 Far from being always opposed to religious views, we more often find an emerging secular discourse on the medical "science" of sex heavily involved in either the conservative project of converting prior religious positions to pseudo-scientific ones (most often to support a continued control and regulation) or in a liberalizing business of finding religious justifications for positive attitudes to sex. Thomas Laqueur, *Making Sex: Body and Gender from the Greeks to Freud* (Cambridge: Harvard University Press, 1990) and the briefer summary of his argument in "Orgasm, Generation, and the Politics of Reproductive Biology," *Representations*, 14 (Spring 1986), 1–41, has demonstrated fully how even biology as a science developed its positions on central issues in sex anatomy less in response to scientific evidence than to ideologies of the time. Less as a result of any new evidence in anatomy than as a general shift of sexual paradigms from a view of women as versions of men to a new view,

beginning around 1800 but in controversy throughout the nineteenth century, of women as fundamentally different from men, biology shifted its entire way of conceptualizing female anatomy, sex functions, and often, sex experience (for instance, the possibility of orgasm-free sex in the later model). In another area of sexual thought, Flandrin, *Le Sexe et l'Occident*, pp. 297–98, notes how the "scientific" discussions of the dangers of masturbation – beginning with the English early eighteenth-century *Onania* and especially the much-copied writing of Tissot of the mid-eighteenth century – picked up, rather late, the new stress in the Church from 1500 on the seriousness of masturbation as a sin. On the variety of medical – religious works in the nineteenth century see n. 69, below.

Rita Goldberg's interesting *Sex and Enlightenment: Women in Richardson and Diderot* (Cambridge: Cambridge University Press, 1984) shows how closely tied religious and secular views can be, even when the secular view is openly hostile to religion: Diderot finds the substance of his secular reduction of religion (the ecstasy of La Religieuse is "explained" as sex) in his deconstructive reading of the pious Protestant Richardson, where sex seems still to carry a full load of religious meaning (Clarissa's spiritual virtue, like that of an early Christian, is manifested in spiritual control of sex). In England generally in the eighteenth century sexual issues continued to be closely related to religious ones, with Enlightenment latitude in sexual behavior connected to a rational religion, where man followed the easy laws of nature, and more traditional religious views strongly opposed to libertine attitudes. See Roy Porter's survey, "Mixed Feelings: The Enlightenment and Sexuality in Eighteenth-Century Britain," in Paul-Gabriel Boucé, ed., *Sexuality in Eighteenth-Century Britain* (Manchester: Manchester University Press, 1982), pp. 1–27.

57 Gardella, pp. 9–24. Protestant accusations of libertine attitudes in such Catholic traditions were among the forces leading to the reaction to more traditional positions in mainstream Catholicism in England and the United States. For the broader history, see Flandrin, *Le Sexe et l'Occident*; Flandrin generally believes that a belief in love in marriage came earlier in England; yet he also cites leading Catholic thinkers before Liguori – Denys le Chartreux and Thomas Sánchez – as well as even a catechism showing the development of alternative attitudes: pp. 83–96, 101–8. His broader perspective indicates how far the position of the Church has changed, from seeing love as a very dangerous and unwanted intrusion in marriage to the present firm belief in love in marriage. Flandrin makes similar points in his more focussed study of peasant love: *Les Amours paysannes: Amour et sexualité dans les campagnes de l'ancienne France (XVIᵉ–XIXᵉ siècle)* (Paris: Gallimard, 1975). There he notes that the Church did defend love matches against the authority of the fathers and the secular law and that its position on love demonstrated a fundamental ambiguity: love (for God) was the finest, love (for one's spouse) one of the least valuable things people possessed.

58 For a summary of works on this issue see n. 83, ch. 3. Alan Macfarlane, *Marriage and Love in England: Modes of Reproduction* (Oxford: Basil Blackwell, 1986), argues that the survival of Teutonic law in England protected marriage traditions of affective choice of the couples from the patriarchal Roman law which spread family control on the Continent. It should be noted, rather against the kind of Protestant ideology about Catholicism that Kingsley initially brought to this question, that the canon law of the Church tended everywhere, as Brundage shows, to oppose patriarchal control in favor of the rights of couples. Macfarlane's observation that patriarchal control was most often asserted in the upper classes in England would confirm that this is even more a social than a religious phenomenon and might suggest that the religious discussion was from the beginning positioned between opposing social ideologies.

59 For this history in England see Lawrence Stone's recent *Road to Divorce: England 1530–1987* (New York: Oxford University Press, 1990).

60 See James Turner, *One Flesh: Paradisal Marriage and Sexual Relations in the Age of Milton* (Oxford: Clarendon, 1987).

61 On the influence of Milton's presentation as a commanding interpretation of religious sexuality see Jean H. Hagstrum, *Sex and Sensibility: Ideal and Erotic Love from Milton to Mozart* (Chicago: Chicago University Press, 1980), pp. 24–34. Milton's influentiality does not mean his position was typical of Protestant or even Puritan thinking, where there was often much controversy or even confusion about the value of sex in marriage, with marriage often still seen as the prophylaxis against fornication (as indeed it *still* was in conservative religious thinkers of the nineteenth century), not a positive celebration of sex. Both Luther and Calvin, both married and supporting marriage, showed no inclination to celebrate the powers of concupiscence which they, only more strongly than the Church, feared as a fundamental trait of man's depravity. Cole's full explications of Luther and Calvin's views on sexual issues are clear and useful: pp. 100–32. On John Wesley's different, but also strong suspicion of sex, and doubts as to the worth even of marriage (despite his own marriage), see Henry Abelove, *The Evangelist of Desire: John Wesley and the Methodists* (Stanford: Stanford University Press, 1990), pp. 49–73.

62 McDannell and Lang, pp. 111–44.

63 Quoted by McDannell and Lang, p. 173, from Hall, *Works* (1837), VI, 197.

64 McDannell and Lang, pp. 195–97, 212. Their model of Renaissance, reaction, eighteenth-century reaction from the reaction overly schematizes an issue that opened alternative positions, as they show, even to an early Lutheran such as Philipp Nicolai. Michael Wheeler, *Death and the Future Life in Victorian Literature and Theology* (Cambridge: Cambridge University Press, 1990), pp. 119–74, offers a closer and more analytical look at nineteenth-century ideas of heaven (and hell, pp. 175–218) in both specifically theological works and in a number of Victorian writers; he finds a continuing conflict between heaven as a place of human

fulfillment (what he calls an anthropocentric view) and heaven as a place of praise (theocentric). Of course, as his own stress on eschatology as offering metaphors for present as well as future experience makes clear, the afterlife can only be imagined in terms of human qualities; we could talk as well of restricted anthropomorphism (the afterlife as a place of some selected human emotions and fulfillments) and broad anthropomorphism (the afterlife as a place of more full or full humanity). However defined, it is in his view, as in McDannell and Lang's, a site of ideological controversy. On an often-related issue, the varying imaginations of Eden in religious and secular thought (including Victorian ideas of heavenly cities here or there), see Max F. Schulz, *Paradise Preserved: Recreations of Eden in Eighteenth- and Nineteenth-Century England* (Cambridge: Cambridge University Press, 1985).

65 The closest thing to a history of this diversity in the nineteenth and twentieth centuries in the many, many works and theories by theologians, preachers, and self-inspired religious originators, popular writers, medical "experts," and plain quacks is Peter Gardella's study of the broad American intellectual history, which offers helpful parallels to the English situation. Gardella looks at Catholic regulation of sexuality (generally positive), the reaction to Protestant attacks on the Catholic system of confession and celibacy as a hidden system of prurience and debauchery, and the cult of the Virgin and virgins as a form of sexuality directed to God (in the medieval tradition); he explores the religious attitudes, generally in the Augustinian tradition, as well as the conversions of religious anti-sexual traditions into pseudo-medical ones, in the respectable sex-negative and regulatory traditions; he looks at a broad spectrum of Evangelical thinkers, from those who brought sex-like ecstasy into conversion to those who explicitly read sex as a positive act in Christian marriage; and he suggestively but very briefly tries to read secular writers on sex, including Freud, Sanger, Marcuse, and Lacan in relation to varying religious traditions (for instance, Freud is closer to the Augustinian tradition of suspicion of nonetheless unavoidable sex; his American introducer and follower, G. Stanley Hall, and American Freudians generally, are closer to sex-positive Protestant traditions that celebrate sex as an event with religious meaning). Gardella's attempt to define one central tradition, a spiritualizing of sex into ecstasy, specifically female ecstasy, in both Catholic cults of the Virgin and in Protestant focus on female conversion is interesting but somewhat overly organizes the great diversity of religious–sexual discussions he surveys.

66 Peter Gay, *The Bourgeois Experience: Victoria to Freud*, vol. I, *Education of the Senses* (New York: Oxford University Press, 1984) and vol. II, *The Tender Passion* (New York: Oxford University Press, 1986): Gay includes broad and useful summaries of sources at the conclusion of his work; Foucault's *Introduction*; Jeffrey Weeks, *Sex, Politics and Society: The Regulation of Sexuality Since 1800* (London: Longman, 1981), rethinks issues in social history by the light of Foucault's conception of sexuality; perhaps

because his work began with earlier studies of the emergence/production of homosexuality in the nineteenth century, Weeks's history of the "respectable" position is especially aware of its competitive place among diverse sexual systems; my own work has appeared in *Charlotte Brontë and Sexuality* – esp. pp. 1–6, ch. 1 – and in a parallel review of the scholarship, specifically the revision of earlier twentieth-century stereotypes, in "The Worlds of Victorian Sexuality: Work in Progress," in *Sexuality and Victorian Literature*, ed. Don Richard Cox (Knoxville; University of Tennessee Press, 1984), pp. 251–65. Similar points have been made in work by Carl N. Degler, Morse Peckham, R. S. Neale, and F. Barry Smith (see *Charlotte Brontë and Sexuality*, p. 229), as well as in the seminal article by Peter Cominos, cited below. A more recent critique of the modernist position, interestingly from a feminist view, is offered by Christina Simmons, "Modern Sexuality and the Myth of Victorian Repression," in Peiss and Simmons, eds., pp. 157–77. The success of the very different approaches to a critique of earlier twentieth-century stereotypes of Victorian sexuality by such very different historians as Gay, Foucault, and Weeks allows a study such as the present one to proceed directly beyond the preliminaries of revising the old stereotypes, as I indeed felt obliged to do in my view of Brontë's interesting secular thinking on sexuality. Because both Gay's work (in a broad European–American context) and my own (for England) offer rather full summaries of scholarship in the various sub-topics of sexuality, I have not repeated general background references to the field here but concentrated on specific documentation or more recent work. Specifically, for works on the general history of sexuality, see my *Charlotte Brontë*, pp. 225–26, to which should be added especially works by Weeks (nn. 2 and 4, above), Coward (n. 7, above), Paglia (n. 3, above), Caplan (n. 4, above), Harpham (n. 17, above), and Niklas Luhmann's somewhat too vague and Parsonian sociological study, *Love as Passion: The Codification of Intimacy* (Cambridge: Polity Press, 1986), works on English history, marriage, and Puritanism (n. 83, ch. 3, below), recent books on sex and religion cited above in this chapter. For works on the general Victorian period, the studies by Gay and Weeks cited above should be added, and also Sander L. Gilman's interesting essays in connecting discourses, *Difference and Pathology: Stereotypes of Sexuality, Race, and Madness* (Ithaca: Cornell University Press, 1985). On the Victorian sexual underworld, see my p. 225; on prostitution, pp. 226–27 and works cited in n. 5, ch. 2, below; on medical attitudes to sexuality, my p. 230, Mort's work cited n. 2 above, Laqueur's work cited n. 56, above, and articles in *Representations*, 14 (Spring 1986), pub. 1987 as a separate volume, *The Making of the Modern Body*, by University of California Press, and, on contraception, Angus McLaren, *A History of Contraception from Antiquity to the Present Day* (Oxford: Basil Blackwell, 1990) – also Sander L. Gilman's book on representation, *Sexuality: An Illustrated History* (New York: Wiley, 1989); on homosexuality, my p. 277 and works cited in n. 13, ch.

3, below; on sexuality and literature, my pp. 230–32, work on the prostitute in literature cited in n. 53, ch. 2, below, and esp. Nancy Armstrong, *Desire and Domestic Fiction: A Political History of the Novel* (New York: Oxford University Press, 1987), Gay Daly, *Pre-Raphaelites in Love* (New York: Ticknor and Fields, 1989), John Kucich, *Repression in Victorian Fiction* (Berkeley: University of California Press, 1987), Robert M. Polhemus, *Erotic Faith: Being in Love from Jane Austen to D. H. Lawrence* (Chicago: University of Chicago Press, 1990), and essays in Regina Barreca, ed., *Sex and Death in Victorian Literature* (Basingstoke: Macmillan, 1990) and in Cox, ed.; on censorship and prudery, my pp. 228–29; on pornography, p. 228, to which should be added Kendrick's work (n. 14, discussed, n. 70, below). I have not tried earlier or here to catalog the very large number of books on the related issues of gender difference, patriarchy, feminism, mothering and fathering, the family, population statistics, or the history of psychiatry – all nonetheless clearly of relevance to sexual issues.

It should be said that there is perhaps now a danger, which I have tried to answer in beginning with Clough's debate with this position, in not giving enough play to the "respectable" positions that come closest to the conservative religious, prudish, and/or pseudo-scientific discussions of sex earlier ascribed to all Victorians. Gay is distinctly involved in finding evidence to support his universalistic, generally Freudian, views of sexual experience; Mabel Loomis Todd's complicated record of intercourse up in Amherst (volume I) or the happy married sex life revealed in the correspondence of Alfred and Emma Wickham Roe during the Civil War (Volume II) are given very heavy weight in his overview, as the Mosher survey of some late Victorian women's sex lives was in my own earlier work (see James MaHood and Kristine Wenburg, eds., *The Mosher Survey: Sexual Histories of 45 Victorian Women* [New York: Arno Press, 1980] – also used by Gay along with the statistical work of the Scot J. Matthews Duncan, *On Sterility in Women* [1884]). Gay does offer a useful survey of the variety of conservative medical positions of the nineteenth century (I, 145–68, on women's sexuality; 294–327, on fears of masturbation and sexual education), but his own commitment to one prominent discourse that developed out of the broad gestation of ideas of sexuality in the nineteenth century, that of Freud himself, is of course written into the very structure and method of his work and places him ultimately as a committed critic of the conservative and especially the religious tradition of sexual discourse in a way, say, that Peter Brown is not in his attempts to recover the thought of the celibate tradition in early Christianity. Flandrin was probably correct in his response to Edward Shorter's similar revisionist view in reminding us that the presence of the Church in Catholic countries, and of varieties of conservative Christian discourse in religiously pluralistic countries, continued to play an important role in creating by repression the subjective world of sexuality in the modern mind: "Christianisme" was the "éducation sentimentale" of the West (see *Le Sexe et l'Occident*, pp, 279–300). Foucault's brilliant opening of the nineteenth-century discourse, which does accept much of it as negative to sex in attitude but clearly demonstrating a great and ever growing interest in producing a world of sexuality, is nonetheless limited in not leaving sufficient space for self-conscious diversity and controversy within that discourse. Foucault's own position, like that of all of us, is indeed involved in the development of the complex discourse of the nineteenth century, so it would have been much harder for him to exercise the meticulous and controlling historicism of his studies of sexuality in ancient Greece or Rome, or even of his earlier inquiries into other, earlier, phases of the modern mind. The historian of the contemporary mind has to risk calling fire even on his or her own position, as I have been aware of doing in risking my personal tradition of skepticism about religion in exploring these Victorian versions of what is obviously a universal phenomenon.

67 All modern historians of medieval sexuality are clear about the large gap between various Christian doctrines and the external reality – a reality of much fornication, for instance, that Church authorities despaired of eliminating. In this the Victorian respectable sexual position, and the purity crusade that followed it, should be understood as involved, even in their rhetorical excesses, in a centuries-old practical attempt to find some ideology strong enough to exert some control over the world of sex out there. Jacques Rossiaud offers a look at the flagrant and abominable practice of gang rapes in fifteenth-century France, generally tolerated as an outlet for young male sexual energies and as a gross form of "rough music" social control over signs of female independence among the poor: "Prostitution, Sex and Society in French Towns in the Fifteenth Century," in Ariès and Béjin, pp. 84–86. The realities of Victorian social life can be garnered amply from Walter's history; or if this seems too excessive not to be in part fiction, one can turn (at the *top* of the social structure) to Charles Greville's diary account of Lord Hertford on the occasion of Hertford's death:

> There has been, as far as I know, no example of undisguised debauchery exhibited to the world like that of Lord Hertford, and his age and infirmities rendered it at once the more remarkable and the more shocking. Between sixty and seventy years old, broken with various infirmities, and almost unintelligible from a paralysis of the tongue, he has been in the habit of travelling about with a company of prostitutes, who formed his principal society, and by whom he was surrounded up to the moment of his death, generally picking them up from the dregs of that class, and changing them according to his fancy and caprice. Here he was to be seen driving about the town, and lifted by two Footmen from his carriage into the Brothel, and he never seems to have thought it necessary to throw the slightest veil over the habits he pursued . . . [E]very day at a certain hour his women, who were quartered elsewhere, arrived, passed the greater part of the day, and one or other of them all the night in his room.
>
> (*The Greville Memoirs*, ed. Lytton Strachey and Roger Fulford [London: 1938], pp. 5, 19–21, quoted in Richard D. Altick, *The Presence of the Present* [Columbus: Ohio State University Press, 1991], p. 596)

The implication in the word "veil" is that Hertford was more remarkable in his age for the openness of his habits than for the habits themselves.

68 Peter T. Cominos, "Later Victorian Sexual Respectability and the Social System," *International Review of Social History*, 8 (1963), 18–48, 216–50. Marcus cites primarily Acton's *Functions and Disorders of the Reproductive Organs* (London, 1857), giving Action unreal centrality in the secular discussion as in the broader, usually religious-oriented, conservative outlook. As a doctor committed to regulation of prostitution Acton was, despite his "respectable" views on female passion, the proponent of a specialized attitude to prostitution which would come under very strong criticism from the mass movement of opponents of the Contagious Diseases Act, who despised both the male inspection of prostitutes and the implicit tolerance of fornication. The crusaders, a powerful political force, were themselves only another controversial position in the varied Victorian display of opinions on sexual issues.

69 The discussions below of four varied, Victorian writers will reveal that the so extensive and influential Christian conservative tradition stemming from the major Church Fathers and especially from Augustine (and in the special case of Patmore, the medieval mystical tradition) was far more centrally positioned as the discourse against which they reacted than a modern pseudo-scientific version of conservative "respectable" positions in a writer like Acton. Clough and Kingsley, as well as Hardy's Jude, found this tradition in the revival of patristic learning in the Tractarian movement, which they experienced as both seductive and deeply troubling. Patmore, a Catholic convert, eventually responded more directly to the even more complex Catholic tradition itself.

Gay, who rightly criticizes the tendency to take Acton as a representative figure, is insufficiently sensitive to the strength of the diverse and age-old Christian discussion in shaping and empowering nineteenth-century formulations; when the wide net of his research into nineteenth-century writers on sex pulls up a number of medical discussions of sex that use religious arguments and a wide range of expert works on sex written not by doctors but by ministers or priests, he notes them, even identifying a new medical–religious genre, without particular remark (I, 304–6, 322, citing, among others, Dr. William Alcott, a physician who recommended the gospel to outwit Satan, a Dr. Cooke, author of *Satan in Society*, the Catholic Carl Capellmann, author of a work translated into English as *Pastoral Medicine*, and Sylvanus Stall, a divine who wrote on sex for the young as late as the turn of the century). His Freudian approach instead turns him to biography as explanation of the genesis of ideas (which are in any case unimportant in themselves because the definition of sexual nature has been definitively provided by the correct discourse that did emerge from the century, the Freudian one) but leaves intact a fairly simple historical structure: medieval Christianity as primarily a repressive force was overturned by the successive attacks of the Enlightenment and the Romantic period (II,

48–51). The tone of his allusion to the Mary tale as "the boldest, most picturesque family romance ever concocted" contrasts strongly to Freud's own very thoughtful and even hesitant explanations in a work like *Moses and Monotheism*. Jeffrey Weeks shows a similar confusion between his awareness of the importance of religious thinking in the nineteenth century and his failure to give it proper centrality in his history of sexuality. In *Sexuality*, for instance, he notes that "medicine and psychology, sexology and pedagogy, took on a role, alongside the Churches, of establishing moral and social standards"; yet he doesn't even list religion in his summary of societal forces shaping sexuality: pp. 12, 27–31. His position in *Sexuality and Its Discontents* is even more conflicted. On the one hand, he sees a new secular discourse of the eighteenth century becoming a scientific discourse in the nineteenth; on the other hand, his own argument deconstructs such pretensions to a science of sexuality based on essentialist views into only so many myths (in Barthes's sense of a myth as an attempt to make discourse natural). But he doesn't probe the consequences of this view, which is that the "scientific" discourses have in fact a similar status to the religious ones, except to quote Alfred Kinsey's penetrating observation on the frequent identity of both religious and scientific discourses: "scientific classifications . . . nearly identical with theologic classifications": pp. 65–66.

Two more recent studies of the conflicting discourses on sexuality in the nineteenth century, Frank Mort's history of the competing and changing attitudes toward sexuality and disease from 1830 to the current discussion of AIDS and Linda Mahood's more narrowly focussed approach to the similarly conflicted discourse over prostitution in Glasgow (cited n. 2, above), have more adequately indicated the continuous and complex interrelations of religious and medical discussions of sexuality. Mahood, p. 33, sees medical reformers casting their regulatory arguments in what she calls a medico-Christian discourse. Mort, on whose work she draws, offers a full history, in the area of disease control through sexual control, of the changing relations between religion and medical discourses: briefly, an alliance in controlling prostitution and the lower classes in the earlier part of the century, then an emerging separate medical discourse – as in Acton – that somewhat ignores moral issues by positing its own mythology in a firmer view of passionless females and sex-driven males that justifies a highly regulated system of prostitution as society's release valve (thus contradicting many religious writers' earlier stress on the value of married sexuality to both males and females), followed by a purity reaction that draws upon religious views and attracts religious support to attack the system of prostitution.

Ian Bradley, *The Call to Seriousness: The Evangelical Impact on the Victorians* (London: Jonathan Cape, 1976), pp. 121–22, discussed Evangelical writers on prostitution, including Thomas Scott and Baptist Noel. In her more recent search for a hegemonic Victorian discourse in the representation of women, Lynda Nead, pp. 155–64, looks at these writers and other Evangelical reformers who wrote on prostitution from a religious viewpoint, John Blackmore and J. Ewing Ritchie, as well as at the earlier William Logan and the Congregationalist Ralph Wardlaw. Her account comes perhaps closest to accepting the religious discussion as the still-dominant one.

There has also been some increasing recognition that medical and scientific discourses are not really different in kind from the traditional religious ones. In their Introduction to essays in *Body/Politics: Women and the Discourses of Science* (New York: Routledge, 1990), p. 9, Mary Jacobus, Evelyn Fox Keller, and Sally Shuttleworth point out that the "scientific" views of women's sexual nature in the nineteenth century were "animated by narratives" – that is, are themselves in the same area of discourse as religious dogmas or myths. Nead, p. 145, similarly looks at doctors' myths of the inevitable medical fall of the prostitute (challenged as a myth by Acton, it should be said, but then only for his different polemical purposes). See also works by Laqueur (on the history of the very ideology-driven development of the science of sexual anatomy) and Flandrin cited above, n. 56. See also Richard Sennett's discussion of Western views on autoeroticism as a reappearance of Christian formulas of subjectivity as explored by him and Foucault in their "Sexuality and Solitude," pp. 16–21.

70 Kendrick (cited n. 14, above), p. 65, interestingly traces ideas of obscenity in the early modern period as usually remarking a (to them even seditious) attempt to unhook sexual ideas from a broader context. It is precisely this deconstruction of systems that seems to mark secular thinking about sex: "one could now conceive of 'sex' in its own right, sorting it out from the moral, legal, and religious contexts in which it had hitherto been embedded." Yet it is just this conceptualization of sex as the parts without a larger meaning that makes pornography such a place of controversy. It implicitly raises the issue of "the separability of sex from all other activities" and usually receives an answer: "it [sex] is so complexly woven with the rest of life as to be separable only by fraud or violence." Yet, as Kendrick also notes, such a position has inevitably emerged in the modern world as an alternative view from, and a necessary point of view on, discussions of sex that still connect it to other areas of thought. Kendrick somewhat misreads Foucault in seeing competing sexual discourses as especially about power; the battles between opposing views on pornography are not so much wars over power as holy wars, with different systems of discourse, including the deconstructed one of sex parts, merely exhibiting their intrinsic conflict. The project, which Kendrick suggests, of separating sex from discourses on it is in some sense necessarily a project against language. Foucault's play of bodies and pleasures, Kinsey's statistics on sex actions move away from language, the one to an admittedly impossible description of sex plain and simple, the other to mere numbers. Similarly, a project such as

Lawrence's in *Lady Chatterley's Lover* to speak the facts of sex leads him logically to four-letter words as the nearest thing in language to the physical facts of sex. If we say more about sex, we begin to make again the kinds of connecting discourses we find everywhere in human culture. The repetitiveness and lack of formal, aesthetic interest in much pornography, which Marcus remarked in his discussion of pornotopia, derives from a fundamental disinterest in representation: pornography prefers to pretend to imagine it discusses the actual part as a thing not a signifier.

71 My indebtedness to the exceptionally intelligent and well-informed writing of another worker in this untilled if not entirely new field, Katherine Stockton, will be clear in my discussion and notes; I came to the work of Renée V. Overholser only as this was going to press but have been pleased to find in her fine work on Hopkins's presentation of sexuality constructions of discourse similar to my own. See her "'Looking with Terrible Temptation': Gerard Manley Hopkins and Beautiful Bodies," *Victorian Literature and Culture*, 19 (1991), 25–53. She generously read parts of this manuscript, though of course bears no responsibility for my faults.

2 FROM CLOISTER TO "GREAT SINFUL STREETS": ARTHUR HUGH CLOUGH AND THE VICTORIAN "QUESTION OF SEX"

1 *The Poetry of Clough: An Essay in Revaluation* (New Haven: Yale University Press, 1963).

2 Michael Timko's study of Clough's satire, *Innocent Victorian: The Satiric Poetry of Arthur Hugh Clough* (Athens: Ohio University Press, 1966), emphasized the "positive naturalism" that Clough asserts through his satire. Evelyn Barish Greenberger, *Arthur Hugh Clough: The Growth of a Poet's Mind* (Cambridge: Harvard University Press, 1970), studied the social and political assertion of Clough's prose.

3 See especially Warwick Slinn's reading, "Fact and the Factitious in *Amours de Voyage*," in his *The Discourse of Self in Victorian Poetry* (London: Macmillan, 1991), pp. 90–118, which the author kindly allowed me to read in manuscript. Anthony Kenny, *God and Two Poets* (London: Sidgwick and Jackson, 1988), has added a philosopher's respect for the breadth and seriousness of Clough's interactions with major issues of his age.

4 The clearest are Frederick Bowers, "Arthur Hugh Clough: The Modern Mind," *Studies in English Literature*, 6 (1966), 709–16, who generally recognizes Clough's outspokenness on sexual issues, and Wendell Stacy Johnson, *Sex and Marriage in Victorian Poetry* (Ithaca: Cornell University Press, 1975), pp. 79–86, who recognizes a pull between physical sexuality and idealism in Clough. Patrick Greig Scott, "The Victorianism of Clough," *Victorian Poetry*, 16 (1978), 32–42, argues rightly that we should not disconnect Clough from his milieu in the interest of calling

him modern. His argument on sexuality, pp. 36–38, however, is misdirected in that it implies that attention to Clough's unusual occupation in his writings with sexuality is a misreading of his Victorianism. Rather, Clough's way of agonizing over sexual issues is a part of Victorian experience that has been too much overlooked in our view of over-counter Victorians. Clough's satirical thrusts at simplistic sexual attitudes in some of his contemporaries place him among the rather large group of Victorian thinkers on sexual issues who found both conservative and liberal positions of the day on sexuality problematic.

5 Fraser Harrison, *The Dark Angel: Aspects of Victorian Sexuality* (New York: Universe Books, 1977), pp. 217–57, argues that the two nations of sexuality were somewhat coterminous with those of rich and poor, with both well-to-do men who accepted the double standard easily, or those who were driven uneasily by the repressions of their milieu to find sexual gratification elsewhere, resorting to working-class women. Walter of *My Secret Life* (New York: Grove Press, 1965) certainly looked on virtually all working-class women as potential recruits to prostitution. In this perspective, prostitution provided one place of meeting of a nation increasingly divided in two. Certainly this aspect of prostitution both interested and troubled Clough. The large areas of working-class prostitution exposed by the local studies of Judith R. Walkowitz, *Prostitution and Victorian Society: Women, Class and the State* (New York: Cambridge University Press, 1980), and Frances Finnegan, *Poverty and Prostitution: A Study of Victorian Prostitutes in York* (Cambridge: Cambridge University press, 1979), in which working-class women largely served working-class men, often from the army or navy, were, however, unlikely to have been known by Clough.

Linda Mahood's more recent, *The Magdalenes: Prostitution in the Nineteenth Century* (London: Routledge, 1990), looks at working-class prostitution more as a site of conflict in discourses on sexuality. In her view, working-class women are subject to a different controlling approach by middle-class (mainly) men: a combined religious and medical discourse against prostitution as a place of immorality and disease. Frank Mort, *Dangerous Sexualities: Medical-Moral Politics in England since 1830* (London: Routledge & Kegan Paul, 1987), on whose approach Mahood builds, looks more broadly at differing views of sexuality and disease in the period from 1830 to the AIDS epidemic. Lynda Nead, *Myths of Sexuality: Representations of Women in Victorian Britain* (Oxford: Basil Blackwell, 1988), devotes much space both to the representation of prostitutes in visual arts and to religious and medical discussions as well as to middle-class fears of prostitutes' intrusion in middle-class life and the male market economy. As I point out below, n. 30, Clough's attitudes to folk courting in Scotland also show no recognition of the very different world of urban prostitution explored by Mahood. For other references on prostitution see below nn. 25, 36, 54, 56.

6 Katherine Chorley, *Arthur Hugh Clough: The Uncommitted Mind: A study of his Life and Poetry* (Oxford: Clarendon, 1962), and Robindra Kumar Biswas, *Arthur Hugh Clough: Towards a Reconsideration* (Oxford: Clarendon, 1972).

7 Chorley, like Biswas, finds them in the concern with sin and allusion to childhood castration in a manuscript version of "Sa Majesté très Chrétienne" and in the first poem of "Blank Misgivings of a Creature Moving about in Worlds Not Realized" with its equation between the mother's first kiss and the will to sin: see Chorley, pp. 352–53. The habit, so frequent in biographers without psychological training, of diagnosing an entire person by a few passages taken out of context, especially here where one is a dramatic monologue, must be deplored. When viewed in relation to Clough's extensive sexual speculations, these texts, interesting as they are, appear as part of a larger anatomy of sexual attitudes rather than as signal neurotic revelations.

8 See esp. pp. 175–89, 337–39, as well as the discussions of "Natura Naturans," pp. 245–48, and *The Bothie*, pp. 279–80. Biswas follows Chorley's discussion of "Sa Majesté," p. 336; he adds a stress on disgust at excremental sexuality based on one notebook entry (see p. 177) that also tends to reduce Clough to a case study in neurotic fixation. Yet he can also recognize Clough's affinity to D. H. Lawrence in his openness to discussion of sexual questions: p. 181.

9 Biswas, p. 337, broadly traces this fear of pollution to the influence of a pious mother, the emotional force of Arnold's version of evangelicalism, and the Tractarian ideal of immaculateness (to which Clough was especially exposed by the excited disputations of his tutor and rather parasitical friend at Balliol, the future Catholic convert W. G. Ward, and by his own great admiration for Newman and his sermons at St. Mary's Church, which Clough frequently attended; when Clough failed to receive a fellowship at Balliol he found a place at Oriel, Newman's own college). These were three common kinds of influence variously at work in shaping the conservative system that Peter T. Cominos, "Late-Victorian Sexual Respectability and the Social System," *International Review of Social History*, 8 (1963), 18–48, 216–50, has called middle-class sexual respectability and that Steven Marcus in *The Other Victorians* broadly identified with the views of Dr. William Acton: especially stress on female asexuality, the advantages of abstinence, the dangers of masturbation. As a proponent of regulation and medical inspection of prostitutes, Acton took a more tolerant view of prostitution than many who shared his general views. As noted in the Introduction, Marcus has been rightly criticized for offering Acton, a conservative among Victorian thinkers on sex, as a representative of a monolithic norm; among conservatives Acton is also a special case in not being much interested in a religious basis for his discourse.

10 Conservatives such as Acton, who both discounted female interest in sex and saw a danger to males in too much sexual activity, hardly espoused

ideals of warmly sexual marriages. Other conservative, though not necessarily representative, medical or religious authorities could become hysterical at the idea of too much loss of sperm or, as in Catholic tradition, could label married sex indulged in for enjoyment as fornication. Again, this is not *the* Victorian position. As we will see, their equally respectable opponents were as prominent and vocal, or more so, especially the two writers studied in succeeding chapters, the very popular Charles Kingsley, and Coventry Patmore during the phase of his career when he authored the best-selling *The Angel in the House* – both of whom put forward an ideal of sexual love in marriage.

11 Quoted in Biswas, p. 128.

12 Biswas, p. 187, citing an article by J. Bertram.

13 *The Correspondence of Arthur Hugh Clough*, ed. Frederick L. Mulhauser (Oxford : Clarendon, 1957), I, 117, 315. Clough speaks of reading Sand's *Jeanne*; Biswas, p. 181, offers it as a source for *The Bothie*.

14 Anthony Kenny, ed., *The Oxford Diaries of Arthur Hugh Clough* (Oxford : Clarendon, 1990), p. 249; slightly earlier entries, p. 246, mention Swedenborg and the Bhavagadghita [*sic*], suggesting that Clough's broadening view of universal religion included awareness of the sexual element in other religions.

15 See *Diaries*: entries esp. on pp. 18, 36, 48, 52, 55–56, 63, 66, 73, 130, 137–39, 141, 146, 151, 158, 161–62, 165, 178, 187–88, 193–94, 196–97, 202, 211, 219–20, 222, 226–29, 231, 239–40, 246 seem to refer to his "darling pleasure," "my worst sin," almost certainly correctly identified by Kenny (pp. lxi–lxii) as masturbation, though individual entries may be uncertain; probably there should be included in this the monk's other fear, of nocturnal emission, since at least one entry speaks of a condition between sleep and waking. Clough specifically identifies this as a problem – temptation he had suffered from since 1833 – i.e., since close to the normal onset of puberty (he was about fourteen). Evidently he even discussed it later with his father and a surgeon as a pathology (*Diaries*, p. lxii). *The Bothie* refers to masturbation (see below). The letter to Blanche Smith before marriage, answering her comments on the coarseness of *Dipsychus*, admits that "feelings of the kind that repel and revolt you" possessed him "for lack of better" from age twenty to thirty-four (1839–53) "more or less" (quoted in Biswas, p. 440, from the Bodleian MS.). This equivocal admission that he was not "unsoiled" only opens more speculation as to what he actually means. The later date does suggest some experience beyond the earlier one of masturbation.

Kenny (pp. lxiii–lxiv) raises the issue of evidence for a relation with a local girl or (perhaps) prostitute, which could explain the age twenty in the confession to his wife. But the evidence is less clear here. There are references in 1841 (when Clough was in his twenty-second year) and after to a visit to a Susan at Woodeaton, which Kenny tentatively identifies as a fifteen- or sixteen-year-old daughter of a shoemaker, and many visits to nearby Shotover, one with a reference to a Bessie Gray, whom he has not been able to identify: suggestive but inconclusive. See n. 18, below, on the availability of prostitutes at Oxford. Finally, Kenny properly raises, from the language and concerns of the diaries, the issue of possible homosexual experience. He rightly sees Clough involved in male–male intimacies of the, of course, all-male institution that require the term love: the older Ward as well as Tylden somewhat bothering Clough with their attachments to him, while he is in turn disturbed by his attraction for his own younger student, Walrond. I would agree with his conclusion that an ambiguous reference in the diaries to "unnatural demonstrations" have reference to Clough's concern, already suggesting that of his future hero Claude, not to speak more than he feels – that is, demonstrate his affection thus unnaturally. On the complicated issues of homosocial and homoerotic, but often non-physical, relations between men in the nineteenth century, see n. 13, ch. 3. Clough's *Diaries* can be compared to G. M. Hopkins's *The Early Poetic Manuscripts and Notebooks*, ed. Norman H. MacKenzie (New York: Garland, 1989), also revealing attempts to control private forms of sexual release.

16 *Diaries*, p. 30. It should also be said that the stars in the diaries seem to become more routine, almost casual quick entries with at most a brief explanation suggesting tiredness or drink as a cause, as Clough moves away from the very earnest and self-accusing period of his first few years at Oxford.

17 *Diaries*, p. 56: a reflection of the day after he went "my full length."

18 Arthur J. Engel, "Immoral Intentions: The University of Oxford and the Problem of Prostitution, 1827–1916," *Victorian Studies*, 23 (1979), 84, estimates that there were perhaps 300–500 common prostitutes in Oxford and others, beyond the control of the university, in nearby towns. Chorley, p. 357, speculates that Venice may have been the scene of a "sordid adventure" with a prostitute on the part of Clough as well as Dipsychus. Obviously, as Engel's study shows, with Oxford's own unrivaled resources he had no need to go so far.

19 *The Poems of Arthur Hugh Clough*, ed. Frederick L. Mulhauser, 2nd edn. (London: Oxford University Press, 1974), pp. 35–38. All other references to Clough's poetry, hereafter cited in the text, are to this edition. This edition is substantially different from the 1951 edition by H. F. Lowry, Norrington, and Mulhauser (essentially the basis of the Oxford Standard Authors version of 1968), especially in providing the unexpurgated full text of *Dipsychus* that restores the central third scene of sexual discussion and temptation.

20 Chorley, pp. 91–93.

21 The poem was dated by Clough "In the Highlands, Sept[r]. 1847" in Norton's copy.

22 Clough resigned in October 1848 when he felt he could no longer subscribe to the Thirty-nine Articles, the condition of his fellowship (he had given up his tutorship at Easter 1848; the resignation of the fellowship was not accepted until February 28, 1849). He had planned,

in any event, to leave in Easter, 1849, when his fellowship expired, unless he took the further step of holy orders (Chorley, p. 95). In not taking that step Clough was choosing, quite apart from all religious scruples, a secular life, open to marriage, rather than the celibacy of the permanent don. "The Lawyer's First Tale" in *Mari Magno* celebrates a similar decision in favor of leaving college for fuller life. I suggest below the relevance of this decision to the poem of the same date.

23 Wendell V. Harris, *Arthur Hugh Clough* (New York: Twayne, 1970), p. 78. Chorley, p. 201, cites Tom Arnold that Clough went through "some violent mental or spiritual upheaval"; this could refer, however, to a religious crisis rather than an amorous one; probably, as my argument generally suggests, the two were both present and related in some manner.

24 Clough arrived in Rome April 16, 1849 and was there to witness the siege of the brief Republic; he arrived in Naples August 18, 1849. He then took up his new position at University Hall, London, but returned to Venice the next autumn. That Italy, the lovely vision of art and history mixed everywhere with a continuing life of communality and civility, should have provided the main theater for the kind of growth in understanding that Clough records, found in great sinful streets of Naples or narrow alleys of Venice, may seem a jarring and discordant fact. Why go to beautiful Italy for vulgar realities that London, and indeed Oxford itself, beneath its medieval spires, could abundantly proffer? Yet in the record of continuous productive interaction that Italy and England offers to us in the nineteenth as in virtually every century since the Middle Ages, Italy's place as a human bottom line, offering an unclouded vision of life in its essentials, has a special importance. For a Samuel Butler or a Browning speaker of "The Englishman in Italy" it was a place where people seemed to live closer to a natural and human order, without the falsities of English civilization. For Ruskin, who came to something like Clough's position over a long period of time, the sensuous realism and reality of Italy since the Renaissance long seemed a dangerous and even evil temptation, as it appears in his attempt to rescue that most sensuous Italian center, Venice, from its own magnificent Renaissance tradition. It was only a good deal later, in very worldly Turin, after enjoying the fleshly delights of Veronese's *Solomon and the Queen of Sheba* "glowing in full afternoon light. The gallery windows being open, there came in with the warm air, floating swells and falls of military music" that Ruskin too saw Italy as the happy and triumphant protagonist over his own narrow religious heritage: *Praeterita* (London: Rupert Hart-Davis, 1949), pp. 459–61.

25 Harrison, p. 217, cites Victorian estimates ranging from 65,000 to 100,000. Peter Fryer, in his edition of William Acton, *Prostitution* (New York: Frederick A. Praeger, 1969), pp. 17–18, considers most such reports exaggerated, presumably by contrast to Acton's citation of police reports. But Acton in fact believed that if full figures could be known "the estimates of the boldest ... would be thrown in the shade" (p. 36).

Gordon Rattray Taylor, *The Angel-Makers: A Study of the Psychological Origins of Historical Change 1750–1850* (London: Heinemann, 1958), p. 66, expresses similar doubts about Michael Ryan's contemporary estimate of 80,000–100,000. Peter Gay, *The Bourgeois Experience: Victoria to Freud*, vol. II, *The Tender Passion* (New York: Oxford University Press, 1986), p. 365, attributes the high estimates to middle-class hysteria and cites W. R. Greg's 1850 review of Parent-Duchâtelet in the *Westminster Review* as more reliable, though it in fact merely expresses similar skepticism. Without more reliable data the issue is likely to remain one of speculative debate. E. M. Sigsworth and T. J. Wyke, "A Study of Victorian Prostitution and Venereal Disease," in Martha Vicinus, ed., *Suffer and Be Still: Women in the Victorian Age* (Bloomington: Indiana University Press, 1973), pp. 77–99, moderately conclude that police statistics clearly are lower than the actual number but that it isn't clear that large figures of *c.* 100,000 are correct.

26 Chorley, pp. 235–37; Harris, p. 34. Harris's is an exemplary introduction to Clough in the Twayne series.

27 Having opened Pandora's box by reading the manuscript that Clough had asked her not to, Blanche wrote Clough: "I did hardly know that good men were so rough and coarse" and later added equally naive reflections on men's love being "so much less personal and enduring, less spiritual" than women's (quoted, Biswas, p. 439). Biswas sees in Clough's response a kind of personal reconstruction and notes that Blanche herself declared him "much improved" (p. 441). Certainly there was energy left over from his marriage for Clough to seek the famous secretarial work for cousin Florence that Strachey, perhaps not too extravagantly, presents as a kind of sadomasochistic distortion of sexual energies.

28 *North American Review*, 77 (1853), 2–5.

29 On the issue of the original title see Chorley, pp. 168–69; Clough, *Correspondence*, I, 185. Biswas says the definition of *fuosich* has been challenged, but doesn't indicate by whom. Clough's letters to Tom Arnold demonstrate the important point, that Clough understood the title to have this obscene meaning and changed it for the 1862 edition accordingly; Clough told Arnold that the man must have said "bairns'" (children's), which he had misunderstood as "bairds'" (probably for bards'), but Chorley explains *feusaq* as Gaelic "bearded" (well of the beard or bearded well, or as the man probably said, beard's well). The howler was first noticed in a review, "English Hexameters," *Literary Gazette*, 66 (Aug. 18, 1849), 606–7, reprinted in Michael Thorpe, *Clough: The Critical Heritage* (London: Routledge & Kegan Paul, 1972), p. 49, which restates the title as Bothie of Tobair na Feosag, attributes it to a "malicious Gael," and imagines some Scots readers now enjoying a "hearty guffaw." The review is rather merciless itself in wittily quoting back Clough's own line in light of the title's meaning: "Study the question of sex in the Bothie of What-did-he-call-it."

30 J. C. Smout's study of "Aspects of Sexual Behavior in Nineteenth Century Scotland," in A. Allan MacLaren, ed., *Social Class in Scotland: Past and Present* (Edinburgh: John Donald, 1976), pp. 55–85, interestingly shows that there was an unusually high rate of illegitimacy in Scotland that raised a Victorian debate over its causes. A Dr. J. M. Strachan explained the illegitimacy as the consequence of a different sexual morality among country working Scots. The pattern is really that associated traditionally with northern peoples, free courting, without chaperones, heavy petting, acceptance of sexuality after troth-plighting, occasional continuation of customs of bundling. A minister complained that, despite all his efforts, "there is no just sense of the soul-polluting, unmanly unwomanly nature of the sin" (quoted, p. 71). The bothie system, which brought farm laborers together in dormitory living apart from their families, was sometimes blamed for patterns of sexual freedom. Whether these qualities were unique to Scotland or also a pattern of unchanged rural England at the time is unclear. They follow some of Lawrence Stone's observations about permissive eighteenth-century patterns of behavior in his controversial *The Family, Sex and Marriage in England 1500–1800* (New York: Harper and Row, 1977) – observations that may themselves only hold true for parts of the society he studied. Jean-Louis Flandrin has discussed at length similar traditions (called *maraîchinage*) among the French peasantry in *Amours paysannes: Amours et sexualité dans les campagnes de l'ancienne France (XVIᵉ–XIXᵉ siècle)* (Paris: Gallimard, 1975); see also his summary of the literature for Europe in *Le Sexe et l'Occident: Evolution des attitudes et des comportements* (Paris: Editions du Seuil, 1981), p. 287. Lest all this suggest an unreal and arcadian picture of Scotland, it should be noted on the other side that the Kirk was often quite fierce far into the eighteenth century in exercising the traditional power of the Church of Scotland to seek out and punish vice and that prostitution was common in Edinburgh just as in London: see Norah Smith, "Sexual Mores and Attitudes in Enlightenment Scotland," in *Sexuality in Eighteenth-Century Britain*, ed. Paul-Gabriel Boucé (Manchester: University of Manchester Press, 1982), pp. 47–73. Linda Mahood's study of prostitution in Glasgow and the society's attempt to regulate and/or reform magdalenes paints a very different picture of urban sex in Scotland, much closer to the English experience.

Two earlier reactions to Scotland suggest Clough's especial interest was from the first in a perceived difference in sexual attitude. A diary entry (*Diaries*, p. 255) that includes the first use of the name of the poem also notices Scots girls showing their "Petticoats [up] to the knee or indeed a trifle over / Shewing their thighs" (used in book II of the poem with some changes); notebook entries (Bodleian) of early attempts at hexameters on the subject of *The Bothie* are about the ease of kissing a Scots girl in a boat: quoted in Patrick Scott, ed., Clough, *The Bothie* (St. Lucia: University of Queensland, 1976), p. 83. In both cases Clough's interest is not so much prurient as curious about a more relaxed attitude toward sex and the female body than he was familiar with. It is interesting to note that Clough's regular diaries, to which he had long secretly confessed his masturbation, perhaps other sexual experience, and even that discussion "[de sexualibus]" with Emerson, end with the beginning of his public statements on the question of sex in the first ideas and lines (above) for *The Bothie*.

31 Scott notes that Clough was deciding to give up his fellowship just at the time of composition of the poem. Adam is made graver and older than the tutor-author and Philip, who though only a student also decides to leave, is the focus of the author's interest. Clough's friends claimed that they recognized him in both parts, though Matthew Arnold also thought an older Dr. W. A. Greenhill was an original of Adam; and Tom Arnold, who had in fact emigrated, was another original of Philip (see Scott, ed., *The Bothie*, pp. 81–82).

32 Perhaps a special case of the general submergence of political issues in domestic or private ones that Nancy Armstrong has found in her study of the English novel: *Desire and Domestic Fiction* (New York: Oxford University Press, 1987). "Citizen Clough" of the forties henceforth has only a sideline role in his written work, including the special passivity of Claude's witness of revolutionary times in Rome in *Amours de Voyage*.

33 The 1862 version, in *Poems by Arthur Hugh Clough* (Cambridge and London: Macmillan), published by Clough's wife after his death, followed revisions Clough made for an American edition brought out with Ticknor and Fields in 1862 by C. E. Norton. This is the basis for Mulhauser's text. Scott, ed., *The Bothie*, presents a photocopy of the 1848 text with useful textual notes indicating readings from the manuscript, the first revises for 1848 and correction made there by Clough, and a copy of 1848 with layers of changes and corrections, similar but not identical to those in the 1862 version (all at Balliol). Clough's wife added some earlier lines back into the 1862 edition in the Macmillan 1863 second edition, which seems therefore a made-up text without author's authority. Scott, p. 24, offers a number of reasons to credit the 1848 edition as an alternative text; his position has been strengthened by recent discussion of textual principles that has increasingly questioned the orthodoxy of author's last intentions in nineteenth-century texts. A particularly good additional reason to consider readings from 1848 is the clear pressure on the later Clough, who is in some sense the more respectable editor of his own young man's work, to create a text less offensive to a prudish audience; indeed, his work on the revisions for the 1862 edition was specifically for a *Boston* audience. Although in my discussion of the poem I have given references to Mulhauser's still-standard text, I have cited readings from the earlier published edition, or the manuscripts, revises, and corrections (for simplicity, from Mulhauser's own textual notes where available) when revisions seemed to me *pro pudore*; the earlier texts in any case sometimes help to clarify Clough's intentions. Scott, "The Victorianism of Clough," p. 38, offers

Clough's revisions as an indication of his withdrawal from sexual issues, but embarrassment is not the same as withdrawal; Clough simply toned down his text without eliminating the sexual issues. Although the poem was generally well received on publication (Thorpe, p. 3), Clough had heard from readers such as his own superior at Oriel, the Provost Hawkins, who was troubled by parts that he considered "rather indelicate": *Correspondence*, I, 247–48; and the embarrassment and attention given to sexual issues from the title doubtless added further pressure.

34 In the 1848 edition this was adjusted: "to me" and "sexual honours." The use of "sex," "sexual," "sexuality" in the sense of erotic desire or activity as opposed to the differentiation of male and female, is a fairly recent one. The *OED* cites "act of sexual intercourse" in the 1799 *Medical Journal*. But this is close still to the root sense of "of the sexes." The first citation for sexuality in the erotic sense is Kingsley in 1848 in *Yeast*: "honest thorough-going sexuality." Clough's use of "sexual" here I take to be an early use of the newer sense, not a way of saying "female glory": certainly his experience is of his own response to the girl, not merely his sense of the glory of that sex.

35 Scott, ed., *The Bothie*, p. 38, takes sex in the first use here to mean the "*social* roles of men and women." Given the context, the potato-rooter episode as Philip's clear history of the development of his sexual desire, this seems a very unlikely reading of Hobbes's wit and the immediate occasion for study in the lines: Philip's being "smit." See n. 34 above, on the use of the word sex. Presumably the discussion with Emerson of summer 1848 "[de sexualibus]" was also, as Kenny translates, "about sex" as well as the sexes.

36 That is, in the positions represented by a work such as Acton's *Functions and Disorders of the Reproductive Organs* (London, 1857). As I indicate in the Introduction, the position taken by writers such as Acton, despite the prominence given to it by Marcus, was not a Victorian monolithic orthodoxy, as Clough's own disagreement with this conservativism shows; and among conservatives, Acton himself is not the only or even the central exponent; he merely represents one version (a highly articulate one) of the conservative "respectable" sexual attitudes on the attack in the 1840s and 1850s. Clough's work, of course, predates Acton's and is probably responding to "respectable" ideas in the air rather than to a specific work. It is also clear that he gives a larger place to religious thinking in the conservative positions than we find in Acton who, as Mort has stressed (p. 79), in effect tries to secularize the conservative discourse – far more than earlier medical writers such as Kay, who had more deliberately combined medical and religious views, as had religious writers on prostitution, as well (see n. 69, ch. 1). Harrison, pp. 42–50, 228, 256, notes that the dual idea of women as chaste angels and also as potential sex fiends appears frequently in conservative ideas of women's sexuality. Peter Gay, *The Bourgeois*

Experience: Victoria to Freud, vol. I, *Education of the Senses* (New York: Oxford, University Press, 1984), pp. 145–68, also summarizes the debate over women's sexuality; Gay offers striking evidence, in this volume and in his second, from personal writings of some individual Victorian women or couples – e.g., Mabel Todd – as well as from surveys of the period to suggest that Victorian female sexuality was not as different from that of males as some Victorian writers believed; he offers male insecurity and fear of women as an underlying reason for the conservative opinions. His argument is similar to Clough's in exposing the underlying failure of logic in the conservative position, which at best can only explain the lubricity of the fallen woman by an implicit identification of other women's asexuality with their lack of sex experience: the discourse that denies women's sexual desire is so strident because it must seek power to make sure it is never activated!

In a similar mode, Mary Poovey, "'Scenes of an Indelicate Character': The Medical Treatment of Women," *Representations*, 14 (Spring 1986), 137–68, explores physicians' hysteria over clinical displays of female sexual desire. See also her similar points about Greg's double thinking on female desire: "Speaking of the Body: Mid-Victorian Constructions of Female Desire," in Mary Jacobus, E. Fox-Kelley, and S. Shuttleworth, eds., *Body/Politics: Women and the Discourses of Science* (New York: Routledge, 1990), pp. 29–36. Peter T. Cominos, "Innocent Femina Sensualis in Unconscious Conflict," in Martha Vicinus, ed., *Suffer and Be Still: Women in the Victorian Age* (Bloomington: Indiana University Press, 1973), pp. 155–72, outlines the complex strategies by which Victorians were supposed to protect their daughters from ever making acquaintance with their sexual selves. His argument is both too schematic and too detached from the complications inherent in the plurality of Victorian sexual worlds. Even on the issue of female sexuality the excessive focus on Acton by Marcus has probably had a distorting effect in making the issue appear less controversial to the Victorians than in general it was. As Mort interestingly points out (p. 79), Acton diverged from the earlier medical–religious discussion by stressing female disinterest in sex (quite against many earlier religious writers of the century on medicine and sex who wished to maintain the importance of healthy sex for males and females in marriage). Acton could then justify a system of medically regulated prostitution as a necessary release for males – a position that purity and religious critics would find both immoral and irreligious.

In view of the strong arguments in Gay and Poovey, a position I also had developed previously after reading the Mosher survey of some Victorian women's attitudes to their experience of sex, I have not followed the conservative Victorian practice, followed by some feminist discourses of our age, of labeling Clough's sex desire, by difference, as "male," though it obviously involved him, especially in the later temptations to sex with prostitutes, in highly gendered worlds of

Victorian discussion of and experience of sex. His own mode, of questioning such ideological and cultural structures, makes it inappropriate to try to explain him by either a universal concept of maleness or one or another of our contemporary stereotypes of the Victorian male.

37 As the examination of Kingsley will show, the position, unlike that represented by both medical writers such as Acton and more religiously preoccupied conservative writers (whether doctors of divinity or of medicine), accepts the strength and necessity of the sex drive and celebrates its expression in marriage, but seems also to accept much of the conservatives' distrust of sex on every other occasion.

38 Houghton, pp. 107–8, first pointed out the Freudian implications of Elspie's images of the bridge and the river. See also the reading by Geoffrey Tillotson, "Clough's *Bothie*" in G. and K. Tillotson, *Mid-Victorian Studies* (London: Athlone Press, 1965).

39 Patricia Ball, *The Heart's Events: The Victorian Poetry of Relationships* (London: Athlone Press, 1976), p. 84, sees the image as about Philip's need to respect, not violate, Elspie's personality; yes, certainly, but in a sexual *and* emotional sense.

40 Scott, ed., *The Bothie*, p. 15, also notes a movement from realism to symbolic structures that allow larger patterns of meaning; there is a similar pattern of symbolic meaning structured into the pastoral allusions of the Latin epigraphs to each chapter, from Virgil, Horace, or Catullus: both worlds, of Bible and pagan greats, seem to endorse the lovers' idealism. Kenny, p. 119, similarly notes a divine hand at work here.

41 Blanche Clough fought hard to try to keep "Natura Naturans" from ever appearing in print (Chorley, p. 263n). Biswas, pp. 245–48, has discussed the poem at length. As Jean H. Hagstrum, *Sex and Sensibility: Ideal and Erotic Love from Milton to Mozart* (Chicago: University of Chicago Press, 1980), pp. 24–34, has shown, Milton's sexual passages in *Paradise Lost* provided a mode of acceptable erotic celebration, a tradition that could survive even nineteenth-century suspicion of earlier literature. *Paradise Lost* was not operated on by Bowdler. As I note in the Introduction, the issue of sexuality and the Fall had been for close to two thousand years the central, much fought-over battlefield for opposing views of sexuality in the history of Christian sexual thought. Clough was an advocate for *Paradise Lost* in an Oxford milieu, he told a friend, certainly hostile to Milton's "opinions or indeed character" and doubtful about his "greatness as a poet": *Correspondence*, ed. Mulhauser, I, 89.

42 Kenny, pp. 81–82, translates the work. His suggestion, with Biswas, that the female figure is Eros Pandemos or vulgar Aphrodite is perhaps not wrong but too mythic for the directness of the poem: she is as "pan," across, the people, in effect the power of sex with other people (with perhaps a look forward to the people Clough will meet most easily in his later poems, women of the people, prostitutes). Clough's complicated,

really rather competitive relation to the Bible as text is repeatedly apparent in his *Diaries*, where he keeps both quoting the Bible in his context and admitting and criticizing his temptation to interfere in the text, to "play with God's word" (p. 13) or to begin the rational reconsideration of the text that his knowledge of German criticism would eventually lead him into in depth. We have perhaps not appreciated sufficiently in general the competitive anxiety of influence that the Higher Criticism allowed to be directed at the ur-text of Western culture; Strauss and the later Renan in effect not only critique the text but, like Clough, are drawn to set up their own competitive gospels.

43 Clough's own experience with the democratic revolutions of 1848 at such close quarters completed his estrangement from politics as public activity, a movement already clear in *The Bothie*. In *Amours*, as in the earlier poem, the private world of (possible) marriage absorbs the public energies of the hero even before the failure of public heroic activity.

44 Arthur Hugh Clough, *Amours de Voyage*, ed. Patrick Scott (St. Lucia: University of Queensland Press, 1974), p. 7, gives an earlier variant. Scott's textual annotation usefully reveals the rather large amount of biblical parody and overwriting in Claude's allusive and difficult discourse, much of it suggesting his half-hidden anticipation of the happy fulfillment in love that he will not achieve. Clough's prefatory poem to Canto III even alludes to the Song of Solomon. Clough's tendency to paraphrase and overwrite biblical texts even ran into James Russell Lowell's mild censorship in regard to l. 143–46. Many of Clough's unused manuscript lines for Claude carry this tendency even further and were perhaps withheld by Clough himself as likely to offend orthodox religious sensibilities. Here again, Clough's conception of an American audience for publication in the *Atlantic Monthly* may have further inhibited him. Although "banned in Boston" is a slogan for a somewhat later, Comstockian period, Clough would have been aware he was writing for progressive people, sympathetic to him, but of Puritan background; more important, he would not have wanted to offend a friendly, foreign audience.

45 In context the line refers to the monastic life Claude observes, with some attraction, in Rome; yet it also reminds us of unreformed Oxford and Clough's own location in the Tractarian hub of Oriel College. John Purkis, ed., *A Selection from Arthur Hugh Clough* (London: Longmans, 1967), rather understandably annotated the line as about "the celibate fellows of Oxford Colleges rather than monks in Rome": corrected by Scott, ed., *Amours*, p. 33. In an unused draft Claude demonstrated his, and doubtless Clough's, own limited sympathy with the monastic ideal; after the return of Catholic power to Rome he sees the Church sacrificing its secular victim for Easter and repeats the line on mild monastic faces, now noting the fierce smile over the sacrifice that momentarily interrupts their mild peace: Scott, ed., *Amours*, p. 72.

46 Of recent studies of the complicated play of language in *Amours*, the best

is Warwick Slinn's deconstructive reading, a sympathetic account of the intensely skeptical and probing texture of Claude's utterances. See also the earlier article by John Goode, "Amour de Voyage: the Aqueous Poem," in Isobel Armstrong, ed., *The Major Victorian Poets: Reconsiderations* (London: Routledge & Kegan Paul, 1969), pp. 275–97.

47 Clough knew the term from two uses of it in the Epistle of James, with its reference to a sinner's unclean and divided state: another indication that the poem is not simply about an intellectual division: Kenny, p. 139; as noted above, the Greek is used repeatedly in the *Diaries* from as early as 1838.

48 The poem was to have been quoted further after VII.15, possibly, as Houghton, p. 191, argues, along with some of "Easter Day II."

49 The Freudian reader will find it hard to avoid the blasphemous sense of Christ not risen as phallic impotence (the common sexual wordplay on raising the dead, etc.). I doubt, but am not entirely sure, that the idea would have occurred consciously to Clough. Certainly, as I note below, there is a psychological connection, rather directly observed by Clough, between sexual frustration and religious belief, with aggravated sexual demands threatening religious belief as much as loss of religious belief threatens sexual continence. The failure to achieve phallic potence because of religious repression could bring in reprisal the "relief" of denying the whole religious scheme.

50 See n. 22 above. Hawkins did not in fact accept the resignation until rather close to this date, February 28, 1849.

51 Kenny, pp. 82–88, provides a most helpful reading of the biblical undertext to Clough's cancelling rewriting. As usual, Clough is very close to a wide range of biblical texts, here mainly from Paul and the New Testament Gospels.

52 Peter Brown has written an attractive history of the many versions of such aspiration to a desexualized but blissfully resurrected self, usually a bodily self included, in Christianity before Augustine: *The Body and Society: Men, Women and Sexual Renunciation in Early Christianity* (New York: Columbia University Press, 1988): discussed in my Introduction, above.

53 As Fryer notes in his Introduction to Acton's *Prostitution*, prostitution was beyond the pale of ordinary Victorian public discussion as late as the 1850s. Obviously *Oliver Twist* or *Mary Barton*, even *David Copperfield*, discuss fallen women, but not the realities of their trade. To discuss one's temptation to prostitutes was decidedly beyond propriety, even in the freer genre of poetry, and probably explains why Clough withheld publication more than any hesitations he may have had over *Dipsychus'* religious iconoclasm. Clough's private opposition to reticence about prostitution is clear from his assessment of Gaskell's *Ruth* as a little too timid. That work was considered sexually bold in the early 1850s (see Chorley, p. 261). On the literature of prostitution see Eric Trudgill, *Madonnas and Magdalens: The Origins and Development of Victorian Sexual*

Attitudes (New York: Holmes & Meier, 1976), ch. 11 and George Watt, *The Fallen Woman in the Nineteenth-Century English Novel* (London: Croom Helm, 1984) – a study of a few major works. In the 1840s and 1850s what treatment there was focussed on the fall, sin, and redemption of the poor magdalene. In the 1860s discussion was somewhat more open, primarily in the form of sensation novels and talk-of-the-town articles about fashionable courtesans, as also in poetry in a work like D. G. Rossetti's "Jenny," which was not harshly received despite Buchanan's notorious attack (see Trudgill, pp. 228–29).

54 Prostitution proved indeed to be the most difficult sexual issue for the conservative "respectable" middle-class sexual morality that was emerging aggressively in the early and middle Victorian period. The difficulty is clear in Acton himself, who, as a physician interested in regulating prostitution, generally downgrades and represses sexuality but still realistically accepts the need of prostitution as the necessary outlet for male passions that might otherwise infect the home. This rationale for preserving the old double standard comes increasingly into conflict with the anti-sexual ideas that Acton and those of his persuasion were promulgating. Acton, as Mort has interestingly shown (p. 79), attempts to assert a more secular position on regulation of prostitution than had earlier medical reformers such as Kay, who worked with religious leaders of various Anglican and especially dissenter Churches to create a jointly religious and medical discourse against vice and disease. Acton justifies a regulatory system that accepts the necessity of prostitution as an outlet by diminishing female sexuality in marriage (which earlier religious writers on prostitution had defended as a good) and certifying male need. This almost inevitably courted a disagreement and backlash from religious thinkers who had earlier worked with physicians for health regulation. The rift emerges historically in the campaign of Josephine Butler against the Contagious Diseases Act, the act supported by physicians like Acton to control and regulate the necessary vice of prostitution. Mort (pp. 93–110) underlines the powerful religious base to Butler's argument or those of Elizabeth Blackwell, author of *The Human Element in Sex* (1884). On the purity movement generally see Paul McHugh, *Prostitution and Victorian Social Reform* (New York: St. Martins, 1980). Given their general disparagement of sex, the regulators had little they could answer to the moral assertions of the repealers that men and women should both avoid illicit sex, except to restate the easily attacked argument that prostitution is the sewer system of male sexuality (see n. 56, below). The crusaders' reasonable position, with its demand for male and female celibacy before marriage and very restrained sexuality in marriage, eventually led to the abandonment of the entire system of universal chastity as logical but unworkable.

55 See n. 36, above.

56 The division in Acton's own thinking is clear in his critique of the standard morality of the whore's descent that had been by and large

accepted by prior medical and religious writers. He noted, pp. 72–76, that prostitutes were often recycled into society: as a lucrative employment relative to other possibilities for women, prostitution attracted many who were also wise enough businesswomen to find a successful way out to a more stable occupation. In her study of prostitution in two southern seaside cities, Walkowitz similarly sees prostitutes as easily merging into their society, though not usually into the affluence Acton might have found among a few enterprising London prostitutes and courtesans. Finnegan's study of common prostitutes in York by contrast finds a more closed system. The difficulty in Acton's realism about prostitution is that it threatens to undermine his unrealism about non-prostitutes' virtual disinterest in sex, a weakness, again, in the general thinking of many sexual conservatives that Clough exploits. If prostitutes are people, then their unfallen sisters might be people, too. A second problem in Acton's social thinking somewhat helps justify the apparent callousness of the Spirit's realism. An argument against regulation was that it tended to freeze the prostitutes' positions as labelled and socially managed outcasts. By contrast, the vulgar humanism of the Spirit's position at least avoids creating such a restricting sexual class. Alain Corbin, "Commercial Sexuality in Nineteenth-Century France: A System of Images and Regulations," trans. Katherine Streip, *Representations*, 14 (Spring 1986), 209–19, explores the implicit meanings in the language used by Acton's predecessor in regulation in France, Alexandre Parent-Duchâtelet (1790–1836), which included the whore as total outcast, an infection, a dead body still present in society, as well as a servant and a public sewer. (The last is a metaphor that goes back at least as far as Aquinas, who used it to justify the need for prostitution: "Take away the sewer and you will fill the palace with pollution": quoted, D. S. Bailey, *Sexual Relations in Christian Thought* [New York: Harper & Brothers, 1959], p. 162.) Mahood has also stressed the development of a dehumanizing and destructive view of the prostitute as "an alien" in her study of middle-class attempts to control working-class prostitutes in Glasgow (p. 10). See also Walter Kendrick's chapter on French regulation in *The Secret Museum: Pornography in Modern Culture* (New York: Viking, 1987). Sander L. Gilman looks at extreme discussions that combined racist stereotyping of Africans and stereotyping of prostitutes into one image that attempted to label both as degenerate: *Difference and Pathology: Stereotypes of Sexuality, Race, and Madness* (Ithaca: Cornell University Press, 1985), pp. 76–108.

57 In this view of marriage as what you have to do to have sex if you can't accept prostitution, Clough implicitly satirizes the more liberal Victorian attitudes toward sex such as those espoused by writers like Kingsley and the Patmore of *The Angel in the House*, and to some extent by Clough himself in *The Bothie*. As I show for Kingsley, especially, their idealization of sex in marriage is a patent, and logically not entirely

tenable, compromise between their felt need for sex and their moral scruples about most of its manifestations. And, of course, Hardy's *Jude the Obscure* more bluntly satirizes this special position of marriage as a license to make love on the premises.

58 Cf. *Amours*, III. 179–80. Biswas, pp. 405–6, is perplexed by the nature of the demon of craving. I think it a clear reference to the sexual need raised so directly in the first three scenes. I believe Biswas is right in arguing the relatively higher quality of those early scenes over the rest of the poem, though wrong in trying to disturb the poem from its central place in the Clough canon despite greater recent critical interest in *Amours*. Many of the problems of plot or of the nature of the characters that have been raised by critics from Houghton on could be at least clarified by recognition of the controlling issue of sexuality in the poem. It provides the motivation for both the explicit discussion of prostitution in the opening scenes and for the broader discussion of gratification through conformity in the rest of the poem. Kenny (p. 145) sees three temptations, to carnality, aggression, and atheism, but this static formula overlooks the degree to which the last two are related to the initial temptation of the flesh: certainly religion, as we have seen, but even the much less discussed issue of aggression takes the form of a male–male confrontation with an Austrian soldier which raises, as in *Amours*, problems of defending women. Or Timko's view (p. 156) of the Spirit as representing the extremes of propriety and uncleanness to be avoided, for instance, doesn't sufficiently acknowledge the logic of his alternate positions as those developed naturally as answers to conservative Victorian sexual codes. The Spirit really endorses neither extreme. He represents more of a reality principle than an ideological position or positions. He tries to offer some solution to Dipsychus' sexual need within the confines of his confused standards. Dipsychus is ultimately forced to choose both extremes, not some better middle position.

59 *Dipsychus Continued*, written in the United States while Blanche was very much in Clough's mind, already shows Clough's movement toward rehabilitation through Blanche and concomitant stress on guilt. I think it is clear, however, that Dipsychus' double fall, as recorded in the continuation, is just what the first poem has led Dipsychus to. The ending of that poem clearly showed Dipsychus led off by the Spirit.

60 Indeed it has been identified as still implicit in Freud's thinking, where a rational self, there reduced to the ego, must deal with the id's different law of the body: Peter Gardella, *Innocent Ecstasy: How Christianity Gave America an Ethic of Sexual Pleasure* (New York: Oxford University Press, 1985), suggestively compares Freud's rather pessimistic thinking to Augustinian religious attitudes toward desire. Clough would have listed, and compulsively does list in his *Diaries*, a host of other, more social sins as warring against his better self. As Kenny notes, the Balliol reports on him are uniform in giving him highest evaluations for moral character; the impression of a reader of the *Diaries* is of excessive scrupulousness by a person whose major sin was against his own talents in being too kind

to his obsessive and emotionally devouring tutor, Ward; only the repeated and rather glaring star entries for masturbation keep telling Clough of a problem of the divided self that he could not master.

61 *Correspondence*, ed. Mulhauser, I, 284.

62 See, for instance, "Lie here, my darling, on my breast," p. 334.

3 SEXUAL CHRISTIANITY: CHARLES KINGSLEY'S *VIA MEDIA*

1 James D. Barry, for instance, gave Kingsley about three pages in the MLA guide (*Victorian Fiction: A Second Guide to Research*, ed. George H. Ford [New York: MLA, 1978], pp. 219–22), and then primarily to note his impending demise as a novelist for posterity. It is an inherent difficulty of such guides that they should force an assessment of a writer in one area – here the novel – rather than, as Kingsley deserves, for his overall place as a central Victorian voice.

2 His thinking and sexual biography have already found a useful place in Peter Gay's revaluation of modern ideas of Victorian prudery: *The Bourgeois Experience: Victoria to Freud*, vol. II, *The Tender Passion* (New York: Oxford University Press, 1986), 297–309. As two additional authentic and documented voices of sexual passion from the Victorian period, Kingsley and his wife Fanny Grenfell serve something like the function of Mabel Loomis Todd in Gay's first volume, a setpiece to show Victorians did enjoy sex. The Freudian universalist assumptions that bring Gay to look for sex as usual in the Victorian period also lead him to take little interest in Kingsley's discourse: he and his wife are cases for Freudian biographical explanation of a version of sublimation that Gay calls displacement: the indulgence of sexual instinct by associating it with a cultural activity, notably religion. Gay's protestations that he is not treating religious thought reductively seem to me obviously countered by his simple association of Patmore and Kingsley together in this chapter, who are very much at opposite ends of permissive Christian thinking about sexuality. (For more general reservations about the theoretical difficulties in this and other Freudian versions of sublimation see n. 54, ch. 4.)

3 Newman's long and difficult struggle for independence within the Church, culminating in his use of the Oratorian tradition in England to insulate himself from the restrictions and machinery of the regular orders, really a version of the English college of the nineteenth century, is well related by John P. Tricamo, "A Second Via Media: John Henry Newman: His Sojourn in Rome," diss. New York University, 1979.

4 A. Dwight Culler, Introduction, John Henry Newman, *Apologia Pro Vita Sua* (Boston: Houghton Mifflin, 1956), ix-xi. Norman Vance, *The Sinews of the Spirit: The Ideal of Christian Manliness in Victorian Literature and Religious Thought* (Cambridge: Cambridge University Press, 1985), pp. 35–41, sketches out the broader context of Kingsley's objection to Newman over issues of celibacy and marriage.

5 John Henry Newman, *Apologia Pro Vita Sua: An Authoritative Text; Basic*

Texts of the Newman-Kingsley Controversy; Origins and Reception of the Apologia; Essays in Criticism, ed. David J. DeLaura (New York: Norton, 1968), p. 349.

6 Kingsley, "Elizabeth of Hungary," unpublished, unfinished prose life with Kingsley's illustrations given as a wedding present to Fanny Grenfell, British Library, Add. 41296, f. 1v. This is the dedicatory letter to Fanny. An undated letter to a Dear Sir, British Library Add. 41298, f. 42, also admits that he longed at one time, probably also this time, "for Rome, + boldly faced the consequences of joining Rome."

7 _Apologia_, ed. DeLaura, pp. 299–300. The sermon on which Kingsley so provocatively commented in his 1864 review of volumes of Froude's _History of England_, "Wisdom and Innocence," was first published in _Sermons, Bearing on Subjects of the Day_ (Oxford: J. H. Parker, 1843). It was preached February 19, 1843, when Newman, of course, was still Protestant. There _was_ some material in the sermon for Kingsley to remember. In a sermon on Christians being wise as serpents if harmless as doves, Newman does speak ambivalently of both "sacramental confession and the celibacy of the clergy": these "aggrandize the priesthood" but "how can the Church be one body without such relation?"

8 _Apologia_, ed. DeLaura, pp. 312–13.

9 _Apologia_, ed. DeLaura, pp. 298, 313. Kingsley's wife, F. E. Kingsley, _Letters and Memories of Charles Kingsley_ (New York: Chesterfield Society, 1899), pp. 12, 29, confirms that Kingsley had focussed, when she first met him in 1839, on the ascetic element in the Tractarian movement.

10 "Note C," _Apologia_, ed. DeLaura, p. 235. Culler, Introduction, pp. ix–x, notes that Newman was in fact much more emotionally committed to celibacy, from adolescence on, than this remark would suggest, and that he deplored the loss of friends to marriage. If Kingsley knew something of Newman's personal life – and I know no evidence that he did – he was foolish to base a controversy on knowledge that he could not adduce in public argument.

11 E.g., Brenda Colloms, _Charles Kingsley: The Lion of Eversley_ (New York: Barnes and Noble, 1975), and Susan Chitty, _The Beast and the Monk: A Life of Charles Kingsley_ (London: Hodder and Stoughton, 1974). Chitty's account is the more helpful here. Robert Bernard Martin, _The Dust of Combat: A Life of Charles Kingsley_ (London: Faber and Faber, 1959), is still the standard account of Kingsley's life and general career. I have found no record of Kingsley actually hearing or meeting Newman – undergoing that very strong personal influence that further complicated the reaction of Clough, Arnold, and so many others. The sermon that provoked him was evidently known in published form only. There is an allusion, without name, to Newman in "a certain remarkable man," recently converted, who appears in _Yeast_, not, apparently, a portrait based on first-hand knowledge (Martin, p. 94). Newman took _Hypatia_ as a criticism of his general position and answered in _Callista_ (1855), but in

no direct or personal way: see Susann Dorman, "*Hypatia* and *Callista*: The Initial skirmish between Kingsley and Newman," *Nineteenth-Century Fiction*, 34 (1979), 173–93.

12 Chitty, pp. 52, 236. Gay, II, 302, attributes to Kingsley "homosexual panic" in a few of his writings.

13 As noted above, Clough's relations with his group of friends at Oxford suggest the same kind of clear affection without an explicit or apparently strong sexual element in a person who would quickly take a clear and sexual interest in women. There is in any case the difficulty of even defining what is meant by homoerotic feeling in a social and historical context where the concept of homosexual is, apparently, not developed. Of recent works, all indebted to Jeffrey Weeks, *Coming Out: Homosexual Politics in Britain from the Nineteenth Century to the Present* (London: Quartet Books, 1977), David F. Greenberg, *The Construction of Homosexuality* (Chicago: Chicago University Press, 1988), is a promising start in a very general survey. Eve Kosofsky Sedgwick, *Between Men: English Literature and Male Homosocial Desire* (New York: Columbia University Press, 1985), and Richard Dellamora, *Masculine Desire: The Sexual Politics of Victorian Aestheticism* (Chapel Hill: University of North Carolina, 1990), have both explored the area of male desire as something other than, or repressed away from, what we now define as homosexuality. Gay, II, 198–219, well explores some individual instances of homoerotic or homosexual experience. See also Louis Crompton, *Byron and Greek Love* (Berkeley: University of California Press, 1985) and the essays in Martin B. Duberman, M. Vicinus, and G. Chauncey, eds. *Hidden from History: Reclaiming the Gay and Lesbian Past* (New York: NAL, 1989). We continue to need more information, which is most difficult to come by, on the degree to which there was already a sub-culture in existence by, say 1850 or 1860, that was self-aware and, absent the name, not so different from modern homosexual enclaves. The danger of our vague thinking here, added to the Victorians' own, is clear enough in both Chitty and Gay on Kingsley and Newman. Gay finds "an erotic ingredient, half joyful and half desperate" in Newman's relation with his friends (II, 236; one wishes *so* much to have Newman's own answer to such another unclear statement about Newman's private life); Chitty believes Kingsley may have reacted against a homoerotic attraction to Newman. But, as noted above, there is in fact no evidence that the Cambridge student even heard him; the sermons he speaks of reacting to seem to have been read.

14 Quoted, Chitty, p. 47.

15 See Arthur J. Engel, "Immoral Intentions: The University of Oxford and the Problem of Prostitution, 1827–1916," *Victorian Studies*, 23 (1979), 79–107; I am assuming relatively similar conditions held at Cambridge, though a similarly detailed study of the other gentleman's university would be desirable.

16 Quoted, Chitty, p. 57. The letter is in the collection of Charles Kingsley's Letters to his Wife at the British Library, at Add. 62552, f. 177

(henceforward cited as Letters with accession number and folio; the total, important collection is Add. 62552–57. It was used extensively by Chitty in a then private collection and in its present location by Gay; for a brief description see C. J. Wright, "'My Darling Baby': Charles Kingsley's Letters to his Wife," *British Library Journal* 10 (Autumn 1984), 147–57. Kingsley is explicit about his not bringing a "virgin body" to his marriage; the experience with a prostitute is the biographer's assumption; Gay, II, 299, who doesn't note this letter, on the dubious authority of material in the novel *Yeast*, assumes a variety of experience; this is possible, though Kingsley's level of guilt suggests he in no way became accustomed to a secret life.

17 Chitty, p. 59.

18 Nice Diary, manuscript diary (including time at Nice) kept by Fanny Grenfell from October, 1842 to September, 1843 as letters to Charles during their enforced separation, with one entry in 1846, private collection of Angela M. K. Covey-Crump: entry for October 22, 1842; Letters, Add. 62552, ff. 71, 46v; Chitty, p. 74. They were married in early 1844; Fanny's entry for July 4, 1843 speaks of four years loving Charles "soul and body."

19 Letters, Add. 62552, f. 97.

20 Letters, Add. 62552, f. 100.

21 Letters, Add. 62552, f. 65; Charles was bothered because of continued guilt over indulgence in his earlier sexual experience; both he and Fanny admitted shyness about appearing naked before the other and he expressed some fear of the man being "struck powerless . . . by modest awe, at the holy thing wh is at last his own": ff. 181v–182.

22 Chitty, p. 159: he claimed to be able to see Ruskin's sexual failure in his face. He was similarly critical of Carlyle, whom he otherwise revered.

23 Letters, Add. 62552, ff. 100, 159v; Add. 62553, f. 41. On this evidence Gay, II, 307–8, assumes the marriage was consummated the first night.

24 Letters, Add. 62552, f. 37v.

25 James MaHood and Kristine Wenburg, eds., *The Mosher Survey: Sexual Histories of 45 Victorian Women* (New York: Arno Press, 1980). In his useful search for authentic voices of Victorian sex Gay finds Kingsley an attractive example; of course Kingsley is not a typical Victorian, as Gay's also universalistic Freudian assumptions might suggest, any more than prudes and celibates (e.g., Fanny's sisters) of the period were, but, as I suggest, a voice from a particular experience and ideology – though clearly a very popular one in his time.

26 Letters, Add. 62553, f. 190.

27 Letters, Add. 62552, f. 130: "how much may be done in a moment *we know!*"

28 "Elizabeth of Hungary," f. 1v.

29 Letters, Add. 62552, ff. 162–63. Susan Casteras confirms the impression we have in Kingsley that the revival of nunneries among Protestants greatly agitated English imaginations; many renditions of nuns in art

appeared in the 1840s, usually focussed on the repression of sexual feeling in the nun: "Virgin Vows: The Early Victorian Artists' Portrayal of Nuns and Novices," *Victorian Studies*, 23 (Winter 1981), 157–83. Walter L. Arnstein, *Protestant Versus Catholic in Mid-Victorian England* (Columbia: University of Missouri Press, 1982), pp. 62–73, 108–22, tells the story of Charles Newdegate's rather hysterical attacks on Catholic nunneries, first over fears of licentiousness, later from fears of excessive severity. The Protestant foundations would develop in numbers substantially over the century: 6 were founded between 1845 and 1851, 9 more between 1851 and 1858, and 15 more by 1900. Newman had accepted the idea of an Anglican sisterhood as early as 1835, though it was Pusey who encouraged them in the early 1840s and they were sometimes called "Puseyite nunneries."

30 Letters, Add. 62552, ff. 62v, 57, 69, 43. See ch. 1 for a brief summary of the Christian history. Peter Brown, *The Body and Society: Men, Women, and Sexual Renunciation in Early Christianity* (New York: Columbia University Press, 1988), pp. 160–77, confirms Kingsley's view of the early third-century Origen; he sees him as a major turning-point in early Christian thought away from tolerance of marriage and sex and toward the more extreme positions of the desert ascetics or even Augustine himself.

31 Letters, Add. 62552, f. 183f. More: the Cambridge Platonist of the seventeenth century.

32 Letters, Add. 62552, f. 208v.

33 Letters, Add. 62552, f. 66. "My beloved is to me a bag of myrrh, that lies between my breasts." As we have and will see, interpretation of the sexual matter of the Song of Solomon was a central issue in the Victorian period that continued sexual discussions in Judaism and Christianity that had been going on for thousands of years; it is rather a pleasure to find one where the work is *not* rationalized as the love of God for Israel or for mankind.

34 "Elizabeth of Hungary" (described n. 6, above), f. 2v. Elaine Pagels's chapter on "The Nature of Nature," *Adam, Eve, and the Serpent* (New York: Random House, 1988), pp. 127–50, gracefully summarizes the earlier debate.

35 Nice Diary, entry for December 10, 1842. Charles's influence as a lover may have been spontaneous; the education of Fanny was deliberate; he writes to his mother in 1841 of Fanny's involvement with "the worst *doctrinal* features of Popery Mr. Newman professes to believe in – Help me to wean her from this pernicious superstition": British Library, Add. 41298, f. 14v.

36 Letters, Add. 62552, f. 159v.

37 Letters, Add. 62552, ff. 201v–202.

38 Chitty, p. 81.

39 Chitty, p. 85.

40 Letters, Add. 62553, f. 56.

41 Letters, Add. 62552, f. 150.

42 Letters, Add. 62553, ff, 128, 211.

43 Letters, Add. 62553, f. 169.

44 Nice Diary, entry for Feb. 21, 1846. Fanny expresses her own fears that this may not last but adds a reassuring P.S.: "I forgot to say we are fitting up a new nursery for our darling."

45 His italics; Letters, Add. 62552, ff. 119–20, 23–23v.

46 See Ian Gibson, *The English Vice: Beating, Sex and Shame in Victorian England and After* (London: Duckworth, 1978). The much more developed and explicit case of Swinburne is well known.

47 Letters, Add. 62552, ff. 113v, 188v; the night was All Saints Eve, 1842, shortly after Fanny's forced departure abroad. Scourging was evidently still a recognized form of (extreme) religious mortification in the nineteenth century; Gladstone also resorted to self-flagellation when, after rescuing prostitutes from the streets, he was disturbed by feelings of temptation himself: Gay, II, 387, citing the *The Gladstone Diaries*.

48 Letters, Add. 62552, f. 126.

49 Nice Diary, entry for September 10, 1843; an entry of December 9, 1842, looks forward to their union as the way to stop "The scourging . . . Oh how I long to kiss away the stripes."

50 Letters, Add. 62552, ff. 201v–202; and this is mainly a metaphor for male-dominant intercourse, not in fact a private sadistic rite. Other letters after marriage show concern on both sides not to overdo ascetic activities; and there is even a reminder from Fanny, acknowledged in one of Charles's letters, that he doesn't fast and pray enough as part of his normal Anglican life: Letters, Add. 62553, f. 89.

51 British Library, Add. 41296.

52 "Elizabeth of Hungary," ff. 9, 12.

53 Letters, Add. 62553, f. 99.

54 Chitty, p. 66.

55 *Letters*, II, 56. Kingsley had criticized Anne Brontë's *The Tenant of Wildfell Hall* for its coarseness and *Shirley* for its opening satire on clergymen. For Kingsley on *The Bothie* see *Fraser's Magazine* (Jan. 1849), 39, 103–10; reprinted in Michael Thorpe, ed., *Clough: The Critical Heritage* (London: Routledge & Kegan Paul, 1972), pp. 37–47; he deliberately compares Clough's wholesome poem, with its central focus on a love story and its faith that this world's facts are put there by God, to the "pale and sickly bantling" of the Tractarian school of poetry found in Keble, Newman and others' anthology, *Lyra Apostolica*; he praises Elspie's "intense and victorious energy" and answers the allegation of "any supposed impropriety" with "*Honi soit qui mal y pense*"; see also *Letters*, I, 168. *The Bothie*, of course, unlike Clough's later works, comes very close to Kingsley's own idealization of sexual marriage. Gaskell's *Ruth* Kingsley called a pure book: Letters, I, 323.

56 Kingsley, "Plays and Puritans," in *Plays and Puritans and Other Historical Essays* (London: Macmillan, 1889), pp. 1–83.

57 John C. Hawley, "Charles Kingsley and Literary Theory of the 1850s," *Victorian Literature and Culture*, 19 (1991), 165–86, has made the point that Kingsley sacrificed permanent fame for contemporary importance – a trade-off he himself came to recognize later in his career.

58 *Letters*, I, 222.

59 *Letters*, II, 54.

60 *Letters*, I, 224. As I note in my Introduction, Catholic ideas of social relations between individuals in heaven in fact varied widely over time.

61 On the very complicated issue of early Christian debates over sexual attitudes see the discussion and references in my Introduction.

62 *Letters*, I, 227, 361.

63 *Letters*, II, 116; the full original is Letters, Add. 62552, f. 147v.

64 Letters, Add. 62552, f. 69. I discuss a few of Milton's ideas in my Introduction above. For a concise account of sexuality in *Paradise Lost* and an assessment of Milton's influentiality as a source of positive sexual norms see Jean H. Hagstrum, *Sex and Sensibility: Ideal and Erotic Love from Milton to Mozart* (Chicago: University of Chicago Press, 1980), pp. 24–34. On issues of sexuality in Milton see James Tuner's comprehensive study, *One Flesh: Paradisal Marriage and Sexual Relation in the Age of Milton* (Oxford: Clarendon, 1987). Colleen McDannell and Bernhard Lang, who draw on Gay's discussion in their *Heaven: A History* (New York: Random, 1988), pp. 228–75, place Kingsley's attitudes toward love in heaven in the broader nineteenth-century context of humanization of heaven. Michael Wheeler, *Death and the Future Life in Victorian Literature and Theology* (Cambridge: Cambridge University Press, 1990), offers a full study of the large literature of Victorians' assertions about the debates over the nature of heaven: Kingsley's preoccupation with the afterlife was shared by many theologians and writers of his age.

65 *Letters*, II, 116; the full original of this letter is Letters, Add. 62552, f. 147v–148. Kingsley also found the ideas on heaven of Swedenborg attractive in their suggestion of survival of usual human experience: Letters, Add. 62553, f. 98.

66 Letters, Add. 62552, f. 147v. This is the letter that specifically cites Milton as an authority in dealing with Jesus' statements on marriage in heaven in Matthew.

67 *Letters*, II, 116.

68 *Yeast: A Problem* (London: Macmillan, 1881), p. 273; hereafter cited in the text.

69 This is cited in the *OED* as the first use of "sexuality" in our modern erotic sense of referring to the physical intercourse of the sexes (as opposed to the sense of gender). As noted in ch. 2, Clough used it in this sense in *The Bothie* in the same year.

70 *Alton Locke: Tailor and Poet: An Autobiography* (London: Macmillan, 1881), I, 245; hereafter cited in the text.

71 The historical Hypatia was in fact brutally murdered by a band of monks loyal to the prominent ascetic leader, St. Cyril of Alexandria.

Cyril's championing of asceticism in the Eastern Church merged with his successful advocacy against Nestorius of a more exalted position for the Virgin Mary, thus furthering the Church system of asceticism and virginity that Kingsley abhorred.

72 Kingsley, *Hypatia or New Foes with an Old Face* (London: Macmillan, 1881), II, 227; hereafter cited in the text. On *Callista* and *Hypatia* see above, n. 11. *Westward Ho!* (1855) is more concerned with the adventure of Elizabethan nationalism than with Kingsley's habitual themes of sexual immortality. The discussion of sex, as we shall see, is more about the problematics of debased sexual customs than about Kingsley's central sexual religion.

73 Kingsley, *Two Years Ago* (London: Macmillan, 1881), II, 446; hereafter cited in the text.

74 Kingsley, *Hereward the Wake: "Last of the English"* (London: Macmillan, 1881), II, p. 340; hereafter cited in the text.

75 Kingsley, *Poems* (New York: J. F. Taylor, 1890), p. 78; all poems cited hereafter in the text are from this edition.

76 For instance, "The Weird Lady" (p. 227) and "The Poetry of a Root Crop" (p. 232). "Hexameters" (p. 304), using Clough's favorite poetic meter and one of his favorite themes, both of which Kingsley had approved, celebrates the return of the old Edenic time when there will be again no shame in passion.

77 Peter T. Cominos, "Late-Victorian Sexual Respectability and the Social System," *International Review of Social History*, 8 (1963), 18–48, 216–50, has called the more conservative position, with its stress on minimizing sexual activity in marriage and on the asexual nature of respectable women, the system of sexual respectability. The more specifically religious movements, whether of Tractarianism or ascetic aspects of Catholicism itself, stood of course somewhat outside, and often socially above this general position, but the broader effect of their interest in religious celibacy was necessarily on the side of the respectable, conservative tendency.

78 Kingsley, *Westward Ho! or the Voyages and Adventures of Sir Amyas Leigh, Knight, of Burrough in the County of Devon, in the Reign of her Most Glorious Majesty Queen Elizabeth Rendered into Modern English by Charles Kingsley* (London: Macmillan, 1881), I, 103; hereafter cited in the text.

79 *Letters*, I, 295. On the general and very strong resonance of this myth for Victorian (usually male) writers see Adrienne Munich's excellent *Andromeda's Chains: Gender and Interpretation in Victorian Literature and Art* (New York: Columbia University Press, 1989). Her study of Kingsley's poem, pp. 55–74, focusses on the way in which the myth enacts Kingsley's system of gender difference, the use to which one ostensible subject of the sexual bond (Aphrodite) is put to create a certain kind of patriarchal structure of society (announced by Athene) – albeit a liberal one in which women are given different but empowering roles. Obviously Kingsley used female voices to register *his* view that this was

the ideology commanded by the universe: bound to seem now a suspicious argument for a male author's point of view. Here as elsewhere Kingsley's tendency is to criticize and then eliminate all other possible cultural structures organizing sexuality and thus to suggest that one system, his own, is a necessary one: the poem in fact celebrates the destruction of an earlier Eastern system and its replacement by the Greek one symbolized by Perseus. I discuss Kingsley's broader relation to feminist issues of his day below.

80 *Letters*, I, 164.

81 Kingsley, *The Roman and the Teuton: A Series of Lectures Delivered Before the University of Cambridge* (London: Macmillan, 1891), p. 38. It is worth noting in passing that Kingsley hangs a great deal on the evidence of Tacitus' praise of the women of the Northern tribes and he overlooks the Roman (and Roman Christian) concern for the dignity of marriage; the implication in his system, that Protestantism uncovered a traditional Northern faith in monogamous sexual marriage that had been briefly repressed by Roman influence in the Catholic Church, also very much simplifies his own English situation, making his liberal position the norm and erasing the history of continuing conservative or even ascetic positions in his country with which he was in fact actively quarreling.

82 Kingsley does not deal with the issue of the origin of courtly love in the South, not North. He would perhaps have claimed the Cathars as early Protestants. Although *The Saint's Tragedy* speaks of courtly love, Kingsley would doubtless have seen that tradition as a deviation from the chivalric marriage tradition he attempts to trace back to the Goths. The Platonic aspect of courtly love, certainly its adulterous direction, would be troubling to him; he would resist seeing in his own views a certain unusual channeling of sexual energies into marital sexuality by the force of an idealism somewhat akin to that generated in courtly love. Instead, like more recent theorists of "English married love" (see next note), he would see courtly love as a mere stage, caused by a system that didn't allow persons to marry for love, in the historical progression toward the new norm of married love.

83 Kingsley's concern with the Puritan art of love, far from seeming eccentric today, is fundamental to major controversies over the nature of marriage and the family in Puritan times. His view of the affective marriage in this period, followed in effect by Ronald Mushat Frye, Charles H. and Katherine George, William and Malleville Haller, and Levin L. Schücking, was challenged by Lawrence Stone's *The Family, Sex and Marriage in England 1500–1800* (New York, Harper and Row, 1977) that argues for a later date for the affective family based on companionate marriage. From another view the stress on contrast between Puritan and Catholic marriage has been criticized by Kathleen M. Davies "'The Sacred Condition of Equality' – How Original Were Puritan Doctrines of Marriage?" *Social History*, 5 (1977), 563–80, as overstated. In *A Happier Eden: The Politics of Marriage in the Stuart*

Epithalamium (Ithaca: Cornell University Press, 1990), ch. 1, Heather Dubrow has reasonably argued a compromise position for Renaissance thought in England – that there is almost certainly more than one discourse within each religious group in such a complex age.

Kingsley reads English sexual history generally as a special case; the case itself has been often repeated by contemporary scholars. See especially Jean-Louis Flandrin, *Families in Former Times: Kinship, Household and Sexuality*, trans. Richard Southern (Cambridge: Cambridge University Press, 1979), who also contrasts Catholic and liberal Puritan positions. Alan Macfarlane's *Marriage and Love in England: Modes of Reproduction 1300–1840* (Oxford: Basil Blackwell, 1986), who disagrees with Stone's revisionist view, argues the uniqueness of the English case from an anthropological analysis, and also argues, as Kingsley in effect does, for a very early date for that uniqueness. Laurence Lerner, *Love and Marriage: Literature and Its Social Context* (New York: St. Martins, 1979), applies the same argument of uniqueness generally to literature, as of course have many critics of individual English writers including those on the Renaissance, cited above, who discuss English marriage as a union of love and sex. For other references, see Gay, II, 503.

84 Kingsley, "Sir Walter Raleigh and His Time," *Plays and Puritans*, p. 141.
85 *Letters*, II, 255–56, 278–83. I should note his less congenial fears that the movement will be hurt by association with either disreputable (i.e., fast) women or with sexually repressed, hysterical women; one grants even here, though, that both associations have of course frequently been used by conservative opponents of feminism. Nikki Lee Manos, "Kingsley's Notorious Yeast," paper delivered to New York College English Assoc., November 13, 1987, offered a helpful, balanced view of Kingsley's sympathetic, though not in any clear sense feminist, position on women's issues.
86 See Kingsley, "The Science of Health," *Sanitary and Social Lectures and Essays* (London: Macmillan, 1880), p. 35.
87 In Kingsley, *Sanitary and Social Lectures*, pp. 7–18.
88 This is repeated in "Thrift," *Sanitary and Social Lectures*, pp. 77–104. Munich's study of "Andromeda," noted above, n. 79, offers a very cogent exposure of the legislating *for* women that lies beneath even Kingsley's rather empowering prescriptions of active roles for women.
89 See my *Charlotte Brontë and Sexuality* (Cambridge: Cambridge University Press, 1984).
90 *Letters*, I, 197.
91 "Plays and Puritans," p. 27; *Two Years Ago*, II, 320.
92 William Acton, *Prostitution* (New York: Frederick A. Praeger, 1969). As Cominos notes, the more secular versions of the "respectable" conservative sexual attitudes of the mid-Victorian age represented by a medical writer such as Acton were tolerant of prostitution as a necessary evil, as many traditional religious commentators had been, including Aquinas. As noted above (n. 54, ch. 2), the medical vision of regulation eventually came into profound conflict with the purity ideals of reformers

for repeal of the Contagious Diseases Act, whose views were closer to Kingsley's on prostitution.

93 Kingsley is interestingly, and characteristically, open in raising this issue despite his conventional and conservative opinion. He recognizes an entire culture of homosexuality in the ancient world and notes that his own society had not yet even given it a name: homosexuality as a term, and in many ways as a full concept of a sexual nature or type accepted by society as a whole, did not come into general specialized use until the end of the century and into common use until the twentieth. As noted above, it remains unclear how widespread were sub-groups of homosexuals in the nineteenth century and to what degree they had a consciousness of themselves as sexually distinct. The view that there were only homosexual acts, not homosexuals or a recognized set of sexual practices, often justified by the fact that the law punished sodomy not homosexuality, runs immediately into contradictory evidence that sodomy itself could be used to refer to a variety of sexual activities: Jeffrey Weeks, *Coming Out: Homosexual Politics in Britain, from the Nineteenth Century to the Present*, p. 10 (see n. 13, above); see also his broader study, *Sex, Politics and Society: The Regulation of Sexuality since 1800* (New York: Longmans, 1981). Dellamora and Sedgwick attempt interestingly to write a history of various forms of masculine desire in a period when the conceptualization of homosexuality is still to us unclearly unclear.

94 As noted above, Chitty, pp. 52, 236, suggests his friendship with Mansfield at school was a homosexual infatuation and that the attack on Newman sprang from his fears of his own tendency to effeminancy. Colloms, *Charles Kingsley*, p. 169, discusses the issue of his brother Henry Kingsley's possible homosexuality. His story "Jackson of Paul's" is in any case an accepted classic of early literature about homoerotic attraction (what Henry Kingsley calls "boy-friendship" – i.e., close bonding between boys in the English school system). The issue was raised by R. L. Wolff in *Harvard Library Bulletin* (1959), 13, and is well discussed in John Barnes's survey of Kingsley, *Henry Kingsley and Colonial Fiction* (Melbourne: Oxford University Press, 1971); see also the discussion of the story by William H. Scheuerle, *The Neglected Brother: A Study of Henry Kingsley* (Tallahassee: Florida State University Press, 1971), pp. 50–51. Kingsley followed a somewhat disreputable set at Oxford, then emigrated to Australia, then offended his brother by marriage to a woman and family whom Charles and Fanny considered beneath them.

95 See Maureen Duffy, *The Erotic World of Faery* (London: Hodder and Stoughton, 1972), pp. 283–84. As Chitty notes, her other sexual interpretations are much more questionable.

96 Kingsley, *The Water-Babies* (New York: Dodd Mead, 1910), p. 172.

97 See esp. John S. Haller, Jr. and Robin M. Haller, *The Physician and Sexuality in Victorian America* (1974: rpt. New York: Norton, 1977), pp. 196–224.

98 I give a very brief and cursory summary of this complicated intellectual

and religious history in the Introduction. I have found Peter Brown's account of Paul's desire to keep his Christian communities within traditional Jewish practice on sex and marriage and of the later non-ascetic philosophy of stoic Christian marriage of Clement of Alexandria suggestive; Brown reminds us of the rather "silent majority" of married Christians, including clergy, in the early Church: pp. 44–57, 122–39. Kingsley is anything but silent and his position clearly would stand out among early Christian anti-ascetics, including Paul, for its outright enthusiasm for married sex and its joys. Even Julian, in his attempt to answer Augustine and demonstrate that sex was merely a part of the normal order of nature, not a force within a man's fallen nature working against his Christian self, shows little of Kingsley's enthusiasm for sexuality as a positive force, where Kingsley is really closer to both pagan or Jewish non-ascetic attitudes, or possibly to suppressed pro-sexual Christian groups (see n. 49, ch. 1).

4 KNOWN AND UNKNOWN DESIRE: COVENTRY PATMORE'S SEARCH FOR EROS

1 Basil Champneys, *Memoirs and Correspondence of Coventry Patmore* (London: George Bell, 1900), I, 21. In his *My Friends and Acquaintance: Being Memorials, Mind-Portraits, and Personal Recollections of Deceased Celebrities of the Nineteenth Century With Selections from their Unpublished Letters* (London: Saunders and Otley, 1854), Peter George Patmore continued to explain and support Hazlitt and continued to speak rather sensationally about the *Liber Amoris* episode (III, 171–88), doubtless assuring his book of sales. The Regency writer who lived on into the more reticent Victorian age also speaks very bluntly about the actual immorality of London, "where no married man in high life is thought the worse of or treated the worse, even by the female friends of his wife, for being suspected of having a mistress or two . . . where every *un*married man in high life is compelled to keep a mistress whether he likes it or not, unless he would put his character in jeopardy" (I, 229). Ian Anstruther's *Coventry Patmore's Angel: A Study of Coventry Patmore, his Wife Emily and The Angel in the House* (London: Haggerston Press, 1992) similarly notes, pp. 37–42, Patmore's involvement in his father's relation to Hazlitt – and interestingly suggests that Patmore's first publication immediately drew him into his father's old quarrels. Also interestingly, he ascribes the anonymous first issue of *The Angel* to Coventry's embarrassment over the current notoriety of his father's memoirs. (Seen only as this was in press.)

2 Champneys, I, 37–38.

3 Champneys, I, 42. Evidently her name was Cecilia.

4 Coventry Patmore, "Dreams," in *Courage in Politics and Other Essays*, ed. F. Page (Oxford: Oxford University Press, 1921), pp. 97–101. Elsewhere he speaks of "The whole of after-life depending very much upon how life's transient transfiguration in youth by love is subsequently re-

garded ": Coventry Patmore, *Religio Poetae Etc.* (London: George Bell, 1907), p. 143. See also the discussion of this theme in the early poems, below.

5 The only record of published work extant seems to be her *Hints to Maid Servants in Small Households, on Manners, Dress, and Duties*; running title: *The Servant's Behaviour Book* (London: Bell and Daldy, 1859), published under the pseudonym of Mrs. Motherly. Commentators speak of other books written under this name, including a *Nursery Rhymes* of 1859. Anstruther, pp. 5–25, offers an attractive portrait of Emily and her family background, based on some unpublished sources – though most were available to Champneys. He cites *Nursery Poetry* and *Nursery Tales* but without any information indicating he saw them. His suggestion that she co-edited *The Children's Garland*, indicated in title-page and catalogs as only by Coventry, is more serious. Again, he gives no evidence.

6 Champneys, I, 128, 137, quotes Emily on Patmore's "haughty manner," and her own mere "appearance of submission," and notes her personal strength in her role.

7 Quoted in Derek Patmore, *The Life and Times of Coventry Patmore* (New York: Oxford University Press, 1949), p. 65.

8 Quoted in Derek Patmore, p. 110 (at Boston College). Patmore expressed similar horror of homosexuality. See Champneys, II, 150. It is remarkable that Patmore would ultimately work his way to a vision of desire that nonetheless modeled man's (man and woman's, but certainly man's) relation to Christ in sexual terms. I have not chosen to reduce this to a release of a defense against latent homosexuality, because I find no clear evidence of the latter in Patmore. It seems rather an expansion of the idea of desire beyond normal polarities.

9 Champneys, I, 122.

10 Champneys, I, 211–12; II, 36.

11 Champneys, I, 213.

12 Champneys, I, 219.

13 See L[ouise] Wheaton, "Psyche and the Prophet," *The Catholic World*, 117 (Dec. 1923), 356: "What really happened was that the second Mrs. Patmore lived in conformity with her vow [of chastity], while for sixteen years the poet used the leisure now secured by his new circumstances, outwardly as a country gentleman improving his estates, inwardly living an ascetic and contemplative life." Sister Mary Anthony Weinig, SHCJ, *Coventry Patmore* (Boston: G. K. Hall, 1981), identifies the author as a friend of Bertha and Harriet Patmore as well as of the biographer Champneys. Earlier studies, e.g., J. C. Reid's generally authoritative *The Mind and Art of Coventry Patmore* (London: Routledge & Kegan Paul, 1957), pp. 27–28, were not aware of the importance of this article as a memoir based on family information; nonetheless it is obviously not at the level of authority that, say, a letter from Patmore discussing his unusual kind of marriage would be. Certainly all that we know of the second wife and the marriage suggests that sex was not an (important)

part of it. Conrad's notorious satirical allusion to Patmore as the "savage sentimentalist" father of Captain Anthony in *Chance* (probably an allusion to Patmore's bad relations with his son Milnes) focusses on the issue of unconsummated marriage. This, though blamed on the father, is the son's, not the father's; yet it suggests Conrad had smelled scandal in what he had heard of Patmore's marriage. It should be said, in light of Conrad's strong language, that the difficult relations with Milnes were not typical of Patmore's relations to his sons. His son by his third marriage, Francis J. Patmore, left warm recollections of his old father: "Coventry Patmore: A Son's Recollections," *English Review*, 54 (Feb. 1932), 135–41.

14 Champneys, I, 263.

15 Champneys, I, 144.

16 A Religious [Louise Wheaton], *A Daughter of Coventry Patmore: Sister Mary Christina, S.H.C.J.* (London: Longmans, 1924), p. 29. Wheaton, who speaks of help from Mrs. C. Patmore (third, surviving wife), is identified as the author by Weinig, p. 24.

17 [Wheaton], *A Daughter*, p. 190; cf. Aubrey Gwynn, SJ, "A Daughter of Coventry Patmore," *Studies* [Dublin], 13 (Oct. 1924), 454.

18 Champneys, I, 278; [Wheaton], *A Daughter*, pp. 131–46, discusses her careful reading and enthusiastic response to his work.

19 Champneys, I, 271; [Wheaton], *A Daughter*, pp. 90, 129–30, 180, 186, 189, cites poems.

20 Quoted Champneys, I, 271. The poems quoted in [Wheaton], *A Daughter*, focus repeatedly on the idea of union with Christ. One (pp. 91–92) speaks of resting on the "breast of God" rather than having to face the "fitful alternatives of fierce love / Short joys and griefs." Another (pp. 129–30) on the "Day of Profession" looks forward to the time when "thy Beloved shall be thine / And thou be His for evermore." It is worth noting that the nun refers in her poems to St. Teresa of Avila as a model, perhaps suggesting that ecstatic union was rather consciously in her mind from other sources than her father's work. See [Wheaton], *A Daughter*, p. 168. Patmore himself was familiar with St. Teresa and echoes her work in the ode "Eros and Psyche" in *The Unknown Eros*, but he alludes far more often to St. John of the Cross. On Patmore's relation to the Spanish mystics, see Reid, pp. 96–100 and n. 90, below.

21 [Wheaton], *A Daughter*, pp. 195–98; cf. Gwynn, p. 455, a similar, probably derivative, account. Obviously we must take the entire story of her blissful death, not just of her vision, with the skepticism due most saintly ends described by partisans.

22 Champneys, I, 276. [Wheaton], *A Daughter*, pp. 136–37.

23 Edmund Gosse, *Coventry Patmore* (New York: Charles Scribners Sons, 1905), p. 123; Champneys, II, 56.

24 Gosse, p. 27.

25 On the vexed issue of Hopkins's influence and Patmore's reaction see Claude Colleer Abbott, ed., *Further Letters of Gerard Manley Hopkins, Including his Correspondence with Coventry Patmore* (2nd edn.; London:

Oxford University Press, 1956), pp. xxxiv–xxxix, xli, 361, 385–86, 390–91, and Derek Patmore, pp. 199–201. Hopkins was bothered by the misapprehension possible with such material – "abuses high contemplation is liable to" – and cited specific sexual problems: sex acts in contemplation, nuns identifying sex and "divine union," Hindu practice. He advised Patmore to consult his spiritual director: which Patmore did (seeing a Dr. Rouse) and found no objection; however, he then decided to destroy the prose work. Abbott's earlier preface, written for the 1938 first edition, understates Hopkins's influence; he was unaware of the contents of the letter of August 21, 1885. Anstruther, p. 100, speaks of the destroyed work as odes, but it seems to have been prose. Whether a collection of odes, on the Virgin, was ever written beyond what is indicated in "The Child's Purchase" remains unclear.

26 Champneys, II, 88; I, 316; italics Patmore's.

27 Derek Patmore, p. 150. The boys were not on the trip. Derek Patmore is correct to assume a propriety in Patmore's long and very likely entirely platonic relation with Robson before his wife's death.

28 Champneys, I, 249–62; II, 79–89: identified by Weinig: the letters indicate that Harriet was not always within the family.

29 Derek Patmore, p. 148. He gives this as the complete *Eroticon Biblion Society* collection, privately printed. It is worth noting that Patmore's patron had been Lord Houghton, one of the great private collectors of pornography – after whom his eldest son, Milnes, had been named.

30 Derek Patmore, p. 205.

31 Derek Patmore, p. 207. Other letters speaking of "*the cultivation of mutual love*" as "that greatest of natural delights within the limits of even the highest Christian perfection" are printed in Champneys, II, 130–37.

32 Weinig, p. 98.

33 Reid, p. 28; Champneys, I, 347.

34 Patmore published an essay on "Mrs. Meynell" as a woman of genius in the *Fortnightly Review*, 1892. She had also been mentioned in an 1889 essay on "Distinction." Both are in Coventry Patmore, *Principle in Art Etc.* (London: George Bell, 1912). Meynell in turn brought out a badly needed selection of his poems in 1895.

35 Derek Patmore, pp. 206–7, prints two letters in which Patmore speaks of her "phantom trouble" (Jan. 3, 1893) and assures her of his continuing love as "in former days"; p. 207 prints a note, evidently accompanying a gift, offering "renewal of entire love and fidelity, which have never been broken for a moment."

36 Quoted in Weinig, p. 99: evidently letters to Louise Wheaton.

37 Quoted in Derek Patmore, p. 234.

38 In "Mrs Meynell's New Essays," in the *Saturday Review*, of June 1896; reprinted in Coventry Patmore, *Courage in Politics and Other Essays*, ed. F. Page (Oxford: Oxford University Press, 1921). The letter supporting Meynell for Poet Laureate is also reprinted, pp. 200–1. Meynell had originally published the poem in the *Pall Mall Gazette* in 1895.

39 Quoted in Derek Patmore, p. 235.

40 Patmore, *Religio Poetae*, p. 165. The collection was originally published in 1893.

41 Derek Patmore, p. 238.

42 Derek Patmore, p. 238.

43 Coventry Patmore, *The Rod, the Root, and the Flower*, ed. Derek Patmore (1950; rpt. Freeport, New York: Book for Libraries Press, 1968), p. 44; first pub. in 1895 by G. Bell.

44 Gosse saw a break; Frederick Page, *Patmore: A Study in Poetry* (1933; rpt. New York: Archon, 1970), argues for continuity, even creating a textual story without textual evidence, that many odes were drafts for *The Victories of Love* (see pp. 109–12). Reid's more judicious study of Patmore's "ideas" takes them as a unit without much regard for their period in Patmore's work. Terence Connolly's useful handbook, *Mystical Poems of Nuptial Love* (Boston: Bruce Humphries, 1938), an avowed work of Catholic piety to a Catholic writer, not surprisingly stresses the growth and change in a Catholic context. E. J. Oliver, *Coventry Patmore* (New York: Sheed and Ward, 1956), also presented as a Catholic work, takes a rare middle position stressing a unity of temperament and to some extent of ideas while noting the major shifts of Patmore's life.

45 See Weinig, p. 30.

46 Letter to Patmore of October 13, 1884: *A Catalogue of the Library of Coventry Patmore Lately Purchased by Everard Meynell* (London: 1921), item 444.

47 See John Holloway, "Patmore, Donne, and the 'Wit of Love'," *The Charted Mirror: Literary and Critical Essays* (1960; rpt. New York: Horizon, 1967), pp. 53–62. For Praz's reading, which also draws parallels to Donne, see "The Epic of the Everyday," in his *The Hero in Eclipse in Victorian Fiction*, trans. Angus Davidson (New York: Oxford University Press, 1969), pp. 413–45.

48 Peter George Patmore, *Chatsworth* (New York: Harper, 1844), pp. 14–15.

49 "Winter" (i.iii), *The Unknown Eros* in Coventry Patmore, *Poems*, ed. Frederick Page (London: Oxford University Press, 1949), 354–55. Further references to the poems in *The Unknown Eros* will be given in the text by volume and number without the unnecessary apparatus of page numbers. Neither Patmore nor Page provided line numbers. Page's text is essentially a reprint of Patmore's final *Poems*, without serious attempt at editing or annotation – and with no attempt to grapple with the major issue of Patmore's incessant revisions.

50 It is worth noting here the familiar argument of literary post-structuralism that all texts generate, by their very nature as texts, multivalent significance. The point here is only that one is, nonetheless, more or less aware of an authorial intention asserted by the shape of the work or the discussion in it. As I shall show, Patmore's early texts seem especially written by the literary traditions in which he writes rather than by any very evident author's intention. If they rather often

deconstruct themselves, it is especially not as a subversion of the author's view but in the sense that we find very evident discrepancies between differing perspectives not necessarily in dialogue with each other.

51 The obvious analogue for us, as it was consciously for Patmore, was of course Wordsworth's Immortality Ode, thus sexualized by Patmore. Seventeenth-century writers' concern with sexual paradise and sexual fall and a counterbalancing search for a paradise within, as well as the specifically sexual quest for religious perfectionism in the nineteenth and twentieth centuries, suggest broadly similar quests for renewal of paradise within, more or less sexualized. See Peter Gardella on perfectionism: *Innocent Ecstasy: How Christianity Gave America an Ethic of Pleasure* (New York: Oxford University Press, 1985), esp. pp. 66–67, 86–90, 92–94, 159–61.

52 Patmore, *Poems* (London: Moxon, 1844), p. 104. Poems from this volume are hereafter cited by page in the text. The prodigal pen suggests Patmore's sense that his sexual exploration became increasingly complicated as it led him into more and more language. One such complication is the anxiety over manipulating that prodigal pen in the first attempts to bring the glory of sex into this world that later readers hear as guilt over masturbation.

53 Georges Bataille, *Erotism: Death and Sensuality*, trans. Mary Dalwood (San Francisco: City Lights, 1986), originally pub. 1957 as *L'Erotisme* and trans. 1962 as *Death and Sensuality: A Study of Eroticism and the Taboo*.

54 The classic discussion is Freud's *Leonardo da Vinci and a Memory of His Childhood*, in *The Standard Edition of the Complete Psychological Works of Sigmund Freud*, trans. Alan Tyson (London: Hogarth Press, 1955), XI, where he finds a total repression of sexual drive due to Leonardo's excessively close relation to his unwed mother. The sublimated libido that drove the researcher and the artist cannot reveal itself to the artist by his work because he rejects all direct sexual activity. It is only available to the analyst who may, as in interpretation of dreams, be able to find hidden revelations of the now-abandoned sexual aim. In "On Narcissism: An Introduction," *Works of Freud*, trans. James Strachey (London: Hogarth Press, 1978), XIV, 94, Freud defines sublimation as "a process that concerns object-libido and consists in the instinct's directing itself towards an aim *other than, and remote from, that of sexual satisfaction*; in this process the *accent falls upon deflection from sexuality*" (italics mine). The awkwardness is in the open question of how much deflection, and also in the large grey area between direct stimulation of the body and remote gratification of instinct. Elsewhere Freud insisted that when "sexual impulses" are sublimated "they are diverted from their sexual aims and directed to others that are socially higher and no longer sexual," and that sublimation substitutes an aim that "is related genetically to the abandoned one but is itself no longer sexual and must be described as social." The artist modifies his daydreams, in Freud's conception, so that "they do not easily betray their origin from

proscribed sources": *Introductory Lectures on Psychoanalysis*, in *Works of Freud*, trans. James Strachey, XV, 23; XVI, 345, 376. A pathbreaker in open discussion of sex, Freud still seems not to see any place for the non-repressed writer on sex or, indeed, the pornographer. Freud generally does not look at sexual discourse – his own is indeed a huge and obvious one – as a form of sublimation.

Freud's idea of religion as a product of sublimation is an especially revealing case of his confusion. Following the ideas of R. Payne Knight, he presents religion as originally an explicit discourse of sexual parts, a phallic worship, that has somehow necessarily been suppressed – in Freud's myth of the return of the repressed murdered father with the death of Moses – in a state of "advanced civilization" just as sex is suppressed in the individual in sublimation (see my discussion of this, n. 7, ch. 1). Lacan's stress on the necessarily linguistic way in which the unconscious is spoken to us puts more focus on the difference between a physical/unconscious level of sex and its representation in words. Foucault's sense of two quite different spheres, bodily acts and discourses of sexuality, is especially clear about their arbitrary relation to each other. He is right in emphasizing that all talk about sex is of course necessarily different from the acts of the body it codifies, articulates, and fictionalizes. But he does not treat the latter as a sublimation of the former. Claire Kehane, "Sublimation, Symbolization, and the Post-modern Body," Paper, MLA, Dec. 29, 1989, interestingly suggested an intermediate position for literature between sex and sublimation: a coded releasing of the rigors of sublimation (in itself a potentially cruel and damaging supremacy of the superego) in symbolic activity – which would apply more or less to more or less explicit sexual discussion. Leo Bersani, "Representation and Its Discontents," in Stephen J. Green-blatt, ed., *Allegory and Representation*, English Institute Essays (Baltimore: Johns Hopkins University Press, 1981), pp. 145–62, drawing on the ideas of Jean Laplanche, has also proposed an interesting alternative scheme for Freudian sublimation by a second reading of Freud's study of Leonardo, in which he finds Freud also offering, self-subversively, an unrepressed model. This is based on a non-Oedipal childhood, which he finds in Leonardo because of the absent father (though Freud probably would not, because for him Leonardo underwent even stronger repressions because of his closeness to his mother). Sublimation is thus a continuation into adulthood, unrepressed, of infantile sexual fantasies that can express sexual content directly. The thinking thus moves here toward "a view of sublimation as coextensive with sexuality, as an appropriation and elaboration of sexual impulses rather than as a special form of renunciation of impulses" (p. 157).

It is perhaps worth noting that in cultures or religions where there is an acceptance of the use of sexual energies in thinking or imagination people find it much easier to recur to the root sense of sublimation as a conscious and desirable transformation of one substance into another. In their theory of sublimation through semen retention Hindus see sex – in this case their abstinence from ejaculation – as directly connected to spiritual energy which they activate consciously in their "raising of the seeds upward": Sudhir Kakar, *Intimate Relations: Exploring Indian Sexuality* (Chicago: University of Chicago Press, 1989), pp. 118–22.

 Peter Gay, *The Bourgeois Experience: Victoria to Freud*, vol. II, *The Tender Passion* (New York: Oxford University Press, 1986), rather confusingly attempts to apply Freud's confused term in a consistent way to a history of sexuality. He moves from sublimation, which he also finds inadequate, to more conscious activities of projection and displacement that he assimilates to sublimation (II, 256–57, 287); but in both cases he is merely talking about discussions of sexuality that make him uncomfortable by their distance from sexual acts. That *all* discussion of sex must have such distance, what I have called sexuality, isn't clear in his versions of sublimation as discourse. His failure, II, 291–311, to distinguish between the sexual–religious discourse of Kingsley (whom he understands well as a man) and Patmore (whom he does not understand as man or writer, especially as Catholic mystic writer – sound unpleasing to a Freudian's ear!) suggests the problems in a history that wishes to reduce sexual discourse to sex. The good sense about the realities of sex among the Victorians, as among all peoples, that makes Gay's account generally a useful corrective to views of Victorian prudery (even correcting Freud on this, II, 351–52!) makes his work reductionistic when it moves from sex biography to sexual discourse; certainly Freud never considered talk about sex expendable much as he, unlike Jung, was suspicious of the illusionary nature of religious discourse.

55 *Tamerton Church-Tower and Other Poems* (London: John W. Parker, 1854), p. 7. Hereafter cited in the text. This is largely a reprint of *Tamerton Church-Tower and Other Poems* (London: William Pickering, 1853) but not, as the British Library catalog and other sources have it, identical. In 1854 Patmore added a new table of contents, omitted the Dedication to Milnes, and added a note on the poems that were sketches for a love poem (*The Angel*). The text itself is identical, including the same pagination, except that "Amanda" (1853) was replaced by "Easter and Lent" (1854), and the topical poem against French imperialist brutality, "The Caves of Oahra" (1853), was replaced by "The Storm," "Night and Sleep," and "The Tragedy of Tragedies" (1854).

56 Holloway pays tribute to Patmore's sophistication in the line of English wit, while also rightly stressing the congealed nature of the verse, the sense of failure to connect metaphysical wit to felt experience.

57 Coventry Patmore, *Poems* (London: George Bell, 1906), pp. 131–32. Hereafter cited in the text. This is Patmore's final version for his *Poems* (London: George Bell and Sons, 1886), reissued by Champneys, with poems by Harriet Patmore, Patmore's son Henry, and the essay on metrics omitted. The quoted lines are identical in the first edition, 1856, cited below, where the bride's meditation occurs, pp. 137–40, and the

groom's, pp. 143–48. Unless otherwise noted, parts of the poem cited from this final version occur in the first edition, sometimes with minor variations.

The Angel in the House: The Betrothal (London, 1854) and *The Angel in the House*. Book II. (half-title); *The Espousals* (London, 1856), first issued anonymously, were sometimes brought together without additional title by the original publisher, John W. Parker and Son, in a single volume (Yale copy). True 2nd and 3rd editions appeared in 1858 and 1860 under that title but now with Patmore's name as author. Patmore revised the 1858 edition considerably and added and omitted many poems; changes in the 1860 edition were relatively less, five added poems and two new ones put in place of those removed. There were publications in Boston of the 1854/1856 London editions in 1856 and of later editions by Ticknor and Fields, presumably of no independent authority. In 1863 Macmillan, London, issued *The Angel in the House* in 2 vols., using text identical with Parker's 1860 edition for the first two of the four total books (vol. I) but now first including the later two books (vol. II). An 1863 Parker issue similarly joins the 1860 Parker edition with the Macmillan edition of the second half of the full *Angel*. In 1866 Macmillan reissued this in a single volume, small-print edition with a new epigraph from Plato, a few poems omitted from Book I, and some changes in the miscellaneous poems at the end. (My notes here are not intended as a substitute for a descriptive bibliography or full study of Patmore's revisions or, Lord bless him or her with the patience, a variorum edition, but are only to suggest how complicated the history of Patmore's revisions is.) Patmore again considerably revised the first two books, omitting and adding poems, and now eliminating the separate sub-titles, for the [1879] *Poems* and made further, but now generally minor, revisions for 1886 (one new poem, "The Unthrift," was added to Book I). There were separate 5th and 6th editions of *The Angel* published with Bell in 1878 and 1885, presumably the same as 1879 and 1886 respectively (not seen). In the 1879 revisions he had the help of Hopkins's suggestions but, as Oliver, p. 168 notes, he acted on few of them. Linda K. Hughes, "Entombing the Angel: Patmore's Revisions of *Angel in the House*," in *Victorian Authors and Their Works*, ed. Judith Kennedy (Athens: Ohio University Press, 1991), pp. 140–68, notes an interesting pattern of suppression of Honoria's voice, so that the independence of the woman in the relation and discussion of the poem is considerably muted. Many of these revisions, it should be noted, began as early as 1858. I find also a pattern of suppression of sexually direct passages in the early revisions – accepted and augmented in 1879.

58 First appearing in London, 1858, p. 274
59 First appearing in London, 1860, p. 154.
60 First appearing in London, 1858, p. 291. Critical statements about the poem in the past twenty years have mainly been directed polemically against the usually misread title. Carol Christ, "Victorian Masculinity

and *The Angel in the House,*" in Martha Vicinus, ed., *A Widening Sphere: Changing Roles of Victorian Women* (Bloomington: Indiana University Press, 1977), pp. 146–62, argues that idealization of women conceals ambivalence about masculinity – the other, masochistic, side.

61 First appearing in London, 1858, p. 259.

62 First appearing in London, 1858, p. 275.

63 The second two books appear in [1879] and the final *Poems* under the single title, *The Victories of Love*, a two-book poem. The two books originally appeared separately under the titles *Faithful for Ever* (London: J. W. Parker, 1860) – revised and reduced from twenty-four to nineteen letters in the Macmillan 1863 edition, and again modestly revised in the final version in *Poems* – and *The Victories of Love* – originally published in *Macmillan's Magazine*, 4 (Oct. 1861), 436–48; 5 (Nov., Dec. 1861), 23–37, 109–19, and, from that (probably pirated), in the identical first book publication (Boston: T. O. P. H. Burnham, 1862). The 1863 edition (London and Cambridge: Macmillan) is much rewritten and enlarged from the serial and 1862 publication, which have only nine letters and even appear to be a kind of work in progress. All four books were published in two volumes, with separate names retained, in the full two-volume Macmillan (and Parker) *The Angel in the House* of 1863, as well as in the one-volume Macmillan edition of 1866. As with the first two books, there were publications by Ticknor and Fields in Boston, in different type and presumably with no independent authority as texts (curiously, the Boston 1863 *Victories* omits the eleventh section of "The Wedding Sermon"). Here again, Patmore is badly in need of a modern bibliography and a modern editor. Page's Oxford edition, as for the first two books, merely reprints Patmore's final versions in slightly different order, though he provides the original titles for the four books and publishes them together under the title *The Angel in the House* – a confusing amalgam. Patmore's persistent rewriting and reorganization of his poems very much need variorum treatment. Reid provides the best checklist of publications but in no sense a descriptive bibliography – indeed, he is especially weak on Patmore's own works. Weinig also contains inaccuracies in her listing of Patmore's own works.

Citations in my text are to the 1906 version of the final (1886) *Poems*; unless otherwise noted these are essentially the same in the 1860 and 1863 editions of *Faithful for Ever* and the 1863 edition of *The Victories of Love*.

64 *Faithful for Ever* (London: Parker, 1860), p. 197: omitted in Patmore's final version. Hughes makes a good case, similar to hers on the first two books, that feminine voices are suppressed in revision, both Honoria's and Jane's. Her conclusion, that Patmore tended to submerge the living presence of Emily after her death and that this follows a movement from individual relationship to more general concern with an eternal feminine, fits the move I chronicle from a Kingsleyan concern with specific marriage to an interest in the nature of desire. Of course Hughes

is right in seeing that this merely weakens the never-too-real texture of this supposedly realistic view of marriage – though it is interesting that one of the lines Patmore censors, at the end of *The Betrothal*, is one in which Honoria censors him *pro pudore* over mention of a kiss. In submerging the female voice he was also partly throwing off the Kingsleyan limits that he had allowed Honoria to represent. (He never deleted the reference to the kiss itself.)

65 First appearing in London: Macmillan, 1863, II, 11.

66 *Faithful for Ever* (London: Parker, 1860), pp. 116–17.

67 For background discussion of this complicated issue see n. 82, ch. 3.

68 Pp. 224–27. In the first version Frederick was also given some fairly technical lines arguing against interpretation of Christ's words to the Sadducees (Matthew xxii.24–30) as a statement against marriage in heaven: the same lines that Kingsley also felt moved to explain away: *Faithful for Ever* (London, 1860), p. 237.

69 London: Macmillan, 1863, II, 164–68.

70 A frequent position of liberal religious thinkers on sexuality in the nineteenth century: see n. 51, above.

71 London: Macmillan, 1863, II, 234. Emily died July 5, 1862.

72 Certain omissions of *recherché* religious themes in the final version of the last two books suggest he later became aware of his own wish to put more speculative thought into these books than their plots would warrant (*The Victories of Love*, 1863, p. 71): he omitted an elaboration of the dean on Christ and marriage, and on the Virgin's crown and the cross, p. 72, as well as Jane's long dream discussed above. He also omitted an epigraph from Hermes Trismegistus on the interrelations of heavenly and earthly things. Patmore turned most fully against his earlier work in 1873 when he purchased and apparently burned some copies (Anstruther, p. 96). Anstruther offers, pp. 74–82, 95–103, an interesting but imprecise and somewhat self-contradictory account of the reception history of *The Angel*. He sees its popular success only in the 1880s when it could represent a conservative position in women question debates and anxieties. But if its first reception by reviewers was surprisingly negative, the subsequent editions, American reprints, and continuing critical attention in the poem's first 10–15 years suggests *The Angel* was even then Patmore's most popular work. Its popularity, of a greater kind, in the 1880s would eventually please him.

73 Published April 17, 1868; Reid, p. 331, lists these reprinted as *Nine Odes* (Priv. printed, May 1870) – not seen by me and no copy listed in the National Union Catalog or the catalog of the British Library: possibly this is a ghost. The odes, untitled in the first version, were "Prophets Who Cannot Sing," "Felicia" (later, "Beata"), "Tired Memory," "Faint Yet Pursuing," "Pain," "The Two Desarts" (later Deserts), "Deliciae Sapientiae de Amore," "Dead Language," and "1867." Most had minor changes when reprinted; only "Tired Memory" was revised in a major way. There is apparently almost no information, other

than terminal publishing dates for the odes, to provide dating. The most personal and immediate, "The Azalea," only appears in the latest, 1878, publication in which additional poems were added. As noted above, there appears to be no evidence to support Page's hypothesis, pp. 109–12, that some of the poems of loss were written in the early 1860s as drafts for *The Victories of Love*. In any event, even if some of these could have pre-dated the loss of Emily, they would have been written out of a sense of her sickness and probable death. I must note again the lack of sound bibliographical scholarship on Patmore. Reid's bibliography in *The Mind and Art of Coventry Patmore* hardly describes the different versions of the odes and cites the 1877 edition as publishing XXI odes, a mistake carried on by Weinig, p. 139. Connolly's useful handbook nonetheless has many inaccuracies, beginning with dating the *Odes* as 1866, also mispresenting the title of the 1877 version and inaccurately reporting the number of *Pall Mall Gazette* publications (p. 148)! I provide minimal publication information here and below.

74 In the *Pall Mall Gazette*: "How It Seems to an English Catholic" (later, "The Standards"), March 8, 1875; "Peace," Jan. 18, 1876; "'Let Be,'" Nov. 3, 1876; "A Farewell," Nov. 7, 1876; "If I Were Dead," Nov. 14, 1876; "The Two Deserts," Nov. 22, 1876; "The Toys," Nov. 30, 1876; "Prophets Who Cannot Sing," Dec. 20, 1876. "Arbor Vitae" was published in *The Week*. There were two miscellaneous poems, "The Rosy-Bosom'd Hours" and "The Girl of All Periods" also published in the *Pall Mall Gazette* (see Champneys, I, 246).

75 [Anon.] *The Unknown Eros and Other Odes. Odes I–XXXI.* (London: George Bell and Sons, 1877). This included "Psyche" (later "Mignonne"), "Semele," and "1877," later excluded from the Odes. Poems in the 1878 edition and the final version (1879 and later) but not in the 1877 edition were: "Vesica Piscis," "'Sing Us One of the Songs of Sion,'" "Eros and Psyche," "The Cry at Midnight," "De Natura Deorum," "Winter," "Psyche's Discontent," "Arbor Vitae," 'Sponsa Dei," "To the Body," "Auras of Delight," "The Azalea," "Saint Valentine's Day," "The Merry Murder" (later "1880–85"), and "The Child's Purchase." Possibly, but only conjecturally, some of these were written, or finished, close to 1877–78. In 1877, "Beata" is titled "Felicia" and "The Two Deserts" is spelled with an a: Desarts. Two poems not among the odes here or later, "The Rosy Bosom'd Hours" and "The After-Glow" were published at the end.

76 *The Unknown Eros* by Coventry Patmore, *Odes I–XLVI* (London: George Bell and Sons, 1878); *Poems by Coventry Patmore* (London: George Bell and Sons, 1886), 2 vols., establishes the final text. The 1878 edition dropped "1877" but included "Semele" and "Psyche" as well as a new poem, "Alexander and Lycon," all three excluded from *Poems by Coventry Patmore* (London: George Bell and Sons, [1879]), IV. In both the 1878 and 1879 editions "Beata" is still titled "Felicia" and "1880–85" "The Merry Murder," but "Deserts" is spelled with an e. The "Proem"

was not numbered in 1879, where there are 42 numbered odes and the new epigraph from Proverbs, as in all succeeding versions. The order of 1878 follows 1877 with additions at the end; both are very different from 1879 and the final version. Page's Oxford edition of *Poems* (1949) is a reprint of the *Poems* of 1886 where Patmore made some changes from 1877, including final titles for "Beata" and "1880–85" and considerable revisions in "1880–85" as well as "Psyche's Discontent."

77 Little has been written on the Victorian sequence poem made up of individual poems. John Woolford provides an introductory survey of what he calls the "structured collection" in his *Browning the Revisionary* (New York: St. Martins Press, 1988), pp. 76–98. Structure, in his definition, may be either biographical or thematic. Presumably it may be both, as in the odes. The case of Patmore's *Angel* suggests the structure may also be narrative rather than the special narrative of the author's biography.

78 See Geoffrey Ashe, *The Virgin* (London: Routledge & Kegan Paul, 1976), p. 26, and the broader view of interpretations in Geoffrey Parrinder, *Sex in the World's Religions* (New York: Oxford University Press, 1980), pp. 197–98. Ashe is influenced by Graves and Campbell in looking for a suppressed Great Mother emerging in later Judaism. Rabbinical tradition could find a middle ground in Wisdom as the Law or Torah existing with God before creation. The Catholic tradition of interpreting the Old Testament Wisdom as a type of the Virgin raises the question of whether Patmore used a motto, itself added only in 1879, that looked forward thematically to his identification with the Virgin as muse at the end of the series of odes.

79 For a broader, but still very cursory treatment of this subject, including exceptions to this logic within the tradition as well as some basic references, see my discussion in ch. 1.

80 Paul H. Fry, *The Poet's Calling in the English Ode* (New Haven: Yale University Press, 1980), pp. 119ff. Fry rightly speaks of the ode's tendency to process and contain other genres. Patmore writes, as we shall see, out of the broad tradition of the ode. It should be said that in doing so he in some sense fulfills some of the goals set for religious poetry by the most articulate Victorian tradition of religious verse, that of the Tractarians who, as G. B. Tennyson, *Victorian Devotional Poetry: The Tractarian Mode* (Cambridge: Harvard University Press, 1981), has reminded us, were a poetic as well as a religious movement. Keble called for strong expression of religious emotion in the poet, who should express yearning and closeness to God; and he even gave Pindar as an example; Newman of course used choric forms in his poetry. Whether they could have seen much connection between their own relatively tame, often Romantic celebration of God's plan in nature or the days of the Christian year, or their solemn prayers in verse, and Patmore's highly imaginative, often quite violent use of the ode tradition to express his idiosyncratic religious vision remains a question. Newman himself, as Catholic,

expressed little sympathy with Patmore's odes "mixing up amourousness with religion, since they are two such very irreconcilable elements" (quoted, Gosse, p. 203).

81 For brief histories of the ode see John Heath-Stubbs, *The Ode* (New York: Oxford University Press, 1969); John D. Jump, *The Ode* (London: Methuen, 1974), as well as the older, more specialized English histories: Robert Shafer, *The English Ode to 1660* (Princeton: Princeton University Press, 1918) and George N. Shuster, *The English Ode from Milton to Keats* (New York: Columbia University Press, 1940). Fry's work is by far the most thoughtful and critically provocative. Though I take issue with some of his conceptions as too constraining for Patmore's use of the ode, I have found his statement of the problem of the ode exceptionally useful.

82 Patmore's "Essay on English Metrical Laws," originally written in 1856 and reprinted in his *Poems*, from [1879] on (but not in Champney's edition), is one of the classic statements of pre-free verse prosody, especially interesting for its openness to new ideas, including full recognition of alliteration as an organizing principle in English based on new knowledge of the Anglo-Saxon poems. Patmore sees both rhymes and alliterations as forms of rhyme allowing line organization in traditional forms. His difficult system of time, based on sounded and unsounded syllables and unsounded pauses, has not caught on, but is an interesting way of explaining the normal irregularity of English poetry. Donald Wesling, *The New Poetries – Poetic Form since Coleridge and Wordsworth* (Lewisburg: Bucknell University Press, 1985), pp. 89–92, recognizes Patmore's centrality but understates his originality.

83 Fry, p. 9. Eric Gould, *Mythical Intentions in Modern Literature* (Princeton: Princeton University Press, 1981), pp. 172, 179, usefully calls attention to the necessary removal from religious presence in all representation of "the numinous – whatever we think that is – in the world of signs"; that is, even traditional myth-makers, or, in the case of the ode, Fry's hymn-makers, whatever the force of their personal beliefs, had to face the problem of how to bring their gods or rites alive in the special world of language.

84 Connolly's work, which is important for providing the only annotation available for these difficult and allusive classics, groups the first three poems, including "Wind and Wave" (i.ii) as poems of nature, following seasons of spring, summer, winter (pp. 151–52). But i and iii are both clearly winter poems and the themes of love generated by absence are central to the entire set of odes; nor are these simply about seasons of natural love to set against later divine ones – a pious mis-statement of both concerns.

85 See Connolly's summary, p. 149.

86 She was originally named Felicia, a less impersonal allusion to the mate of Felix of *The Angel*; Hopkins's questions about the name led to the more abstract, certainly less personal, Beata: Abbott, ed. *Further Letters*, pp.

341, 345. The original name also suggests there is no reason to identify this specifically earthly love with the Virgin.

87　Abbott, ed., *Further Letters*, pp. 341, 344. Hopkins was not happy with Patmore's playful half-sins, half-damnations; Patmore excused the mythology as poetry: "the harmless expression of a poetic mood."

88　A longer, more awkward explanation was revised out after 1868. Twenty-three lines spoke of the hope for some kind of acceptable triple relationship in heaven. The late narrative poem, "Amelia," deals with a similar situation in a slicker, less problematic and, yes, patriarchal way. "Tired Memory's" uncertain, questioning approach is far closer to Patmore's best work in allowing his own conflicts and questions over a special subject of infidelity that very much troubled a writer like Kingsley to be displayed rather than covered up. Michael Wheeler's *Death and the Future Life in Victorian Literature and Theology* (Cambridge: Cambridge University Press, 1990), one of the very few general studies in many years to give Patmore's odes the attention they deserve, interestingly finds echoes of Luke in the lines accepting uncertainty about having his first wife again (in heaven): those troubling lines – to Patmore's dean of the Wedding Sermon and to Kingsley generally – on not marrying in heaven; and also in the sign offered by finding a new love – a parallel to signs offered to the disciples of Christ after his death. These work to validate Patmore's troubling experience, yet it is still left explicitly problematic in the conclusion.

89　Abbott, ed., *Further Letters*, p. 345.

90　Katherine B. Stockton, "Spiritual Discourse and the Work of Desire: Feminine Sexual Economies in Theory and the Victorian Novel," diss., Brown Univ., 1989, esp. pp. 33–47, has outlined the most useful history, for the period roughly since the Renaissance, for this idea of spiritual longing based on putting off the ultimate gratification of a union with God, generally imaged in sexual terms. In Revelation, the Bridegroom, Christ, is to marry the Church at the *end* of time, a consummation and ending that Christian history has been obliged to keep deferring from closure. In an excellent rewriting, or really overwriting, of M. H. Abrams's study of secular transformations of religious structures in Romanticism, Stockton explains how this Christian myth of the Church and Christ easily became internalized in Christian spiritual auto-biographies as the marriage of the individual to Christ, also generally postponed until the end of time and thus creating a powerful system of desire and absence heightening desire. Stockton's interesting compari-sons between this dis-closure in Christian mystical thinking and the prominence of absence, lack, and deferral in postmodernist theory is suggestive, without being reductive and dismissive.

　　As a Catholic convert Patmore had, of course, a more direct access to a generally older tradition that converted union of Church and God to a sexual union of individual and God, especially in Catholic mystical writers, many of whom he knew. Reid, pp. 90–100, summarizes parallels and possible influences on the odes from St. Bernard of Clairvaux (whose work he and his second wife translated as *St. Bernard on the Love of God*, London: Kegan Paul, 1881), St. John of the Cross (known before the odes were completed, despite Gosse's observation to the contrary), and St. Teresa of Avila (dear to Patmore's religious daughter and whom Reid believes at least offered ideas for the Psyche poems). St. Bernard's sermons on the Canticles could have suggested an interpretation of the Song of Solomon as about the individual's love with God, rather than the conventional interpretation of these apparent love poems as about marriage of the Church or Israel to God. Reid also suggests St. Augustine, whom Patmore knew fairly well, as source for some of Patmore's own assertions of the individual's relation to God as a parallel to the marriage of Christ and Church forecast in the Bible (e.g., 2 Corinthians xi.2–3). Reid's other connections between Patmore and Augustine are interesting but somewhat confusing. Patmore moves from sexual energy in human love to that with God; Augustine redirects sexual energy but does so while and by insisting on the dangers of lust's power, since the Fall, over man's rational control (sex in Augustine before the Fall was to have been a rational act, not one of passion). Reid is probably right in asserting that Patmore took comfort in Augustine's directness about sex in his own attacks on the prudery of parts of Victorian society. Reid mentions Patmore's lesser familiarity with St. Catherine of Genoa, St. Francis de Sales, and St. Catherine of Siena (pp. 107–11). Reid rightly stresses Patmore's tendency to look in Catholic texts for confirmation of his ideas after he had formulated them; and he generally stresses Patmore's fresh thinking, rather than mere copying, in his use of such sources. Although he identifies some echoes of Church writing in the odes, mainly the Psyche poems, most of the specific references are in Patmore's late prose work. On a non-Catholic source, Swedenborg, whom Patmore studied before his conversion and whom he later claimed to be essentially in harmony with Catholic thinking, see Reid, pp. 66–81. Swedenborg's idea of purified marriages in heaven fits Patmore's Kingsleyan thinking at the time of *The Angel*, when he read Swedenborg, better than his work in the odes. (See n. 96, below.)

91 The issue of the relation of sex to the Fall is, of course, a central bone of contention and crux in Christian discussions of sex, from extreme views that the descent into the body caused the Fall or at any rate was the cognate of Fall from a paradise of virginity (St. Jerome) to more liberal positions, such as Clement of Alexandria's or Milton's, that sex was healthily enjoyed in paradise. See my brief discussion and references for these major and extremely complicated issues in Christian sexual thinking in ch. 1. Reid, pp. 89–90, glosses Patmore's view by Aquinas (whom Patmore read): sex was natural, not bad in itself, but had not been indulged in before the Fall; after the Fall it was degraded by passions released by the Fall – itself a result of pride, not sex. Central to much Christian, especially Catholic, thinking was Augustine's con-

servative innovation in finding sex after the Fall a force that overwhelmed man's rational will, even, as Elaine Pagels has emphasized,
that of the baptized Christian. Patmore's entire strategy consciously
builds a case for virginity as a greater sexual experience, better than the
obviously still attractive sex of the fallen world – an idea quite alien to
Augustine's of rationally chosen sex (sex like a handshake) – as it was to
have been before the Fall.

92 On the mythology of Joseph and the Virgin's virgin marriage see n. 105
below.

93 Champneys, II, 133.

94 Abbott, ed., *Further Letters*, p. 349.

95 I have corrected "atta" to "attar" as in [1879]. That this obvious error
should stand even in the Oxford edition (p. 406) shows the state of
Patmore's studies of the past forty years.

96 Connolly, pp. 249–50, rightly calls attention to Patmore's transposition
of God's love for Israel to the individual soul and the parallel to the same
move in St. Bernard of Clairvaux's sermons on the Canticles. Wheeler
also identifies biblical echoes in this ode and rightly identifies them with
an element of hymnody, which he, independent of Fry's work, explores in
relation to Victorian assertions of heaven as something to be realized by
the Christian here and now. His assertion, p. 168, that Patmore fails here
to write such a hymn is correct, but is a sign of the success, not failure, of
this work as a poetic ode, rather than a ritualistic hymn. When Patmore
attempts to make his language work, as Wheeler interestingly finds that
of Victorian hymns working, to cancel the distance between here and
heaven, absence and presence, he fails as a poet – as we shall see below.
Patmore mentions Swedenborg's *Deliciae sapientiae de amore conjugiale* in
a note at the end of volume I of the Macmillan full (1863) *Angel*. Now,
of course, the love is not merely conjugal – so the qualifier is dropped.

97 See n. 90, above.

98 Gardella, pp. 9–24. Gardella provides the broader Continental context
for the realistic acceptance of sexuality in the Catholic Church in
America in the early nineteenth century. He also chronicles the move to
be more puritan than the Puritans following Protestant criticism of
Catholic leniency (see pp. 37–38). On the Protestant attacks on the
Catholic Church generally see also Walter L. Arnstein, *Protestant Versus
Catholic in Mid-Victorian England* (Columbia: University of Missouri
Press, 1982). Professor Donoghue informed me that Patmore was still
read as a Catholic author in Ireland when he was in school but that most
of the reading was from the (Protestant) *Angel* rather than the odes,
which were treated as something a bit dangerous and not for the lay
reader.

99 Richard Dellamora, *Masculine Desire: the Sexual Politics of Victorian
Aestheticism* (Chapel Hill: University of North Carolina Press, 1990), pp.
50–57, does find repression – of homosexual feeling – in Hopkins's life
and work, and also goes on to read some of his poems as at least

homoerotic diversions of sexual desire to Christ. In the readings there is nothing approaching the very direct treatment of the theme of sexual desire directed to God that Patmore expresses, though Hopkins himself had been chastised for sermons preaching God's love for man as that of a lover for a sweetheart. Renée V. Overholser, "'Looking with Terrible Temptation': Gerard Manley Hopkins and Beautiful Bodies," *Victorian Literature and Culture*, 19 (1991), 25–53, provides a fuller account, in both Hopkins's life and writing, of similar themes and persuasively suggests the redirection of (homo)sexual desire.

100 Stockton, pp. 39–40, citing M. H. Abrams *Natural Supernaturalism* for what is commonplace in any case in Church writing: Patmore liked to quote Augustine, "Christ is the Bride as well as the Bridegroom, for he is the Body": *Religio Poetae*, pp. 55–56. Stockton's more specific, and more interesting, points here about Christ's varying gender roles are cited again below. She and Abrams both note Patmore's odes as a case in point, both of the nuptial theme and the sometime reversal of sex roles (though they both also misread his clear reference to Mary as to Christ).

101 *The Rod, the Root, and the Flower*, p. 20. The essay "Ancient and Modern Ideas of Purity" in *Religio Poetae* is a splendid attack on practical and religious sexual prudery in Victorian society – as contrasted to the sexual "outspokenness" of the early Church, the Bible, or Bacchic mysteries (p. 69). In *The Rod, the Root, and the Flower* he attacks the prudish tendency even in the Catholic Church that leads to human love, the "precursor and explanation of and initiation into the divine" being demeaned as "carnal and damnable" and the Incarnation itself being "emasculated" (p. 197). In *Religio Poetae* Patmore emphasizes the literal mystery meaning of the Sacrament, where man "affirms and *acts* a familiarity [with God] which is greater than any other that can be conceived" (p. 174).

102 Connolly, p. 228, reads "Heaven high" as Christ; it is rather the sense of experience of heaven set together with that of the latest lowly Maude or Cecily that makes the odd bridal-bed. Christ, not appropriate here before the revelation that follows, would be both together.

103 The passage is in John iii.2. Connolly, p. 229, rightly notes a reference to the same passage in Patmore's *Religio Poetae* with his more direct suggestion of a third dispensation: "A voice of the Bride and the Bridegroom shall be heard in our streets."

104 On the many versions of the myth, see Elizabeth Hazelton Haight, *Apuleius and His Influence* (New York: Cooper Square, 1963), and the study of the myth in the late eighteenth century and Romantic period by Jean H. Hagstrum, "Eros and Psyche: Some Versions of Romantic Love and Delicacy," in his *Eros and Vision: The Restoration to Romanticism* (Evanston: Northwestern University Press, 1989).

105 As Hagstrum discusses, from the richly fleshly and sexual presentations in a Renaissance work, such as Giulio Romano's stunning frescoes on

the walls of the Palazzo Te in Mantua, the myth had altered by the beginning of the nineteenth century, in the representation in the sculpture of Canova or the use of the motif in Shelley, into one that suggested a mixing of male and female characters, even qualities of incest, homoeroticism, and narcissism. Patmore's reestablishment of a gendered meeting of dominant god male and submissive human female thus reverses the norm Praz long ago suggested for development from male dominance to female dominance in the imagination of the nineteenth century. His use of the myth is paralleled by Burne-Jones's representations of the myth in art, where Cupid is given authority over Psyche: see Joseph Kestner, *Mythology and Misogyny: The Social Discourse of Nineteenth-Century British Classical Subject Painting* (Madison: University of Wisconsin Press, 1989). The story itself was retold from Apuleius in Patmore's time by Morris in *The Earthly Paradise* (before Patmore's poems) and by Pater in *Marius the Epicurean* (after Patmore) – and also by Robert Bridges.

106 This poem was considerably revised between [1879] and the final 1886 version, which is not true of any of the other important odes. Patmore came back to it to give Eros rather than Psyche the last word: perhaps troubled by the force of her pleas for a warm but sex-free intimacy (ending lines omitted in 1886). Patmore's division on gender and human/God relations is perhaps built into the myth he chose: Carol Gilligan has very interestingly reread the Psyche myth as just such a myth of justified feminine resistance to male authority; Psyche demands to know, whereas Oedipus, in the parallel male myth, is left in the dark – where Psyche begins ("Psyche and Oedipus," Paper, MLA Meeting, December 28, 1989).

107 Hoxie Neale Fairchild, *Religious Trends in English Poetry*, IV (New York: Columbia, 1964), 332. Patmore had been studying the lore of the Virgin and follows learnedly much of the traditional Catholic story of the Virgin and the definition of her significance. He stresses her permanent virginity (thus accepting the Church's view that the apparent brothers and sisters of Jesus are cousins by the "other Mary") and her part in the crucifixion (see note 111, below), and seems to accept her Assumption. He seems to allude broadly to the apocryphal traditions of her girlhood and is rightly impressed by the power of her response to Gabriel – the Magnificat – in Luke. He avoids mythmaking over her life during Christ's own life and after the crucifixion, where he rightly notes that her main contribution in the record is silence. Her doctrinal position is the central Catholic role for her, of intercessor with Christ and God; as the new Eve, as Patmore emphasized in "The Contract," she undoes the ill of Eve's fall in parallel to Christ's work with Adam and is in some sense mother of all. She is associated with wisdom – traditionally connected with the figure of wisdom in Proverbs that is used as an epigraph for Patmore's odes as a whole (see n. 78, above) – and she is cited, as was common, as a hard test of orthodox faith. Patmore nonetheless stresses boldly two aspects

of the traditional description that make his use of the Virgin idiosyncratic though not totally unprecedented. The first is his emphasis on her sexual relation to God in all the senses possible. She is traditionally mother of God, but Patmore will stress the spousehood as well.

Almost in the other direction, as I show below, he insists on her representative humanness. Catholic tradition has tended to expand her history, inventing a story for her girlhood and for her life after the crucifixion; Patmore emphasizes how little she has to say or do. His is an extreme version of her traditional role as one of us who can intercede with the more distant figures of Christ and God ("our only Saviour from an abstract Christ"). As I show below, the logic of his position leads him to stress and stretch the ends of the traditional view, both her human absence (silence) and her ultimate role as at least a name for fulfillment, human married to God, queen and spouse. Despite Hopkins's and Patmore's own nervousness over his approach to Mary, there were other extreme precedents in the Church, for instance the rather broad tradition of St. Bernard of Clairvaux, which did sexualize God's relation to the Virgin (as noted above his work was translated by Patmore and his second wife), St. Catherine of Siena, who speaks of God's seduction by the Virgin, or the eighteenth-century work of St. Alphonsus Liguori, which stressed the Virgin's love with God as a model for all humans' relation to God. The nineteenth century was a time of intense development of the love of the Virgin, both in popular visions and cults and in the expansion of papal control over the discourse in hitherto disputed areas, especially the Immaculate Conception of the Virgin. On the former see Gardella, pp. 95–101. For general, and readable, histories of the cults of the Virgin, see Ashe, and Marina Warner, *Alone of All Her Sex: The Myth and the Cult of the Virgin Mary* (New York: Vintage, 1983).

108 The deliberate emphasis on transgression can be compared to Bataille's sense of a place of transgression where the sexual and sacramental meet.

109 Abbott, ed., *Further Letters*, p. 351. Hopkins, far from criticizing the poem as a whole, classed it among the few odes he especially praised: "Nothing so profound can be found in the poets of the age." It was the quality of Patmore's "insight" in *The Unknown Eros* that Hopkins generally rated most highly, indeed highest, among the living poets.

110 Susan A. Handelman, *The Slayers of Moses: The Emergence of Rabbinic Interpretation in Modern Literary Theory* (Albany: New York State University Press, 1983), draws an influential and generally helpful distinction between Rabbinic tradition, where the word is the center of the religion, and the Christian substitution of flesh (miracle) for word. Patmore's admission of failure to call down this flesh to replace the word also suggests how in practice Christian thinking quickly substitutes text for flesh, though the Catholic Mass is, of course, a constant reminder of the theoretical primacy of the latter.

111 I am indebted to Stockton's observations on these lines for this point, as

also for the general feminization of Christ's sexual role here, though she misreads Christ for Mary. Patmore follows the *stabat mater* theme and the interpretive tradition that took Simeon's prophecy (Luke ii.35), "a sword will pierce through your own soul also," as a prediction of her sympathetic participation in the crucifixion.

5 CONCLUSION: HARDY'S *JUDE*: DISASSEMBLING SEXUALITY AND RELIGION

1 Wendell Stacey Johnson, *Sex and Marriage in Victorian Poetry* (Ithaca: Cornell University Press, 1975), in a general study of sexual issues in Victorian poetry and Richard Dellamora, *Masculine Desire: The Sexual Politics of Victorian Aestheticism* (Chapel Hill: University of North Carolina Press, 1990), in the special area of homoerotic writing, have surveyed a number of writers on religious–sexual issues; see also excellent studies by Katherine B. Stockton, "Spiritual Discourse and the Work of Desire: Feminine Sexual Economies in Theory and the Victorian Novel," diss. Brown Univ., 1989 and Renée Overholser, "'Looking with Terrible Temptation': Gerard Manley Hopkins and Beautiful Bodies," *Victorian Literature and Culture*, 19 (1991), pp. 25–53.

2 Stockton, pp. 175–83.

3 I am thinking of the difference between the work in *Three Contributions to the Theory of Sex* (1905), and the later speculations on the origins of religion, beginning with the fairly simple myth of origins of religion in *Totem and Taboo* (1913) and continuing in more complex attempts to explain the desire for the comforting "illusion" of religion in *The Future of an Illusion* (1927) and *Moses and Monotheism* (1939).

4 See the discussion of Walter Kendrick's interesting thinking about pornography, esp. in relation to Foucault's radical hypothesis of what sexuality would be outside of language in ch. 1, n. 70, above. The relatively successful efforts of some scientists at an independent discourse have not discouraged a good deal of "science" as myth-making on these subjects in our century as well: Jeffrey Weeks, *Sexuality and Its Discontents: Meanings, Myths, and Modern Sexualities* (London: Routledge & Kegan Paul, 1985), usefully describes the continuing variations of thought in the twentieth century, following nineteenth-century theology and sexology alike, that attempt to stabilize cultural opinions on sex by the claims of nature, for instance the guru-like development of sociobiology or the social-sexual myth-making of Reich or Marcuse. Paul Robinson, *The Modernization of Sex* (New York: Harper, 1977), in his essay on Masters and Johnson also points out the amount of sexual morality and bias that creeps into the objectivity of even these sexual experimentalists.

5 Contrast Rosemarie Morgan's interesting revisionist reading, *Women and Sexuality in the Novels of Thomas Hardy* (London: Routledge, 1988), pp. 30–57, to Susan Beegel's more conventional, and on the whole more – but not entirely – persuasive reading, "Bathsheba's Lovers: Male

Sexuality in *Far from the Madding Crowd*," in *Sexuality and Victorian Literature*, ed. Don Richard Cox (Knoxville, the University of Tennessee Press, 1984), pp. 108–27. John Goode, *Thomas Hardy: The Offensive Truth* (Oxford: Basil Blackwell, 1988), p. 25, interestingly sees Hardy playing a "scientific game" in a subversive rewriting of a popular novel. In his reading, the merely theatrical Troy nonetheless raises a sexual response in Bathsheba, though the novel questions its own *Bothie*-like resolution.

6 Hardy's personal interest in, and sympathy for, the Tractarian movement has been outlined in Raymond Chapman, "'Arguing About the Eastward Position': Thomas Hardy and Puseyism," *Nineteenth Century Fiction*, 42 (Dec. 1987), 275–94. Hardy's well-known concern over Bishop William How's own medieval revival – burning the book – may relate to his sense that he was expressing through Jude his own former sincere feeling *for* the Church; of course Bishop How was only returning Jude's own burning of Church Fathers in the novel. It is worth noting once again in this study that with Hardy, as with Clough and Kingsley, the important conservative "respectable" tradition of sexual lore that has to be confronted continues to be the conservative Church tradition itself and not primarily the new pseudo-scientific discourse of, say, William Acton, on which twentieth-century discussion has tended to focus: as I have noted in the first two chapters, in the broad perspective of Western tradition, his discourse is in many ways merely a minor variant of, or parasite on, the major Augustinian one.

7 That Hardy sees Jude's Christian faith as very much in the Augustinian conservative Church tradition on sexuality is underlined by Jude's later decision not to pursue apostleship after kissing Sue: "It was glaringly inconsistent for him to pursue the idea of becoming the soldier . . . of a religion in which sexual love was regarded as at best a frailty, and at worst damnation."

8 Hardy adds his comment to the history of the other Oxford that we have considered with Clough (as well as with Kingsley's apparently parallel experience at Cambridge). The carter who tells young Jude of the Christminster for which he is amorous "like a young lover alluding to his mistress" makes a very explicit reference to "wenches in the streets o' nights" available to those young parsons being raised there "like radishes in a bed."

9 Modern scholarship distinguishes between the martyr Jude, one of the twelve disciples, and both the author of the Epistle of Jude and the Judas called the brother of Jesus by Matthew and Mark. His obscurity in this confused tradition allows Hardy to evoke a sense of brotherhood of sorrow with Jesus, of martyrdom with the saint, and, especially, of ordinary human obscurity in his imitation of the suffering human side of Jesus. David Lodge usefully summarizes parallels between the passion play of Hardy's Jude and that of Jesus, including the return to *Christminster* as coming into Jerusalem and his "sermon" to the crowd: *Working with Structuralism: Essays and Reviews on Nineteenth- and Twentieth-*

Century Literature (London: Routledge & Kegan Paul, 1981), pp. 112–13. Goode, pp. 143–44, notes frequent references to the apocrypha, a tendency to reduce the Bible, when it is alluded to, to a merely human text, and interesting parallels between the working brother of Christ, Hardy's Jude, and Gibbon's account of the discovery of St. Jude's grandsons in Rome as ordinary laboring men, who were saved from persecution themselves by their very "obscurity" – laborers' rough hands.

10 Here as elsewhere Hardy's commentary on Christian attitudes to sex is very much within the tradition of discussion; a drunken Arabella is grotesquely given the conservative and Kingsleyan religious position on divorce: "I feel I belong to you in Heaven's eye, and to nobody else, to death us do part." Or to take another fine point: when Jude and Sue consider marriage they find there are many other customers, which Hardy relates to Lent being over, thus giving us a little reminder of traditional Christian regulation of sexual seasons. Or, finally, there is Sue's attack on marriage as a right to make love on the premises; she is, as always, very knowledgeable in Church tradition which she everywhere interestingly opposes or cancels. Here she takes on the long tradition in canon law of the marital debt, a current subject in the feminism of her day as in ours: see Dellamora, p. 214.

11 See Leo Bersani's interesting general study of the deconstruction and instability of character in modern literature, *A Future for Astyanax: Character and Desire in Literature* (Boston: Little Brown, 1976). In Victorian literature this critical issue has been most fully raised in discussions of Browning's characters, especially by Warwick Slinn, *Browning and The Fictions of Identity* (London: Barnes and Noble, 1982). On Hardy see Ramón Saldívar, "*Jude the Obscure*: Reading and the Spirit of the Law," in Harold Bloom, ed., *Thomas Hardy's Jude the Obscure* (New York: Chelsea House, 1989), pp. 103–18; reprinted from *ELH*, 50 (1983) and, on Sue Bridehead as a constantly changing signifier, Anne B. Simpson, "Sue Bridehead Revisited," *Victorian Literature and Culture*, 19 (1991), 54–65. A number of books have looked at Hardy's treatment of women or erotic issues. Penny Boumelha, *Thomas Hardy and Women: Sexual Ideology and Narrative Form* (Brighton: Harvester, 1984), a study of Hardy's commentary on the new woman theme, works with a one-sided conception of Victorian sexuality as a scientific discourse (that presented by Marcus in Acton's thinking with additions from later, Darwinian, conceptions). Morgan, pp. 110–54, sees the reformist, rather than the gloomy side, of Hardy seeking redefinitions of gender and sex roles which he opposes, with the more militant and radical feminist extremes of his day, to forms of patriarchal control; her revisionist but somewhat one-sided readings of male characters from Oak to Jude (Bathsheba and Sue-sided readings) usefully show male and patriarchal biases even in such attractively untraditional males. Kathleen Blake, "Sue Bridehead 'The Woman of the Feminist Movement,'" in Bloom, ed., pp. 81–102, is

better balanced in seeing Hardy's tragic sense of the problems posed by gender and sexual conflicts between the sexes. Boumelha, Morgan, and Blake, along with earlier work by Mary Jacobus – "Sue the Obscure," *Essays in Criticism*, 25 (1975), 304–28 – importantly insist on Sue's possession of a sexual nature against a long critical tradition of her sexlessness. In some sense this began with Lawrence's famous study of Hardy, though Lawrence's position is not really the apparent one that Sue is sexless but that her sexuality is a matter of consciousness, not body – a prime case of Lawrence's "sex in the head." My discussion below agrees with Boumelha, Morgan, and Blake, that Sue is anything but sexless, but also follows Lawrence's sense of her sexuality as especially clearly a matter of discourse. In this I also agree with the general approach to an "erotic" in Hardy presented by T. R. Wright in his Introduction on "Wessexuality" to *Hardy and the Erotic* (London: Macmillan, 1989), though I found the chapter on *Jude* disappointing precisely in not fully applying this concept. Lawrence's quest for a modern myth, in the sense that Perry Meisel has defined it, as a search for something essential and beyond discourse, his desire to find a pagan sexual reality to set against a Christian tradition, made him especially anxious to confront Hardy's display in Sue of sex as a thing of words; it is for this reason that he surprisingly finds her a Christian product, even to the extent of quoting her echo of Swinburne against her: "In her the pale Galilean had indeed triumphed."

12 On the various states of Hardy's text, from much-expurgated serial (in *Harper's Magazine*) to the blunt 1895 American and English texts, to the subsequent softening in Macmillan's English text of 1903 and the 1912 Wessex text, see Robert C. Slack, "The Text of Hardy's *Jude the Obscure*," *Nineteenth Century Fiction*, 11 (March 1957), 261–75. Unless otherwise noted, quotations in my text are taken from the Wessex edition.

13 Hence the early view, certainly shared by a libertine writer like de Sade, that pornography was an act of sedition, an act of anarchy. See n. 70, ch. 1.

Index

Index 379

sexuality, 39, 77, 83–84 (*bibliographic information*), 324–25n4, 332–33n33, 340n58; skepticism, 40, 291; Houghton on, 40; and post-structuralist thinking, 40; as satirist, 40, 324n2; poet of religious perplexity, 40; career-long preoccupation with sexual–religious issues, 40, 46–47; relation to his society, 41, 42, 44, 46, 324n2; sexual biography, 42–46; restless at Oxford, 43; worldly friends and reading, 43; anxiety over masturbation, 44, 327–28nn15–17, 340–41n60; possible relation with prostitutes and pimps, 44, 45, 327n15, 328n18; love affair of 1846, 44; in Scotland, 44–45, 331n30; resigns fellowship, 45, 328–29n22, 337n50 (reflected in work), 67–69; in Italy, 45, 329n24; marriage to Blanche Smith and doubts about marriage, 45–46, 77, 339–40n57; on modern poetry, 47; decorum, 56, 78, 101, 332–33n33, 335n41, 336n44, 337n53; overwrites Bible, 59, 69–70, 335–36n42, 336n44, 337nn47, 51; parallel problem of sexual and religious commitment, 60; commitment to facing experience, 77, 110; silent period, 78; his voice moved from clerical to priest of world, 80, 83; summary of interpretations of career and poems, 82–85; Kingsley on, 102, 346n55; compared to Kingsley, 137–39; compared to Patmore, 141–42; compared to Hardy, 279, 281 (summary), 291; quest for meaning in sexuality and religion, 291; and homosexuality, 328n15; editions of works, 328n19; and Milton, 335n41

WORKS

"Adam and Eve," 77
"Addenda to the Apocalypse," Revelation rewritten for the body, 59, 66, 335n42
Ambarvalia (with Burbidge), 43, 47, 56, 57–59
Amours de Voyage, 45, 59, 71, 83; relations to Clough's life, 46; Claude's religious–sexual irresolution, 60–62; fear of the "factitious," 62–63; Clough's critique of idealism of sexual

marriage, 63–64; recognition of sexual craving, 64–65; decorum, 336n44; editions, 336n44
"Blank Misgivings of a Creature Moving about in Worlds Not Realized," 326n7
The Bothie of Tober-Na-Vuolich, sexual focus, 40; Adam like a priest, 43, 44; howler in original title, 47, 56, 330n29; Scotland as inspiration, 47, 330–31n30; Adam, 48–49, 71; social context, 48–49, 332n32; Philip's sexual growth, 49–56, 61, 66, 122; masturbation, 50, 327n15, 332n30; critique of Victorian ideas of seduction/idealization of women, 51–52; psychology and imagery of sexual awakening, 53–55, 335n38; Elspie's sexual growth, 54, 335n39; romance ending, 55–56, 62; Clough's division over, 56; summary, 83; verse novel, 197; editions, 332–33n33; use of word "sexuality," 333nn34–35; epigraphs, 335n40; Kingsley on, 346n55
Diaries, 44, 327–28nn14–17, 340n60
Dipsychus, 59, 292; use of Greek term, 44, 66, 68; Venetian setting, 45; major dramatic poem in *Faust* tradition, 65; dialectical critique of confused sexual ideas of his time, 65–66, 71–75; Spirit (Mephistopheles, Cosmocrator) related to Dipsychus, 66, 340n58; Dipsychus related to Clough, 66–67; relation to "Easter Day," 66–71, 337n48; central focus on Dipsychus' sexual–religious dilemma, 67–74; temptation of sinful streets, 67–68; play of language, 71–73; on purity, 72; romantic idealization, 72; women's sexuality, 73; conservative "respectable" discourse questioned, 73–75, 338n54; seduction and the whore's progress, 74; Dipsychus forced to acknowledge desire, 74, 340n58; marriage legal prostitution, 75; ascetic alternative impossible, 75–76; visit to prostitute, 76; summary, 83–84; editions of, 328n19
Dipsychus Continued, demon of craving and guilt, 76–77; written in United States, 340n59
"Easter Day. Naples, 1849," 45; relation to *Dipsychus*, 66–71;